This interdisciplinary collection of essays does indeed rethink neoliberalism. Through an interrogation of ideologies, policies, and practices, the contributors challenge not only neoliberalism itself but also established forms of academic and activist critique. At a time when developing progressive political alternatives is ever more imperative, the thought-provoking contributions to this book are essential reading.

> — *Wendy Larner, Provost and Professor of Human Geography, Victoria University of Wellington, New Zealand*

With Trump's election ensuring we are nowhere near the twilight of neoliberal capitalism, this interdisciplinary collection provides astute and compelling fodder for understanding and countering its theoretical premises, uneven spatialities, and modes of governance. Attentive to the varying grounds and effects of neoliberalism in social policy, subject formation, and everyday life, the essays in this volume offer timely and original insights into issues such as policing, neoliberal urbanism, "commanded individuality," and "critical counter-conduct" that recognize the stickiness and instability of neoliberalism and the possibilities for its undermining in multiple heres and nows.

> — *Cindi Katz, Professor of Geography in Environmental Psychology and Women's Studies, City University of New York, Graduate Center, USA*

RETHINKING NEOLIBERALISM

Neoliberalism remains a flashpoint for political contestation around the world. For decades now, neoliberalism has been in the process of becoming a globally ascendant default logic that prioritizes using economic rationality for all major decisions, in all sectors of society, at the collective level of state policymaking as well as the personal level of individual choice-making. Donald Trump's recent presidential victory has been interpreted both as a repudiation and as a validation of neoliberalism's hegemony.

Rethinking Neoliberalism brings together theorists, social scientists, and public policy scholars to address neoliberalism as a governing ethic for our times. The chapters interrogate various dimensions of debates about neoliberalism while offering engaging empirical examples of neoliberalism's effects on social and urban policy in the USA, Europe, Russia, and elsewhere. Themes discussed include:

- Relationship between neoliberalism, the state, and civil society
- Neoliberalism and social policy to discipline citizens
- Urban policy and how neoliberalism reshapes urban governance
- What it will take politically to get beyond neoliberalism.

Written in a clear and accessible style, *Rethinking Neoliberalism* is a sophisticated synthesis of theory and practice, making it a compelling read for students of Political Science, Public Policy, Sociology, Geography, Urban Planning, Social Work and related fields, at both the advanced undergraduate and graduate levels.

Sanford F. Schram teaches at Hunter College, CUNY where he is Professor of Political Science and Faculty Associate at the Roosevelt House Public Policy

Institute. He also teaches at the CUNY Graduate Center. His published books include *Words of Welfare: The Poverty of Social Science and the Social Science of Poverty* (1995) and *Disciplining the Poor: Neoliberal Paternalism and the Persistent Power of Race* (2011) – co-authored with Joe Soss and Richard Fording. Both books won the Michael Harrington Award from the American Political Science Association. His latest book is *The Return to Ordinary Capitalism: Neoliberalism, Precarity, Occupy* (2015). Schram is the 2012 recipient of the Charles McCoy Career Achievement Award from the Caucus for a New Political Science.

Marianna Pavlovskaya is Professor of Geography at Hunter College and CUNY Graduate Center. She has an MA in Geography from Moscow State University and a PhD in Geography from Clark University. Her major fields include urban geography, feminist geography, and critical GIS (Geographic Information Science). Her current research examines neoliberalism and the production of economic difference in post-Soviet Russia, the role of the census, statistics, and geo-spatial data in constitution of the social body, the relationship between gender, class, and work-related migration, and the emergence of the solidarity economy in the United States. Her work has appeared in the *Annals of the American Association of Geographers*, *Geoforum*, *Europe-Asia Studies*, *Environment and Planning A*, *Cartographica*, *Urban Geography*, and many edited volumes. She has worked on international research projects with colleagues from Norway, Uganda, and Russia.

RETHINKING NEOLIBERALISM

Resisting the Disciplinary Regime

Edited by Sanford F. Schram and Marianna Pavlovskaya

Routledge
Taylor & Francis Group

NEW YORK AND LONDON

First published 2018
by Routledge
711 Third Avenue, New York, NY 10017

and by Routledge
2 Park Square, Milton Park, Abingdon, Oxon OX14 4RN

Routledge is an imprint of the Taylor & Francis Group, an informa business

© 2018 Taylor & Francis

The right of Sanford F. Schram and Marianna Pavlovskaya to be identified as
the authors of the editorial material, and of the authors for their individual
chapters, has been asserted in accordance with sections 77 and 78 of the
Copyright, Designs and Patents Act 1988.

Library of Congress Cataloging-in-Publication Data
Names: Schram, Sanford, editor. | Pavlovskaya, Marianna.
Title: Rethinking neoliberalism : resisting the disciplinary regime /
Sanford F. Schram and Marianna Pavlovskaya, editors.
Description: New York, NY : Routledge, 2017. | Includes bibliographical
references.
Identifiers: LCCN 2017007974 | ISBN 9781138735958 (hardback) |
ISBN 9781138735965 (pbk.) | ISBN 9781351736480 (epub) |
ISBN 9781351736473 (kindle)
Subjects: LCSH: Neoliberalism. | Neoliberalism--Social aspects. | Free
enterprise--Social aspects. | Free enterprise--Political aspects.
Classification: LCC HB95 .R48 2017 | DDC 320.6–dc23
LC record available at https://lccn.loc.gov/2017007974

ISBN: 978-1-138-73595-8 (hbk)
ISBN: 978-1-138-73596-5 (pbk)
ISBN: 978-1-315-18623-8 (ebk)

Typeset in Bembo
by Taylor & Francis Books

CONTENTS

ILLUSTRATIONS

Figures

Tables

CONTRIBUTORS

Dorte Caswell is Associate Professor, Head of Section at the Department of Sociology and Social Work, Aalborg University (Copenhagen Campus) and Head of SAB (Social Work at the Frontline of Social and Employment Policy) at Aalborg University, Denmark. Her current research is focused on an interest in bridging political science and sociological approaches in understanding social work practice. Her research interests include welfare state developments, especially the organizational and professional aspects, as well as understanding the implications for the most vulnerable clients. The research is informed by a theoretical perspective paying attention to the translation of policy in interaction at the frontline of the welfare state in meetings between clients and professionals. See http://personprofil.aau.dk/117637 for more information.

Barbara Cruikshank is Associate Professor of Political Science at the University of Massachusetts, Amherst. She is the author of *The Will to Empower: Democratic Citizens and Other Subjects* (Cornell University Press, 1999) and of a forthcoming book titled *Machiavellian Optimism: Cultivating and Sustaining the Spirit for Political Life as an Endless Struggle*. She serves on the editorial boards of *Foucault Studies* and *Polity*.

Sophie Danneris teaches at Aalborg University in Denmark, Department of Sociology and Social Work, where she is a postdoctoral researcher, with a PhD in Social Science. Her special interest fields are social policy and labor market research with a focus on vulnerable clients, and the methodological development of qualitative research. Her published work includes "Ready to Work (Yet)? Unemployment Trajectories among Vulnerable Welfare Recipients" and "One Size Doesn't Fit All: Diversifying Research on Active Labor Market Policies" as well as several publications in Danish and contributions to books within the fields of sociology and social work.

Jodi Dean is the Donald R. Harter '39 Professor of Humanities and Social Sciences at Hobart and William Smith Colleges in Geneva, NY. She is the author or editor of twelve books, including *Democracy and Other Neoliberal Fantasies* (Duke, 2009), *Blog Theory* (Polity, 2010), *The Communist Horizon* (Verso, 2010), and *Crowds and Party* (Verso, 2016).

Mitchell Dean is Professor of Public Governance at the Copenhagen Business School. He has held Chairs of Sociology at the University of Newcastle and Macquarie University, where he also was Dean of Society, Culture, Media and Philosophy from 2002 to 2009. He is author of seven books, including *Governmentality: Power and Rule in Modern Society* (Sage, 1999/2010), *Critical and Effective Histories: Foucault's Methods and Historical Sociology* (Routledge, 1994), and *The Signature of Power: Sovereignty, Governmentality and Biopolitics* (Sage, 2013). Stanford University Press has published his most recent book, co-authored with Kaspar Villadsen, *State Phobia and Civil Society: The Political Legacy of Michel Foucault* in 2016. He also edited, with Barry Hindess, *Governing Australia: Studies in Contemporary Rationalities of Government* (Cambridge University Press, 1998), the first national work of "governmentality studies." His work stands at the nexus between political and historical sociology and political theory and philosophy.

Leonard Feldman is Associate Professor of Political Science at Hunter College and the Graduate Center, CUNY. His research is focused in contemporary political theory and public law, with an interest generally in the relationship between legal order and executive, police, and popular powers. He is the author of *Citizens Without Shelter: Homelessness, Democracy and Political Exclusion* (Cornell, 2004). He is currently the Associate Editor for Political Theory of *Polity*. His work has appeared or is forthcoming in *Political Theory, Law, Culture and the Humanities, Polity, Theory & Event* and many edited volumes. Prior to CUNY he was a Mellon Foundation post-doctoral fellow at Grinnell College, and an assistant and an associate professor at the University of Oregon. From 2007 to 2008 he was a member of the Institute for Advanced Study in Princeton.

Bettina Leibetseder is Assistant Professor at the Department of Politics and Social Policy of the Johannes Kepler University in Linz, Austria. Her work covers social policy in comparative perspective, especially aspects of minimum income schemes and gender. Bettina was Fulbright-Botstiber Visiting Professor of Austrian-American Studies at Hunter College, Department of Politics in spring 2015. Recent publications include an article on territorial fragmentation of welfare in Austria (*Journal of Social Policy*), the impact of functional and territorial subsidiarity on welfare in European countries (*International Journal of Social Welfare*) and an analysis of the policy instruments embedded in the European Social Investment Package (*Comparative European Politics*).

Maureen T. Matarese, an Associate Professor of Academic Literacy and Linguistics at BMCC, City University of New York, specializes in the analysis of institutional, practitioner–client interaction in social work and education. She examines how bureaucratic, neoliberal policies surface in face-to-face, street-level organizational communication. She has been published in *Discourse Processes*, the *Journal of Applied Linguistics and Professional Practice*, and the *British Journal of Social Work*, and is a co-editor of and co-contributor to the book *Analysing Social Work Communication: Discourse in Practice*, published through Routledge (2014). She is a member of the DANASWAC network of researchers in discourse and narrative analysis in social work and counseling, and she is the Vice President (and current acting President) of the International Linguistic Association.

Joshua Page is an Associate Professor of Sociology and Law at the University of Minnesota. He is the author of *The Toughest Beat: Politics, Punishment, and the Prison Officers Union in California* (Oxford, 2011) and *Breaking the Pendulum: The Long Struggle over Criminal Justice* (Oxford, 2017). He's currently studying the bail bond industry and, with Joe Soss, writing a book titled *Criminal Debts: Predatory Governance and the Remaking of American Citizenship* (Chicago). He can be contacted at page@umn.edu.

Marianna Pavlovskaya is a Professor of Geography at Hunter College and CUNY Graduate Center. She has an MA in Geography from Moscow State University and a PhD in Geography from Clark University. Her major fields include urban geography, feminist geography, and critical GIS (Geographic Information Science). Her current research examines neoliberalism and the production of economic difference in post-Soviet Russia, the role of the census, statistics, and geo-spatial data in constitution of the social body, the relationship between gender, class, and work-related migration, and the emergence of the solidarity economy in the United States. Her work has appeared in the *Annals of the American Association of Geographers*, *Geoforum*, *Europe-Asia Studies*, *Environment and Planning A*, *Cartographica*, *Urban Geography*, and many edited volumes. She has worked on international research projects with colleagues from Norway, Uganda, and Russia.

Jamie Peck is Canada Research Chair in Urban & Regional Political Economy and Professor of Geography at the University of British Columbia, Canada. With long-term research interests in urban restructuring, geographical political economy, labor studies, the politics of policy formation and mobility, and economic geography, his current research is focused on the financial restructuring of US cities, the politics of contingent labor, and the political economy of neoliberalization. Recent books include *Offshore: Exploring the Worlds of Global Outsourcing* (Oxford, 2017); *Fast Policy: Experimental Statecraft at the Thresholds of Neoliberalism* (Minnesota, 2015, with Nik Theodore); *Constructions of Neoliberal Reason* (Oxford, 2010); and the *Wiley-Blackwell Companion to Economic Geography* (Wiley, 2012, co-edited with Trevor Barnes and Eric Sheppard). A Fellow of the Royal Society of Canada, and previously the holder of Guggenheim and Harkness fellowships, Peck is the Editor-in-Chief of the *Environment and Planning* series of journals.

Sanford F. Schram teaches at Hunter College, CUNY where he is Professor of Political Science and Faculty Associate at the Roosevelt House Public Policy Institute. He also teaches at the CUNY Graduate Center. His published books include *Words of Welfare: The Poverty of Social Science and the Social Science of Poverty* (1995) and *Disciplining the Poor: Neoliberal Paternalism and the Persistent Power of Race* (2011) – co-authored with Joe Soss and Richard Fording. Both books won the Michael Harrington Award from the American Political Science Association. His latest book is *The Return to Ordinary Capitalism: Neoliberalism, Precarity, Occupy* (Oxford University Press, 2015). Schram is the 2012 recipient of the Charles McCoy Career Achievement Award from the Caucus for a New Political Science.

Jillian Schwedler is Professor of Political Science at the City University of New York's Hunter College and the Graduate Center, and Nonresident Senior Fellow of the Rafiq Hariri Center for the Middle East at the Atlantic Council. She is a member of the Board of Directors and the Editorial Committee of the Middle East Research and Information Project (MERIP), publishers of the quarterly *Middle East Report*. Dr Schwedler's books include the award-winning *Faith in Moderation: Islamist Parties in Jordan and Yemen* (Cambridge, 2006) and (with Laleh Khalili) *Policing and Prisons in the Middle East* (Columbia, 2010). Her articles have appeared in *World Politics, Comparative Politics, Middle East Policy, Middle East Report, Journal of Democracy*, and *Social Movement Studies*, among many others. Her research has received support from the National Science Foundation, the United States Institute of Peace, the Fulbright Scholars Program, the American Institute for Yemen Studies, and the Social Science Research Council, among others.

Joe Soss is the inaugural Cowles Chair for the Study of Public Service at the University of Minnesota, where he holds faculty positions in the Hubert H. Humphrey School of Public Affairs, the Department of Political Science, and the Department of Sociology. His research and teaching explore the interplay of democratic politics, societal inequalities, and public policy. He is particularly interested in the political sources and consequences of policies that govern social marginality and shape life conditions for socially marginal groups. His books include *Disciplining the Poor: Neoliberal Paternalism and the Persistent Power of Race* (2011) and *Unwanted Claims: The Politics of Participation in the U.S. Welfare System* (2000). In addition to his scholarship, Soss has been named to the University of Minnesota's Academy of Distinguished Teachers and, as a musician, recently released an album, *The Sound of Sweet Ruin*. He can be contacted at jbsoss@umn.edu.

Kaspar Villadsen is a Professor at the Department of Management, Politics and Philosophy, Copenhagen Business School. Villadsen is doing research on the concept of the state and civil society in Michel Foucault's authorship. He has published *Statephobia and Civil Society: The Political Legacy of Michel Foucault* (Stanford University Press, 2016, with Mitchell Dean). He is also the author of *Power and Welfare: Understanding Citizens' Encounters with State Welfare* (Routledge, 2013, with Nanna Mik-Meyer). Villadsen's work has appeared in journals such as *Economy and Society*, *Theory, Culture and Society*, *Body and Society*, and *New Political Science*.

Heather Whiteside is Assistant Professor of Political Science at the University of Waterloo and Fellow at the Balsillie School of International Affairs, Canada. Her research and publications center on the political economy of privatization, financialization, and fiscal austerity. She has published articles in journals such as *Economic Geography*, *Studies in Political Economy*, and *Health Sociology Review*, and her books include *About Canada: Public-Private Partnerships* (Fernwood, 2016), and *Purchase for Profit: Public-Private Partnerships and Canada's Public Health Care System* (University of Toronto Press, 2015). She is currently a co-investigator on two multi-year Social Sciences and Humanities Research Council of Canada grants investigating varieties of austerity and alternatives to austerity. She is a co-editor of the journal *Studies in Political Economy*.

INTRODUCTION

Rethinking Neoliberalism: Resisting the Disciplinary Regime

Sanford F. Schram and Marianna Pavlovskaya

This book is a collection of essays about neoliberalism as the governing ethic of our time. The focus is on neoliberalism's disciplinary regime that seeks to regiment subordinate populations into a market-centered society. Neoliberalism has been ascendant for some time as the default logic that prioritizes using market logic for making the critical decisions across all spheres of society, at the collective level of state policymaking as well as the personal level of individual choice-making (Schram 2015). Neoliberalism promotes a market-centered society and disciplines people to be compliant in adhering to its strictures, incentivizing market consistent behavior, and punishing people when they fail to comply. Already controversial, neoliberalism came under intense scrutiny as it had not before with the surprising election of Donald Trump as President of the United States. When Trump won, some commentators noted that he had run as an outsider against the Washington Establishment that had favored neoliberal approaches to governing, and his victory signaled a repudiation of the neoliberal orientation that had for several decades dominated national politics (Fraser 2017; Klein 2016; and Lynch 2016).

To be sure, Trump's election was already controversial in other many ways. Perhaps most disturbing was the role played by racism, xenophobia, and sexism that evidently helped propel his candidacy to victory. Trump's candidacy was also profoundly provocative because he cut such a controversial profile as an outsider with no real qualifications for governing the country. He lacked both governmental experience and rudimentary knowledge of policy. He seemed to be extremely temperamental and talked in over-simplified and emotional terms. He proved to be a pathological liar, especially about things that made him less great than his constant boasting claimed. He made the controversial claim that as a successful businessman he could apply his business skills once in office to undo failed policies. He would make the USA a winner on the world stage in both foreign and economic policy. He would, as his slogan claimed, "Make America Great Again," which many of his white nationalist supporters could interpret as "Make America White Again." His calls to crack down on illegal immigration, ban Muslims from the Middle East, and other xenophobic policy proposals suggested that that might have been what he actually meant. There was a lot to not like. In fact, Trump ultimately lost the popular vote to his opponent Hillary Clinton by almost 3 million votes but won the Electoral College by outpolling her ever so slightly in the three Rust-Belt states of Michigan, Pennsylvania, and Wisconsin where deindustrialization turned some voters against Clinton toward Trump, perhaps if only out of desperation for change in economic policy in particular.

Irrespective of how unconventional a candidate Trump was, once in office his cabinet appointments and early policy positions suggested not the end of neoliberalism but its continuation and even perhaps its intensification. As president, Trump stayed loyal to the corporate class and hired wealthy supporters to head key agencies that they often were poised to dismantle. He took a pronounced big business approach to rolling out his administration. He continued to tout the idea that businessmen like himself knew best how to govern. In his autocratic style, he claimed only he could save us. He said he would be the people's voice. Yet his demagoguery was founded on claiming to be a man of the people while acting on behalf of the corporate class to actually intensify the neoliberal approach to governing that the people had voted against. He was proving to be a master in playing those contradictions to his political advantage. He claimed he would end policies that served the interests of what he had characterized in the campaign as a global corporate class, while now he emphasized that he would remove barriers to corporate profit-taking. His was at best a faux populism, consistent with the right-wing demagogues in Europe who were seeking to impose autocratic rule on their countries as a way of addressing their social and economic problems (Müller 2016).

The political context not only in the USA but across the globe had in fact made it possible for Trump to exploit people's frustrations with existing neoliberal approaches that worked largely for a privileged few. In the USA, both major political parties had failed to stand up for ordinary Americans while global economic change was wreaking havoc for middle Americans for several decades. The frustration cut across all groups of people other than the wealthy who seemed to be the only winners in the economic shift that had been going on since the 1970s. But Trump appealed most successfully to whites who thought that the eight years of the presidency of Barack Obama, the country's first black president, meant their concerns were being ignored in a changing political economy that featured inclusion of women and minorities but not displaced white workers. Many of these people were not happy with the Republicans who championed integration into a global economy without social protections for those left to the wayside.

But the Democratic Party was not much better. The Party looked to have betrayed white workers by focusing only on amending neoliberal policies with an identity politics that sought inclusion for out-groups, women, and racial and sexual minorities but left economic change off the table as a non-issue not meriting serious discussion. Bernie Sanders had tried to redress this but his failed candidacy now served only to remind people how the Democrats ended up being proponents of a "progressive neoliberalism" that simply put a smiling face of racial and gender inclusion on the economic transformation (Fraser 2017).

People who had struggled to maintain their standard of living after the Great Recession were among those vulnerable to being seduced by Trump's bombastic lying about what he would do to "drain the swamp" of Washington and bring back prosperity to middle America (Edsall 2017). Some people were attracted to his bellicose approach to foreign threats, whether it was illegal immigration that was allegedly taking away jobs from American citizens or the radical Islamic terrorists who periodically were killing people in the Middle East, Europe, and in the USA. Trump said he was just the vessel of a social movement, that he heard what people wanted and he promised to give it to them. But like most demagogues, his understanding of "the people" was self-serving (Müller 2016).

Trump ran hard, even violently, against Clinton, accusing her of crimes and using her gender to shame her as weak and identify her as part of the Washington Establishment (or Cartel, as one of Trump's defeated Republican opponents for the nomination called it). Hillary was too inside-the-beltway. She was a proponent of the dreaded neoliberalism (the "progressive" version that added multiculturalism to the mix in ways that seemed more aimed at rationalizing the elite-dominated status quo than actually producing progressive change for most people). Yet, by the time Trump got around to picking his cabinet, it was clear he was transparently telling the public one thing but was never intending to "drain the swamp," and his policy initiatives were now, all of a sudden, strikingly and explicitly neoliberal on any number of fronts across the policy spectrum, from charter schools, to privatizing Social Security and Medicare, to tax cuts for the rich, to enforcing personal responsibility on the poor to be market compliant actors who overcame their adversity by being successful in the deregulated economy. Neoliberalism was not evidently ever in retreat, and now it appears to be ever ascendant.

How could it be otherwise? Trump embodied neoliberalism; he lived and breathed the idea that government should be run like a business by a businessman just like himself. He believed in blurring boundaries including and especially between the market and the state. Trump refused to relinquish his business holdings while president, forcing the issue into the courts, his wife hawked her jewelry line on the White House webpage the very first day of his presidency, and Trump insisted on making the taxpayers pay the Trump Organization (his own personally owned company) for security for his wife and son to continue living in Trump Tower and not the White House (Honig 2017). Trump insisted he would govern by making better business deals with other countries and international institutions and actors. In fact, he treated all government decision-making as if it were a form of business deal-making. He was marketizing the state in real time and in an iterative fashion, day by day, or even at some moments it seemed hour by hour. His initial actions as president showed he saw governing strictly through the lens of his best-selling book *The Art of the Deal*. If this is not neoliberalism, it is not clear what is.

Neoliberalism in fact has been variously defined, but arguably it is first and foremost about making market logic hegemonic as the touchstone for decision-making – personal and collective – in all spheres of life, including the public sector and the managing of state operations (Schram 2015). It is significantly about blurring the boundaries between the market and the state, bringing in market actors to reorganize the state along market lines, and marketizing state operations to run consistent with market logic and make those public policies and programs more specifically directed to buttress, rather than counter, markets by getting people as clients or citizens more generally to be more market compliant. While Keynesian liberal economics relied on the state to counter markets and mitigate their worst effects, especially on the least advantaged in society, neoliberalism saw the state as buttressing markets to enable them to become more profitable in a globalizing world (Krinsky 2008). If that is neoliberalism, Trump embodied it like no president before.

People may have voted against Clinton for her stubborn commitment to the neoliberalism of her husband, the former President Bill Clinton, the champion of a finding a "Third Way" between left and right (as his friend Tony Blair in England did) to work within the existing structure of consolidated power by being a "New Democrat." Hillary did promise to make neoliberalism work for ordinary people even if it had failed them in the past. She epitomized, though, at best that limited effort of "progressive neoliberalism" (Fraser 2017). Yet, Trump quickly turned out to be much more a neoliberal than Clinton ever imagined, especially since he ran against her progressive version of neoliberalism and its commitments to multiculturalism. She may have cravenly fallen into sticking with Clintonian neoliberalism as its own desperate, if moderate, Third Way, New Democrat approach to squeezing benefits from the prevailing power structure for middle America. But Trump more fulsomely lived and breathed a cutthroat neoliberalism, perhaps even thoughtlessly, or even somatically, as if it were the only way to act in the world.

Trump's ascendancy is very much associated with the rise of far-right, nativistic demagogues in Europe and Asia, all seemingly reacting to neoliberal policies that promote globalization, immigration, and multiculturalism while leaving native workers more economically vulnerable (Müller 2016). His friendship with Russian President Vladimir Putin showed Trump was attracted to leaders who ruled autocratically. Some of the more demagogic leaders of these movements are more explicitly fascistic in their orientation, and many take an autocratic approach to governing. Some say Trump is a fascist, but neoliberalism has strong affinities with fascism, especially in using state disciplinary power on subordinate classes so that they will be market compliant in ways that serve corporate interests (Chaudhary and Chappe 2016). The long wave of structural change from the

1970s until Trump's election has concentrated wealth and power at the top, and elites have used that shift to re-make the state to run consistent with market principles to benefit those who dominate the market system (Schram 2015). The autocrats might run against neoliberalism but end up ruling consistent with it.

With Trump as president, we can now clearly see that neoliberalism has not gone away and is not likely to any time soon. It remains hegemonic as the largely unstated public policy orientation of our time. While much has been written about neoliberalism as ideology and as a public policy orientation, much more remains to be said and needs to be said in an age of Trump where the president embodies that ideology and orientation without perhaps even knowing it and without ever saying its name or defending its perspective.

In fact, neoliberalism, it turns out, is more of an implicit orientation to governing than a full-blown, explicit ideology. It is more the *zeitgeist* for making decisions in a market-centered society (Schram 2015). Whereas President Richard Nixon said we are all Keynesians now, it goes without saying that today we are all neoliberals, increasingly under pressure to make key life decisions, publicly and privately, collectively as well as individually, according to market logic. It remains the case that in today's neoliberal society, people are expected to become entrepreneurs of the self who can take full responsibility for their personal choices. In this way, we enact what has come to be called "neoliberal governmentality" (Foucault 2008). Trump is that neoliberal man-child who instinctively acts in a neoliberal fashion, now as president, performing his incessant and highly insecure market-centered approach to his own life and applying it to his public decision-making.

Trump, therefore, is part of something larger. Nancy Pelosi, the leader of the Democrats in the US House of Representatives, affirmed that after the 2016 election when she responded to a question about doing more to appeal to dis-enchanted young voters: "We're capitalists, and that's just the way it is" (Seipel 2017). Neoliberalism is today's most significant manifestation of the capitalism Pelosi says reigns supreme. Therefore, this volume's important intellectual resources can have profound pertinence to the politics of our time. The essays in this volume were in most cases completed before Trump was elected and do not specifically address his policy proposals. Yet, their relevance is likely to endure beyond a Trump presidency. Neoliberalism remains hegemonic irrespective of what happens to his incendiary approach to governing. Both parties remain focused on proposing neoliberal approaches to addressing social and economic issues at home and issues of economic development and political stability abroad.

Each chapter makes an important contribution to the growing literature on neoliberalism, especially as it relates to social policy, and most especially regarding the self-making processes enacted by neoliberalism via social policy. This volume brings together a diverse set of essays that examine both the theory and the practice of neoliberalism in this regard. The essays use theory to interrogate neo-liberalism critically and therefore can provide resources for political resistance in an age of neoliberalism.

The lessons for thinking critically about neoliberalism today come from a wide range of sources. The chapters are authored by an interdisciplinary group of scholars from political science, sociology, geography, social work, and related fields. Included in this diverse group are scholars from the United States and Europe, who offer theoretical and empirical accounts of the rolling out of neoliberalism as a policy regime in different parts of the world.

The chapters range across issues of theory and practice, but have a keen focus on how neoliberalism puts in place a disciplinary regime for managing subordinate populations. The beginning chapters provide a theoretical context for thinking about neoliberalism as promoting a highly individualizing form of population management. The next set of chapters considers the ways in which neoliberalism has relied on social policy to discipline citizens as particular types of compliant subjects within subordinated populations. This is followed by a section that includes two chapters on the role of policing in disciplining individuals of these most often racialized, subordinated populations. Next are three chapters on urban policy and how neoliberalism reshapes urban governance to focus on issues of disciplining the subordinated to be complaint, economically as well as socially and politically. The final set of chapters asks what it will take politically to get beyond neoliberalism.

The Origin

These chapters did not come to us randomly but originated in a two-year-long faculty seminar on neoliberalism at Hunter College, CUNY, where we worked to bring the best people to talk about their specific research efforts on neoliberalism. The seminar was an ongoing event of significant scholarly attention at Hunter. It started in the fall of 2014 when a select group of Hunter College faculty and CUNY doctoral students began meeting to present their work on and discuss neoliberalism as the influential ideological orientation it had become in theory and practice in the USA and across the globe. To further this process of reflection and discussion, the faculty decided to invite additional scholars who had written on the topic to make presentations.[1]

The seminar presentations took place from the fall of 2014 through the spring of 2016 and included scholars from a widening geographic network: Mimi Abramovitz, Leonard Feldman, Marianna Pavlovskaya, Sanford Schram, and Jillian Schwedler, from Hunter College; David Harvey, Ruthie Gilmore, and Cindi Katz from the CUNY Graduate Center; Nancy Fraser, from New School for Social Research; Bernard Harcourt, Columbia University; Jodi Dean, Hobart and William Smith Colleges; Lester Spence, Johns Hopkins University; Carolyn Fraker and Joe Soss, University of Minnesota; Barbara Cruikshank, University of Massachusetts; Jamie Peck, University of British Columbia; Mitchell Dean and Kaspar Villadsen, Copenhagen Business School; Sophie Danneris, Aalborg University in Denmark; Maureen Matarese and Dorte Caswell, presenting together from Borough of Manhattan Community College and Aalborg University,

Copenhagen, respectively; François Ewald, French Technological Academy and Columbia University Center for Contemporary Critical Thought; Bettina Leibetseder, Johannes Kepler University, Linz, Austria; Katherine Gibson, Western Sydney University, Australia; and Guy Feldman, Tel Aviv University.

This volume reflects some the best presentations of our seminar. It adds significantly to the literature on neoliberalism. While there is a burgeoning literature on neoliberalism, there is a dearth of books that bring theoretical analysis to bear on concrete social policy issues. There are fewer that provide a comparative analysis such as we offer in this book, with chapters on the EU, Denmark, Jordan, Russia, the USA, and elsewhere. Our great group of seminar presenters provide the opportunity to offer this more international and comparative perspective. The essays included here also provide a good mix of theoretical and policy-related analyses of neoliberalism that are specifically focused on neoliberalism's disciplinary regime for regimenting subordinate populations into a market-centered society.

While a variety of work by prominent scholars informs the scholarship showcased here, a few jump out as most significant. The volume reflects the long shadow Michel Foucault (2008) has cast over the study of what he calls "neoliberal governmentality," where the state is marketized in order to get subordinate populations to be market compliant. Foucault is at the center of a number of chapters in this volume. A very critical, recent work that draws heavily from Foucault but also re-works and extends his thinking is that of Wendy Brown (2015). Almost as influential is Philip Mirowski (2014). Other chapters draw from a wide variety of sources including several of the seminar participants whose work is not included in this volume but who made significant contributions to the seminar. Prominent among these are David Harvey (2007) and Bernard Harcourt (2012). Also, key contributor to the existing literature Jamie Peck (2011) has a co-authored chapter in this volume. Drawing on much of this literature another contributor to the present volume, Mitchell Dean (2014), raised the question of "rethinking neoliberalism" in an important paper some years ago. A common theme in these writings is that neoliberalism is not mere market fundamentalism that emphasizes liberating markets from state control. Instead, neoliberalism involves centrally re-orienting the state to use its coercive power to discipline people to be market compliant in furtherance of creating a more thorough, robust market-centered society, where market logic reigns supreme over all decision-making across all social spheres and at all levels, personal and political, individual and collective.

Drawing on these and other sources and this orientation toward understanding neoliberalism, our contributors offer a rich set of essays that can help understand the challenges for resisting the neoliberal disciplinary regime in an age of Trump. We say this in particular since Trump's neoliberalism is likely to be extremely harsh for those on the bottom of the socio-economic order. It is all the more pertinent then that a prominent unifying theme to the included essays is the relationship of neoliberalism to social welfare and related public policies that affect people's opportunities to thrive socially and economically.

The Chapters That Follow

The chapters that follow are organized into sections. The first section lays theoretical groundwork on the issue of neoliberalism to social policy. Jodi Dean provides a theoretically rich examination of how the left has failed to come to grips with the individualization that neoliberalism enacts on public discourse today. Her chapter, titled "Nothing Personal," takes up what she sees as neoliberalism's anti-political assault on collectivity. She looks at shifts in "commanded individuality" from the 1970s to the present, highlighting the political, economic, social, and cultural challenges on the individual as she becomes "the overburdened remainder of dismantled institutions and solidarities – the survivor." Revisiting Christopher Lasch's *The Culture of Narcissism* (1996), Dean notes that it underscored incisively the ways capitalist processes simultaneously promote the individual as the primary unit of capitalism and unravel the institutions of solidaristic support on which this unit depends. She puts later sociologists in conversation with Lasch to extend the implications of Lasch's account. The chapter concludes by examining the effects of neoliberalism's individuation for the left. Dean provides an incisive critique of the fragmentation of a collective perspective under the weight of reasserted capitalist class power. She draws on Elias Canetti's (1984) work on crowds to introduce the power of the many as a productive response to the demands for individuality. Dean emphasizes that her chapter aims to "dislodge from left thinking the individualism that serves as an impasse to left politics" (p. 4).

Mitchell Dean's chapter follows in direct relationship to Jodi Dean's analysis. In "The Secret Life of Neoliberal Subjectivity," Dean addresses *both* Michel Foucault's contribution to the current debate on neoliberalism, together with its legacy in governmentality studies, *and* the intellectual-historical context of his own engagement with it in the later part of the 1970s. The chapter examines Foucault's view of liberalism and neoliberalism as sharing an orientation toward the "art of government" as manifested in post-war Europe and the United States. In particular, Dean notes how neoliberalism operated within such political movements as the French "Second Left" of the 1970s. Dean uses this historiography to critically examine the still contested legacy of Foucault in what has come to be called "governmentality studies." Dean concludes:

> Foucault can seem insightful and prescient about neoliberalism because he would come to share so many of its premises: the impossibility of a science of the human that does not intensify domination, the economy – not the public, or the state – as the generator and manifestation of truth, at least for liberal or even modern governance, and the occlusion of the question of inequality. Foucault both acutely diagnosed and to some extent could be said to have participated in what amounted to a counter-revolution in public policy.

The last of the three chapters in this first theoretically oriented section of the book is by Kaspar Villadsen: "Foucault's Three Ways of Decentering the State."

This chapter extends Dean's analysis to think how Foucault's evolution enables us to think about power, politics, and policy in an age of neoliberalism. Villadsen explains how Foucault reached a "decentered position on the state." For Villadsen, the later Foucault reflected his evolution away from state-centered political analyses to the point that Foucault seemed to conclude that neoliberalism would allow greater space for difference and individual self-formation. Villadsen concludes that Foucault's theorizing, while not without problems, ends up being prismatic in ways that can help study and challenge power in a neoliberal era.

Building on the theoretical investigations of the first section, the second section of the book includes chapters organized around the role of social policy in constructing individuals as compliant citizens. Chapter 4, "Investing in Social Subjects: The European Turn to Social Investment as the Human Capital Theory of Social Citizenship," by Bettina Leibetseder examines critically the self-making involved in what is called the EU's "Social Investment Package." The EU's Social Investment strategy places the newer conceit of social investment on equal footing with the established idea of social protection. Leibetseder notes that critics of the scheme argue that social investment over-invests in an economic governing rationality that threatens established understandings of social citizenship (and its welfare state protections) as grounded in solidarity as a basis for binding citizens and societies together, especially in the emerging and fragile European community. Theoretically, the social investment perspective could actually help perpetuate commitments to social citizenship, even as it endorses a human capital approach and redistributive aims concomitantly. Leibetseder argues that this remains possible due to the EU's "polysemic" notion of social investment; however, it may instead advance neoliberal approaches to social welfare that would limit redistribution to the poor. Analyzing EU policy documents, Leibetseder finds four types of subject formation variously affected by the EU's social investment approach. Not only do the unemployed face an activation regime, but also the young and old, sick and healthy, are targeted in neoliberalizing individuating ways. Leibetseder concludes that the European Commission's Social Investment Package moves human capital theory into mainstream European social policy and with less than positive implications for sustaining a commitment to an inclusionary, solidaristic social citizenship.

The issue of targeting populations is extended in Chapter 5, "Ontologies of Poverty in Russia and Duplicities of Neoliberalism," by Marianna Pavlovskaya. For Foucault, neoliberal governmentality centrally involved the state creating populations and then getting people to populate these as compliant members of particular groupings, all in the service of stabilizing the social order. Pavlovskaya notes that in contrast to the Soviet past, when differences in material wealth were relatively limited, the post-Soviet transformation has produced a dramatically polarized society with a large impoverished population including working poor. Consequently, Russia has to develop from scratch new metrics and policies to deal with this emerging population that is a result of regime change at the state level. This chapter examines how these metrics of poverty have evolved in ways that both normalize and obscure the extent of poverty produced by the twenty-five years of the arduous transition from state socialism to free-market capitalism and in the end reinforce this large population. During this transformation, the Soviet system of universal welfare, arguably the most complete and comprehensive in the world, was radically transformed as well, through regulations largely guided by neoliberal ideologies adopted by the Russian state. The authorities implemented a shift to means-tested and targeted welfare provisioning following Western societies who built their welfare systems under capitalism over decades. The chapter concludes by comparing unemployment benefits in Russia with those in the United States (a common reference point for Russians) in order to highlight the deleterious effects of neoliberal reform creating and normalizing the poor as an distinct population. Pavlovskaya suggests that, given its growing influence on the world stage, the Russian neoliberal regime that the state has rapidly and successfully built, and continues to support with an increasingly consolidated authority, may indeed set the development path for the rest of the world unless we learn to resist and divert this trajectory.

Chapter 6, "Neoliberalism Viewed from the Bottom Up: A Qualitative Longitudinal Study of Benefit Claimants' Experiences of the Unemployment System," by Sophie Danneris, drills down more concretely into the neoliberalizing effects of the unemployment system in Denmark. Arguing that it is pivotal to look at neoliberal policy from the bottom up, this chapter explores the lived experiences of program participants. Through a qualitative longitudinal study on the effects of recent welfare reforms in Denmark, Danneris explores how neoliberalism is experienced from the viewpoint of the people subject to it on a daily basis. She focuses on vulnerable long-term unemployed benefit claimants. Through an in-depth analysis of client interviews, Danneris highlights how clients are coping by adjusting to the new rules, and in the last instance working as best they can to make the system work for them personally. Thus, by looking at policy through the eyes of the people who are directly affected by the new regime, the chapter offers an "everyday world" perspective to the analysis of how active labor market reforms involve self-making and re-making. In the process, the study reveals a multitude of hidden dimensions to the way neoliberalism manifests itself in the daily life of the unemployed.

Chapter 7, "Neoliberal Talk: The Routinized Structures of Document-Focused Social Worker–Client Discourse," by Maureen T. Matarese and Dorte Caswell drills down even further to examine how the interactions between social workers and clients involve issues of self-making. This chapter uses conversation analysis to examine this issue. Analyzing naturally occurring data from social work interactions in a homeless shelter, the authors argue that combining a bottom–up, street level bureaucracy perspective with a conversation analytical approach enables us to discover new aspects of form-related interaction. The analysis shows how standardization, routinization, time, and documentation function in concert to accomplish social work goals that end up consciously or not having good as well as bad implications for client self-understandings.

The third section brings together two chapters that examine issues of governance via population management when the subordinated are constructed as a deviant, racialized other. In Chapter 8, "Criminal Justice Predation and Neoliberal Governance," Joshua Page and Joe Soss examine how the racialized US state system systematically operates not just to discipline but also to exploit. They focus on the predatory practices associated with the carceral regime today that end up making subordinated blacks vulnerable to becoming indentured citizens. Here the state is the flip side of the social citizenship state that accords people social protections. Instead, for those who do not meet the threshold conditions for inclusion in the social citizenship state, often because they are poor, non-white, and sequestered in marginal neighborhoods, the state is more Janus-faced and operates to discipline more than to uplift. But it goes further to exploit their subordination to serve the state's need to sustain itself financially. We see this most especially through the operations of the criminal justice system (though it is by no means limited to that). Page and Soss note that this was forcefully brought before the American public in 2015, when the US Department of Justice (DOJ) concluded in a detailed report in response to the shooting of Michael Brown by police officer Darren Wilson that the city of Ferguson, Missouri, had been operating a "predatory system of government." Police officers were acting as street-level enforcers for a program – aggressively promoted by city officials – in which fines and fees were used to extract resources from poor communities of color and deliver them to municipal coffers. Page and Soss argue that what the DOJ discovered in Ferguson should not be seen as anomalous, either in relation to US history or governance in contemporary America. They highlight how the predatory state relies on "targeted mechanisms of resource extraction, organized by race, class, and gender," and deployed in specific communities, relying at times on private actors. They argue that "the neoliberal era of governance has been marked by a resurgence and transformation of state predation on poor communities of color." They conclude that neoliberalism will be misunderstood if we fail to develop a theoretical and empirical account of its distinctive predatory forms and the new model of the resulting form of "indentured citizenship" it is constructing.

In Chapter 9, "Neoliberalism and Police Reform," Leonard Feldman pursues the issues of neoliberal criminal justice further by examining how quantitative performance measurement and surveillance combine to be redeployed in the service of police reform. Relying on Bernard Harcourt (2012) and others, Feldman describes how neoliberalism as a political form involves the development of particular technologies of measurement and observation. He considers two specific reforms: (1) DOJ investigations of police departments to establish evidence of unconstitutional, illegal conduct; and (2) policy-violating uses of force through a CompStat-like approach to quantitative performance measurement. He turns to the debate about how police body cameras redeploy contemporary surveillance technologies in the service of making state actors accountable. In arguing that neoliberal governance technologies play a role in police reform efforts, Feldman recognizes the well-documented role of neoliberal policies in facilitating or producing the intensified policing of urban space and the refocusing of punitive and carceral mechanisms on subjects who fail to self-regulate according to market norms. But he supplements that picture with an account of how neoliberal governance logics can become attached to different political projects. In conclusion, he considers the limitations of such redeployed neoliberal technologies by arguing that, even as they promise to restrict excess police violence, they "enframe" it in an administrative logic that prevents consideration of broader questions of the legitimacy of police use of force.

The fourth section of the book turns to the urban scene as the site for the most intensified forms of neoliberal disciplining of the subordinated. In ways reminiscent of David Harvey's analysis of New York City (2007), in Chapter 10, "Neoliberalizing Detroit," Jamie Peck and Heather Whiteside provide a critical study of Detroit as a test case for a domesticated form of neoliberal structural adjustment in the United States. They note that Detroit was one of the first cities to "entrepreneurialize" after the early 1970s, as a largely defensive response to economic decline, white flight, and state withdrawal. Detroit has since experienced its own version of corporate failure, having declared the largest municipal bankruptcy in US history. The authors diagnose that the city has been subjected to a "politically steered and racially targeted process of financialized restructuring," based on a neoliberal model of technocratic governance, and involving court-administered municipal downsizing and public asset stripping. They explain that Detroit is now being repurposed, in leaner form, for new markets. "In the wake of the Wall Street crash of 2008, Detroit has become a strategic target in an evolving regime of austerity urbanism, with important implications for cities near and far, as well as for emergent modalities of market rule."

In Chapter 11, "Political Dissent in Amman, Jordan: Neoliberal Geographies of Protest and Policing," Jillian Schwedler turns the analysis of neoliberalism toward the regulation of street protest (which became a staple of resisting Trump's policies). Schwedler notes that in the case of the city of Amman, its dramatic expansion over the past thirty years led to its population more than doubling through growth of the indigenous population being supplemented by an influx of two new waves of refugees (from Iran and now Syria). King Abdullah II, who gained the throne in 1999, has sought to address the growing economic disparities of the city with neoliberal reforms, notably developing a foreign real estate market, attracting foreign finance services, and implementing incremental austerity programs. The result has been a dramatic altering of the locations and repurposing of public space, with attendant effects on the ability to mobilize politically, especially for public demonstrations and street protests. Schwedler notes that with the shifting of the city's built environment in the course of advancing neoliberal projects, the visibility and availability of public spaces in which citizens can protest has been significantly reduced. In other words, this chapter examines the changing geography of the city through the lens of political protests. It utilizes original field research to illustrate how the neoliberalization of the city – or, what turns out to be half of the city, to be precise – has a profound depoliticizing effect, rendering some protests invisible as it eliminates the spaces previously available for enacting protest.

The final section of the book includes two chapters about responding to the challenges of neoliberalism. Both offer heterodox responses that transgress the convention of a left–right continuum. In Chapter 12, "The Knight's Move: Social Change in an Age of Consolidated Power," Sanford F. Schram discusses the challenges for getting meaningful social policy change in an age of neoliberalism where power is increasingly concentrated among market actors in highly unequal ways and only incremental policy change is likely. Using the neoliberalization of social welfare policy in the USA as his main example, Schram goes on to suggest that the key to progressive policy change is trying to figure out how to make incremental changes that lay the basis for more dramatic transformation which helps us get beyond the limitations of existing power relationships. This is not a "progressive neoliberalism" that seeks to rationalize the existing neoliberal policy regime (Fraser 2017). Instead, it is a "radical incrementalism" that looks to identify which incremental changes have radical potential to lay the basis for eventually getting beyond the neoliberal disciplinary regime. The chapter suggests how we can build on such incremental changes to rework power relationships and begin the process of creating more inclusive, solidaristic, and equitable policies that address fundamental problems rather than papering over them and rationalizing them. The contentious example of Obamacare is put forward as a site for thinking about radical incrementalism even as it faces its greatest threat of repeal in the first moments of the Trump administration.

The last chapter in the book, Chapter 13, "Neoliberalism: Towards a Critical Counter-Conduct" is by Barbara Cruikshank. It extends the consideration of how to respond to neoliberalism as hegemonic and does so by returning to the insights of Michel Foucault. Cruikshank asks, as did Foucault, why we tend to only focus on neoliberalism as always an instrument of subjection. Cruikshank argues that that sort of critical conduct – in activist and academic alike – too often remains under the spell of what Foucault called the "repressive hypothesis" and the questionable presumption that freedom and knowledge – in this case movements against and critical studies of neoliberalism – are external to power. Cruikshank thoughtfully suggests such a presumption mistakenly unifies neoliberalism as an object of resistance and essentializes it as self-evidently real, stable, and bad, thereby closing off the door to contingent forces of change. For these reasons, Cruikshank says, critical conduct under the spell of a neoliberal repressive hypothesis has become an obstacle to the kind of critical thought and action much needed in the current era. This kind of intransigent stance leads to the devaluation and disparagement of ongoing struggles that are deemed insufficiently critical of neoliberalism. Cruikshank uses examples of current movements challenging neoliberalism from within as models for a more politically effective "critical" counter-conduct.

Cruikshank's analysis is profoundly protean in a number of ways that make for a fitting last chapter of this book. For instance, it opens the door to considering other voices to move beyond the so-called "capitalocentrism," that is, the tendency to examine capitalism as a homogeneous economy while disregarding the significance of the ongoing non-capitalist economic practices that over time could prove to be critical to constructing "post-capitalist" politics (Gibson–Graham 2006; Roelvink et al., 2015).

In conclusion, these chapters reflect a diverse set of voices, examining issues both theoretical and empirical. They share a focus on neoliberalism, especially as manifested in social policy and how those policies work to target subordinated populations for discipline. They provide resources for countering neoliberalism in the current era. While we may have thought the age of neoliberalism was fading away, it seems ever more ascendant, making these essays profoundly politically pertinent.

The current political climate is undoubtedly challenging and those seeking to resist the perpetuation of a neoliberal system of subordination need all the help they can get. But it is important to keep in mind that opportunities for political resistance are still available. It is important to remember, for instance, that Trump's victory does not mean that American society as a whole has endorsed his faux populism and cutthroat neoliberalism. The speed at which protests greeted his ascendancy has indicated otherwise. The opposition comes from a variety of sources, opposing his racism, sexism, and class politics that reinforce some of the most oppressive dimensions of how neoliberalism gets enacted through state policy today. Even without Trump, neoliberalism's grip on policy is not likely to be loosened without ongoing active resistance to the disciplinary regime. Critical analyses of neoliberalism, therefore, will continue to be relevant to the ongoing struggles. Our hope is that readers will find important political insights in these essays, especially for combating neoliberalism as the defining way to govern still today.

Note

1 The seminar was funded by the Hunter College Dean of Arts and Science. Guy Feldman and Araby Smyth provided critical assistance.

References

Brown, W. (2015). *Undoing the Demos: Neoliberalism's Stealth Revolution*. Cambridge: Zone Books.
Canetti, E. (1984). *Crowds and Power*. Trans. C. Stewart. New York: Farrar, Straus, and Giroux.

Chaudhary, A. and Chappe, R. (2016). The Supermanagerial Reich. *Los Angeles Review of Books*, November 7. Retrieved from: https://lareviewofbooks.org/article/the-superma nagerial-reich/

Dean, M. (2014). Rethinking Neoliberalism. *Journal of Sociology*, 50(2), 150–163.

Edsall, T. (2017). The Peculiar Populism of Donald Trump. *New York Times*, February 2. Retrieved from: www.nytimes.com/2017/02/02/opinion/the-peculiar-populism-of-donald-trump.html?ribbon-ad-idx=3&rref=opinion&module=Ribbon&version=con text&region=Header&action=click&contentCollection=Opinion&pgtype=article

Foucault, M. (2008). *The Birth of Biopolitics: Lectures at the Collège de France 1978–1979*. London: Palgrave.

Fraser, N. (2017). The End of Progressive Neoliberalism. *Dissent*, January 2. Retrieved from: www.dissentmagazine.org/online_articles/progressive-neoliberalism-reactionary-populism-nancy-fraser.

Gibson-Graham, J. K. (2006). *A Postcapitalist Politics*. 1st edition. Minneapolis: University of Minnesota Press.

Harcourt, B. (2012). *The Illusion of Free Markets: Punishment and the Myth of Natural Order* (Reprint edition). Cambridge, MA: Harvard University Press.

Harvey, D. (2007). *A Brief History of Neoliberalism*. New York: Oxford University Press.

Honig, B. (2017). The President's House Is Empty. *Boston Review*, January 17. Retrieved from: http://bostonreview.net/politics/bonnie-honig-president%E2%80%99s-house-empty

Klein, N. (2016). It Was the Democrats' Embrace of Neoliberalism that Won It for Trump. *The Guardian*, November 9. Retrieved January 30, 2017, from: www.thegua rdian.com/commentisfree/2016/nov/09/rise-of-the-davos-class-sealed-americas-fate

Krinsky, J. (2008). *Free Labor: Workfare and the Contested Language of Neoliberalism*. Chicago: University of Chicago Press.

Lasch, C. (1979). *The Culture of Narcissism*. New York: Norton.

Lynch, C. (2016). Neoliberalism's Epic Fail: The Reaction to Hillary Clinton's Loss Exposed the Impotent Elitism of Liberalism. *Salon*, November 19. Retrieved January 30, 2017, from: www.salon.com/2016/11/19/neoliberalisms-epic-fail-the-reaction-to-hillary-clintons-loss-exposed-the-impotent-elitism-of-liberalism/

Mirowski, P. (2014). *Never Let a Serious Crisis Go to Waste: How Neoliberalism Survived the Financial Meltdown*. London: Verso Books.

Müller, J-W. (2016). *What is Populism?* Philadelphia: University of Pennsylvania Press.

Peck, J. (2011). *Constructions of Neoliberal Reason*. London: Oxford University Press.

Roelvink, G., St. Martin, K., and Gibson-Graham, J. K. (Eds.) (2015). *Making Other Worlds Possible: Performing Diverse Economies*. Minneapolis: University Of Minnesota Press.

Schram, S. F. (2015). *The Return of Ordinary Capitalism: Neoliberalism, Precarity, Occupy*. New York: Oxford University Press.

Seipel, B. (2017). Pelosi Town Hall Question on Capitalism Wasn't Planned: Report. *The Hill*, February 2. Retrieved from: http://thehill.com/blogs/blog-briefing-room/news/317639-pelosi-town-hall-question-on-capitalism-wasnt-planned-report

PART I

Theorizing Neoliberalism

The Individual, the Subject, and the Power of the State

1

NOTHING PERSONAL

Jodi Dean

The era of communicative capitalism is an era of commanded individuality. The command circulates in varying modes. Each is told, repeatedly, that she is unique and encouraged to cultivate this uniqueness. We learn to insist on and enjoy our difference, intensifying processes of self-individuation. No one else is like us (like me). The "do-it-yourself" injunction is so unceasing that "taking care of oneself" appears as politically significant instead of as a symptom of collective failure – we let the social safety net unravel – and economic contraction, in a viciously competitive job market we have no choice but to work on ourselves, constantly, just to keep up. Required to find out, decide, and express it all ourselves, we construe political collectivity as nostalgia for the impossible solidarities of a different era. The second-wave feminist idea that the "personal is political" has become twisted into the presumption that the political is personal: how does this affect *me*?

Individualism has not always been so intense and unmitigated. As Jefferson Cowie (2010) details in his history of the United States in the 1970s, "reformed and diversified individualisms" undermined class-based approaches to economic rights over the course of the decade.[1] This chapter takes up the assault on collectivity. Looking at shifts in commanded individuality from the 1970s to the present, I highlight the enormous strains placed on the individual as it becomes the over-burdened remainder of dismantled institutions and solidarities – the survivor. I revisit Christopher Lasch's *The Culture of Narcissism* (1979), marking the ways capitalist processes simultaneously promote the individual as the primary unit of capitalism and unravel the institutions of solidaristic support on which this unit depends. Putting later sociologists in conversation with Lasch, I draw out the limits of Lasch's account. Even as Lasch's descriptions of celebrity culture,

competition, and consumerism still resonate, individualism is today less an indication of narcissism than it is of psychosis. The last sections of the chapter find
possibilities of collectivity in the ruptures of the fragile individual form. With help
from Elias Canetti's (1984) indispensable study of crowds, I introduce the power
of the many and the relief it provides from the unbearable demand for individuality. This chapter aims to dislodge from left thinking the individualism that
serves as an impasse to left politics.

Two commercials illustrate the celebration of personal uniqueness characteristic of communicative capitalism. Both are for soft drinks. Both, in different ways, engage the limits conditioning the very individuality that they
command.

On January 9, 2012, Dr Pepper announced a new advertising campaign,
"Always One of a Kind." The campaign's first commercial features hundreds of
people in red T-shirts with white lettering converging in a crowd to march down
streets and through a park. The T-shirts have slogans like "I'm One of a Kind,"
"I'm a Cougar," "I'm a Fighter," and "I'm a Pepper" (one of Dr Pepper's earlier
slogans). The accompanying music is a cover of the 1968 Sammy Davis, Jr. hit
"I've Gotta Be Me." According to the press release accompanying the campaign's
launch, the red T-shirt wearers are Dr Pepper fans "proudly showing off their
own original expressions on T-shirts describing what makes them unique and
different from the rest of the crowd."[2] In the optimistic words of the company's
director of marketing, the campaign "should serve as a catalyst for expressing
originality and being authentically you." Dr Pepper also offered fans the
"opportunity to express their originality by ordering their own 'Always One of a
Kind' T-shirts on DrPepper.com."

Putting aside the designation of customers as "fans," the targeted demographic
appears to be people who want to express their uniqueness. The commercial hails
them as individuals, inviting them to identify with particular slogans and identities.
Within Dr Pepper's commercial imaginary, going to the streets isn't collective
rage; it's individual self-expression, an opportunity to assert one's individuality
and stand out. Crowds are that against which individuals define themselves. The
Dr Pepper Brand, in this imaginary, is a natural continuation of primary urges
to establish unique identities, a helpful, vital supplement for the crucial task of
distinguishing oneself from others.

The commercial's presumption that people need support in expressing their
originality – an authenticity catalyst of the kind a T-shirt might provide – gives
it an ironic inflection. Augmented through the retro turn to Sammy Davis, Jr.,
the irony of expressing one's authenticity via a branded soft drink invites
another identificatory twist: are you like the crowd of those who *really* think
that Dr Pepper T-shirts make you unique, or does your capacity to get the joke,
to recognize that originality necessarily exceeds any branded media image, make
you different from, even superior to, the rest of the crowd? The fact that some
of the slogans are reappropriations of offensive labels – "cougar" and "mamma's

boy," for instance – opens up this alternative. The wearers of these shirts are unique in their strength, confident enough to assert the labels, to *own* them. Thus, a further irony: their courage is amplified by the crowd. The energy of the commercial, its *feel*, comes less from what's written on the T-shirts (the majority of which can't be read) than from the sea of red that carries people along. The celebration of difference and creativity comes from the enthusiasm of a crowd where people march shoulder to shoulder, pumping their fists and taking confidence in their collectivity. Even as collectivity as a trope is coopted into the service of amplifying individual courage, the fact of, the *need for*, this amplification cuts through the individualist message as it acknowledges the power of the crowd.

Coca-Cola's "Share a Coke" campaign likewise takes individuality as its theme, targeting a demographic the company presents as preoccupied with the assertion of personal uniqueness.

"For teens and Millennials, personalization is not a fad, it's a way of life," explains the press release announcing the campaign. "It's about self-expression, individual storytelling and staying connected with friends" (Moye 2014). Launched in Australia in 2011 and expanded into some fifty additional countries, the campaign alters the Coke iconography by replacing the Coke logo with personal names. It encourages young consumers to find cans and bottles with the names of themselves and their friends, photograph them, and share them online.

In the campaign, personal names take the place of the brand. Consumers aren't called on to show their individuality by wearing the brand. The brand comes to them, taking on their individual identities, letting individuals see themselves in it. The icon becomes abstract enough to carry individual identities while nonetheless transcending them. The appeal of the campaign arises not just from the personal name but from the personal name in the place of the known and popular. The social media dimension of the campaign testifies to the continuation of the place of the brand. The Coke icon is still there, now riding on and circulating through individual uploads of personal self-expression, less viral marketing than free product placement in the intimate moments of everyday life.

When the left echoes injunctions to individuality, when we emphasize unique perspectives and personal experiences, we function as vehicles for communicative capitalist ideology. "Left" becomes nothing but a name on a bottle, the shape of which is determined for us and which relies on us for its circulation. Making individual difference the basis of our politics, we fail to distinguish between communicative capitalism and emancipatory egalitarian politics. Even worse, we strengthen the ideology that impedes the cultivation of politically powerful collectivities. To call on people to ground their politics in the personal experiences that differentiate them from others is to reinforce capitalist dynamics of individuation. Offering the fantasy of customizable politics, such a call says: look at yourself from the specific position and interests given to you by capitalism and do what you want. In so doing, it pushes away from the collectivity on which left politics depends.

Individualism without Individuals

The injunction to individuality is so ubiquitous that it's easy to forget its histories and modulations (Seigel 2005). The research of sociologists such as Christopher Lasch, Richard Sennett, Jennifer M. Silva, and Carrie M. Lane treads a path through this history as it attends to the pathologies accompanying capitalist processes of individuation. As I detail below, key sites along this path – rugged individual, corporate gamesman, flexible temp worker, and sole survivor – open up the ways economic turmoil, changes in the structure of authority, and the loss of self-sufficiency give a tenuous quality to personal identity. The shifts from one site to another demonstrate moreover how the competitive pressures of capitalist processes become increasingly displaced onto and concentrated in the individual. The forces enjoining individuation undermine it. The more the individual, that fictitious subject of capitalism, is glorified, the more strained and impossible it becomes.

Lasch's influential book *The Culture of Narcissism: American Life in An Age of Diminishing Expectations* presents an individualism that has self-destructed. Appearing in 1979, the book highlights the rise of a therapeutic sensibility. The economic man of the nineteenth century "has given way to the psychological man of our times – the final product of bourgeois individualism" (Lasch 1979, p. xvi). For Lasch, the preoccupations with self, authenticity, and personal growth that became prevalent over the course of the 1970s are symptomatic of an individualism collapsing in on itself as commanded individuality struggles to realize the ever-increasing expectations coming to burden it.

Lasch describes his critique of the therapeutic individual as "radical," even as he shares conservative concerns with the weakening of the family and the rise of dependency. This overlap is worth noting. Not only does it point toward an increasing convergence among critics of the basic institutions of the welfare state, but it also indexes the common object of their concern: the fragile individual. The difference between Lasch's analysis and the conservative critique of welfare liberalism consists in their targets. Where conservatives attack the bureaucracy of the welfare state, Lasch attacks the bureaucracy of the corporation. He expands this attack into a full assault on the broader impact of corporate culture on American life. Lasch's innovation stems from his diagnosis of the "me decade's" preoccupation with psychic health as a symptom of the more fundamental intellectual and political bankruptcy of welfare state capitalism's liberal paternalism. The end of the individual in narcissistic hedonism and aggression is the outgrowth of capitalism, inclusive of and exacerbated by the liberal welfare state. Capitalism's own injunctions to individuality overburden and undermine the individual form.

Locating changes in the individual in the context of political and economic change, Lasch contrasts the narcissistic personality of the twentieth century with the rugged individual of the nineteenth century. His vision of the nineteenth-century American psyche (clearly an ideological figure or organizing motif) comes from the settler colonialism of the frontier. The pioneer fights to tame the West, to subdue nature, and eliminate the native threat. This fight requires an attendant internal battle: domination over more immediate appetites and impulses. Lasch writes:

> Through compulsive industry and relentless sexual repression, nineteenth-century US Americans achieved a fragile triumph over the id. The violence they turned against the Indians and against nature originated not in unrestrained impulse but in the white Anglo-Saxon superego, which feared the wildness of the West because it objectified the wildness within each individual.
>
> (p. 10)

He continues, "Capital accumulation in its own right sublimated appetite and subordinated the pursuit of self-interest to the service of future generations." The frontier American is egoistic and brutal, this brutality tied to a self-constraint on behalf of civilized community. Violence is channeled, put to internal as well as external use.

Lasch positions the corporation as the twentieth-century parallel to the frontier. In contrast to the fierce and rugged pioneers fighting for survival, seventies Americans are stuck in a boring, ordered, and banal society. Because the struggle for success has replaced the struggle to survive, they have lost the capacity to desire. Nonetheless Americans in the seventies seethe with an inner rage that bureaucratic society and its injunction to cheerful getting along prevents them from expressing the violent forces of the id, now lacking an outlet.

Lasch uses the "executive" as a figure for twentieth-century narcissism. Unlike the "organization man" associated with mid-century American anxiety about conformism, Lasch's executive is the bureaucratic "gamesman." Seeking competitive advantage, the gamesman wants to get ahead of everyone else. He values quickness and mobility. He construes power in terms of momentum. He replaces craftsmanship with socials skills that involve seducing, humiliating, and manipulating others. The gamesman doesn't interiorize rules as socially valid norms; he experiences both work and personal relations as power struggles. Bureaucratic emphases on rules and cooperation couple with personal exceptionalism – *rules don't apply to me*. The gamesman thus looks for ways to exploit conventions for his own benefit. "Activities ostensibly undertaken purely for enjoyment often have the real object of doing others in" (p. 66). A friendly demeanor, an air of compassion, and an open, participatory approach to decision-making all conceal a power game that the majority will lose.

The sense that a game is being played extends beyond the corporation. The lower orders, Lasch writes:

> internalize a grandiose idea of the opportunities open to all, together with an inflated opinion of their own capacities. If the lowly man resents those more highly placed, it is only because he suspects them of grandly violating the regulations of the game, as he would like to do himself if he dared. It never occurs to him to insist on a new set of rules.
>
> *(p. 186)*

The "lowly man" acquiesces uneasily to expectations of friendly cooperation, suppressing dissatisfaction into a growing emptiness.

Lasch's psychoanalytic explanation for the rise of the narcissistic personality highlights changes in the paternal function. Unlike the materially self-sufficient frontier family, the family in the second half of the twentieth century depends on help and advice from experts. Whether as medical and therapeutic child-rearing guidance or educational and juridical intervention in the domestic sphere, expertise dislodges symbolic patriarchal authority. This dislodging continues broader patterns associated with industrial development, more specifically with the separation of production and reproduction, the distancing of children from labor, and the diminution of opportunities for fathers to teach the technical skills associated with their work directly to their children. The father's absence "encourages the development of a harsh and punitive superego based largely on archaic images of the parents, fused with grandiose self-images" (p. 178). The child doesn't identify with parents; it introjects them, holding itself up to idealized standards and punishing itself for failing to achieve them. Put in Lacanian terms, the change in the paternal function is a decline in authority such that the symbolic law can no longer provide a site of relief from superegoic demands (Žižek 1999, pp. 322–334).

The decline of symbolic authority in liberal therapeutic society induces cultural narcissism. Welfare capitalism's bureaucratic rationality replaces the previous era's hierarchy with administrators, technicians, and experts. The struggle to succeed within the confines of the corporate bureaucratic game takes the place of survival under frontier conditions. Rather than having symbolic authority, experts and administrators have knowledge. This knowledge is generally contestable and provisional: experts disagree; what a bureaucrat knows may not be useful. The culture of technocratic expertise and management absolves individuals of responsibility, making everyone a victim of sickness or circumstance. More broadly, narcissistic culture infantilizes by promoting dependence on the paternalist bureaucracies of welfare liberalism (corporation and state) and at the same time encouraging the pursuit of pleasure. The narcissistic person admires the strong and rich – celebrities – for their independence, their capacity to do and have whatever they want. Mass media encourages the fascination with celebrity, amplifying the narcissist's tendency to divide society into two groups: winners and losers, the great and the crowd. Self-fulfillment and hedonism are celebrated, yet unsatisfying and, increasingly, unattainable. In response, people absorb themselves in a search for authenticity, their skepticism toward the falsity of mass culture's manufactured illusions manifesting as an ironic detachment that further distances them from meaningful connections with others.

What Lasch diagnoses as pathological or secondary narcissism is a reactive individuality that accompanies changes in capitalist society associated with mass production and consumption. When consumption is a way of life, work need not be meaningful, fair, or morally necessary (as a previous generation held). Instead, the purpose of work is acquisition. Consumption solves all problems, fills all needs. Rather than postponing pleasure, consumerism enjoins gratification now. The concomitant growth in management and proliferation of technicians, experts, and knowledge professionals presents "new forms of capitalist control, which established themselves first in the factory and then spread throughout society" (p. 235). Having lost its role in production, the family is stripped of its role in reproduction as its social tasks either become matters in need of expert intervention or reducible to problems solved by the right commodities. The effect of these developments is a realization of the logic of capitalism such that "the pursuit of self-interest, formerly identified with the rational pursuit of gain and the accumulation of wealth, has become a search for pleasure and psychic survival" (p. 69). The result, which Lasch says was already foreseen by the Marquis de Sade, is the reduction of people to objects. Each person is to be used for the enjoyment of another: "pure individualism thus issues in the most radical repudiation of individuality" (p. 70). The culture of narcissism erodes the individual it ostensibly celebrates.

In sum, Lasch links changes in the individual form to changes in capitalism. The shift from the rugged individual of the frontier to the gamesman of the corporation is economic and psychic. As the struggle to survive becomes a drive to consume, the self-reliance of the frontier morphs into dependence on corporate and state bureaucracy. Frustrated individuals narcissistically strain against their traps, identifying with celebrities and searching for authenticity. They want to be unique, exceptional. The rules don't apply to them, so they need not abide by them. They can focus on themselves, their own well-being, using others as means to achieve it.

A quarter of a century later, Richard Sennett (2006) suggests that deepening inequality and economic insecurity have further changed the contemporary individual. Where Lasch highlights the bureaucratic corporation for its cultivation of gamesmanship and dependency, Sennett considers the so-called "new economy" of temporary workers, technology workers, and entrepreneurs (before and after the bursting of the dot-com bubble). These workers aren't dependent on bureaucracy. They aren't locked into the banal security of the corporation and its internal machinations. Their lives and work are unstable, without guarantees, precarious. They lack a narrative for adulthood. Many work on short-term contracts. Companies want to be flexible – and to avoid providing health insurance and pensions. The critique of dependency has become itself an interiorized norm. Whether a firm employs the winner-take-all dynamic of internal markets, relies on subcontractors and temporary labor, or uses consultants and a revolving door of executives, primary business values are autonomy and self-direction. Workers worry about keeping their skills up-to-date, having the potential to learn new tasks quickly, and cultivating easily transferable capacities such as "problem-solving."

Surprising, though, is the resonance of Sennett's account with Lasch's. One might expect the enforced self-reliance of the new economy to induce a sense of purpose and direction along the lines of the rugged individualism of the frontier. Instead, Sennett's sociological investigations into late capitalism suggest a self oriented toward the short term, focused on potential, and capable of jettisoning the past. This echoes Lasch's highlighting of immediacy, flexibility, and a break with historical continuity. Like Lasch, Sennett emphasizes the separation of power from authority, the diminution of trust, and the growth of anxiety. But where Lasch presents the pressure confronting the individual as an effect of a corporate culture that breeds gamesmanship and dependence, Sennett attributes the problem to the *loss* of corporate culture and the unmooring of individuals from the intelligible patterns of everyday life that results. The corporation no longer provides a stabilizing point of reference for the narrative of working life.

Lasch of course observes that the Protestant work ethic eroded decades ago. Sennett, however, links its disciplinary effects to the corporate structuring of life patterns (even for those working outside the corporation).

On the one hand, insofar as he attends to a certain loss, Sennett signals the decline of the symbolic that subtends Lasch's analysis of the change in paternal authority. With the vantage of two more decades, Sennett detects that this change is a loss. He analyzes this loss in terms of meaning and language: the absence of a place from which to narrate one's life. On the other hand, because Sennett concretizes this loss as a loss of narrative rather than of symbolic authority, he overlooks the real changes to the individual form that Lasch already diagnosed. Sennett wants to shore up the individual. Lasch recognizes the form's obsolescence. By emphasizing the missing narrative of adulthood, Sennett thus covers over the more fundamental disruption at the level of the symbolic.

For Sennett, the new economy has an upside. It allows for the emergence of new personal qualities such as "repudiation of dependence, development of one's potential ability, the capacity to transcend possessiveness" (p. 182). Accentuating the bright side of the post-welfare state technologized economy, Sennett tries to redeem the project of the New Left, making its critique of bureaucracy, cult of individuality, and celebration of emotional authenticity into not simply vanishing mediators of communicative capitalism but real achievements to be continued. He packages his recommendations for this continuation as the cultural values that individual workers require to sustain themselves in the fast-paced and volatile economy: narrative, usefulness, and craftsmanship.

Sennett's advocacy of a "cultural anchor" for an economy he recognizes as productive of extreme inequality and social instability puts Lasch's critique of monopoly capitalism in stark relief: Lasch's rejection of capitalism really is radical.

Jennifer M. Silva (2013) draws out an alternative to Sennett's emphasis on a missing narrative of adulthood. The narrative isn't missing. The narrative has changed, morphing into a more extreme version of the therapeutic self Lasch already identified in the collapse of its material and symbolic supports. What matters in the twenty-first century is individuation itself. "In a time when suffering is plentiful and work and family unreliable," Silva writes, competent adulthood is defined "not in terms of traditional markers like financial independence, a career, or a marriage, but rather in terms of psychic development: achieving sobriety, overcoming addiction, fighting a mental illness, or simply not becoming one's parents" (p. 125). Silva's alternative account of the pressures on contemporary adults draws from her ethnographic study of working class adults in Massachusetts and Virginia. Her interviewees emphasize self-reliance, making it on their own. They can't rely on experts or institutions. Other people are likely to fail or betray them. Individualism preserves and protects their own best thing, the only thing they can rely on, themselves. Their repudiation of dependence is a reaction to the loss of dependable others. Rather than an achievement, independence is a fetish barely holding together the fragile individual form.

Silva's account of a transition to adulthood marked not by "entry *into* social groups and institutions but rather the explicit rejection *of* them" provides a poignant rejoinder to Sennett (p. 84). One man tells Silva that "the hardest part about being an adult is finding a real fucking job" (p. 98). People aren't lacking *a narrative* for adulthood. Capitalism presents adulthood as an individual project. For the young working people Silva interviewed, individualism equals dignity. They tell heroic tales of self-sufficiency, turning inward as they manage feelings of betrayal, accept flexibility and flux, and buttress their sense of being utterly alone. Although the dependencies of the welfare state and corporate bureaucracy that Lasch associates with the therapeutic sensibility have been dismantled and replaced by a harsher, more competitive capitalism, therapeutic language remains the vocabulary through which to account for individual success and failure.

Instead of the jettisoning of the past that Lasch and Sennett observe, Silva's subjects embrace the past as they narrate the challenges they have had to overcome in order to realize their authentic selves. Understood in terms of familial and personal experiences, the past provides an open field of explanations for hardship, failure, and the diminution of what they see as success. Unlike Lasch's empty narcissists, Silva's young adults have lives of inner purpose – surviving on their own in a context where the odds are against them. They struggle with illness and battle with addiction. They overcome dysfunctional families and past relationships. The fight to survive is the key feature of an identity imagined as dignified and heroic because it has to produce itself by itself.

Silva's young adults point to an imaginary identity beyond the rugged individualist and the narcissistic gamesman: the survivor. Unlike the symbolic identity of institutions (the place from which one sees oneself as acting), imaginary identity is the image one adopts of oneself. Since so many of Silva's informants feel they have had to do it all by themselves, in contexts of poverty and diminishing opportunity, they take the fact of their survival as the morally significant fact: making it on one's own is what bestows dignity. Some of the white survivors Silva interviews resent "socialists" like US President Barack Obama for trying to take away their last best thing, the special something that is all they have left, namely, the dignity they have because they are completely self-reliant. The black survivors, too, narrate their experiences in individual rather than collective terms. They, too, seek to hold on to the only person they can count on – themselves. Betrayed by schools, the labor market, and the government, Silva's working class informants in general feel "completely alone, responsible for their own fates and dependent on outside help at their peril." For them, surviving means internalizing the painful lesson that "being an adult means trusting no one but yourself" (p. 9).

What Sennett lauded as a repudiation of dependence appears in Silva's account as a deep skepticism of solidarity. Reliance on other people requires acknowledging one's insufficiency as an individual, one's inability to survive alone. The hostility to the needy expressed by some of Silva informants suggests a defense against their own need. Hostility lets them displace their need onto others and thereby shore up a fragile and impossible individuality. Having learned that they can't rely on anyone, these young working class adults try to numb their sense of betrayal by affirming the worst cultural scripts of individualism, personal responsibility, and self-reliance, hardening themselves to the world around them. Their hostility to various forms of government intervention, particularly affirmative action, makes them ideal supports for neoliberal capitalism. Incidentally, those of us who write and circulate critical exposés – stories of governmental corruption, university failure, and corporate malfeasance – may not be helping our cause. We may be affirming what some in the working class already know to be true: they are being betrayed.

Likewise countering Sennett's happy rendering of the repudiation of dependence, Carrie M. Lane's (2011) research on white-collar technology workers in Dallas situates the emphasis on individual responsibility in the context of wide-scale layoffs and unemployment. Insecurity is a primary feature of the lives of these tech workers. Most alternate through contract positions of varying duration, unemployment, and self-employment.[3] Lane notes how the technology workers she interviewed embrace a "career management" ideology that casts "insecurity as an empowering alternative to dependence on a single employer" (p. 13). They construe loyalty as a thing of the past: since everyone is a victim of economic forces beyond their control, neither companies nor employees owe each other anything. Owners and workers both want to make money however they can. No one should expect a company to provide employment security or opportunities for professional development. Such an expectation indicates a childish attitude of dependence. According to one executive, "To give my employees job security would be to disempower them and relieve them of the responsibility that they need to feel for their own success" (p. 51). Laid-off and job-seeking tech workers adopt the corresponding individualist mindset: success comes from doing "whatever it takes" to get by, get through, get that next job.

The survivor is a compelling identity under conditions of extreme competition and inequality. It validates surviving by any means necessary. Survival is its own reward. Setbacks and lapses are new challenges, ultimately greater proof of one's survival skills. Popular culture provides a wide array of survivors to emulate (as well as examples of those who have been unable to get themselves together): from Katniss in *The Hunger Games*, to the winners of uncountable reality television competitions, to games like *Day Z* and *Fallout*, to victims of illness or crime. Emotions of anger, suspicion, and defensiveness are justified – one can rely only on oneself – and potentially useful as the psychic weapons that can help maintain an impossible individuality.

The survivor is a figure not for a culture of narcissism but for a psychotic culture. If narcissistic culture is characterized by the dislodging of symbolic authority, psychotic culture is characterized by its foreclosure (see Dean 2009). In brief, Lacan (1997) defines psychosis in terms of the foreclosure of the Name-of-the-Father or master signifier. That the master signifier is foreclosed means that it does not stabilize meaning; the signifying chain lacks an anchor that can hold it together. The generalized loss of symbolic power impacts the subject such that he feels this now-missing authority to be all the closer, more powerful, and intrusive. In a psychotic culture, then, mistrust is pervasive, all-consuming. Each confronts power directly and alone.

To compensate for the missing symbolic authority, the psychotic turns to the imaginary. He positions himself in relation to a "captivating image," perhaps of one whom he hates, admires, or fears. This imaginary other would then be a rival to defeat or destroy. The psychotic may try to mimic those around him, particularly as he grapples with intense fear and aggression. And he may also become captivated by an image of himself. Here the psychotic imagines himself not *as* anyone or anything in particular: *I am my own worst enemy*. What matters is persistence, survival, for its own sake.

Whether rendered as caring for oneself or looking out for number one, the captivating image of the individual enjoins its own maintenance. For all their emphases on self-reliance, Silva's interviewees nonetheless want to be recognized. They want someone else to hear their stories, validate what they've accomplished. Communicative capitalism supplies the necessary infrastructure, the crowd of many who might view, like, or share.

The Pressure Is Killing Me

The intensification of capitalism amplifies pressures on and for the individual. These pressures are political: the individual is called on to express her opinion, speak for herself, get involved. She is told that she, all by herself, *can make a difference*. Her responses to ubiquitous demands for feedback take the place of collective action, rendered as either impossible or too repressive to constitute a real alternative. The pressures on the individual are also economic: even in the absence of significant social mobility, the individual is offered up as the most significant determinant of success or failure. In competitive labor markets, attracting buyers for one's labor power is a challenge. One has to distinguish oneself to get hired or, for some of us, to maintain the fantasy of something like a fair competition (it would be horrible to think that all that debt was for nothing). No wonder that communicative capitalism enjoins us to uniqueness: we are the product we make of ourselves. At the same time, specialization supports marketeers' interests in ever more granular access to customers, police efforts to locate and track, and capital's concern with preventing people from coalescing in common struggle. Identification is inseparable from surveillance, personalization absorbed in commerce. Capitalism's injunction to individuate is the most powerful weapon in its arsenal.

The pressures are also psychological, as we have already seen. Franco Berardi (2009) highlights the "conquest of internal space, the interior world, the life of the mind" endemic to communicative capitalism. Informational intensification and temporal acceleration saturate our attention to "pathological levels." Berardi associates panic, aggressiveness, depression, and fear with this saturation. He finds symptoms of it in waves of suicide, escalating Viagra use among those with no time for affection, tenderness, and sexual preliminaries, "millions of boxes of Prozac sold every month, the epidemic of attention deficit disorders among youngsters, the diffusion of drugs like Ritalin to school children, and the spreading epidemic of panic" (Berardi, p. 82). People respond to overload with drugs and technology, trying to do more, be more, keep up and on top, but the pressure is relentless. The more they do, the more they are expected to do. Swamped under the overproduction of signs, the human receiver is overloaded to the point of breakdown.

I agree with much of Berardi's description, but I want to suggest an alternative approach to the psychopathologies he observes. Drugs, depression, ADHD, and panic are not merely pathologies. They are also defenses. The real pathology is the individual form itself. Drugs attempt to maintain it, keep it going. The individual is pathological in the sense that it is incompatible with its setting, incapable of responding to the pressures it encounters without pain, sacrifice, or violence (psychoanalysis stems from this insight, hence the primacy of castration). The problem of contemporary subjectivity arises not from the extremes of a capitalism that has merged with the most fundamental components of communicativity. It's not that the saturated, intensified, and unbearably competitive circuits of communicative capitalism are making us depressed, anxious, autistic, and distracted and that we need to find ways to preserve and protect our fragile individualities. Depression, anxiety, autism, and hyperactivity signal the breakdown of a form that has always itself been a problem, a mobilization of processes of individuation and interiorization in a reflexive inward turn that breaks connections and weakens collective strength. The individual form is not under threat. It is the threat. And now it's weakening.

In *Alone Together: Why We Expect More from Technology and Less from Each Other*, Sherry Turkle (2011) documents some of the ways social media provide relief from individualist expectations. To be sure, she does not describe her findings in terms of such relief. Rather than construing the individual form as a problem, she presents it as a vulnerability in need of protection. So she echoes dominant injunctions to individuality. Nonetheless, her explorations of "networked life and its effects on intimacy and solitude, on identity and privacy" open up paths she doesn't follow, paths to collectivity (p. 169).

Reporting on her interviews with teenagers, Turkle describes young people waiting for connection, fearful of abandonment, and dependent on immediate responses from others even to have feelings. For example, seventeen-year-old Claudia has happy feelings as soon as she starts to text. Unlike a previous generation that might call someone *to talk about* feelings, when Claudia wants *to have* a feeling, she sends a text (p. 176). Turkle reports the anxieties people express about face-to-face interactions as well as about expectations associated with the telephone, that is to say, about speaking to another person in real time. The multitasking inseparable from contemporary communication, the fact that people may be texting and talking simultaneously, looking at something else while ostensibly listening to their interlocutor, implants an uncertainty as to whether another is even paying attention. Combined with pressures for immediate response and the knowledge that the "internet never forgets" (most of us are unable to eliminate all traces of our digital identities after they've been uploaded, archived, and shared), our new intimacy with technology, Turkle demonstrates, is affecting the kinds of selves we become. We experience solitude, privacy, connection, and others differently from how we did before.

For Turkle, these new experiences are pathological. Drawing from Erik Erikson's work on personal identity, she argues that networked technologies inhibit the kind of separation necessary for maturation. Parents are always in reach, available, even if they are not actually present but themselves overworked, distracted, and overextended. Young people do not learn how to be alone, how to reflect on their emotions in private. Fragile and dependent, they fail to develop the sense of who they are that they need to have "before" they "forge successful life partnerships" (p. 175). Rather than inner-directed and autonomous (Turkle refers to David Riesman), the culture of mobile phones and instant messaging has raised other-directedness "to a higher power" (p. 167). The expectation of constant connectivity eliminates opportunities for solitude even as people are "increasingly insecure, isolated, and lonely" (p. 157). Turkle concludes, "Loneliness is failed solitude. To experience solitude, you must be able to summon yourself by yourself; otherwise you will only know how to be lonely" (p. 288).

If we do not give normative priority to the individual as the proper or exclusive form of subjectivity, we can read the evidence Turkle offers differently. We can read it as an indication that a political form of separation and enclosure is changing, mutating, becoming something else. Michael Hardt and Antonio Negri (2000) follow Gilles Deleuze in describing this change as the passage from disciplinary society to the society of control. They point out how disciplinary logics worked primarily within the institutions of civil society to produce individuated subjects. By the end of the twentieth century, disciplining and mediating institutions – the nuclear family, the school, the union, and the church – were in crisis (Lasch's cultural narcissism is one diagnosis of this crisis). The spaces, logics, practices, and norms previously coalescing into social and economic institutions broke down and apart. In some instances, the release of an institutional logic from its spatial constraints gave it all the more force; in other instances, the opposite occurred. Thus, Hardt and Negri argue that pervasive institutional dissolution has been accompanied by an "indeterminacy of the *form* of the subjectivities produced" (p. 197). Hardt and Negri conclude that the bourgeois individual – the citizen-subject of an autonomous political sphere, the disciplined subject of civil society, the liberal subject willing to vote in public and then return home to his private domesticity – can no longer serve as a presupposition of theory or action. They suggest that in its place, we find fluid, hybrid, and mobile subjectivities who are undisciplined, who have not internalized specific norms and constraints, and who can now only be controlled.

Hardt and Negri are right to point to the changes in the settings that produced the bourgeois individual. Yet they underplay the emergent ferocity of commanded individuality. Their fluid, hybrid, and mobile subjectivities appear as loci of freedom, as if their singularity were a natural property rather than itself enjoined, inscribed, and technologically generated in the service of capitalism. As the decline of discipline weakened individuating structures, new technologically mediated techniques of individuation took their place. An easy example (one prominent in Turkle's discussion) is the adoption of mobile phones as personal communication devices for kids. Enabling parents to keep track from a distance, phones fill in for the direct supervision and contact that has diminished in the wake of increasing work demands on parents, particularly mothers. Additional such techniques and technologies of individuation include competition in intensified labor markets as they induce a marketing relation to oneself; targeted advertisements that urge consumers to differentiate and specify themselves; locative technologies associated with mobile phones and GPS; cookies and other data-gathering techniques associated with transactions on the internet; political injunctions to personal participation; and, in the USA, a rights-based political culture focused on personal identity, harm, and exclusion as opposed to common, collective, and systemic injustice – within this culture, systemic problems such as exploitation in the workplace and amplified personal indebtedness are treated as the effects of individual choices, preferences, and luck. The fluidity that Hardt and Negri observe, then, is accompanied by the technologies and practices of commanded individuality. The result is that the expectation of unique individuality exerts demands that are as constant and unyielding as they are impossible to meet.

That the young people Turkle interviewed express anxieties associated with autonomy and connection is not surprising. They are enjoined to individuality, told each individual is selfsame, self-creating, self-responsible: one is born alone and one dies alone; you can rely on no one but yourself. Yet the technologies that further individuation – smartphone, tablet, laptop – and the platforms that encourage it – Twitter, Facebook, Instagram, Tumblr – provide at the same time an escape from and alternative to individuation: connection to others, collectivity.

Crowds

Turkle thinks that people's aversion to talking on the phone (as opposed to texting) and conversing face-to-face reflects their need for filters, for ways to handle sensory and information overload. They reflect, she suggests, not only a longing for solitude but also the way that in a stimulation and simulation culture we have become cyborgs (p. 209). Elias Canetti (1984) suggests an alternative interpretation: we may be coming to prefer the crowd, the presence of many that opens us to collectivity and relieves us of anxiety. One-on-one conversations may feel too constraining insofar as they enclose us back in an individual form. Rather than part of a group, of many, we are just ourselves.

If this is plausible, then we have an alternative way to think about preoccupations with numbers of friends, followers, blog hits, shares, and retweets. They do not indicate personal achievement or popularity. They mark our absorption in the crowd, how densely we are enmeshed in it. So, to be clear, we can think of these counts in the individualist terms given us by capital. We can also recognize them as something else, as markers of belonging to something larger than oneself. In this latter sense, they reassure us that we are not unique but common.

For Canetti (1996), the relief we feel in a crowd is paradoxical. It arises from a fear of others, a feeling that others are threatening, which "reverses into its opposite" in the crowd. In a discussion with Adorno, he explains that he believes that people like to become a crowd because of "the relief they feel at the reversal of the feeling of being touched" (p. 185). From this vantage point, the craving for dopamine Turkle describes seems more like the relief we may feel when we shake off the fears associated with individuation – isolation, exposure, vulnerability.

One might object that Canetti's crowd is physical and the networked crowd is virtual. This objection is absolutely right and compelling – part of the power of the occupations of Tahrir Square, Syntagma Square, and the Occupy movement's multiple parks and sites came from the force of bodies out of doors in collectivities authorized by neither capital nor the state. But this is not the end of the story. Most crowd theorists attend to physical and virtual crowds. They draw out "crowd" as a verb, as dynamics, and as affects that traverse and constitute collectivity. Canetti himself describes invisible crowds of the dead and spermatozoa. Gustave Le Bon's (1896) influential (albeit notoriously reactionary) work on crowds treats the crowd primarily as a psychological concept. Le Bon goes so far as to claim enigmatically that "crowds, doubtless, are always unconscious, but this very unconsciousness is perhaps one of the secrets of their strength" (p. 6). Furthermore, technologies of presencing have developed so as to make our mediated interactions feel all the more present and intense. We are interacting with others, not just screens. When we register trending hashtags and multi-shared stories, we experience the force of many. In social media, the many flow across our screens, waves of images and expressions of feeling with effects that accumulate, resonate, and consolidate into patterns irreducible to any particular position or utterance. Canetti (1992) notes "how *gladly* one falls prey to the crowd" (p. 148). The crowd, virtual and physical, moves and intoxicates. Canetti (1982) writes:

> you were lost, you forgot yourself, you felt tremendously remote and yet fulfilled; whatever you felt, you didn't feel it for yourself; it was the most selfless thing you knew; and since selfishness was shown, talked, and *threatened* on all sides, you needed this experience of thunderous unselfishness like the blast of the trumpet at the Last Judgment.
>
> *(p. 94)*

The experience of flow that overwhelms the conscious experience of self that Turkle finds so threatening, then, might also be understood as a breaking out of the illusion that the individual is and can be a subject of action (rather than a form of enclosure and containment) and a giving-over to a crowd.

We've Got to Be We

The crumbling of capitalist realism – the shaking off of Margaret Thatcher's destructive mantra that "there is no alternative" to unfettered capitalist competition – has led to mainstream acknowledgement that capitalism is a system that takes from the many and gives to the few (Fisher 2009). Today no one denies the fact that some always lose in the capitalist economy. The system produces losers – the unemployed, the homeless, the indebted, the conned, the wiped out, the abandoned, the sacrificed. It runs on debt, foreclosure, expropriation, eviction, dispossession, destruction – these are just other words for privatization. But then what? Ever since the left started looking at itself and the world in terms of individual specificity and the efficiency of markets, it has seemed easier to imagine the end of capitalism than it is to imagine an organized left.

Some find collectivity to be undesirable because of its opposition to individual responsibility and freedom. Rejecting the communisms of Badiou as well as Hardt and Negri, Vanessa Lemm (2011) warns, "in both these trends, the process of subjectivation tends to dissolve the individual into a 'multitude' or a 'cause' that is supra-individual and that, far from assuming responsibility for one's freedom, demands that one surrender it" (p. 96). Lemm offers a Nietzschean "counterforce to the radical egalitarianism" of the communists, emphasizing how Nietzsche's "aristocratic conception of culture" relies on "cultivating the responsibility of singular individuals." Others position collectivity as undesirable by insinuating that collectivity has to be imposed; any collective employs a state logic. Banu Bargu's (2011) bold deployment of Max Stirner's egoist view of liberation as an individual project of self-valorization best exemplifies this view: to realize their own uniqueness and potential, egoists "should direct their efforts not only against the state, but against any collectivity and collective project" (pp. 114–115).

In the place of an undesirable collectivity, left realism offers up diversity, plurality, and multiplicity. To this end, Eugene Holland (2011) wants to create a "multiplicity of multiplicities." Jimmy Casas Klausen and James Martel (2011) likewise encourage expressions of human diversity and view thriving political and economic associations as those that are adaptable, contingent, and multiple. And Andrew Koch (2011) claims that anarchism is the "only justifiable political stance" because of its defense of the infinite pluralism of individuated meaning (p. 38). Such views proceed as if such multiplicity were primarily ontological, rather than also stimulated by capitalism for its benefit and preservation. They also underplay state interest in plurality, particularly the fragmentations that hinder collective opposition and the individuations that facilitate targeting, isolation, and control.

Left realism's second premise is that collectivity is impossible. We are so different, so singularized in our experiences and ambitions, so invested in the primacy of one set of tactics over another that we can't cohere in common struggle. At best we can find momentary affinities and provisional coalitions. Politics should thus involve cultivating our own unique point of view – or the point of view of our sect, tribe, or locale – rather than trying to organize these views into something like a strategy. Left realism implies that coming together itself should be exposed as a fantasy covering over a hidden Hobbesian impulse to transcendence, a myth some use to manipulate others into fighting for their interests.

A further variation on the premise of impossibility is that fundamental changes in the world economy preclude collectivity (Clover and Benanav 2014). Rather than concentrating workers in centralized locations, contemporary capitalism disperses them across the globe. It relies on long supply chains and global capital, using complexity to dissolve sites of accountability. Workers in ever more sectors of the capitalist economy are thus isolated, immiserated, and politically disorganized. To be sure, immiseration and political disorganization also characterize the early decades of revolutionary socialism. Karl Marx, Friedrich Engels, and Rosa Luxemburg all emphasize how competition means that workers tend to remain isolated, lack solidarity, and take a long time to unite. This is why unions and parties have to be created and why creating them is a struggle. Left realism's one-sided emphasis on the objective dimension of our present capitalist setting fails to acknowledge the subjective dimension of perspective, organization, and will: our perspective is part of the setting it sees. This subjective dimension has always been crucial to the Marxist tradition. The communist response to isolation is not to let the reality that produces individualism determine our political horizon. Instead, it is to build solidarity.

The assumptions that collectivity is both undesirable and impossible derive from an even more insidious assumption of left realism: that politics involves the individual. Manuel Castells (2012), for example, treats as a key cultural transformation "the emergence of a new set of values defined as individuation and autonomy, rising from the social movements of the 1970s, and permeating throughout society in the following decades with increasing intensity" (p. 230). Exactly how politics involves the individual varies – *no one speaks for me but me; the personal is political; if I can't dance, I don't want to be part of your revolution*. But the premise remains the same: a left politics has to encourage and express the multiplicity of individual projects. Individuals have to choose and decide – even as the left fails to provide something anyone could actually choose. Leaders, vanguards, and parties are modes of politics for a time not our own, we are told. They are remnants of a political-economic assemblage that has already crumbled (Gilbert 2014).

Left realism feels realistic to some because it resonates with the prevailing ethos of late neoliberalism that tells us to do it ourselves, stay local and small, and trust no one because they will only betray us. It affirms capitalism's insistence on immediacy and flexibility and the state's replacement of long-term planning and social services by crisis management and triage. Left realism is good on spontaneous outrage. But it fails to organize itself in a way that can do something with this outrage. Disorganized, it remains unable to use crises to build and take power much less construct more equitable and less crisis-prone social and economic arrangements.

The realism in which the Left has been immersed in the neoliberal decades has meant that even when we are fully conscious of the deep inequity of the system in which we find ourselves, we confirm and conform to the dominant ideology: turn inward, enclave, emphasize the singular and momentary. Sometimes we don't feel like we can do anything about it (maybe we have too much work to do already). Or we find ourselves participating in individuated, localized, or communicatively mediated activities without momentum, duration, or a capacity for political memory. Or we presume that we have to focus on ourselves, start with ourselves and thereby redirect political struggle back into ourselves. In a brutal, competitive, and atomized society, psychic well-being is so difficult that success on this front can feel like a significant accomplishment. Trying to do it themselves, people are immiserated and proletarianized and confront this immiseration and proletarianization alone.

This chapter has sought to dismantle the assumption of the political primacy of the individual that binds left politics to the dominant capitalist imaginary and that prevents us from seeing the concentration of politics onto the individual as symptomatic of left defeat. Rather than a locus for creativity, difference, agency, and responsibility, the individual is the overburdened remainder of dismantled institutions and solidarities. Commanded individuality obscures individual incapacity even as it amplifies the contradictions barely congealed in the individual form. At the same time, these commands and incapacities attest to another force, the power of collectivity that manifests in crowds.

Notes

1 Throughout this chapter, I blur together individualism, individuality, and individuation, treating them as component aspects of capitalist society's requirement for and production of individuals.
2 Product release: "Dr Pepper Celebrates Its Legacy Of Originality With The Launch Of The New 'Always One Of A Kind' Advertising Campaign," news.drpeppersnapplegroup.com, January 9, 2012.
3 Lane's subjects were men and women, in their twenties through sixties, from different racial and ethnic backgrounds – African American, Asian American, Latino, Indian, Pakistani, Chinese, and Japanese. Most, however, were white men between the ages of thirty and fifty.

Bibliography

Bargu, B. (2011). Max Stirner, Postanarchy avant la lettre. In J. Klausen and J. Martel (Eds.) *"How Not to Be Governed": Readings and Interpretations from a Critical Anarchist Left.* Lanham, MD: Lexington Press.
Berardi, F. (2009). *Precarious Rhapsody*. London: Minor Compositions.
Bernes, J. (2013). Logistics, Counterlogistics, and the Communist Prospect. *Endnotes*, 3 (September). Retrieved from: https://endnotes.org.uk/issues/3/en/jasper-bernes-logistics-counterlogistics-and-the-communist-prospect
Canetti, E. (1982). *The Torch in My Ear*, trans. Joachim Neugroschel. New York: Farrar, Straus and Giroux.
Canetti, E. (1984). *Crowds and Power*, trans. C. Stewart. New York: Farrar, Straus, and Giroux.
Canetti, E. (1992). *Crowds and Power*. London: Penguin Books.
Canetti, E. (1996). Discussion with Theodor W. Adorno. *Thesis Eleven*, 45, 1–15.
Castells, M. (2012). *Networks of Outrage and Hope: Social Movements in the Internet Age.* Cambridge, UK: Polity Press.
Clover, J. and Benanav, A. (2014). Can Dialectics Break BRICS? *South Atlantic Quarterly*, 113, 743–759.
Cowie, J. (2010). *Stayin' Alive: The 1970s and the Last Days of the Working Class.* New York: The New Press.
Dean, J. (2009). *Democracy and Other Neoliberal Fantasies: Communicative Capitalism and Left Politics*. Durham, NC: Duke University Press.
Fisher, M. (2009). *Capitalist Realism*. London: Zero Books.

Gilbert, J. (2014). *Common Ground: Democracy and Collectivity in an Age of Individualism.* London: Pluto Press.

Hardt, M. and Negri, A. (2000). *Empire.* Cambridge, MA: Harvard University Press.

Holland, E. (2011). *Nomad Citizenship.* Minneapolis: University of Minnesota Press.

Klausen, J. and Martel, J. (2011). Introduction. In J. Klausen and J. Martel (Eds.), *"How Not to Be Governed": Readings and Interpretations from a Critical Anarchist Left.* Lanham, MD: Lexington Press.

Koch, A. (2011). Poststructuralism and the Epistemological Basis of Anarchism. In D. Rousselle and S. Evren (Eds.), *Post-Anarchism: A Reader.* New York: Pluto Press.

Lacan, J. (1997). *The Psychoses: 1955–1956, Seminar III,* ed. Jacques-Alain Miller, trans. Russel Grigg. New York: Norton.

Lane, C. (2011). *A Company of One.* Ithaca, NY: Cornell University Press.

Lasch, C. (1979). *The Culture of Narcissism.* New York: Norton.

Le Bon, G. (1896). *The Crowd: A Study of the Popular Mind.* Kitchener, ON: Baroche Books.

Lemm, V. (2011). Nietzsche, Aristocratism and Non-Domination. In J. Klausen and J. Martel (Eds.), *"How Not to Be Governed": Readings and Interpretations from a Critical Anarchist Left.* Lanham, MD: Lexington Press.

Moye, J. (2014). Summer of Sharing: "Share a Coke" Campaign Rolls Out in the U.S., June 10. Retrieved from: coca-colacompany.com

Sennett, R. (2006). *The Culture of the New Capitalism.* New Haven, CT: Yale University Press.

Seigel, J. (2005). *The Idea of the Self: Thought and Experience in Western Europe Since the Seventeenth Century.* New York: Cambridge University Press.

Silva, J. (2013). *Coming Up Short: Working-Class Adulthood in an Age of Uncertainty.* New York: Oxford University Press.

Turkle, S. (2011). *Alone Together: Why We Expect More from Technology and Less from Each Other.* New York: Basic Books.

Žižek, S. (1999). *The Ticklish Subject.* London: Verso.

2

THE SECRET LIFE OF NEOLIBERAL SUBJECTIVITY

Mitchell Dean

Neoliberalism has been called a "rascal concept – promiscuously pervasive, yet inconsistently defined, empirically imprecise and frequently contested" (Brenner, Peck, and Theodore 2010, p. 182). While the term is usually employed as a critical tool, those who are its supposed agents do not accept the epithet and (at least since the mid-1950s) prefer instead to regard themselves as classical liberals in the tradition of Adam Smith (Mirowski 2009, p. 427; Dean 2014b, p. 154). In general, and in its most explicit form, it refers to a kind of "economic theology" (Agamben 2011) consisting of a faith in the providential order of the free-market economy and individual economic freedom and self-government – but to stop there would be very misleading, as Michel Foucault's work (2008) would point out. While it is often attributed to the Chicago School of the mid-twentieth century, particularly in Europe, many Americans use the term "liberal" to denote the progressive side of politics, supporting enhanced freedoms of individual lifestyle and, to some extent, a level of federal governmental intervention in the provision of healthcare, education, and social welfare. With the administration of President Obama, and in particular Hillary Clinton's 2016 presidential election campaign, however, it often seemed that the Democratic Party sought to reconcile these two kinds of liberalism: a political liberalism offering a rights-based progressive "identity politics" of diversity and an economic liberalism that would be a pro-corporate, pro-financial capital, version of free-trade globalism.

Some are more used to the term "neo-conservative" to describe a certain recent form of the New Right, at least since the administration of President George W. Bush. Here, we find the advocacy and implementation, often through executive orders, of enhanced security mechanisms such as intensified surveillance of populations, stronger border controls, the use of detention camps, extra-territorial "black sites," "enhanced interrogation techniques" (more commonly referred to as torture) and extra-juridical killings in the treatment of enemies. All this hardly seems consistent with the rosy end-of-history gospel of global free-trade and prosperity. Indeed, neoliberalism often seems to refer to quite contrary things: the principle that the state should be rolled back in the name of individual freedom coexists with the mistrust concerning whether many individuals are capable or responsible enough to use that freedom and a continuum of paternalist, authoritarian, and coercive treatment of the latter. If this is the case, the new Trump administration may not be a case of a rascal concept going full "loony tune." Rather than a fundamental departure from a neoliberal paradigm it could be approached as a nationalist and protectionist inflection and intensification of it: at the same time de-regulatory and protectionist toward the national economy, further marketizing healthcare, insurance, and social provision, while re-enforcing borders and (further) restricting immigration, reviving the hyper-security state, and working through executive order rather than legislation. But rather than announce yet another death of neoliberalism, it might be better to think of recent developments as a kind of national neoliberalism.

More broadly, there are the "roll back" and "roll out" phases or dimensions of neoliberalism, as Jamie Peck (2010a, pp. 21–25) puts it, not to mention the simple rolling on – or rolling with. As Philip Mirowski (2009, 2013) has pointed out, the claim of the vanity of human knowledge in the face of the market as the great information-processor seems to except those who advance that truth, including much of the economics profession. While justifying itself as preventing the slippery slope to totalitarianism, neoliberalism has often found itself preferring liberalism to democracy, a "liberal dictator" to an anti-liberal demos, as F. A. Hayek (1981) did during the Pinochet regime in Chile. At the onset of the financial crisis of the 2000s, it called for bank bailouts and quasi-nationalizations of certain industries deemed "too big to fail." In fact, some have spoken of a "zombie neoliberalism" that lives on in an undead form after its much proclaimed death as that crisis unfolded (Peck 2010b). In the course of that crisis, it appeared both to lose its legitimacy and gain a source of renewal. While initially a marginal political ideology, it has become so embedded in governmental practices, everyday politics, and culture, and perhaps even our subjectivities that it has proved very difficult to resist and redirect. Even allowing for its contingent appearance and operation, once established it follows uneven forms of development with particular path dependencies, feeding on the roiling crises it seems to provoke (Brenner, Peck, and Theodore 2010).

For those working with Foucault and particularly his work on governmentality, there are some additional complications. Taking some sustenance from Foucault, a group of scholars in the United Kingdom and Australia produced a literature on what might be called "neoliberal governmentality" or, rather less pointedly, "advanced liberal rule" (Rose 1996), by the end of the twentieth century, although the latter term seemed often to depoliticize neoliberalism, systematically downplaying its authoritarian side and its rootedness in robust intellectual-political movements and action taken to appropriate political sovereignty. Nevertheless, we did this without much of Foucault's work on the topic being either published or widely available. Hence, our work was exciting as a conceptual and analytical invention provoked by Foucault rather than a fidelity to his text. In any case our main objective was not the scholastic interpretation of Foucault's texts but the development of an analytical perspective – an "analytics of government" as I called it at the time (Dean 1999, pp. 20–27) – that could be applied successfully to many different spheres of governing, from education, indigenous issues, bureaucracy, auditing, and accounting to the reform of welfare-state measures. While the initial heyday of this now much cited literature was the 1990s, the lectures Foucault delivered in the 1970s on governmentality and neoliberalism would only become widely available after the initial development of what Michel Sennelart later dubbed "governmentality studies" (2007, p. 390) – in French in 2004 and English in 2007. In fact his lectures on neoliberalism, *The Birth of Biopolitics*, would appear in English in the fateful year 2008. As a result destiny has tied these lectures, which were concluded a month prior to the election of the Thatcher government in the UK and almost two years before the Reagan administration took office in the USA, to a wholly different context. That was the worst economic crisis in the North Atlantic world since the Great Depression and the subsequent revaluation of the legacy of neoliberalism and its poster girl and boy. If the crisis was good for some businesses – predatory moneylenders, debt collection and insolvency firms, private employment service providers engaged by governments, to name some – it was also propitious for academics trading or hoping to trade in Foucault's analysis of neoliberalism, themselves under the pressures of a university system they felt was also "neo-liberalizing."

A further complication is that these very lectures are made available under the general editorship of his former student and assistant François Ewald, thus making him perhaps Foucault's most influential follower. The apparent irony here is that Ewald, in his work with the employers' association *Medef* would promote what Maurizio Lazzarato describes as the "policies and mechanisms for … reconstructing society according to neoliberal principles" that were first revealed to him in Foucault's very lectures of 1979 (2009, p. 110). While the case of Ewald as a neoliberal has been raised for some time in Parisian circles by Lazzarato, Antonio Negri (2001), and Jacques Donzelot (Donzelot and Gordon 2008, p. 55), among others, the question of Foucault's own critical but positive appreciation of aspects of neoliberalism has been put on the agenda by none other than Ewald himself. Ewald suggested in 2012 in conversation with the Chicago economist Gary Becker that Foucault had offered an "apology of neoliberalism" (Becker, Ewald and Harcourt 2012, p. 4; Dean 2014a) – a suggestion he seems to have sought more recently to retract (Ewald 2016). One very small lineament of our present is that this topic of Foucault's possibly affirmative reading of neoliberalism has now become a matter for public debate, following the publication of two books endorsing this view in French, one embracing it as the way forward for the Left (de Lagasnerie 2012), the other suspecting Foucault of undermining the Left's core commitments to health and social rights (Zamora 2014b; see Hansen 2015). The Foucault blogosphere would be lit up by an interview with the editor of the latter book, the then PhD student Daniel Zamora, in *Jacobin* (Zamora 2014a). In 2015, this debate reached the pages of the *Los Angeles Review of Books* (Steinmetz-Jenkins and Arnold 2015) under the title "Searching for Foucault in an Age of Inequality" and continues with the revised English version of Zamora's book (Zamora and Behrent 2016) and commentaries on it in *History and Theory*, among other places.

Despite all this, Foucault is still, at least in the United States, imagined as an unadorned radical. On the day of the inauguration of Donald Trump, anthropologists held "read-ins" of the final lecture of *Society Must Be Defended* (Foucault 2003; Jaschik 2017). Whether or not this amounts to one of those "facile gestures" that Foucault himself warned against, this practice perhaps raises the question of Foucault's relation to our political present. After this lecture, Foucault had a year on sabbatical that cemented his relationship with the United States. On his return to the lectern in 1978, his concern was no longer with the inscription of a genocidal racism in the modern state in the combination of biopolitics and sovereignty but with a new framework of power, "governmentality," and the genealogy of liberalism or the liberal arts of government that would culminate in a discussion of the variants of neoliberalism. Is it possible, I want to ask, that Foucault discovered or foreshadowed the possibility of a form of politics that would incorporate neoliberal technologies of government and would be highly influential on the Left over the last three or even four decades, but which has left those democracies vulnerable to the type of nationalist neoliberalism and acclamatory populism we witness today?

To do this, I shall leave the question of the empirical adequacy of his genealogy of liberalism aside for another time. I want to ask instead, what is the distinctive contribution of Foucault's approach to neoliberalism, and by those who followed him? And what are the strengths and limits of this work on neoliberal governmentality today, in the wake of crisis, heightened inequality, and populist insurgence, and, in Europe, reborn nationalism, continuing austerity, massive youth unemployment, and economic stagnation? In answer to the first question, I shall argue that there are several strengths we can build on in Foucault's work on neoliberalism: first, his intellectual-historical approach to it; second, his view of neoliberalism as an art of government; and third, his focus on its critical ethos. At the heart of my way into the more critical assessment is a fourth theme found in much of the secondary literature, that Foucault acutely posed the problem of the production of neoliberal subjectivity. The focus on questions of subjectivity and the problematic of subjection/subjectification takes us to the heart of the current problem for the Left: that its support of contestation against the (often welfare state) institutions and forms of social scientific knowledge as the major forms of domination since the 1970s brought it into a critical alignment with the libertarian dimension of neoliberalism and rendered it relatively useless in preventing the authoritarian populist rise.

Foucault, Governmentality, and Neoliberalism

To start with the obvious, Foucault's analysis alerts us to the plurality of forms of neoliberalism, their emergence within but movement across particular national borders and temporal contexts. Foucault demonstrates the worth of an intellectual-historical and even biographical study of the variants of neoliberalism and their key figures, which he himself recognizes as something of a departure from his usual methods (2008, p. 10). This brings neoliberalism down to earth as something that is identifiable and study-able, as something that is more plural, contingent, and historically rooted than a narrative of neoliberalization might indicate.

With the publication of excellent intellectual-historical studies of neoliberalism such as those found in Mirowski and Plehwe's *The Road from Mont Pèlerin* (2009) and Jamie Peck's *Constructions of Neoliberal Reason* (2010a), this point might seem redundant. But if we allow Foucault the status of a thinker of the Left, which I think he remained (see below), this project was almost unique at the time of his lectures. On the other side of the Channel, there was Andrew Gamble's (1979) paper in *The Socialist Register* in 1979. But what is interesting is that despite Laclau and Mouffe's 1985 recognition (2001) that neoliberalism was a "new hegemonic project," there was little Left engagement with the sources of this project. This was despite the fact, as Foucault's lectures (2008) would report, that such a project had become a practical doctrine of government from the very beginning of the Federal Republic of Germany, that is, some almost forty years before. For Foucault this neglect was due to mistaking neoliberalism as a mere revival of classical liberalism or simply another ideology of market capitalism. The Left, still in thrall to something like a base-superstructure model of ideology, was not able to grasp neoliberalism "in its singularity" (Foucault 2008, p. 130). As Foucault put it: "Neo-liberalism is not Adam Smith; neo-liberalism is not a market society. Neo-liberalism is not the Gulag on the insidious scale of Capitalism" (2008, p. 131).

In paying serious attention to the intellectual-historical sources of neoliberalism, Foucault anticipates those who would regard neoliberalism as a "thought collective" (Mirowski 2009, p. 428), that is, as I understand it, as an empirically and histori-cally identifiable group of thinkers pursuing a common project and ambition but within a certain space of conversation and dissension. As the contributors to *The Road from Mont Pèlerin* have shown, the neoliberal thought collective proved to be one of the most successful, if not the most successful, political movements of the second half of the twentieth century in the influence, capture, and appro-priation of the powers of national states and other governmental organizations (above and below the nation state).

Yet almost contrary to this careful intellectual-historical method, with its emphasis on plurality and historical contingency of the various strands of the neoliberal thought collective, is another of Foucault's bold masterstrokes, the identification of neoliberalism – and indeed classical liberalism – as an "art of government," something he announces at the very beginning of *The Birth of Biopolitics* (2008, pp. 1–2). Citing Benjamin Franklin's notion of "frugal government" (2008, pp. 322, 319), Foucault defines liberalism as neither philosophy nor ideology but as an art of government animated by the suspicion that one always governs too much – or, as Barry Hindess and I argued, that the state is doing too much of the governing (Dean and Hindess 1998, pp. 3–7). This general framework allows him to distinguish between classical economic liberalism and the varieties of neoliberalism. Whereas classical liberalism seeks the limitation of the state in the face of the necessary and natural processes of the economy, neoliberalism will either seek to found the legitimacy of the state on the market, as the Ordoliberals would in post-Nazi Germany, or to extend the market and its rationality to all forms of social existence and to test and evaluate every single act of government, as in the case of American neoliberalism. But to regard neoliberalism as an art of government is to shift the frame decisively from the theory of ideology to the practical orientation of neoliberalism as a form of governmentality. To put this in other words, neoliberalism is a form of *statecraft*. What is important about this move is that it displaces the tendency to view neoliberalism as something merely super-structural in relation to the capitalist economy and forces us to look at it as a practical and technical exercise concerned with governing states. Neoliberalism is not simply a philosophy of freedom and the market that happens to have implications for governing states. It is all about governing states – or about governing states and other organizations. It is a doctrine, or set of doctrines, concerned with a practice centered first and foremost on the exercise of political sovereignty (Foucault 2008, p. 3).

In a recent paper, I have used these two insights – neoliberalism as a thought collective and as an art of government – to arrive at a particular way of characterizing neoliberalism (Dean 2014b). In the first instance, neoliberalism as thought collective conducts a form of what Max Weber called "politically oriented action": that is, action which "aims to exert influence on the government of a political organization; especially at the appropriation, redistribution or allocation of the powers of government" (1978, p. 55). Its target is the control of the exercise of their powers by states and other organizations, from school boards to political parties, universities, and international government organizations. Rather than applying the term "neoliberal" to a form of state, I prefer to suggest that neoliberalism is most appropriately described as a way of governing the state and a way of governing by the state. Against the anti-statism of much current political thought, it is necessary to distinguish between "regime" and "state" (Du Gay and Scott 2010) and view neoliberalism as a regime of government *of* and *by* the state. In this way, we can protect ourselves from the dangers of an analytical anti-statism.

There are many other more general and specific aspects of Foucault's lectures on neoliberalism one could focus on to define the distinctiveness of his contribution. A further set I want to mention contains issues Foucault raises about the critical ethos of neoliberalism. Here we find that at least one part of his orientation to neoliberalism is the identification of what it criticizes or, to put it even more bluntly, what it problematizes. These problematizations are of course national-context dependent – the Ordoliberals (Foucault 2008, pp. 107–108) oppose ideas of national economy derived from Friedrich List in the 1840s, Bismarkian state socialism, and the wartime planned economy, for example, while Hayek displays a particular animus towards the New Deal and the programs of Beveridge in England (Foucault 2008, p. 110). The American school opposes both the latter and the economic and social programs of the postwar federal administrations in the United States, particularly Democratic ones (Foucault 2008, p. 217). However, their common enemies are even more interesting – especially the economics and policy prescriptions of John Maynard Keynes. This approach to neoliberalism underlines its political nature and the relations of antagonism that animated it, against all those who would reduce its concerns to economic, technical, or even ethical ones. It also indicates that liberalism and neoliberalism vary according to context that has among its conditions of existence, the targets of their critique.

The three points I have derived from Foucault emphasize the political character of neoliberalism as a diverse movement or network with no doubt differences of opinion but united by common aims and enemies seeking to institute a particular "regime of government" in various organizations above and below the state but most particularly in national states and their agencies. The fourth proposition concerning the distinctiveness of Foucault's contribution concerns the production of neoliberal subjectivity. This is where Foucault's view, and his legacy, becomes quite confused and confusing, and where, if we were to follow him too closely, we might end up fighting the battles of a previous war.

If one consults contemporary books on neoliberalism, whether they are sympathetic to Foucault, such as Dardot and Laval's *The New Way of the World* (2013) or more critical, such as Philip Mirowski's *Never Let a Serious Crisis Go to Waste* (2013) and Maurizio Lazzarato's *The Making of Indebted Man* (2012), they all concur that one of the strengths of Foucault's work on neoliberalism is that he concerned himself with the production of neoliberal subjectivity. Dardot and Laval devote a chapter to "Manufacturing the Neoliberal Subject" (2013, ch. 9), while Mirowski writes of an "everyday neoliberalism" that takes its cue from his appraisal of Foucault's view of neoliberal identity (2013, pp. 89f.). Mirowski (2013, pp. 95–96) even allows that Foucault "got there first" with regard to key propositions about this neoliberal subjectivity, including the fragmentation of identity attendant upon the neoliberal version of the self, the indefinite extension of the entrepreneurial regime of the self to all aspects of life, the relationship of the entrepreneurial self to risk, and the general malleability of the self. My reservation here is that while Foucault elsewhere described his general project as one concerned with the ways in which the subject is produced, there are only two sets of indications about the theme of neoliberalism and subjectivity in *The Birth of Biopolitics*, which we will summarize in a moment. Nonetheless, I take Mirowski's point that many critical thinkers – whether Marxist or otherwise – want to portray neoliberalism as something more than a deployment of class power and use Foucault to specify "the chains of causality stretching from the executive committee of the capitalist class to the shopper at Wal-Mart" (2013, p. 99). Foucault presents a sophisticated take on how neoliberal governmentality reaches into the very "relation of self to self," of every individual as worker, consumer, and just about any other social identity they might find themselves inhabiting. Let's look more closely at this.

Foucault on Neoliberal Subjectivity

The problem of neoliberal subjectivity does not appear until halfway through the ninth lecture of *The Birth of Biopolitics*, which is also the first lecture concerning American neoliberalism. Even here it does not constitute the main topic, which is simply an exposition of the central components of American neoliberalism and the difference between it and Ordoliberalism. It is introduced in the discussion of the theory of human capital, associated with Theodore Schultz, Jacob Mincer, and Gary Becker, and first emerges in the account of the worker's relation to work.

Foucault contrasts the treatment of labor in Marx and the human capital theorists. In Marx, abstract labor (or "labor power") is a result of the logic of capital and of its historical reality; for American neoliberalism this abstraction is not a product of capitalist production but of the economic theory that has been constructed upon it (Foucault 2008, p. 221). The latter "adopts the task of analyzing the form of human behavior and the internal rationality of this human behavior" (Foucault 2008, p. 223). In other words, it takes the viewpoint of the worker in economic theory rather than regarding labor as simply one of the variables that enters into production. Foucault concludes that these American neoliberals "for the first time, ensure that the worker is not present in the economic analysis as an object – the object of supply and demand in the form of labor power – but as an active economic subject" (2008, p. 223).

It is at this point that Foucault announces that American neoliberalism undertakes a new approach to the economic subject. *Homo œconomicus* is no longer "a partner of exchange" explicable in terms of "the theory of utility based on the problematic of needs" (Foucault 2008, p. 225). Rather *homo œconomicus* is "an entrepreneur, an entrepreneur of himself" (Foucault 2008, p. 226). This means that whether we approach them as producers or consumers, economic subjects should be regarded as their own capital, which is the source of both their own income and satisfaction. Even consumption must be regarded as an activity and consuming individuals are producers of their own satisfaction. What is crucial to remember here is that this is a supposition of economic theory not a concrete technology of government such as the disciplinary practices and forms of knowledge that "subjectify" the individual as criminal, homosexual, and so on.

Foucault then goes on to show the breakdown of human capital into innate and acquired elements. With respect to the former, he suggestively argues that even the genetic makeup of individuals and its manipulation will come to be regarded as a component of human capital. After discussing the augmentation of the acquired elements of human capital through education, parenting, maternal care, family life, migration, and mobility, he concludes that all these aspects of human life can enter into economic analysis "as behavior in terms of individual enterprise, of enterprise of oneself with investments and incomes" (Foucault 2008, p. 230). In this lecture, then, the entirety of Foucault's analysis of neoliberal subjectivity concerns the implication of human capital *theory*. The lecture concludes with an analysis of the implications of this for problems of economic growth and development, but there remains no discussion of the strategies and programs that might seek to enhance human capital nor technologies that work on what he would later call "the relation of self to self."

But, as we shall see, it is not the absence of technologies of creating subjects that makes neoliberal interventions de-subjectifying.

At the beginning of the next, second lecture on American neoliberalism Foucault returns to Ordoliberalism in order to contrast it with the American use of the market economy to decipher all aspects of non-market relations. In the course of a discussion of the promotion of small and medium size enterprises in Ordoliberal social policy (*Gesellschaftpolitik*) he again raises the question of the generalization of the enterprise to all aspects of "the individuals' life itself – with his relationships to private property ... family, household, insurance, and retirement" (Foucault 2008, p. 241). The individual becomes "a permanent and multiple enterprise."

Again, Foucault's principal concern is not with the formation of neoliberal subjectivity but with the contrast between Ordoliberalism and American neoliberalism. On the one side, there is the "economic-ethical ambiguity" of Ordoliberalism with its idea of a "society for the market and a society against the market, a society oriented towards the market and a society that compensates for the effects of the market in the realm of value and existence" (Foucault 2008, pp. 241, 242). On the other, this ambiguity will be resolved by the radical nature of American neoliberalism that seeks an "unlimited generalization of the form of the market" and uses the economic form of the market as "a principle of decipherment of social relationships and individual behavior" (Foucault 2008, p. 243). Insofar as Foucault is concerned with something like a neoliberal subjectivity, it is as but one feature of the broader generalization of economic rationality he finds, to varying extent, in the texts of the different schools of neoliberalism. It is a second-order form of the observation of human behavior, not a first-order description of a new kind of subject. And, we might add, it is a form of observation with potentially "liberatory" aspects, particularly from forms of subjectification – at least for Foucault.

Foucault finishes this lecture by discussing the question of crime and punishment. This part of the lecture is crucial because it makes clear what he derives from American neoliberalism. It also shows that what is at stake is not so much a form of neoliberal subjectification but the potential of de-subjectification.

Here, Foucault argues that penal reformers such as Jeremy Bentham and Cesare Beccaria advanced a notion of *homo penalis* that is a kind of correlate of *homo œconomicus* in so far as the objective of their reform is "to find the least costly and most effective form of obtaining punishment and the elimination of conducts deemed harmful for society" (2008, p. 249). However, the search for this ideal legal framework has the "paradoxical effect" that it opens the possibility of a subjectification of the offender. Penalty and law have meaning not only as punishment of an act but also as a treatment of "an individual, an offender who must be punished, corrected and made to serve as a possible example to other offenders" (Foucault 2008, p. 249). In the course of the nineteenth century, and under the effect of multiple and reciprocal problematizations of the different social sciences, *homo penalis* gives ways to *homo criminalis*. The idea of the criminal is thereby born: someone who through their innate makeup or environment, through their deviation from a norm, their membership of a population or a class, their social deviance or psychopathology, embodies a certain identity. There is thus "an inflation of forms and bodies of knowledge, of discourse, a multiplication of authorities and decision-making elements, and the parasitic invasion of the sentence in the name of the law and the norm" (Foucault 2008, p. 250). Foucault concludes, almost as an afterthought, that "[a]nyway, this is how I would see things were I to adopt a neo-liberal perspective on this evolution" (2008, p. 250). Nevertheless such a perspective bears a strong resemblance to the emergence of the epistemological-juridical complex of the power to punish addressed in *Discipline and Punish* (1977, p. 23).

There is nothing like this in the neoliberal approach to the entrepreneurial subject for Foucault – no bodies of knowledge, no new authorities, no forms of normalization. According to Foucault, the genius of the human capital approach to crime and punishment is precisely that it forgoes the translation of economic theory into an ideal legal-institutional form. The source of the problem is that by invoking the principle of utility, Bentham and Beccaria had thought they had found a justification for the exercise of authority by the state. Indeed one might say, utility is a principle of "veridiction" or truth-production by the state, something Foucault's approach to liberalism rules out with its privilege of the market as the site of veridiction for liberal governing. Becker, by contrast to the eighteenth-century reformers, will keep to a purely economic analysis in which crime is simply that which makes the individual run the risk of penalty. By adopting the point of view of the person who commits the crime, Becker moves to the side of the individual subject in a manner that evades the determinations of subjectivity found in psychopathology or criminal anthropology. Foucault argues that considering the subject as *homo œconomicus* neither means that the whole subject becomes *homo œconomicus*, nor is it based on an anthropological theory of the subject. It simply means that "economic behavior is the grid of intelligibility that one will adopt on the behavior of the new individual ... power gets a hold of him to the extent, and only to the extent, that he is *homo œconomicus*" (Foucault 2008, p. 252).

This neoliberal de-subjectification of the idea of the criminal leads Foucault to draw some larger implications regarding the forms of power he had been pursuing in the previous decade: sovereignty, discipline, and biopolitics. Because of his supposition that power is omnipresent, Foucault's problematic is not one that seeks a freedom from *all* sorts of power but rather an alternative to *particular kinds* of power and regulation. At the end of the lecture in question, Foucault finds in American neoliberalism a rather precisely defined alternative to the other kinds of power and regulation he had analyzed:

> You can see that what appears on the horizon of this kind of analysis is not at all the idea of a project of an exhaustively disciplinary society in which the legal network hemming in individuals is taken over and extended internally by, let's say, normative mechanisms. Nor is it a society in which the mechanism of general normalization and the exclusion of those who cannot be normalized is needed.
>
> *(2008, p. 259)*

This statement directly addresses the governing of crime, but not *just* that. It can be read in terms of the movement of Foucault's thought through forms of power. What is envisaged by American neoliberalism then is a form of regulation that is not one of a *sovereign* power exercised through law, or of *disciplinary* society with its norms, or even of the general normalization of a *biopolitics* of the population. It is not one of the major forms of regulation discussed by Foucault prior to these lectures on governmentality in 1979 and nor is it the framework of biopolitics still attributed to the 1979 lecture course (no doubt due to its rather misleading title). Rather it is a new program and vision:

> On the horizon of this analysis we see instead the image, idea, or theme-program of a society in which there is an optimization of systems of difference, in which the field is left open to fluctuating processes, in which minority individuals and practices are tolerated, in which action is brought to bear on the rules of the game rather than on the players, and finally in which there is an environmental type of intervention instead of the internal subjugation of individuals [de l'assujettissement interne des individus].
>
> *(Foucault 2008, pp. 259–260; 2004, p. 265)*

It would be mistaken to suggest that Foucault does not have reservations about the project of the manipulation of choice through environmental interventions of the behavioral type – as he indicates at the beginning of the next lecture (Foucault 2008, p. 271). Yet these would seem simply to be the costs – in his language, the "dangers" – of a form of neoliberal regulation that he finds has certain benefits – or "potentials." Chief among these potentials is that regulation no longer entails the internal "subjectification" (*assujettisement*) of the individual. We need to attend to the French phrase translated in English as "of the internal subjugation of individuals." *Assujettisement* has a specific dual meaning in Foucault's thought: it is not only subjection in the sense of "submission to" or "subjugation" but also entails the fabrication or production of subjectivity. This dual meaning is underlined by the adjective "internal" that emphasizes not the mere external forms of subjugation (as the equivalent of domination) but the internal forms of subjugation as "subjectification," as the fabrication of subjectivity through relations of power and knowledge. Thus Foucault here distinguishes the neoliberal program from those forms of power and knowledge such as discipline and the human and social sciences that subjugate individuals through the production of subjectivity, that is through tying individuals to the truth of their identity, for example the occasional criminal, the recidivist, the dangerous individual, the invert, and so on. For Foucault in this passage neoliberalism does not subjectify in this sense. In doing so, it opens up the space for tolerating minority individuals and practices and optimizing systems of differences.

This conclusion is an astonishing one. Michael Behrent (2016, p. 53) suggests it shows how far Foucault had come from *Discipline and Punish* with its foreshadowing of a society of normalization. I would add that it marks an astonishing end – even a *telos* – to Foucault's thinking of power over the previous decade. He now foresees a "way out" of the struggle against the "forms of subjection ... the submission of subjectivity" he identified as the central concern of his own epoch in his essay "The Subject and Power" (1982, p. 782) – with the help of this neoliberal rationality, logic, and future imaginary. It is mistaken to think that Foucault offers us an account of neoliberal subjectivity. What he thinks that neoliberalism offers us instead is a way out of subjectification, a way out of the double bind that ties the production of who we are to our domination, the tethering of subjectivity to subjugation.

I realize this reading cuts against the grain of much Foucault scholarship but, at least in this one respect, that scholarship is haunted by a phantasm that simply is not supported by the text. While Foucault is not entirely clear, and his thought has a continuing experimental character and often takes on chameleon colors, the main thrust of his analysis here is that viewing the self as an enterprise and the generalization of this entrepreneurial self is not a new form of subjectification, equivalent to the subjectivity produced by the individualizing and normalizing knowledges of the disciplines and related sciences. Rather it is a way of theorizing and thinking about the subject that does not view subjects from the outside as something to be managed, classified, and divided, but from their own point of view, and makes minimal assumptions about their nature, for example Becker's assumption of the non-randomness of the individual subject's reaction to changes in its environment (Foucault 2008, p. 269). While power can never be entirely limited, and from the viewpoint of the social sciences this way of viewing individuals is reductive, it does cast aside the straightjacketed subjects of the disciplinary and normalizing powers he had fought against, allows difference, and tolerates minority groups.

Some Implications

Foucault, of course, was not entirely uncritical of American neoliberalism. Nor would it be correct to say that he became a card-carrying member of the Neoliberal Thought Collective. Yet there is no doubt that these are crucial and almost secret passages in his work: textual passages and intellectual passageways. In this sense, his conclusions regarding neoliberal regulation can be read as a kind of exclamation point on ten years of concept formation and analyses of relations of power. It is also possible that Ewald, and Andrew Dilts (2011), are correct in viewing the encounter with human capital theory as a passageway to the later texts on subjectivity and ancient practices of the self. The flipside of neoliberalism's imaginary of a form of regulation without subjectification is the idea of a domain in which individuals form their own subjectivity by technologies of the self with or without the help of others.

What are the political and the policy implications that should concern us here? The work of Michael Behrent (2010, 2016) has demonstrated the close association between Foucault and the so-called Second Left in France at the time of these lectures. The Second Left was a faction of socialists and unionists that sought a new approach to socialist politics based on the decomposition and distribution of the state into voluntary associations according to the principle of self-management, *autogestion*. Their principal concern was to free the Socialist Party, forever the bridesmaid on the verge of forming government for the first time, from "social statism." Foucault participated in their conferences and mobilizations and praised the work of their major theorist, Pierre Rosanvallon. Indeed in the course summary of *The Birth of Biopolitics*, Foucault credits Rosanvallon with the discovery of liberalism as critique of government that employs the market as a site of truth production or "veridiction" (2008, p. 320). The Second Left would have shared Foucault's incredible – and unargued for – claim that there is no "autonomous socialist governmentality" (2008, p. 92) and that the only alternatives for the Left were to latch onto a liberal governmentality or be condemned to a "police-state" or "party" one. Hardly, one might say, much of a choice! While of course it is difficult to identify Foucault's politics, he shows an affinity with a kind of "libertarian Left" that is both willing to engage in anti-statism and anti-institutionalism as very much part of France's anti-totalitarian moment of the 1970s and willing to experiment with neoliberal technologies of government. In some ways he can be viewed as anticipating, and participating in, early experiments on the

French Left that will have more enduring manifestations in the Anglophone world in the idea of the Third Way in British Labour politics and President Clinton's administration. While this political formation for a time seemed like the only possible position of the institutional Left in its struggle to take government, the recent rise of nationalism and acclamatory populism suggests its two flaws. First, the focus on a politics of identity and subjectivity, and the local struggles that accompany them, left an opening for populist movements with large segments of the working class with little sympathy for those concerns. Moreover, second, it is precisely the latter whose standard of living and basis of subsistence in the labor market has been substantially eroded with the fostering of neoliberal trade policies and the growth of inequality. It is perhaps no longer possible to prefer Foucault's specific and partial transformations in the fields of subjectivity (1984, pp. 46–47) to questions of inequality and the struggles concerning the state.

Finally, consider the implications for public policy. In an interview for a Second Left collection in 1983, Foucault diagnoses the current problem of social security as one of "facing economic obstacles that are only too familiar," as being limited against the "political, economic and social rationality of modern societies" and having the "perverse effects" of "an increasing rigidity of certain mechanisms" and "a growth of dependence" (Foucault 1988, p. 160). This dependence arises not from marginalization, as it historically had, but from *integration* in the social security system itself (Foucault 1988, p. 162). His answers to these problems are framed in terms of a "way of life" and deploy the language of "lifestyles" (Foucault 1988, pp. 164–165). They seek a "social security that opens the way to a richer, more numerous, more diverse, and more flexible relation with oneself and one's environment," that guarantees a "real autonomy" (Foucault 1988, p. 161). To combat welfare dependency, Foucault also suggests "a process of decentralization" that would lead to a closer relation between users of services and "decision-making centers" (1988, p. 165). In short, the structural economic problems of the fiscal crisis of the welfare state were to be met with new forms of relations to oneself and the decomposition of the state. He stops short of advocating marketization here but he concludes the welfare system should become a "vast experimental field" and that the "whole institutional complex, at present very fragile, will probably have to undergo a restructuring from top to bottom" (Foucault 1988, p. 166). In this same interview, as Zamora points out (2016, pp. 74–75; Foucault 1988, pp. 169), he rejects "the right to health" in terms closely related to free-market arguments against universal health care. Because of the technical growth of medicine and the demand for health, Foucault argues (1988, p. 169), "it is not possible to lay down objectively a theoretical, practical threshold, valid for all, on the basis of which it might be said that health needs are entirely and definitively satisfied." This, again, reminds us of the implications of these arguments for a present in which the faltering attempts at universal coverage in the United States are being abandoned. These few remarks, consonant with the orientation of the Second Left (and not altogether alien to what became Ewald's practice in the 1990s), give us a clue to what his planned book on the art of government and socialist politics might look like. They also have a certain familiarity for those of us who have taken more than a passing interest in the so-called "reform" of welfare states in the name of combatting their self-produced dependency in recent decades and the inflationary tendencies of demands on them.

Let us say that the countercultural and political movements of the sixties and early seventies placed the question of subjectivity – the "politics of experience," as R. D. Laing called it – on the agenda in a time of relative prosperity. With the crisis of the 1970s neoliberalism would appropriate themes around individual freedom, empowerment, and the potentiality of the forces of civil society against the state. Influential sections of the institutional and party Left would seek, just as Foucault predicted, to appropriate and experiment with elements, rationalities, and technologies from neoliberalism, particularly in regard to the welfare state. What emerged over the ensuing period was the flooding of social policy and the welfare state by the neoliberal use of self-technologies, so that the entrepreneurial subject indeed became the elusive goal of many neoliberal social and economic programs, contrary to Foucault's analysis, and we have witnessed an idolatry of the narcissistic individual – from the Me Generation of the 1980s to the "selfies" of today – in popular culture to the point that the ultimate one occupies the White House itself. While the latter subject has indeed occupied a key space in our public culture during this time a more subterranean movement, called by some "neoliberal paternalism" (Soss, Fording, and Schram 2011), has sought to nudge, hector, shame, discipline, and coerce the victims of structural inequality, class and race, into adopting certain forms of subjectivity manifested by their betters and thought to be necessary to contemporary social and economic life. Foucault's lectures on neoliberalism and comments on the welfare state belong to this crucial hinge-moment in recent political culture. In this sense there is a Faustian pact here: Foucault can seem insightful and prescient about neoliberalism because he would come to share so many of its premises: the impossibility of a science of the human that does not intensify domination, the economy – not the public, or the state – as the generator and manifestation of truth, at least for liberal or even modern governance, and the occlusion of the question of inequality. Foucault both acutely diagnosed and to some extent could be said to have participated in what amounted to a counter-revolution in public policy.

As the *Los Angeles Review of Books* has argued in respect of this case, our task is to think for ourselves rather than criticizing intellectuals of the past for our contemporary problems, or believing that they held a magic bullet to solve them. Nevertheless Foucault's work has been massively influential in the contemporary social sciences – and in that part that continues to imagine itself as critical – at the same time in which those sciences have proved largely acquiescent in the face of this neoliberal counter-revolution. Since 1980, the institutional Left – what used to be called "social democracy" – has been one of the main agents of this counter-revolution and allowed itself to become identified with it. This has facilitated the current reconfiguration of the conservative right that can extend the everyday, embedded, and routinized form of neoliberalism with its focus on competition and its low-tax, deregulatory ethos, at the same time as it mobilizes popular movements against global trade agreements, action on global environmental problems, and the possibility of the movement of subjugated peoples on our planet.

Bibliography

Agamben, G. (2011). *The Kingdom and the Glory: For a Theological Genealogy of Economy and Government*, trans. L. Chiesa with M. Mandarini. Stanford, CA: Stanford University Press.

Becker, G., Ewald, F., and Harcourt, B. (2012). *Becker on Ewald on Foucault on Becker: American Neoliberalism and Michel Foucault's 1979 "Birth of Biopolitics" Lectures*. Institute for Law and Economics Working Paper No. 614. Chicago: University of Chicago Law School.

Behrent, M. C. (2010). Accidents Happen: François Ewald, the "Anti revolutionary Foucault," and the Intellectual Politics of the French Welfare State. *Journal of Modern History*, 82(3), 585–624.

Behrent, M. C. (2016). Liberalism without Humanism: Michel Foucault and the Free-Market Creed. In D. Zamora and M. Behrent (Eds.), *Foucault and Neoliberalism* (pp. 24–62). Cambridge: Polity.

Brenner, N., Peck, J., and Theodore, N. (2010). Variegated Neoliberalization: Geographies, Modalities, Pathways. *Global Networks*, 10, 182–222.

Dardot, P. and Laval, C. (2013). *The New Way of the World: On Neoliberal Society*, trans. G. Elliot. London: Verso.

Dean, M. (1999). *Governmentality: Power and Rule in Modern Society*. London: Sage.

Dean, M. (2014a). Michel Foucault's "Apology" for Neoliberalism. *Journal of Political Power*, 7(3), 433–442.

Dean, M. (2014b). Rethinking Neoliberalism. *Journal of Sociology*, 50(2), 150–163.

Dean, M. and Hindess, B. (1998). Introduction: Government, Liberalism, Society. In M. Dean and B. Hindess (Eds.), *Governing Australia: Studies in Contemporary Rationalities of Government*. Cambridge: Cambridge University Press.

de Lagasnerie, G. (2012). *La Dernière Leçon de Michel Foucault: Sur le Néolibéralisme, la Théorie et la Politique*. Paris: Fayard.

Dilts, A. (2011). From "Entrepreneur of the Self" to "Care of the Self": Neo-liberal Governmentality and Foucault's Ethics. *Foucault Studies*, 12, 130–146.

Donzelot, J. and Gordon, C. (2008). Governing Liberal Societies: The Foucault Effect in the English-speaking World. *Foucault Studies*, 5, 48–62.

Du Gay, P. and Scott, A. (2010). State Transformation or Regime Shift? *Sociologica*, 2. Retrieved from: www.sociologica.mulino.it/journal/issue/index/Issue/Journal:ISSUE:10

Ewald, F. (2016). François Ewald on Foucault and Neoliberalism. January 24. Retrieved from: http://blogs.law.columbia.edu/foucault1313/2016/01/24/ewaldneoliberalism/

Foucault, M. (1977). *Discipline and Punish: The Birth of the Prison*, trans. A. Sheridan. London: Allen Lane.

Foucault, M. (1982). The Subject and Power. *Critical Inquiry*, 8(4), 777–795.

Foucault, M. (1984). What is Enlightenment? In P. Rabinow (Ed.), *The Foucault Reader* (pp. 32–50). London: Penguin.

Foucault, M. (1988). Social Security. In L. Kritzman (Ed.), *Politics, Philosophy, Culture: Interviews and Other Writings 1977–84* (pp. 159–177). New York: Routledge.

Foucault, M. (2003). *"Society Must be Defended": Lectures at the Collège de France, 1975–1976*, trans. D. Macey. New York: Picador.

Foucault, M. (2004). *Naissance de la Biopolitique: Cours au Collège de France, 1978–1979*. Paris: Gallimard Seuil.

Foucault, M. (2008). *The Birth of Biopolitics: Lectures at the Collège de France 1978–1979*, trans. G. Burchell. London: Palgrave Macmillan.

Gamble, A. (1979). Free Economy and the Strong State. *The Socialist Register*, 16, 1 25.

Goldschmidt, N. and Rauchenschwandtner, H. (2007). *The Philosophy of the Social Market Economy: Michel Foucault's Analysis of "Ordoliberalism". Freiburg Discussion Papers on Constitutional Economics, 07/4.* Freiburg: Walter Eucken Institute.

Hansen, M. P. (2015). Foucault's Flirt? Neoliberalism, the Left and the Welfare State. *Foucault Studies*, 20, 291–306.

Hayek, F. A. (1981). Interview, *El Mercurio*. April 12. Retrieved from: www.fahayek.org/

Jaschik, S. (2017). Anthropologists and Other Scholars Plan Read-in of Michel Foucault to Protest Inauguration of Donald Trump. *Inside Higher Ed*, January 16. Retrieved from: www.insidehighered.com/

Laclau, E. and Mouffe, C. (2001). *Hegemony and Socialist Strategy: Towards a Radical Democratic Politics.* London: Verso.

Lazzarato, M. (2009). Neoliberalism in Action: Inequality, Insecurity and the Reconstitution of the Social. *Theory, Culture and Society*, 29(6), 109–133.

Lazzarato, M. (2012). *The Making of Indebted Man: An Essay on the Neoliberal Condition*, trans. J. D. Jordan. Los Angeles: Semiotext(e).

Mirowski, P. (2009). Postface: Defining Neoliberalism. In P. Mirowski and D. Plehwe (Eds.), *The Road from Mont Pèlerin: The Making of the Neoliberal Thought Collective* (pp. 417–455). Cambridge, MA: Harvard University Press.

Mirowski, P. (2013). *Never Let a Serious Crisis Go to Waste: How Neoliberalism Survived the Financial Meltdown.* London: Verso.

Mirowski, P. and Plehwe, D. (Eds.) *The Road from Mont Pèlerin. The Making of the Neoliberal Thought Collective.* Cambridge, MA: Harvard University Press

Negri, A. (2001). Interview. *Le Monde*. October 3. Retrieved from: libcom.org/library/interview-le-monde-negri/

Peck, J. (2010a). *Constructions of Neoliberal Reason.* Oxford: Oxford University Press.

Peck, J. (2010b). Zombie Neoliberalism and the Ambidextrous State. *Theoretical Criminology*, 14(1), 1–7.

Rose, N. (1996). Governing "Advanced" Liberal Democracies. In A. Barry, T. Osborne, and N. Rose (Eds.), *Foucault and Political Reason: Liberalism, Neo-Liberalism and Rationalities of Government* (pp. 37–64). London: UCL Press.

Sennelart, M. (2007). Course Context. In M. Foucault, *Security, Territory, Population: Lectures at the Collège de France 1977–1978* (pp. 369–401). London: Palgrave Macmillan.

Soss, J., Fording, R. C., and Schram, S. F. (2011). *Disciplining the Poor: Neoliberal Paternalism and the Persistent Power of Race.* Chicago: University of Chicago Press.

Steinmetz-Jenkins, D. and Arnold, A. (2015). Searching for Foucault in an Age of Inequality. *Los Angeles Review of Books.* Retrieved from: https://lareviewofbooks.org/

Weber, M. (1978). *Economy and Society: An Outline of Interpretative Sociology*, 2 vols. Berkeley: University of California Press.

Zamora, D. (2014a). Can We Criticize Foucault? *Jacobin*. Retrieved from: www.jacobinmag. com/2014/12/foucault-interview/

Zamora, D. (Ed.) (2014b). *Critiquer Foucault: Les Années 1980 et la Tentation Néolibérale.* Brussels: Éditions Aden.

Zamora, D. (2016). Foucault, the Excluded and the Neoliberal Erosion of the State. In D. Zamora and M. Behrent (Eds.), *Foucault and Neoliberalism* (pp. 63–84). Cambridge: Cambridge University Press.

Zamora, D. and Behrent, M. (Eds.) (2016). *Foucault and Neoliberalism*. Cambridge: Polity.

3

FOUCAULT'S THREE WAYS OF DECENTERING THE STATE

Kaspar Villadsen

Currently, we witness certain tendencies to valorize society over the state. In relation to the collapse of the former communist states in Eastern Europe and authoritarian regimes in Northern Africa and the Middle East, there were hopes for democracy arising from below. In several cases, however, ethnic and religious conflicts have displayed the dark side of a civil society "freed from" the state. Across welfare states from New Zealand to Canada, universal social services provided by the state have been increasingly dismantled as governments reduce funding, tighten eligibility criteria, and delegate service provision to market agents and voluntary associations. Within social science, intellectual streams like governance theory, governmentality studies, and Actor Network Theory dissolve the unity of the state. Instead, it is argued that the state should be viewed as "decentered" or decomposed into transient policy networks and global circulations, hence problematizing the idea of centralized political sovereignty exercised over a territory. All of this would seem to imply a diminishing importance of the state. Conversely, however, we have recently witnessed the irruption of nationalism across Europe, the closing of borders around national territories, and the proclamation of protectionism in the USA, all of which puts back the state – and state-centered governance – at the center of the political and intellectual agenda.

It is well known that Michel Foucault challenged the centrality of the state. Instead, he advanced a view of the state as decentered: "I must do without a theory of the state, as one can and must forego an indigestible meal" (2008, pp. 76–77). Foucault further declared: "The state has no heart, as we well know, but not just in the sense that it has no feelings, either good or bad, but it has no heart in the sense that it has no interior" (Foucault 2008, p. 90). Given Foucault's continuous influence over new generations of social science scholars who study problems of the state, and related issues such as territoriality, borders, social policy, and welfare services it is pertinent to evaluate the legacy of his writings on the state. At the outset it should be noted that Foucault's approach is neither a history of the state nor is it a sociology of the state and its institutions. Instead, he recovers from the historical archive different frameworks, "the reflexive prisms," or the grids of intelligibility, though which something called "the state" appears.

Foucault does not undertake these investigations from a mere historical interest. On several occasions, he mentions that he wishes to "test" the potentials of a particular perspective on the state. This aspiration is evident in his 1976 lecture series, where Foucault wanted to test to what extent politics could be conceived as war by other means (2003), or to be more precise, the question of which insights could be achieved by analyzing state formation and the preservation of the state as resulting from struggles between social groups. Foucault's experimental approach to analyzing the state could be said, then, to follow this explorative question: What if we imagine that the state rests upon perpetual social struggle? Or, as he would ask in 1978, what would happen if we imagine the state as pervaded by contradictory governmental rationalities? It is by excavating a body of historical texts, confronting the reader with a particular reflexive prism, that Foucault shows us the potential of a particular framework of analysis. It is this analytical testing that I wish to foreground in this chapter.

In this context, I am neither interested in reifying the idea of Foucault's "decentered state" nor in discussing the historical accuracy of Foucault's analyses regarding the state. The question is instead which resources Foucault's evolving thought on the state offers for contemporary analysis of urgent political issues. The following sections examine the three main routes by which Foucault in the 1970s reached his famous "decentered" approach to the state. I suggest that through these routes Foucault excavates distinct analytical frameworks, and I discuss them in light of contemporary issues. In particular, I consider the question of how Foucault's political thought can be used to study the relationship between the state, civil society, and contemporary neoliberalism. The issues discussed include first, the resurrection of European populism and its connection to economic reforms, second, the EU's reaction to the "refugee crisis," and, third, the rise of Occupy Wall Street and the Tea Party movements in the USA.

First Decentering: The State Rests Upon Social Struggle

> (B)eneath the formal facade of the State, there were other forces and ... they were precisely not forces of the State, but the forces of a particular group with its own history, its own relationship with the past, its own victories, its own blood, and its own relations of domination.
>
> *(Foucault 2003, p. 224)*

The problem of the state's pretentions to universality has been a key question ever since the emergence of the modern state in Western Europe in the seventeenth century and remained urgent with the coming of constitutional democracy. A longstanding problem is how the state can safeguard universal norms while at the same time being responsive to particular individuals with specific needs and demands. In political theory, it has been acknowledged that any universal claim inscribed into the state's laws and institutions will always, inevitably, emanate from particular groups and their values. The 1976 lecture series *Society Must be Defended* (2003) is where Foucault most directly addresses the problem of how the state may represent the totality – that is, reflect the multiplicity of heterogeneous groups and identities. However, Foucault follows a route that disallows any support of the state as the unrivalled instrument necessary to end centuries of confessional conflicts and safeguard against social and ethnic rivalries. Instead, in the 1976 lectures, Foucault presented the social body as a site of perpetual struggles for dominance. In this context, the state does not at all appear as the safeguard against these struggles but rather as the vehicle and crystallization of them.

This is the first decentering of the state that Foucault would perform during the late 1970s. In *Society Must be Defended*, Foucault (2003) breaks down the idea of a unified state sovereignty by presenting a version of society as traversed by perpetual social rivalries. These lectures have been commented upon by a range of scholars, offering quite diverse readings (Pasquino 1993; Marks 2000; Badiou 2012; Karlsen and Villadsen 2015; Dean and Villadsen 2016). Here, I focus on how Foucault argues for a fundamental transition in the legitimation of territorial sovereignty. The fundamental shift is from the absolute monarch's sovereignty to the precarious construction of "the people" under democratized sovereignty.

To frame the whole lecture series Foucault performs a, for him, typical narrative move: He describes a radical discursive break which he subsequently complicates, demonstrating its porosity and contingency. This happens by way of a counter-positioning of Hobbes and Clausewitz as emblematic for two competing discourses on politics and state-formation. Leaving aside whether Foucault's interpretation of Hobbes was correct (Pasquino 1993), we notice that Hobbes is type-cast as emblematic of the centrist-juridical model that Foucault seeks to move beyond: "We have to study power outside the model of Leviathan, outside the field delineated by juridical sovereignty and the institutions of the State" (Foucault 2003, p. 34). On Foucault's account, the Hobbesian model of sovereignty established as break in political discourse which was both temporal and spatial. Implicit in this model was the relegation of war to a pre-modern, barbarian past or to the outside of the civilized territories of the modern West: "Increasingly, wars, the practices of war, and the institutions of war tended to exist, so to speak, only on the frontiers, on the outer limits of the great State units" (Foucault 2003, p. 48).

Foucault then advances his key proposition: There is a continuation of war within a society that has allegedly been pacified. Foucault makes this point by exploring two historical sources, namely "race-war" historians and the modern medical sciences with their normalizing effects. The first textual source centers on the premise that any universalizing erection of the state's legal and constitutional order is inevitably based on a singular project originating from a particular group, a people or a "race." Foucault aligns himself with seventeenth-century race-war writers who approached state-formation as a question of writing-up victorious narratives of the people and nation. Notably, in this textual archive, "race" does not designate a specific ethnicity, but rather figures in discursive battles for mobilizing one social group against another in struggles over territorial control. Foucault thus finds a discursive resource, a kind of "counter-history" that tears society apart. Race war discourse comprises a range of very diverse writers, including the Puritans, the Levellers, and the Diggers in England, and it is represented by reactionary French aristocrats who fought against the monarchy. Foucault also forges a link to later supporters of biological racism and state eugenics appearing in the late nineteenth century.

The significance of this discourse is that it undermines the constitution of the state by rendering its universalism the outcome of contingent struggles and impossible totalizations. The race-war writers also resonate with Foucault's Nietzschean view of history as perpetual struggle for dominance (Marks 2000). In his essay on Nietzsche, Foucault thus wrote: "humanity installs each of its violences in a system of rules and thus proceeds from domination to domination" (Foucault 1981, p. 85). Race-war discourse disrupts the idea of history as progressing towards a pacified universality. There is no claim for a truthful, non-partisan writing of history here. Instead, the historian is "a subject who is fighting a war" (Foucault 2003, p. 54). Hence, the race-war writers are recognized to be in absolute partisanship, writing against defined adversaries.

Across Foucault's authorship, one finds several analyses that potentially undermine the foundations of the modern, constitutional state as a guarantor of liberal rights, the system of representation, and civic peace (Foucault 2000a, 2000b). This undermining can be related to Foucault's rather fundamental distrust in the social body to be safeguarded (Gordon 1996). Society appears, on Foucault's account, to be fundamentally pervaded by relations of domination, suspicions, exclusions, denunciations, and mutual surveillance. The unity of "the people" is rendered as an immanent field of perpetual and multiple force relations that seem to disallow being constituted as a legitimate subject of democratic politics.

Austerity, "Populism," and the Greek Crisis

The theme of "race-war discourse" opens up the study of the formation of statehood around notions of national identity, the people, race, blood, and rightful inheritance (Dean and Villadsen 2016, pp. 67 ff.). This is certainly an urgent issue in our present. Across Europe, right-wing populism has gained influence demanding the suspension of universal rights in their quest to control or expel individuals who allegedly threaten the state's unity from inside. We have witnessed the rise of nationalist parties in countries like the Netherlands (Wilders), France (Le Pen), Denmark ("The Danish People's Party"), and Austria (Haider). In the last decades, we have also seen an upsurge of ethnic nationalism and bloody religious persecution in the former Yugoslavia, in Ukraine, in parts of Africa, and in the Middle East. One may also observe a continuation or resurgence of "populist" political regimes, particularly in Latin America, including Venezuela, Argentina, Equador, and Bolivia. In the USA, the situation is very different, yet the Occupy movement, the Tea Party, and Donald Trump have all been designated "populist."

If we focus on the European context, we may relate the recent rise of populism to neoliberal reforms implemented in certain countries that have drastically reduced expenditures on health and welfare. Greece and Spain, in particular, have witnessed the re-emergence of social issues such as general poverty, rapidly rising youth unemployment, and an increasing amount of indebted and even homeless families. These reforms that rest on neoliberal principles have triggered increasing popular discontent and given rise to massive protests – at times addressed to national governments, at other times addressing the"troika" of the European Central Bank, the European Union, and the International Monetary Fund. We have witnessed the discursive construction of two camps, that is, "the people" suffering under severe austerity and "the establishment" consisting of domestic elites and the EU institutions. As in the race-war discourse studied by Foucault, we see competing narratives of the historical process leading to the crisis, just as we see irreconcilable representations of who constitute legitimate political actors, and who are represented as irresponsibly populist.

Let us briefly consider the Greek government-debt crisis, which was also termed "the Greek Depression." It is well known that an agreement was reached on October 27, 2011 in which extensive austerity measures where requested by the European Central Bank, the EU leaders, and the International Monetary Fund in return for a bailout. From 2010 to 2016, the Greek government undertook twelve rounds of tax increases, implemented cuts in public spending, and major welfare reforms. Between 2008 and 2012, the Greek GDP diminished by 20 percent, and youth unemployment reached as high as 60 percent. These effects triggered sustained public discontent, evident in the Indignant Citizens Movement, and nationwide protests centered on issues like pension cuts and youth unemployment. The EU-group and IMF represented the Greek problem as one about returning to normality and securing the (otherwise) successful EU-collaboration by taking "unavoidable measures." In the discourse formulated by Greeks in opposition to the austerity measures, the Eurogroup and IMF allegedly performed a drastic shift towards Greece from the encouragement to spend to an "overnight declaration" of the Greek debt as irresponsible and unsustainable (Stavrakakis 2015, p. 276).

The anti-austerity and anti-EU elite-discourse can be reconstructed along the following lines: In late 2009, upon a global economic crisis, the Greeks were suddenly faced by the declaration of their debt as unsustainable and disruptive of the whole EU project. The Greeks were unjustly denounced as unproductive "over-spenders," a behavior contrasting with sound European values. The policies that were enforced upon the Greek government resulted in an economic and social situation which no population should be subjected to. According to a prolific critic, Yannis Stavrakakis, this was a "gigantic disciplining operation – a huge experiment in violent downward social mobility and neoliberal adjustment and restructuring" (Stavrakakis 2013, p. 315). Greece was in effect faced with an alliance between the European economic elite and a technocratic EU system that had no regard for common people's suffering. This alliance relied on the "there is no alternative" doctrine which was only challenged by the Syriza party who allegedly voiced the real interest of the Greek people:

> Syriza promised to restore their dignity and represent their interests against the Greek and European establishment, thus breaking the omertà that surrounded the "success story" of the Eurozone, which had been declaring the end of the crisis and a return to "normality."

However, returning to normality in fact implied "the normalisation of the effects of the crisis, a perpetual continuation of crisis within other means" (Stavrakakis 2015, p. 277). The anti-austerity discourse would point out factors, or failures, for which the Greeks were not responsible, since they were in fact inherent to the EU-construction or resulting from the recession of the global economy. We notice that this anti-austerity discourse constructs a defined enemy, presents a distinct historical narrative, and holds the promise of bringing dignity back to the Greek people as they regain control of their country and destiny.

By contrast, the "administrative" discourse represented the Greek crisis in what at first glance would appear to be more neutral or non-antagonistic (economic) terms. It emphasized that the Greek crisis was caused by structural weaknesses in the Greek economy, and that the gravity of government deficits had remained unexposed by the data previously released by the Greek government. At the center of this discourse was that the Greek government had requested bailout loans in 2010, 2012, and 2015 from the Euro-group, the International Monetary Fund, and the European Central Bank, and that it in 2011 agreed to a 50 percent "haircut" on debt owed to private banks. The austerity measures were presented as something akin to a surgical operation performed on Europe's "sick man": "We can clearly observe the operation of a medical metaphor: the crisis is declared a serious illness, the result of an inherent social pathology; 'contagion' or 'contamination'" (Stavrakakis 2013, p. 315). The Greek illness, it was hypothesized, might spread to other European states with comparable government debts and structural problems such as Italy, Spain, or France. Despite this fear, the "administrative" discourse had no recognition of any possible economic failures or systemic faults at the level of the EU.

Placed in the very foreground were innate pathologies of the Greek nation such as irresponsibility and immorality. This construction made it possible to place the fault of unemployment and indebtedness on the Greeks themselves in a process of stigmatization or shaming.

A pertinent perspective on this construction of pathology and stigma can be found in Foucault's *Society Must be Defended* and his rendering of biopolitics (2003, pp. 61–63). There, Foucault argues that the advent of modern biopolitics understood as a strategy for optimizing the vitality of the living population implied the attempt to control, normalize, and persecute elements within the population that threatened it from the inside. In modern societies, sovereign intervention can precisely be justified when such threats to the population are detected, and the Greek pathology could indeed be viewed as such a deleterious element. The Greek crisis proves the point that in liberal times, authoritative interventions can take place with the justification of a "disease of the will," the detection of a pathology in which the will-power is no longer in charge of an individual or a group (Valverde 1996). The logic of sovereign intervention is hence not to *suppress* the individuals governed but to bring them back to rational self-government. This discourse in effect represents the Greeks as a collective subject without rational self-control and responsibility, but the latter can be reinstalled by neoliberal management of the country's economy and public spending. Voices that contest this cure are depicted as enemies of Europe: "(W)hoever diverges from the dominant neoliberal administration of the crisis is immediately discredited and denounced as an enemy of European values" (Stavrakakis 2015, p. 275). Notably then, while the Eurozone institutions purport "technocratic" solutions and rely upon economic calculation this is certainly still a discourse partaking in a battle. This is perhaps most clearly evident in the use of the negative term "populist" about the Syriza party and its supporters, which delegitimizes contestation of the neoliberal narrative, its demands, and the social order that it defends. Just as in the "populist," anti-austerity discourse, we see the construction of history, an enemy to be defeated, a rightful victory, and a just juridical-economic order to be achieved.

These are merely tentative analyses that would require further development. The race-war perspective offers a critical lens through which other, similar discursive political battles could be studied, for instance in Spain around Podemos or in Poland and its right-wing populism (Shields 2012). There are, however, certain limitations to this framework for studying politics and statehood which Foucault excavates in 1976. Insofar as this perspective assumes that social positions and interests are constituted not outside, but inside discursive practices, we cannot speak of identifiable material interests, on the basis of which we can advance critique (Dean and Villadsen 2016, p. 80). Hence, taken to its logical conclusion, this framework can only address the persuasive force that particular discourses may possess which we can analytically deconstruct but not substantially criticize or reject.

Second Decentering: A Gamut of Secular, Administrative Rationalities

> In reality you have a series of complex edifices in which, of course, the techniques
> themselves change and are perfected, or anyway become more complicated, but in
> which above all changes the dominant characteristic, or more exactly, the system of
> correlation between juridico-legal mechanisms, disciplinary mechanisms, and
> mechanisms of security.
>
> *(Foucault 2007, p. 22)*

Foucault's second decentering of the state occurs in his 1978 lecture series, *Security, Territory, Population* (Foucault 2007). There, he argues that the discovery of "the living population" was a decisive event in the history of Western political thought and government. Foucault describes how in the seventeenth and eighteenth centuries a new episteme emerged for reflecting upon political rule, one shared by a diverse range of thinkers, including physiocrats, demographers, hygienists, and political economists. Common to these streams of thought was their departure from the cosmological world-view of what, in short, may be termed "princely rule." Schematically, superseding the doctrine of a divine providence, the object of political government became a living population which possessed inherent mechanisms and regularities that should be studied empirically. I wish to give attention to one analytical potential which these lectures offer. Instead of the ultimate premise of sovereign rule in God's providence, Foucault describes the emergence of several competing governmental rationalities. This situation renders problems of governance indeterminate and complex in a way that is very recognizable from our present viewpoint.

At the start of the 1978 lectures, Foucault introduces three governmental rationalities or "major technologies of power": "law," "discipline," and "security" (Foucault 2007, pp. 5–24). Reading eighteenth-century texts about town planning, Foucault then describes how these governmental rationalities offer very different lenses for turning phenomena like theft or illness into objects of calculation and intervention. Law, discipline, and security each constitute distinct lenses to such an extent that stealing or illness come to appear as fundamentally different objects. The legal rationality institutes "a binary division between the permitted and the prohibited, and a coupling, comprising the code, between a type of prohibited action and a type of punishment" (2007, p. 5). In the gaze of discipline, we see "a series of adjacent, detective, medical, and psychological techniques appear which fall within the domain of surveillance, diagnosis, and the possible transformation of individuals" (2007, p. 5). Finally, security calculations take as their object the living population, that is, the regularities by which populations procreate, produce, consume, migrate, and so on. The security rationality appears as the most modern of the three governmental rationalities. The fundamental aim is to foster and strengthen the self-regulating capacities of the population, insofar as security targets the population as both "object and subject" (Foucault 2007, p. 11).

Law seeks to reinstate an order that has been violated, whereas discipline strives to prevent the unwanted from happening by normalizing bodies and actions. Hence, in its fundamental form, law targets the totality of subjects who inhabit a given territory. It is prohibitive and operates the binary distinction of the allowed versus the forbidden. In contrast to this binary of legal/illegal, security instead "establishes an average considered as optimal on the one hand, and, on the other, a bandwidth of the acceptable that must not be exceeded" (Foucault 2007, p. 6). Security also diverges from disciplinary normalization, since security starts from the reality as given and entails the more tempered aspiration of optimizing the processes already operative in this reality:

> This given will not be reconstructed to arrive at a point of perfection, as in a disciplinary town. It is simply a matter of maximizing the positive elements, for which one provides the best possible circulation, and of minimizing what is risky and inconvenient, like theft and disease, while knowing that they will never be completely suppressed.
>
> *(Foucault 2007, p. 19)*

Foucault then moves on to risk a broad generalization, stating that the emblematic object of legal rationality is a territory, discipline works upon bodies, and security relates to the totality of the living population (2007, p. 11). The major governmental rationalities do not appear historically in a sequential order: "There is not a series of successive elements, the appearance of the new causing the earlier ones to disappear" (2007, p. 8). Importantly, then, instead of outlining irretrievable breaks from one epoch or rationality to another, Foucault emphasized the co-existence and dynamic interplay between governmental rationalities. Accordingly, he wishes to study gradual transformations in "the system of correlation between juridico-legal mechanisms, disciplinary mechanisms, and mechanisms of security" (Foucault 2007, p. 22). This analytical framework offers a very fruitful perspective for analyzing modern problems of political governance, foregrounding the interplay, reverberations, and frictions between several co-existing governmental rationalities (2007, pp. 6–24). Compared to Foucault's previous study of "disciplinary society," he opened up more complex descriptions of mobile and heterogeneous configurations of state power.

Clearly, Foucault's explorations took part in his attempt to challenge the idea of the state as unified and static by retracing the genesis of our modern governmental rationalities and displaying their distinct modalities of knowledge:

> We should not be looking for some sort of sovereignty from which powers spring, but showing how the various operators of domination support one another, relate to one another, at how they converge and reinforce one another in some cases, and negate or strive to annul one another in other cases.
>
> *(Foucault 2003, p. 45)*

Notably, this emphasis on multiple forms of governmental rationalities extends to Foucault's general Nietzschean conception of history as perpetual struggle between divergent forces (Bussolini 2010, p. 88). The plurality of rationalities renders social space fractured by different imperatives, at times reinforcing and assimilating, at other times undermining and contradicting one another. Foucault's second decentering of the state leaves ample space for studying indeterminacy and dynamic repercussions in regard to governmental problems that have become indeterminate.

Refugees, Migrants, and the EU

I suggest that this framework can be put to use to understand the EU's difficulties in regard to how to regulate border-crossers in the shape of migrants and refugees. This is a problem that situates itself in a fundamental paradox characteristic of twenty-first-century European welfare states which emerged as both capitalist-expansive and territorially enclosed entities (Lessenich 2011). The thorny questions of how to react to migrations are shaped by the fundamental contradiction between, on the one hand, the capitalist logic of free circulation and, on the other hand, the national-territorial order of inclusion and granting of social rights via citizenship. At the EU level, one finds problems that reflect the deep-seated tension between supranational mobility and the perpetuation of national borders. This tension may elucidate why concrete problems of how to regulate migration are so hard to determine and manage within the EU-collaboration.

Historically, the EU was established principally as a structure that would facilitate trade, particularly by securing greater mobility of goods, capital, and labor. This key objective of facilitating the effective functioning of the EU's internal market could, in Foucauldian terms, be understood as a security problem, insofar as the EU's creation of an internal market is comparable to a "milieu," that is "a space in which a series of uncertain elements unfold" (Foucault 2007, p. 20). Yet, the citizens of EU member countries are still mainly assigned fundamental rights according to a political-legal rationality of inclusion which is territorially delimited (Lessenich 2011, p. 307). Accordingly, it would appear as if the EU's regulatory practices in relation to cross-border mobility are overdetermined by the legal rationality premised on sovereign territoriality and security rationality which centers on mobility and circulation.

However, the recent attempts to arrest the streams of people on the move already before they reach the outer EU borders and to channel those who do reach EU countries and distribute them in a planned fashion could be viewed as guided by a disciplinary rationality. Hence, Foucault said about discipline that "it arrests or regulates movements; it clears up confusion; it dissipates compact groupings of individuals wandering about the country in unpredictable ways; it establishes calculated distributions" (1977, p. 218). The disciplinary strategy rests on the hope of being able to plan, guide, control, and arrest the individuals who are on the move. By contrast, the rationality of security entails a different set of reflections and solutions, since it inserts phenomena (crime, grain production, or moving individuals) into a series of probable events. Relevant for present concerns in the EU to secure "good" supranational circulation, Foucault argued in regard to early modern town planning: "(T)he concern of government became that of making cities open to wider circulations, freed from their earlier spatial, juridical, administrative and economic enclosure" (Baerenholdt 2013, p. 24). Upholding territorial enclosures would be viewed as detrimental to the imperative of allowing free circulations.

The interplay and shifts between the rationalities of law, discipline, and security may help understanding the difficulties at the EU level in responding with a common voice and in a consistent manner. For instance, this perspective could make intelligible why migrant workers are today often conceived as a threat by national governments who increasingly base their policies on the protection of national boundaries and restricted access to social rights and permanent residency. Stricter military and police measures are put in place to deter, control, arrest, isolate, and survey border-crossers at the exterior EU border and at borders of member states. These measures could be understood as guided by legal and disciplinary rationalities, often contradicting the aspirations of security. Instruments like "fast-mover," green card arrangements, and schemes for attracting specific types of skilled labor can be viewed as solutions resonating with a security rationality, that is, as techniques for "securing" beneficial transnational circulation. The field of regulation of migration and border-crossing in all its diverse manifestations is characterized by rapid technical inventions. It is also marked by contradictions and paradoxes which could be further analyzed as arising from the intersections of the rationalities of law, discipline, and security which pervade the EU.

This analytical perspective can challenge what has been termed "the meta-physics of the border" (De Genova 2013, p. 255), since it displays that neither the exterior EU borders nor the national borders of member states are simply tangible demarcations. Instead, these borders appear in their contingency, continually the object of controversy and redefinitions. We begin to recognize that a sovereign-territorial border is not the same as a disciplinary border, which again is not the same as a security border. Hereby, the apparent fixity of the border is problematized, and instead we may speak of unstable practices of "bordering." On this perspective, the EU regulation of migrants straddles between the governmental logics of law, disciplinarity, and security. Such a perspective on European discussions of refugee management could also elucidate why refugees can simultaneously appear as vulnerable *and* criminalized, be spoken about as a resource *and* a threat. Finally, it would be pertinent to explore how sovereign measures tend to become routinized and embedded in administrative and bureaucratic (disciplinary) systems. Indeed, the debates about how to deal with refugees and migrants at the EU borders often emphasize the importance of avoiding excessive military and police violence against vulnerable civilians displaced by catastrophes. At the same time, bordering practices are enframed in an administrative logic that makes difficult more serious discussion of the legitimacy of violent militarized deterrence and police measures.

Third Decentering: The Infinite State and Political Eschatology

> The state is at once that which exists, but which does not yet exist enough.
> *(Foucault 2008, p. 4)*

In his 1979 lectures, Foucault performs a third decentering of the state (2008). Methodologically, he does so by presenting the state as not a universal but as a "transactional reality." In terms of historical material, Foucault explores different variants of liberal and neoliberal thought with a focus on how they conceive of the state's role vis-à-vis society.

Foucault begins by stating his general approach which avoids basing analyses of historical processes on pre-given "universals" such as sexuality, the economy, civil society, or the state (Foucault 2008, pp. 2–3). We must reject the assumption of the state as a universal, Foucault argues, viewing it as if it were a primary reality existent prior to social and historical events. Instead we must view the state as a historical "singularity" which emerged at a particular moment and develops in response to particular problems.

Perhaps, the 1979 lectures is the place where Foucault most effectually decenters the state through conceptual innovation. He invented the category "transactional reality" to designate "things that do not exist, and yet which are in reality and follow a regime of truth" (2008, p. 20). Instead of assigning a substantial quality to sexuality, the economy, civil society, or the state, Foucault foregrounded practices organized around that "something" which is supposed to exist (2008, p. 3). By this move, Foucault seeks to escape the choice between idealism (the state as a mere abstraction) and realism (particular institutions constituting the state). Instead, he takes as a starting point that the notion of the state is embedded in a series of real practices from which it cannot be isolated, a whole "set-up" which comprises laws, actions, and words (Veyne 2010, p. 31). Like madness and sexuality, the state can be viewed as a transactional reality which does not "exist in-itself," but which saturates real practices that are organized in relation to it (Villadsen 2016, p. 9).

As a transactional reality, the state is subject to a permanent critical reflection regarding its role, its functions, and its limits. This is because the state became inserted into a particular regime of truth, which we may broadly term modern political economy, according to which questions of the state's functions, proper size, its limits, and so on are deliberated. Hence, Foucault describes how political economists, from the eighteenth century onwards, began to subordinate the exercise of state governance to a permanent test with reference to society's self-regulatory mechanisms: "I think that fundamentally it was political economy that made it possible to ensure the self-limitation of governmental reason" (Foucault 2008, p. 13). Henceforth, there will be a permanent testing of the government of the state, which means that the state becomes an infinite project, a mobile object. Hence, Foucault says: "The state is nothing else but the effect, the profile, the mobile shape of a perpetual statification (étatisation) or statifications, in the sense of incessant transactions which modify, or move, or drastically change" (Foucault 2008, p. 77). In 1978, Foucault similarly suggested that in contrast to historical teleology, we now live in an infinite political time that is "not temporally oriented toward a final unity" (Foucault 2007, p. 379). This is what could be termed an "indefinite governmentality." It rests on the belief that the state will always be there, residing in a system of infinite inter-state competition. There would henceforth be a governmentality "with no foreseeable term or final aim" (2007, p. 342). This is a kind of liberal governmentality in which contestations of government may lead to incremental changes, but in which grand ideas of a completely different social order are excluded.

Some critics argue that Foucault's analyses in 1979 depict the neo-liberal social order as more flexible and open, and that he implicitly endorses it as preferable compared to state-centered political ideologies (Behrent 2009; Dean and Villadsen 2016). Alain Badiou counts Foucault among those intellectuals who always caution against the twentieth century's major political projects for creating a "new man," and who risk effectively supporting the technical and "apolitical" biopolitics of the twenty-first century, a purely economic-administrative protection of life (Badiou 2007, pp. 8–9). Notwithstanding their horrific outcomes, the grand political and humanistic projects of the twentieth century were at least "passionate" and genuinely political, insofar as they represented man's aspiration to transcend himself and create a new society. By comparison, the current political order is "depoliticized" which entails "the disappearance of the political," a situation in which diverse political demands are embraced as long as they do not fundamentally contest the dominant neoliberal economic order (Swyngedouw 2014, p. 123). Instead of contestation between substantially divergent political ideologies, we now live in a state of "managed democracy" characterized by conservative, technocratic solutions.

It should be noted, however, that Foucault presents an alternative to this liberal governmental order. At the end of the 1979 lectures, he counter-positions modern, liberal governmentality with what he terms statist and national politics that invoke political eschatology. Conventionally, eschatology designates the theological study of the dramatic end of the world and its rebirth in a perfected form, usually according to a divine plan or a pre-designed history (Villadsen 2016, pp. 14–15). Foucault speaks of a "lingering rationality" which comprises political ideologies that invoke a truth which will reveal itself in the course of history. He mentions Marxism, which invokes "a rationality of history progressively manifesting itself as truth" (2008, p. 313). Hence, the conception of time is pivotal. Crucially, political eschatology asserts the coming of a final time, when a new world or society will be realized. By promising the irruption of the existing order political eschatology is a forceful political discourse that "corresponds" to the infinity state-reason and liberal governmentality. On Foucault's account, eschatological beliefs constituted one of the counter-conducts which developed in relation to the Christian pastorate. With the emergence of state reason in the seventeenth century, eschatological themes were excluded from political discourse. But eschatological thinking was reactivated to contest the "indefinite time" of modern governmentality. In its modern forms, political eschatology designates quasi-religious political ideas of a perfect social order that interrupts the present or is awaiting its realization in the final culmination of history.

Modern political eschatology would be found among extreme and utopian political movements which adhered to the hope of the coming of a new human world. These movements were premised on the hope for a day when the state would transform into a united, non-antagonistic community; a specter that included communitarian theologians, libertarians, utopian socialists, and later on Stalinism, Fascism, and National Socialism. For the purpose of contemporary political analysis, Foucault's notion of "political eschatology" can be used to analyze movements that promise a dramatic break with the emergence of a new order; one that unifies state and society. Whereas liberal governmentality assumes a permanent split between state and civil society and the economy, eschatological ideologies dream of a unification of state and society (Villadsen 2016, p. 13). Eschatological visions may be articulated by diverse forms of political action against existent governmental structures. Particularly relevant for the present discussion, the dramatic idiom of eschatology offers a potentially disruptive weapon in the face of technocratic "post-politics."

The emergence in recent years of radical and utopian political movements could possibly be analyzed through the lens of political eschatology. It has been suggested that the Occupy movement was a reaction to a situation of depoliticization and the monopolization of power by the economic and political elite in contemporary liberal-capitalist society. Occupy succeeded in instituting a moment of re-politicization by entirely rejecting the system of representation and by refraining from formulating demands that could be accommodated within the existing political structure. Hence, Occupy never mobilized around something like a defined political program. Instead the movement articulated broad notions of equality and revived democracy in the face of political-economic inequality. The proclamation of equality, universal solidarity, and the insurrection of a whole new form of politics gave the Occupy movement an eschatological tenor.

> Occupy succeeded in a kind of re-politicization exactly by way of its inclusive and open character. OWS and related movements invoke a decidedly universalizing logic. Although they would admit to constitute a minority in number, they nevertheless claim to speak for "everyone," for "the majority," or giving voice to "the 99%." Evident here is a strive to transcend the

particularism of the local issues of poverty, debts, home evictions and labour struggles and insert them in an overall political spectacle.

(Turner and Villadsen 2016, p. 162)

There was something distinctly non-pragmatic, unnegotiable, and utopian about the messages communicated by the Occupy movement. It articulated the belief that it was better to achieve nothing at all than succumb to the pragmatism of achieving something small within the existent structure. Occupy staged a dramatic spectacle in opposition to pragmatic politics. Occupy's attempt to disrupt the political ontology of representation could be seen as an intervention with eschato-logical connotations, insofar as it carried the message that the liberal–capitalist order as we know it will henceforth be impossible. It promised, as it were, to halt the infinite governmentality of liberal constitutionalism and ushered a new world.

A democratic government derives its just power from the people, but cor-porations do not seek consent to extract wealth from the people and the Earth; … no true democracy is attainable when the process is determined by economic power. We come to you at a time when corporations, which place profit over people, self-interest over justice, and oppression over equality, run our governments.

(Occupy Wall Street General Assembly cited in Creech 2014, p. 466)

Occupy managed to unite and intensify popular protests against a world where corporate capital corrupts and misuses the state apparatus, suppressing the expres-sion of popular will. Banks and big corporations were posited as the absolute antitheses of collectivist, democratic politics. Often the movement used public displays and images of poverty, discrimination, and police brutality, transmitted through social media technology, in order to "dramatize key issues in a given society" (Kellner cited in Creech 2014, p. 463). It was a staged battle between the forces of good and evil. The two-headed monster of abusive corporate capital and the undemocratic political elite was confronted with the mass of protestors united merely in the axiomatic demand for equality.

At another part of the political spectrum, the Tea Party movement, which reached its peak in 2008–2010, similarly demanded a fundamentally different political order. It attacked "big governance" and made reference to an original (lost) America based on the wise doctrines of the founding fathers. Broadly similar to Occupy, the Tea Party managed to generate mass support, it articulated utopian visions some of which displayed quasi-theological and eschatological themes, and it often connected to evangelical movements or congregations (Turner and Villadsen 2016, p. 166). In both cases, "the people" served as an empty signifier for mass mobilization. However, the Tea Party rallied around an anti-government message, requested tax-cuts, and claimed to represent the "small people" of suburban and rural America. Its reactionary and conservative components can be seen in its attempts "to defend and retain traditional identities and statuses based on race, patriarchy and hetero-normativity that have been under assault by late modern 'network society'" (Langman 2012, p. 469). The Tea Party can thus be viewed, at least in part, as a reaction to the dissolution of cultural certainties and the sweeping process of globalization.

In the Tea Party's ideology, society is imagined as an almost mythical space, that is, the original white, rural, and Christian America, which regrettably has been distorted and needs regeneration. Of course this vision was invoked variously across the different parts of the Tea Party movement. Christian conservatives found in the Tea Party a confirmation of their longstanding convictions about the theological signification of the founding of the American constitution and of American exceptionalism. On their view, the juridical-theological foundation of the "real" America has been perverted by politicians, bureaucracy, and the cultural decay of big cities: "Indeed, there has been a long tradition in which the conservative, 'idyllic' countryside where people are more 'authentic' and 'virtuous' has counterpoised the nefarious cosmopolitan city with its toleration of diversity, sophistication, and above all, decadence and sites of transgression" (Langman 2012, p. 473).

Political movements guided by Christian conservatism in the USA are intriguing since they typically praise an original, natural, God-ordained (but now lost) social order. This idea of the loss of "real America" makes possible the claim that the movement is in a sense non-partisan, insofar as it simply aspires to reinstate the founding fathers' intentions and the ordained plan, also articulated as American exceptionalism. Notably, the Tea Party's vision of recovery of lost America is connected with a particular set of fiscal and economic policies, evident in Tea Party members' calls for a severe reduction of the US federal budget deficit by reducing government spending and lowering taxes. This ideological construct is hence premised on "a consistent set of identifications that link the founders – and the particular forms of fiscal and moral probity they are understood to exemplify – with contemporary tea party conservatism" (Wilson and Burack 2012, p. 182). The claim of defending the original constitution also justifies the representation of political opponents as violators of the constitution. This is the case, for instance, with President Obama whose socialist aspirations allegedly disrupt the very constitution: "Mr. Obama's problem is that the Constitution of the United States stands in his way" (Wilson and Burack 2012, p. 48). In brief, then, the Tea Party's political eschatology revolves around the rebirth of God's America.

Future work could use the notion of political eschatology to expand our vocabulary for analyzing the formation of political identities. In particular, it could help rendering current left- and right-wing populist movements and their ideologies intelligible. The notion points to the totalizing and populist character of movements that rely on eschatological visions which promise to annul the permanent contestation of pluralistic politics and institute a new, non-antagonistic society. However, political eschatology can rally both egalitarian movements and radical right movements. It may also constitute a potent critical weapon for forming radical political subjectivities in the face of an economic-administrative order premised on the "there is no alternative" ideology. When social groups suffering from austerity are stigmatized as irrational and resistance is blocked insofar as they are segregated as being individually responsible for their misfortune, eschatological visions may unify people in a common vision that spurs the kind of genuine politics that Badiou hopes for. In brief, political eschatology must be analyzed as a flexible and polyvalent discursive resource.

Conclusion

Readers of Foucault have routinely stated that he turned the analytical focus away from the state. Some have argued that his numerous statements on the state are ambiguous and fail to constitute a coherent position. In this chapter, however, I share Steven Sawyer's aspiration to read Foucault's ambivalences towards the state positively as a resource (2015, p. 140). At a moment where many social scientists shy away from theorizing and studying the state, a non-coherent approach which offers different analytical frameworks for exploring the state and state-centered politics may be very timely. This chapter has explored three ways of approaching the state. In the first, the state was wedded to narratives of the nation or the people. This helped us to elucidate how the Greek nation was constructed in forceful narratives of what constitutes "the people," their history, and their rightful future. In the second approach, the state was decentered into administrative rationalities in which the state and state-action appear entirely differently as a solution to mundane problems. The EU's present difficulties with handling migration served as a window for considering how contemporary (supranational and national) governance straddles between several incongruous rationalities. Third, we explored Foucault's diagnosis of the modern state as embedded in an "infinite governmentality," and we discussed how political eschatology in the preset context may constitute a disruptive force of political agency. Assuming that the state is neither a specific structure, nor an inherently "cold" or "warm" monster, means that the state can unfold in a plethora of ways. Foucault's thinking on the state is certainly not coherent, neither is it without shortcomings. But I hope that this chapter indicates some less acknowledged potentials for exploring current issues of state, civil society, and neoliberalism.

References

Baerenholdt, J. O. (2013). Governmobility: The Powers of Mobility. *Mobilities*, 8(1), 20–34.
Badiou, A. (2007). *The Century*, Cambridge: Polity Press.
Badiou, A. (2012). *The Adventure of French Philosophy*. New York: Verso.
Behrent, M. C. (2009). Liberalism without Humanism: Michel Foucault and the Free-market Creed, 1976–1979. *Modern Intellectual History*, 6(3), 539–568.

Biebricher, T. and Vogelmann, F. (2012) Governmentality and State Theory: Reinventing the Reinvented Wheel? *Theory & Event*, 15(3), 1–18.

Bussolini, J. (2010). What is a Dispositive? *Foucault Studies*, 10, 85–107.

Cohen, J. and Arato, A. (1992). *Civil Society and Political Theory*. London: MIT Press.

Creech, B. (2014). Digital Representation and Occupy Wall Street's Challenge to Political Subjectivity. *Convergence: The International Journal of Research into New Media Technologies*, 20(4), 461–477.

Dean, M. and Villadsen, K. (2016). *State Phobia and Civil Society: The Political Legacy of Michel Foucault*. Stanford, CA: Stanford University Press.

De Genova, N. (2013). Spectacles of Migrant "Illegality": The Scene of Exclusion, the Obscene of Inclusion. *Ethnic and Racial Studies*, 36(7), 1180–1198.

Foucault, M. (1977). *Discipline and Punish*. New York: Penguin.

Foucault, M. (1980). *Power/Knowledge: Selected Interviews and Other Writings*. New York: Pantheon.

Foucault, M. (1981). Nietzsche, Genealogy, History. In P. Rabinow (Ed.) *The Foucault Reader*. New York: Penguin.

Foucault, M. (2000a). Lives of Infamous Men. In *Power: Essential Works of Foucault, 1954–1984*, Vol. 3. London: Penguin Books.

Foucault, M. (2000b). Truth and Juridical Forms. In *Power: Essential Works of Foucault, 1954–1984*, Vol. 3. London: Penguin Books.

Foucault, M. (2003). *Society Must Be Defended: Lectures at the Collège de France, 1975–76*. New York: Picador.

Foucault, M. (2007). *Security, Territory, Population: Lectures at the Collège de France 1977–78*. New York: Palgrave Macmillan.

Foucault, M. (2008). *The Birth of Biopolitics: Lectures at the Collège de France 1978–1979*. London: Palgrave.

Gordon, C. (1996). Foucault in Britain. In A. Barry, T. Osborne, and N. Rose (Eds.), *Foucault and Political Reason: Liberalism, Neo-Liberalism and Rationalities of Government*. London: UCL Press.

Karlsen, M. P. and Villadsen, K. (2015). Foucault, Maoism, Genealogy: The Influence of Political Militancy in Michel Foucaul"s Thought. *New Political Science*, 37, 91–117.

Langman, L. (2012). Cycles of Contention: The Rise and Fall of the Tea Party. *Critical Sociology*, 38(4), 469–494.

Lessenich, S. (2011). Constructing the Socialized Self. Mobilization and Control in the "Active Society". In Ulrich Bröckling, Susanne Krasmann, and Thomas Lemke (Eds.), *Governmentality: Current Issues and Future Challenges*. New York: Routledge.

Marks, J. (2000). Foucault, Franks, Gauls: "Il faut défendre la société": The 1976 Lectures at the Collège de France. *Theory Culture Society*, 17(5), 127–147.

Pasquino, P. (1993). Political Theory of War and Peace: Foucault and the History of Modern Political Theory. *Economy and Society*, 22(1), 77–88.

Sawyer, S. W. (2015). Foucault and the State. *The Tocqueville Review/La revue Tocqueville*, 36(1), 135–164.

Shields, S. (2012). Opposing Neoliberalism? Poland's Renewed Populism and Post-communist Transition. *Third World Quarterly*, 33(2), 359–381.

Stavrakakis, Y. (2013). Dispatches from the Greek Lab: Metaphors, Strategies and Debt in the European Crisis. *Psychoanalysis, Culture & Society*, 18(3), 313–324.

Stavrakakis, Y. (2015). Populism in Power: Syriza's Challenge to Europe. *Juncture*, 21(4), 273–280.

Swyngedouw, E. (2014). Where is the Political? Insurgent Mobilisations and the Incipient "Return of the Political". *Space and Polity*, 18(2), 122–136.

Turner, B. S. and Villadsen, K. (2016). Counter Movements and Space: The Settlement, Occupy Wall Street and the Tea Party. In H-J. Sander, K. Villadsen, and T. Wyller (Eds.), *The Spaces of Others – Heterotopic Spaces*. Göttingen: Vandenhoeck & Ruprecht.

Valverde, M. (1996). "Despotism" and Ethical Liberal Governance. *Economy and Society*, 25(3), 357–372.

Veyne, P. (2010). *Foucault: His Thought, His Character*. Cambridge: Polity.

Villadsen, K. (2016). Michel Foucault and the Forces of Civil Society. *Theory, Culture & Society*, 33(3), 3–26.

Wilson, A. R. and Burack, C. (2012). "Where Liberty Reigns and God is Supreme": The Christian Right and the Tea Party Movement. *New Political Science*, 34(2), 172–190.

PART II

Reconstructing the Individual via Social Policy

4

INVESTING IN SOCIAL SUBJECTS

The European Turn to Social Investment as the Human Capital Theory of Social Citizenship

Bettina Leibetseder

Under the Belgian presidency of the Council of the European Union, the idea of a social investment perspective was initially stipulated in 2001. Frank Vandenbroucke (2002) presented the new concept as a way to promote "sustainable social justice" in the field of social policy. The discursive establishment of a productive notion was to guide member states to transform their welfare states.[1]

Social investment was also introduced to politically buoy the European social model (Hemerijck 2002; Vandenbroucke 2002). This model, as Tony Judt identified (2005, p. 748), "binds Europeans together" and creates a source of solidarity. It has been disputed whether the model upholds strong systems of social protection for all (Vaughan-Whitehead 2015).

Politically, social investment served the purposes of facilitating European integration and enabling new avenues of solidarity in an age of neoliberalism in which market-based approaches to social inclusion are gaining favor. Nonetheless, such a shift inevitably raises the question of whether social investment undermines the inclusionary commitments of a social protection approach. In that respect, social investment may alter policies that promote what theorists call social citizenship, whereby the state compensates those who are left out or left behind by market practices.

In the first decade of the twenty-first century, social investment faced three challenges: First, three enlargement rounds[2] led to a more heterogeneous landscape of welfare states, creating new cleavages (Copeland 2012; Kvist 2004). Second, European and national elections have favored conservative and far right wing and/or Eurosceptic parties (Szczerbiak and Taggart 2008), in which the latter opposes the European integration and the former is less supportive of social issues at the European level. Third, the economic crisis has threatened the sustainability of many welfare states and national and European (social) cohesion (Streeck 2012).

Under these less-than-favorable political and economic circumstances, the European Commission (EC) has introduced the social investment idea. After consultation with stakeholders, panels of experts, and political negotiations, the EC issued its Social Investment Package in 2013 to promote human capital investment as a new goal of social policy in addition to social protection and economic stabilization (EC 2013a). The EU defines social investment as "strengthening people's current and future capacities" (2013a, p. 3).

Although proponents claim that refocusing on social investment assists in maintaining social protection schemes and solidarity (Hemerijck 2013; Morel, Palier, and Palme 2012a; Palier, Vandenbroucke, and Hemerijck 2011; Van Kersbergen and Hemerijck 2012), its critics argue that such a focus cultivates social inequality and dismantles social citizenship (Beckfield 2012; Bothfeld and Rouault 2015; Cantillon 2011; Deeming and Smyth 2015; Jenson 2009; Pintelon, Cantillon, Van den Bosch, and Whelan 2013; Saraceno 2015). Some voices even state that social investment encourages neoliberal reforms (Barbier 2012).

Neoliberalism, on the one hand, promotes free markets, privatization, and competition, leading to retrenchment policies and greater income inequality (Harvey 2010; Peck 2013). Conversely, neoliberalism manifests an economically driven rationality for individuals, societies, and states alike (Dean 2014b; Schram 2015). Wendy Brown (2015, p. 32) defines neoliberalism as "an order of normative reason that, when it becomes ascendant, takes shape as a governing rationality extending a specific formulation of economic values, practices, and metrics to every dimension of human life."

Such economic government rationality may be proposed by social investment thinking, which in turn can challenge current assumptions of social citizenship and alter the goals of social policy. In welfare states, this social investment thinking can even introduce a rationality that re-forms the citizen subjects on the grounds of potential rates of return on (social) investment.

In this chapter, I assert the changing rationality that portrays the social investment subject in the EC's documents on the Social Investment Package. However, the documents do not define a singular subject. Moreover, each report problematizes diverse aspects, proposes unique instruments, and deploys different normative reasons and shapes, with the ultimate aim of achieving a distinct ideal subject.

The focus on multiple subjects rather than a single one emphasizes the empirical variety which lacks in many studies portraying only one type (Brady 2014; Mckee 2009; Whitworth 2016). Furthermore, the plurality acknowledges that social investment subjects cannot be set up in a societal vacuum because "the residues of pre-existing social formations will never be entirely erased or rendered inert" (Peck 2013, p. 154). Therefore, how economic belief systems for governing human lives reshape conceptions of social citizenship for diverse groups is ripe for substantial debate.

Because the social investment perspective spans numerous documents with diverse target groups, I compare the varied expectations about the citizen that needs to be shaped. First, I outline Michel Foucault's ideas on human capital theory and then connect these to social investment strategy and social citizenship. I then frame the analytical grid that assists in delineating the proposed practices and deconstructing the social investment subjects, describing ontology, ascetics, deontology, and teleology. Next, I present the results of the analysis. My discussion pinpoints the term's ambivalent subject formations in relation to social citizenship, and my conclusion recapitulates the changing subjectivity.

Economic Government Rationality and Social Investment

In the following section, I present Foucault's much-discussed thinking on human capital and how neoliberalism encourages changes in our conceptions of subjectivity. I then connect Foucault's analysis of neoliberalism to the theoretical foundations of the social investment strategy. Then, I formulate the questions for the empirical analysis.

For Wendy Brown (2015), Foucault provides an incisive analysis of human capital theory, and I too rely on Foucault. His analysis centers on how neoliberalism offers the recurring notion of individuals as subjects for investment by the state in the name of furthering economic growth. For individuals to be seen as worthy of economic investment, they need to be disciplined to behave consistently with the ideals of an economic actor, that is, as "*Homo oeconomicus.*" This conception of the citizen/subject as worthy of economic investment redefines the political agenda to shift to the background the issues of citizenship rights implied by liberal democratic notions of social justice. To focus on making citizens into economic subjects worthy of investment modifies the established understandings of the liberal-democratic social contract among citizens and between them and the state because today human beings are not perceived as intrinsically valuable but are instead constructed and re-construct themselves as human capital.

Wendy Brown follows the considerations of Michel Foucault (2008, p. 219), who refers to human capital theory as distinctive "American neoliberalism," most notably theorized by Gary Becker's writing (1962). Foucault (2008, p. 219) designates idiosyncratic characteristics to this theoretical school of thought, the "extension of economic analysis into a previously unexplored domain" and "the possibility of giving a strictly economic interpretation."

In this interpretation, labor is seen as capital that has to be developed and that requires investment – as with machinery – "to improve human capital" and "to preserve and employ it for as long as possible" (Foucault 2008, p. 230). Furthermore, Foucault observed new policy aims for the state. By introducing human capital thinking, it is observed that "the economic policies of all the developed countries, but also their social policies, as well as their cultural and educational policies, [are] being orientated in these terms" (Foucault 2008, p. 231).

This shift in policies of Foucault's alters the strategic use of power at the micro level. Individuals are perceived as "manageable" in a systematic, predictable manner with the right (dis)incentives. One of the merits that Foucault perceives is the reduction of punitive actions, an aspect that is foregrounded by Gary Becker (in Becker, Ewald, and Harcourt 2012, p. 17), who attributed human capital theory to "freeing up individuals" and to self-development after reading Foucault's critique. Such an angle pertains to a "soft" libertarian approach that primarily engages in enabling individuals to make choices within behavioral constraints (Whitworth 2016).

From this perspective, human capital theory manifests a world that "is not at all the ideal or project of an exhaustively disciplinary society in which the legal network hemming in individuals is taken over and extended internally by, let us say, a normative mechanism" (Foucault 2008, p. 259). In contrast to Foucault's assumptions in the late 1970s, neoliberalism is now seen as establishing a strong state with rigid regulative structures (Peck 2010; Schmidt and Thatcher 2013).

In the field of welfare, the punishing ideas of Lawrence M. Mead (1986), in whose perspective the right work ethic has to be taught to the unemployed poor and unconditional benefits curtailed, led to the ascendance of workfare regimes (Peck 2010). For Soss, Fording, and Schram (2011, p. 27), the coalescence of neoliberalism and paternalism marks a distinctive regime of neoliberal paternalism: "[T]hey define a strong state-led effort to bring discipline to the lives of the poor so that they can become competent actors who recognize and act on their interests as freely choosing agents on the market."[3]

In addition to extending governing instruments, human capital theory also redefines the addressees of policy interventions based on their earning power. Interventions, such as James Heckman's proposals (Carneiro and Heckman 2003; Heckman 2000), must be evaluated, and those that are most effective and offer the best rate of return must be put forward. Therefore, Heckman (2000) advocates education policies as a means of developing human capital; reducing economic inequality; and achieving, especially, in the case of early childhood interventions, greater equal opportunity.

Taken to its extreme, the welfare state would be re-envisioned as a system of return on investment. Reconstructing citizens as human capital may defy contemporary perceptions of merit or redistribution in social protection schemes. To date, traditional approaches of reciprocity and quid pro quo have translated into greater support in cases of social risk (Ewald 1991). That is to say, by pursuing pure investment logic, the assessment would recast the individual's value in terms of the expected rate of return. Those categorized as unworthy – that is, less "cost-effective" – of investment would obtain minimum income support, whereas those in the "deserving" group would have access to the services that they need to boost their productivity.

Distinct from the market logic, T. H. Marshall (1972, pp. 18–19) argues that "it is a fundamental principle of the welfare state that the market value of an individual cannot be the measure of his [or her] right to welfare." Marshall defined social rights as part of citizenship; these rights vary and can provide benefits from "the right to a modicum of economic welfare and security to the right to share to the full in the social heritage and to live the life of a civilized being according to the standards prevailing in the society" (Marshall 1950, p. 11). Although they aim to build a broad middle class, the rights can mark individual minimums or averages and also extend from unemployment and old age to health services and education. They also oblige the individual to work, although their intention is to restrain market forces (Jenson 2009).

In a contemporary social policy, the notion of social investment dates to Anthony Giddens' (1998) proposal of a "Third Way" for New Labour. In his opinion, "[g]overnment has an essential role to play in investing in the human resources and infrastructure needed to develop an entrepreneurial culture" (1998, p. 99). Human capital investment should be strengthened, to create a "redistribution of possibilities" (1998, p. 101) and replace, if possible, income maintenance.[4]

Social investment does not advance redistribution; for Giddens, economic inequality may be acceptable when it fosters economic and employment growth. Conversely, Esping-Andersen highlights the need for redistribution and strong welfare states that maintain security and social justice as "a *precondition* for an effective social investment strategy" (2002, p. 5, original emphasis). However, he also argues that social policy spending has to be identified as more than consumption alone and refers to human capital theory. Although traditional conceptions classify social expenditures as pure unproductive consumption, these can also "yield a dividend because they (make) citizens more productive" (Esping-Andersen 2002, p. 9). It may not be always easy to distinguish between these two traits (Nolan 2013). However, in his view, social investments provide individual and social benefits over the life course, especially in education and child care. Next to higher fertility rates and women's labor market participation, Esping-Andersen (2015) stresses social mobility and equal opportunity in referring to James Heckman.

In contemporary ideas on social investment, the goals of "[raising] the human capital stock" and introducing "policies serving to make efficient use of human capital" (Hemerijck and Vandenbroucke 2012, p. 205) are embedded. From a life course perspective (Kvist 2015), the social investment approach seeks to prepare individuals, families, and societies to adapt to various transformations and "enable the creation of more and better jobs" (Morel, Palier, and Palme 2012b, p. 354).

To stimulate the economy, full employment, and social cohesion simultaneously, the investment perspective wants to re-channel welfare state resources to address skill demand and to provide social security and social services that support a more flexible labor market and raise overall employment rates. It promotes social inclusion, the creation of high-quality employment, and equal opportunity through human capital investment (Morel et al. 2012a, p. 12).

Social investment policies do not abolish income provisions, which "must remain an important function of the welfare state that works as a necessary complement to activation and which cannot be substituted by activation" (Morel et al. 2012b, p. 359). Although income security over the life course should be preserved, social investment seeks to uphold social rights in reference to their productive impact or economic efficiency (Morel et al. 2012a, p. 5). The perspective may preach sacrifice now, with "the focus being more on the life cycle and on the future than on equality of outcomes in the present" (Morel et al. 2012a, p. 11).

Because the diverse accounts vary on what social investment should achieve, the perspective constitutes a "polysemic" vessel (Jenson 2010): It is reinterpreted, crossing the boundaries of academic and political arenas. Beyond traveling across epistemic communities, the common-sense meaning helps to adapt the concept and ties together diverse actors in the political sphere, who may translate it in any number of ways.

For some, social investment emerges as an answer to classic neoliberal concepts by which fiscal austerity and price stability dominate the macroeconomic agenda and the welfare state is portrayed as redundant (Jenson 2010; Mahon 2013; Morel et al. 2012a). From that perspective, social investment combines traits of human capital investment and social protection beyond income relief for the poor (Mahon 2013).

Social rights and redistribution may be challenged by the potential of economically driven reclassification of citizens and the strict enforcement of work. Pertaining to the theoretical debate, two questions arise for the empirical part. First, the analysis has to explore extending the economic reclassification of the subjects, in greater detail, to the soft and disciplining governing modes put forward to alter citizens' behavior. Second, the inquiry has to consider the impact on redistribution, that is, whether or not the subjects are perceived as intrinsically valuable and endowed with social rights.

The transformations, as indicated by the Commission's SIP, reframe the conception of citizens and may severely alter subjectivity. In the next section, I briefly sketch the content of the European Union's social investment policy documents, which indicate multiple routes of self-formation, and the analytical steps. Then, I depict the empirical analysis in greater depth.

Advocated Subjects of Social Investment

For the European Commission, social investment should complete and modernize contemporary welfare states. Instead of a short-term perspective, welfare states should engage in reforms that "have lasting impacts by offering economic and social returns over time, notably in terms of employment prospects or labour incomes" (EC 2013a, p. 3). Additionally, not only should social policy intervene ex post, but individuals should be prepared to face uncertainties in their lives ex ante. In more detail, a "systematic" adaptation should ensure a preventative approach to financing and spending and enforce a life course perspective in social policy.

The EC has published numerous documents as part of the SIP; two papers set the general framework and address diverse target groups (EC 2013a, 2013e). Other documents single out specific policy fields and relate to distinct groups, such as children (EC 2013b), the homeless (EC 2013d), the unemployed (EC 2013f), and persons with long-term care needs (EC 2013h) and health issues (EC 2013g).[5]

Analyzing these policy documents, I use a discursive approach (Rapley 2007) because official papers provide unique material on how they portray subjects, define problems, and achieve solutions (Sapsford and Jupp 2006). Drawing on a Foucauldian method, I investigate how the diverse subjects are understood.

Analytically, the focus for each group lies on four linchpins determined by Mitchel Dean (1995), which allows for a systematic review of the proposed government practices for each target group: ontology, ascetics, deontology, and teleology. First, *ontology* defines the subject who is to be governed or has to govern him-/herself. It covers any form of problematization that is to be (self-) governed, typically related to the unemployed, the sick, or the poor in social policy. The focus shifts from the subject's situation toward the circumstances, the behavioral assumptions and effects of policy interventions (Dean 1995). Ontology can address the wrongful or suboptimal choices of "rational" subjects who retire too early, are out of work for too long, or suffer from ill health. Conversely, ontology can portray a deviant subject who does not want to live up to responsibilities (Whitworth 2016).

Second, the aspect of *ascetics* denotes the various techniques the documents recommend for governing subjects (or having them self-govern). It specifies the types of instruments needed to achieve individual normalization, for example, client contracts or benefits adjustments, soft governance, or discipline (Dean 1995). Therefore, ascetics can propose an optimum of (dis)incentives to steer individual choices or it can opt for disciplinary actions and coercion (Whitworth 2016).

Third, *deontology* specifies the role or position of the subject within the process, that is, why, in moral or normative terms, one ought to partake in the mode of subjectification. In relation, the position raises questions concerning rules and norms (Dean 1995); for example, one governs oneself to fulfill potential as a productive citizen, to develop human capital, and to strive for entrepreneurial capacities.

Finally, *teleology* characterizes the subject who should be shaped. It addresses understanding what the practices aim for and what vision of the subject the practices aim to produce (Dean 1995); in that respect, the produced subject is, for example, employed and active (Whitworth 2016). The telos also influences notions of an active or disciplinary society.

For each of the four criteria, I coded the documents, and thus, they encompass a distinct range in regard to the subject; for each document, I first marked the text passages and then exported them into a word processing program that categorized the content into one of the four criteria I discuss above. I then compared the exported passages and scanned the original document a second time to increase consistency.

Based on these four traits of subject formation, I present the diverse target groups. I start with the general document that outlines the Commission's overall perspective on social policy, followed by the documents that address children, health and long-term care, homelessness, and unemployment. I subsequently compare these diverse aspects and then discuss the findings.

Investing in Society

The policy document *Towards Social Investment for Growth* portrays the EC's overall envisioned policies (2013a). The paper describes a common line of argument for all target groups and specific routes for distinct problems, which are then outlined in greater depth in subsequent papers.

Broadly, the EC addresses the subjects as being "at risk." In this perception, social policy has to "cover the challenges faced at various stages of people's lives" (EC 2013a, p. 6). Specifically, the paper consistently mentions groups such as children in poverty, young people, the long-term unemployed, the working poor, women, the disabled, and migrants as facing hardships and not having the necessary resilience to conquer these risks; these groups are not to blame for their plights. However, the lack or inadequacy of services and benefits plays a decisive role in creating these situations of social distress. Moreover, the labor market accelerates segmenting processes and further intensifies inequalities.

Ontology stresses that current social policy does not adequately address the risks people face over the life course. Out of this problematization, social investment means "adapting integrated services, cash benefits, and assistance to the critical moments in the life of a person, and preventing hardship from materializing later" (EC 2013a, p. 13). Therefore, ascetics promotes investment in human capital and protection, and human capital purposes to enhance people's skills and enable them to overcome situations of distress on their own or at least to mitigate the negative effects.

The techniques aim at establishing people's self-governing capacity. In contrast, welfare states are still expected to provide adequate and accessible benefits and services, which marks the traditional governance technique of social protection. However, transformations are supposed to pinpoint "critical junctions" (EC 2013a, p. 8) in the life cycles of all groups and provide support that increases life chances and independent living and "provide[s] an exit-strategy, so they should in principle be temporary" (EC 2013a, p. 3). To limit the time of receiving benefits, any support is expected to be conditional, with mandatory job searching, participation in training programs, or education; the degree of coercion is not stipulated, and the restrictions and conditions are not limited to the unemployed but also affect children and those in need of health and care services.

Decisive appears to be the long-term economic impact of social policies; the subject is subjugated to the public code of productivity. The moral code for individuals is to realize or make the most of their potential (EC 2013a, p. 14), to actively participate to the best of their abilities, and to confront life's risks (EC 2013a, p. 3). Nevertheless, the right "to live a life in dignity" (EC 2013a, p. 7) is still declared, which preserves human beings as entitled to social rights.

The telos, as implied in this document, is one that furthers active subjects, although the active role of the subject is not limited to employment but also entails participation in society. Next to the "active" subject, the "dependent" one still exists. Any form of dependency links the subject to a wide array of interventions that raise his/her human capital or at least want to ensure the greatest independence from the welfare state, creating a "temporary dependent subject."

Investing in Children

The policy document on children (EC 2013b) deviates in its scope from all other papers, which concentrate on responsibilities. Instead of conditionality, this document understands children as right-bearing citizens and integrates principles and requirements laid down in the UN Convention on the Rights of the Child.

Children are understood as being more at risk of poverty or social exclusion (EC 2013b, p. 2) than the general population. The ontological claim is that experiencing poverty in childhood reduces school achievement, increases health risks, and, overall, lowers life chances. Parts of the causes of children's risk of poverty are rooted in their parents' employment status. The document puts forward the strong link between parents' participation in the labor market and children's living conditions (EC 2013b, p. 5). Consequently, two aspects are problematized: first, the lack of equal opportunity for children who live in poverty and, second, the inadequate labor market participation of parents.

The policy document states that investing in children should break the cycle of disadvantage (EC 2013b, p. 2). Ascetically, a broad range of instruments covers care, education, health, and social services. The tools aim to provide universal high-quality services and early investments for all children but to specifically support those with greater needs or who come from disadvantaged backgrounds. Furthermore, participatory approaches cultivate engagement in society and decision making in that policy makers should "consult [children] on relevant policy planning" (EC 2013b, p. 9).

Next to children, parents become a key focus, albeit in a fairly divergent manner; all parents, but especially single ones, should be engaged in the labor market, and hence, taxes and benefits are proposed to be redesigned to increase employment rates for parents. However, any purposed conditionality or curtailment intends not to punish children; punitive actions are set to "the child's best interest" (EC 2013b, p. 5).

In the deontological dimension, children are safeguarded, but they themselves do not have specific moral obligations. The norm addresses the state and society, which are expected to enable children to live up to their full potential and contribute to their resilience (EC 2013b, p. 2). The public's obligation is to foster equal opportunity and protect, a trajectory that should limit the adverse effects of families of origin. The grounds for justification suggest an instrumental and ethical argument. Instrumentally, investing in children should maintain economic growth in the short and long terms, boosting the productivity of parents today and of children in the future. Ethically, individuals' life chances should be increased and equalized irrespective of social background.

For parents, good parenthood and supportive family environments are relinquished and economic responsibility strengthened. "[W]hilst fully acknowledging the importance of supporting families as primary carers" (EC 2013b, p. 4), parents' subjectification is to work to lift their children out of poverty.

The paper intends to promote social justice and protection (EC 2013b, p. 1), but the practices propose to shape children as citizens and prospective workers. The telos creates a society of equal opportunity and reframes children as right-bearing subjects independent of their families of origin. The parents are delimited as workers and earners, eliminating the vision of caretaking within families.

Investing in Health and Long-Term Care

The documents on elder care and health (EC 2013g, 2013h) employ identical thoughts on all four comparative aspects. The problematization puts forth the rising need in care and health services due to sociodemographic changes. Moreover, the escalating costs of health care threaten universal coverage of services, but informal care provision is portrayed as declining because of the increase in female employment. Thus, it is paramount "to find ways to limit growth in public spending … while avoiding a rapidly widening gap between the need … and the supply available" (EC 2013h, p. 16).

The papers also address users and employees. For users, the inaccessibility of quality services increases the potential of social exclusion (EC 2013g, p. 2), and employees in health and long-term care services suffer from poor working conditions. As a result, society faces economic impairment because of ill health in the working-age population and informal care lowers productivity (EC 2013g, p. 5; 2013h, p. 8).

Various techniques are employed to govern the subject: Improved employment conditions and formalization of care are expected to support female labor market participation and job retention (EC 2013g, p. 16; 2013h, p. 13). To counteract the rising costs, prevention is singled out as the gold standard. Healthy, physically and mentally active lifestyles are proposed, in particular, for disadvantaged groups (EC 2013g, p. 17).

These processes, though, shift responsibilities toward the individual. Within health, patient empowerment aims to enable patients to live independently; within long-term care, strategies are planned to foster users' coping capabilities given that "becoming dependent is influenced by a person's *perception* of their ability to manage despite functional limitations" (EC 2013g, p. 11).

The deontology of the two papers is never lucidly expressed; the opaque moral understanding that drives the reform is phrased cautiously. Individuals are obliged to maintain healthy lifestyles, avoid any risky behavior, and act preventatively. In case of need, they are expected to regain the utmost independence from health and care services. Deontologically, individuals strive for healthy, independent, and productive lives.

Ideally, policies aim "to boost economic growth by improving the health status of the population and enabling people to remain active and in better health for longer" (EC 2013h, p. 7). The telos again validates an active subject, which implies an independent, self-managing one, with extended employability. The stipulated values of such a policy conversion anticipate the improved quality of life for individuals from all social backgrounds and the sustainability of universal health and long-term care services. Overall, the papers plan for a healthy and productive society.

Investing in Housing

The document on homelessness (EC 2013d, p. 12) sets out from another angle. In the beginning, it accentuates the engrained support against homelessness at the European level. Then, it initiates with the remark that "(h)omelessness is an extreme manifestation of poverty and social exclusion which reduces a person's productive potential and is a waste of human capital" (EC 2013d, p. 5).

The problem description first underscores the destructiveness of homelessness, which affects health and reduces life expectancy and employability. Second, any lack of affordable housing and inadequate preventative services leads to more costly interventions at a later point. Third, the typical stage-based service approach for homeless persons, whereby clients must first visit shelters and only later move on to more permanent residences, is criticized for prolonging the experience of homelessness (EC 2013d, p. 12).

Structural constraints are repeatedly stressed in this document. Homelessness is rooted in a lack of affordable housing, regulations that favor landlords and mortgage lenders, inadequate housing benefits, and the current construction of services for homeless people. In the specific mode of problematization, subjects' behavior is mentioned as one factor (EC 2013d, p. 23), but is addressed to a lesser degree.

The problematization addresses the social and economic costs of homelessness and the lack of social and political rights for clients. The techne of government foremost encourages restructuring housing markets and social services for the homeless; in detail, measures to prevent homelessness, such as low-cost housing and revised eviction policies, are put forward. For the homeless, a rapid transition into permanent housing should shorten negative experiences in shelters, minimizing the human and social costs of homelessness (EC 2013d, pp. 23–26).

The process of normalizing homeless individuals furthermore intends voice and choice. Policies are supposed to aim at "(e)mpowering homeless people through their participation in service delivery and relevant policy-making" (EC 2013d, p. 30).

The subjectification of the homeless does not mark the target group itself. As in the case of the children's document, this policy document shifts the normative obligations toward policy makers and implementers, who are expected to perceive the homeless as rights-bearing citizens who are anticipated to have the same access to basic goods and services.

The subject who should be shaped is a social and political citizen who obtains status equality with people who have housing. First, the services propose to subjugate users no longer than necessary; they ideally transform the clients into tenants and bring them instantly into the ranks of "ordinary" people. Second, the statements stipulate an active, political homeless citizen in social service delivery and in the political process.

Investing in Work

The document on active inclusion for people outside the labor market (EC 2013f) presents a sequel to a previous EC recommendation paper (EC 2013e). It outlines at great length the advantages of the then proposed strategies.

In the realm of work, inactivity is seen as a problem; any non-participation in the labor market, not merely unemployment, is portrayed as "dormant human capital" (EC 2013f, p. 8). The problematization, however, gives a more nuanced perspective on the subject and widens the field; it refers to barriers to employment and to poverty in and out of work.

The cause for inactivity is traced back to the institutional design of the welfare state, which prevents job entry. Institutionally, employment is hampered by lack of work enforcement, mediocre employment services, and the exclusion of certain groups from services. So-called financial disincentives may obstruct the "labour friendliness" (EC 2013f, p. 25) of the benefit system. High benefit withdrawal rates may erect traps of inactivity (EC 2013f, p. 24), unemployment, low wages (EC 2013f, p. 25), dependency, and, overall, poverty (EC 2013f, p. 10).

Too-generous benefits are asserted to hinder employment, and "inadequacy, low coverage, and non-take-up of minimum income" and "in-work-poverty" (EC 2013f, p. 3) are argued to lead to poverty. What is the suggested techne to incentivize work for so-called dormant human capital without jeopardizing minimum income provisions? On the individual level, the right to a benefit is proposed to be tied to "the willingness to work and a minimum commitment to seeking a job" (EC 2013f, p. 35). Rights and responsibilities are to be laid out in individualized contracts that should consider personal circumstances, and these contracts are supposed to follow a staircase approach that intensifies social services over the duration of unemployment (EC 2013f, p. 35). Such agreements are understood to empower clients, but they may provide reasons for imposing sanction policies as well.

Profiling techniques are intended to advance effectiveness. For example, statics is proposed to assist with the selection of the program, which is "expected to have the largest effect in reducing the length of periods of unemployment for a particular individual with given personal characteristics" (EC 2013f, p. 19). The document even excludes some groups from services: "For instance, extensive educational programmes could be made available only to young people who are unemployed and do not have formal education" (EC 2013f, p. 13). Despite the paper's acknowledgement that longer training shows better outcomes in the medium run (EC 2013f, p. 12), budgetary concerns limit the instruments, aiming to "shorten the time a person needs to find a job, while cutting the cost of activation" (EC 2013f, p. 13).

To ensure access to activating and enabling services, the document proposes "one-stop shops" that merge job centers and social assistance offices. Less stigmatizing, these single entry points are expected to boost labor market attachment, "address the need of those least likely to get a job" (EC 2013f, p. 4), and ease the access to a minimum income. High take-up rates of benefits are anticipated to lower the poverty rate.

The policy paper proposes a set of instruments so that individuals may obtain a minimum income without eroding incentives to take up work (EC 2013f, p. 37). In addition to job search and training, the benefit levels are planned to adapt to individual and household needs while avoiding traps of any kind. To circumvent the inactivity, unemployment, low-wage, dependency, and poverty traps, the benefit and tax systems are envisioned to contribute to "mak[ing] work pay" (EC 2013f, p. 8).

To incentivize work, any benefit should be set at the 40 percent median income, and the minimum wages should be tied to the 60 percent median income, with both poverty thresholds grounded in the European context; the gap between these two limits intends to ensure that people choose work over benefits. Taking these suggestions, per year, in Germany, the former group would obtain 7,900 Euro in benefits and 11,900 in low-wage work; in the United Kingdom, the groups would receive 8,200 and 12,400 Euro; in Sweden, 10,800 and 16,300 Euro; and in Greece, 3,100 and 4,600 Euro, all respectively.[6]

"Providing adequate, well-designed income support for those who need it, while helping them back into jobs" (EC 2013f, p. 4) recapitulates the ascetics of the social investment strategy. The deontology is not addressed in the document; the moral argument for partaking in activation and in employment appears to be taken for granted.

The formed subject ought to work, whenever and as quickly as possible. The telos, nevertheless, does not inhibit provision and take-up of benefits and frames out-of-work citizens as entitled to social support. In this ideal scheme, the suggestions lead to two sets of subjects. First, the rational unemployed subjects should govern themselves and seek employment because the optimal design of benefits incentivizes work over inactivity. Second, irrational subjects who do not conduct themselves according to the system's logic are bound to reposition themselves as rational and self-governing subjects over time as services and conditionality transform their behavior into either disadvantage or discipline.

Investment Subjects

Comparing these six documents (or five groups), the notion of an active, productive subject flourishes (see Table 4.1). Not only do the unemployed face an

TABLE 4.1 Social investment subjects

	Ontology	Ascetics	Deontology	Teleology
Society	At risk	Benefits and services at critical moments	Make most of their potential, right to live with dignity	Active, life-risk-managing subject, temporarily dependent subject
Children	Intergenerational transmission of poverty, future lack of human capital	Equal opportunity for children, employment for parents	State's moral obligation to enable children's potential and resilience, parents' norm to earn to lift children out of poverty	Children as citizens and upcoming working subjects under the wings of state services, parents as working subjects
Health and Long-Term Care	Limited access to health and long-term care services	Benefits and services that prolong labor market participation and independence from services	Uphold independence and health	Healthy, independent, employable subject
Housing	Manifestation of poverty and social exclusion	Restructuring housing markets, social services, voices, and choices	State's obligation to create citizen	Social and political citizen subject
Work	Dormant human capital	Avoiding any trap, conditionality	–	Working, rational (incentivized) subject or irrational (disadvantaged, disciplined) subject

activation regime, but also the young and old, sick and healthy are targeted. The proliferation of human capital thinking, however, problematizes, alters governmental techniques, and redefines norms away from a singular subject. Although social investment challenges social citizenship, it does not abolish social rights.

Children and the homeless have not been morally obliged to govern themselves toward activity. Both are first and foremost right-bearing citizens, and it is the state's obligation to enact these subjects; all other subjects are morally obliged to make the most of their potential, although they are still entitled to live lives with dignity.

The documents themselves do not clarify how much paternalism the member states should establish. The paper on the unemployed distinguishes between an optimized route for rational subjects and a disciplinary regime for non-complying ones. In contrast, the recommendations for children stoop lower to sanctioning the parents and put the child's well-being and development first.

The degrees of coercion make explicit that the policy papers do not present a uniform thinking. Another example depicts empowerment: Barbara Cruikshank (1994) understands empowerment as an instrument of subjection, a way to work upon the citizen. In all four cases, empowerment aims at clients' independence and self-governing, but the extent and direction vary. For the frail, empowerment means regaining self-sufficiency so that they can manage their daily lives with less or no help from services (EC 2013h, p. 17). Patient empowerment for people with chronic illness signifies greater self-management of the condition in consultation with health staff (EC 2013g, p. 13). The elderly and sick are depicted as gaining the means to shape their everyday lives. In the case of self-management, a new form of moral obligation that introduces "permanent activeness" may be introduced (Fersch 2015).

The contracts with the job centers should empower the unemployed, with rights and responsibilities defined on an individual basis (EC 2013f). In practice, the unemployed should alter their behavior as outlined in the contracts, which are designed to be more constraining and standardized than individualized and empowering (Minas, Wright, and van Berkel 2012; van Berkel and Valkenburg 2007). In contrast, the homeless should be empowered politically (EC 2013d) and are expected to obtain political strength.

Social investment thinking, as displayed in the documents, clearly aspires to improve human capital and to employ it to the fullest. In doing so, the thinking in the documents also redefines the worthiness of citizens according to rates of return, which is exemplified in comparing the papers on children and the unemployed. Evidently enunciated is the human capital development approach for children and the young unemployed who have no formal education; here, the expected individual and societal gains from longer and costly trainings are assessed to be greater than those for the older or already educated workforce. Yet despite this economic argument, both documents stress that policies are expected to target the worst off as well, eliminating pre-existing inequalities and pushing for equal opportunities.

Social investment's potential to reposition social inclusion and equality, as indicated by Jenson (2013) and Mahon (2013), is curtailed severely, at least in the paper on work. On the one hand, the disciplinary approach promotes sanctions and does not recapitulate the right to live in dignity. On the other hand, the soft-governance approach optimizes the benefits levels to incentivize reentry and thus proposes a rather low benefit.

Taking the optimization by labor market participation and emphasizing the expected rates of return, these approaches may contradict the recommendation to assist disadvantaged groups at a greater rate. Instead of social inclusion, such advice may reinforce exclusionary tendencies and create a second tier of beneficiaries who can only access limited benefits and mediocre services.

Social investment concentrates on equal opportunities for children, which in the future should ensure both social justice and competition. The question remains whether equal opportunity alone is decisive given that the policy documents highlight certain minimum income provisions that address poverty as well. A pure neoliberal policy would resist any further interference in redistribution (Plant 2010), whereas the social investment perspective goes beyond that: It upholds social citizenship and is aware that merely equal opportunity may ruthlessly mutilate social and democratic rights.

To facilitate enablement and redistribution concurrently, services hold a pivotal position in the SIP. Many types of services may stimulate job creation and then provide good job opportunities and raise overall productivity, especially as women's employment flourishes. Separate from the upswing in female labor market participation, the services contribute to caring for children and the elderly irrespective of social background.

Though the redistributive capacity of benefits and services may be curtailed, using the example of merging social assistance and unemployment services to a one-stop shop, the higher take-up and improved services for social assistance recipients may be offset by modest support and less generous compensation for unemployment beneficiaries. Correspondingly, flat-rate universal or, more likely for the unemployed, targeted provisions may replace other benefits and services that previously upheld an element of status security and valued merit.

Not only might merit be replaced completely in the long run, but universal services and benefits may also be perpetually examined to "increase the effectiveness and efficiency of social policies" (EC 2013a, p. 3). Although this economic belief system is deemed necessary to uphold social inclusion, it may ultimately value social investment more than social rights. Because of the lack of explicitly stated social rights in the documents, the challenges of the social investment approach for social citizenship may be best analyzed in consideration of the implementation in the European Union member states. Nevertheless, the two recommended levels of income between those in and out of work might indicate the proposed way forward.

Conclusion

Theoretically, the social investment perspective may perpetuate social citizenship by concomitantly endorsing a human capital approach and redistributive aims, which caters to all societal groups and extends beyond employability. However, social investment may also advance neoliberal policies; these policies may limit redistribution to the poor and advance a human capital approach that values its positive impact on labor market participation and economic growth.

The European Commission's SIP backs an ambivalent adaptation of the social investment perspective. It moves human capital theory into mainstream European social policy and labels it more temptingly as "social investment," and its pivotal element is eliminating all kinds of traps so that people will incentivize work over benefits. Additionally, education policies are expected to align children for early entry into a competitive workforce but also foster equal opportunity. Moreover, preventative and enabling policies are intended to further the independence and employability of the general population, especially the elderly. Clearly, these subjects should raise a dividend and lead more productive lives.

Expanding human capital theory, children, the elderly, and the general population are addressed as social investment subjects, but the documents do not portray a singular version: subjects are active and life-risk managing versus temporarily dependent, citizens and future workers, working parents, healthy, independent, and employable, social and political, rational, disciplined and disadvantaged.

For most subjects, soft-governing mechanisms prevail, although the unemployed may face a disciplining, paternalistic approach; still, social services should provide training for the disadvantaged unemployed. Despite all that, the policy papers accentuate universal services and social rights, particularly for children and the homeless. Such services may deliver indispensable resources for individuals to participate in society.

Thus, the SIP not only carries forward a neoliberal agenda but still supports and protects subjects accordingly. Ultimately, though, this notion of support may depend on budgetary decisions more than on a belief that human beings are intrinsically valuable, which may hamper a genuine European social model and provide scarce, minimal social protection.

Notes

This chapter was presented at the conference "Self-Responsibility in European Welfare Institutions – Concepts, Methods and Trends," University of Hamburg, 19–21 May 2016. I thank the participants and also Sanford Schram and Mathias Herup Nielsen for insightful comments.

1 Owing to the multi-tier system, the European Union often introduces reform agendas with the open method of coordination. Policy coordination should "softly" make policy at the national level with comparisons, guidelines, benchmarks, expertise, and the involvement of relevant stakeholders (Wallace and Reh 2015).

2 In 2004, Czech Republic, Estonia, Cyprus, Latvia, Lithuania, Hungary, Malta, Poland, Slovakia, and Slovenia were added; in 2007, Bulgaria and Romania; and in 2013, Croatia.
3 Moreover, whereas the shift is state led, private-sector institutions themselves apply market logic. Private and public actors combine and competition rules are introduced, which fosters the need for permanent innovation, and then management and surveillance tools are strengthened (Schram, Fording, and Soss 2011; Soss et al. 2011). .
4 Such a productivist notion of social policy has a long tradition in social science, as Smyth and Deeming (2016) stress with the ideas of Myrdal in the 1930s and Tawney in the 1960s.
5 Three policy documents were excluded from the analysis: One because it addresses legal issues for social services (EC 2013c); another one outlines proceedings of the European social funds (EC 2013i); and one only describes problematizations, which are then repeated in all other documents, but it does not give notes on the other three aspects (EC 2013e).
6 I made these calculations using EU-Survey on Income and Living Conditions, 2014 data.

Bibliography

Barbier, J.-C. (2012). Comment on Anton Hemerijck/2. Social Investment, a Problematic Concept with an Ambiguous Past. *Sociologica*, 1, 1–11.

Becker, G. S. (1962). Investment in Human Capital: A Theoretical Analysis. *Journal of Political Economy*, 70(S5), 9–49. doi:10.1086/258724

Becker, G. S., Ewald, F., and Harcourt, B. E. (2012). *Becker on Ewald on Foucault on Becker. American Neoliberalism and Michel Foucault's 1979 "Birth of Biopolitics" Lectures*. Coase-Sandor Institute for Law & Economics Working Paper (614).

Beckfield, J. (2012). Comment on Anton Hemerijck/3. More Europe, Not Less: Reversing the Long, Slow Decline of the European Social Model. *Sociologica*, 1. doi:10.2383/36890

Bothfeld, S., and Rouault, S. (2015). Families Facing the Crisis: Is Social Investment a Sustainable Social Policy Strategy? *Social Politics: International Studies in Gender, State & Society*, 22(1), 60–85. doi:10.1093/sp/jxu014

Brady, M. (2014). Ethnographies of Neoliberal Governmentalities: From the Neoliberal Apparatus to Neoliberalism and Governmental Assemblages. *Foucault Studies*, 18, 11–33.

Brown, W. (2015). *Undoing the Demos. Neoliberalism's Stealth Revolution*. New York: Zone Books.

Cantillon, B. (2011). The Paradox of the Social Investment State: Growth, Employment and Poverty in the Lisbon Era. *Journal of European Social Policy*, 21(5), 432–449. doi:10.1177/0958928711418856

Carneiro, P. M., and Heckman, J. J. (2003). *Human Capital Policy*. IZA. Discussion Paper (821).

Copeland, P. (2012). EU Enlargement, the Clash of Capitalisms and the European Social Model. *Comparative European Politics*, 10(4), 476–504.

Cruikshank, B. (1994). The Will to Empower. Technologies of Citizenship and the War on Poverty. *Socialist Review*, 23(4), 29–55.

Dean, M. (1995). Governing the Unemployed Self in an Active Society. *Economy and Society*, 24(4), 559–583.

Dean, M. (2014a). Michel Foucault's "Apology" for Neoliberalism. *Journal of Political Power*, 7(3), 433–442. doi:10.1080/2158379X.2014.967002

Dean, M. (2014b). Rethinking Neoliberalism. *Journal of Sociology*, 50(2), 150–163.

Deeming, C., and Smyth, P. (2015). Social Investment after Neoliberalism: Policy Paradigms and Political Platforms. *Journal of Social Policy*, 44(2), 297–318.

Esping-Andersen, G. (2002). Towards the Good Society, Once Again? In G. Esping-Andersen, D. Gallie, A. Hemerijck, and J. Myles (Eds.), *Why We Need a New Welfare State* (pp. 1–25). Oxford: Oxford University Press.

Esping-Andersen, G. (2015). Welfare Regimes and Social Stratification. *Journal of European Social Policy*, 25(1), 124–134. doi:10.1177/0958928714556976

EC (2013a). *Communication from the Commssion to the European Parliament, the Council, the European Economic and Social Committee and the Committee of Regions: Towards Social Investment for Growth and Cohesion – Including Implementing the European Social Fund 2014–2020*. Brussels.

EC (2013b). *Investing in Children: Breaking the Cycle of Disadvantage*. Brussels.

EC (2013c). *Social Investment Package Commission Staff Working Document: 3rd Biennal Report on Social Services of General Interest*. Brussels.

EC (2013d). *Social Investment Package Commission Staff Working Document: Confronting Homelessness in the European Union*. Brussels.

EC (2013e). *Social Investment Package Commission Staff Working Document: Evidence on Demographic and Social Trends. Social Policies' Contribution to Inclusion, Employment and the Economy*. Brussels.

EC (2013f). *Social Investment Package Commission Staff Working Document: Follow-up on the Implementation by the Member States of the 2008 European Commission Recommendation on Active Inclusion of People Excluded from the Labour Market – Towards a Social Investment Approach*. Brussels.

EC (2013g). *Social Investment Package Commission Staff Working Document: Investing in Health*. Brussels.

EC (2013h). *Social Investment Package Commission Staff Working Document: Long-term Care in Ageing Societies – Challenges and Policy Options*. Brussels.

EC (2013i). *Social Investment Package Commission Staff Working Document: Social Investment through the European Social Fund*. Brussels.

Ewald, F. (1991). Insurance and Risk. In G. Burchell, C. Gordon, and P. Miller (Eds.), *The Foucault Effect. Studies in Governmentality with Two Lectures By and an Interview With Michel Foucault* (pp. 197–210). Chicago: Chicago University Press.

Fersch, B. (2015). Expectations Towards Home Care Re-ablement in Danish Municipalities. *International Journal of Sociology and Social Policy*, 35(3/4), 126–140. doi:10.1108/IJSSP-06-2014-0045

Foucault, M. (2008). *Birth of Biopolitics. Lectures at the College de France 1978–79*. Basingstoke: Palgrave Macmillan.

Giddens, A. (1998). *The Third Way: The Renewal of Social Democracy*. Cambridge: Polity Press.

Harvey, D. (2010). *A Brief History of Neoliberalism*. Oxford: Oxford University Press.

Heckman, J. J. (2000). Policies to Foster Human Capital. *Research in Economics*, 54(1), 3–56.

Hemerijck, A. (2002). The Self-Transformation of the European Social Model(s). In G. Esping-Andersen, D. Gallie, A. Hemerijck, and J. Myles (Eds.), *Why We Need a New Welfare State* (pp. 174–213). Oxford: Oxford University Press.

Hemerijck, A. (2013). *Changing Welfare States*, 1st edn. Oxford: Oxford University Press.

Hemerijck, A., and Vandenbroucke, F. (2012). Social Investment and the Euro Crisis: The Necessity of a Unifying Social Policy Concept. *Intereconomics/Review of European Economic Policy*, 47(4), 200–206. http://link.springer.com/journal/volumesAndIssues/10272

Jenson, J. (2009). Redesigning Citizenship Regimes after Neoliberalism. Moving Towards Social Investment. In N. Morel, B. Palier, and J. Palme (Eds.), *What Future for Social Investment? Research Report* (pp. 27–44). Stockholm: Institute for Futures Studies.

Jenson, J. (2010). Diffusing Ideas for After Neoliberalism: The Social Investment Perspective in Europe and Latin America. *Global Social Policy*, 10(1), 59–84. doi:10.1177/1468018109354813

Jenson, J. (2013). Changing Perspectives on Social Citzenship: A Cross-time Comparison. In A. Evers and A.-M. Guillemard (Eds.), *Social Policy and Citizenship. The Changing Landscape* (pp. 57–79). New York: Oxford University Press.

Judt, T. (2005). *Postwar – A History of Europe Since 1945.* New York: The Penguin Press.

Kvist, J. (2004). Does EU Enlargement Start a Race to the Bottom? Strategic Interaction among EU Member States in Social Policy. *Journal of European Social Policy*, 14(3), 301–318. doi:10.1177/0958928704044625

Kvist, J. (2015). A Framework for Social Investment Strategies: Integrating Generational, Life Course and Gender Perspectives in the EU Social Investment Strategy. *Comparative European Politics*, 13(1), 131–149. doi:10.1057/cep.2014.45

Mahon, R. (2013). Social Investment According to the OECD/DELSA: A Discourse in Making. *Global Policy Volume*, 2, 150–159.

Marshall, T. H. (1950). *Citizenship and Social Class. And other Essays.* Cambridge: Cambridge University Press.

Marshall, T. H. (1972). Value Problems of Welfare-Capitalism. *Journal of Social Policy*, 1(1), 15–32. doi:10.1017/S0047279400002166

Mckee, K. (2009). Post-Foucauldian Governmentality: What Does it Offer Critical Social Policy Analysis? *Critical Social Policy*, 29(3), 465–486. doi:10.1177/0261018309105180

Mead, L. M. (1986). *Beyond Entitlement: The Social Obligations of Citizenship.* New York: The Free Press.

Minas, R., Wright, S., and van Berkel, R. (2012). Decentralization and Centralization: Governing the Activation of Social Assistance Recipients in Europe. *International Journal of Sociology and Social Policy*, 32(5/6), 286–298.

Morel, N., Palier, B., and Palme, J. (2012a). Beyond the Welfare State as We Knew It? In N. Morel, B. Palier, and J. Palme (Eds.), *Towards a Social Investment Welfare State?: Ideas, Policies and Challenges* (pp. 1–31). Bristol: Policy Press.

Morel, N., Palier, B., and Palme, J. (2012b). Social Investment: A Paradigm in Search of a New Economic Model and Political Mobilisation. In N. Morel, B. Palier, and J. Palme (Eds.), *Towards a Social Investment Welfare State?: Ideas, Policies and Challenges* (pp. 353–376). Bristol: Policy Press.

Nolan, B. (2013). What Use is "Social Investment"? *Journal of European Social Policy*, 23(5), 459–468. doi:10.1177/0958928713499177

Palier, B., Vandenbroucke, F., and Hemerijck, A. (2011). *The EU Needs a Social Investment Pact.* OSE Paper Series. Opinion paper (May 5, 2011).

Peck, J. (2010). *Construction of Neoliberal Reason.* Oxford: Oxford University Press.

Peck, J. (2013). Explaining (with) Neoliberalism. *Territory, Politics, Governance*, 1(2), 132–157. doi:10.1080/21622671.2013.785365

Pintelon, O., Cantillon, B., Van den Bosch, K., and Whelan, C. T. (2013). The Social Stratification of Social Risks: The Relevance of Class for Social Investment Strategies. *Journal of European Social Policy*, 23(1), 52–67. doi:10.1177/0958928712463156

Plant, R. (2010). *The Neo-liberal State.* Oxford: Oxford University Press.

Rapley, T. (2007). *Doing Conversation, Discourse and Document Analysis.* London: Sage.

Sapsford, R., and Jupp, V. (2006). *Data Collection and Analysis* (2nd edn.). London: Sage.

Saraceno, C. (2015). A Critical Look to the Social Investment Approach from a Gender Perspective. *Social Politics: International Studies in Gender, State & Society*, 22(2), 257–269. doi:10.1093/sp/jxv008

Schmidt, V. A., and Thatcher, M. (2013). Theorizing Ideational Continuity: The Resilience of Neo-liberal Ideas in Europe. In V. A. Schmidt and M. Thatcher (Eds.), *Resilient Liberalism in Europe's Political Economy* (pp. 1–52). Cambridge: Cambridge University Press.

Schram, S. (2015). *The Return of Ordinary Capitalism. Neoliberalism, Precarity, Occupy.* Oxford: Oxford University Press.

Schram, S., Fording, R. C., and Soss, J. (2011). Neoliberal Paternalism: Race and the New Poverty Governance. In M.-K. Jung, E. Bonilla-Silva, and J. H. Costa Vargas (Eds.), *State of White Supremacy. Racism, Governance, and the U.S.* (pp. 130–159). Palo Alto, CA: Stanford University Press.

Smyth, P., and Deeming, C. (2016). The "Social Investment Perspective" in Social Policy: A Longue Durée Perspective. *Social Policy & Administration*, 50(6), 673–690. doi:10.1111/spol.12255

Soss, J., Fording, R. C., and Schram, S. (2011). *Disciplining the Poor: Neoliberal Paternalism and the Persistent Power of Race.* Chicago: University of Chicago Press.

Streeck, W. (2012). *Gekaufte Zeit. Die vertagte Krise des demokratischen Kapitalismus.* Berlin: Suhrkamp.

Szcerbiak, A., and Taggart, P. (Eds.) (2008). *Opposing Europe? The Comparative Party Politics of Euroscepticism.* Oxford: Oxford University Press.

van Berkel, R., and Valkenburg, B. (Eds.) (2007). *Making it Personal: Individualising Activation Services in the EU.* Bristol: Policy.

Van Kersbergen, K., and Hemerijck, A. (2012). Two Decades of Change in Europe: The Emergence of the Social Investment State. *Journal of Social Policy*, 41(3), 475–492.

Vandenbroucke, F. (2002). Foreword: Sustainable Social Justice and "Open Co-ordination" in Europe. In G. Esping-Andersen, D. Gallie, A. Hemerijck, and J. Myles (Eds.), *Why We Need a New Welfare State* (pp. xiii–xxiv). Oxford: Oxford University Press.

Vaughan-Whitehead, D. (2015). The European Social Model in Times of Crisis: An Overview. In D. Vaughan-Whitehead (Ed.), *The European Social Model in Crisis: Is Europe Losing Its Soul?* (pp. 1–65). Cheltenham: Edward Elgar Publishing.

Wallace, H., and Reh, C. (2015). An Institutional Anatomy and Five Policy Modes. In H. Wallace, M. A. Pollack, and A. R. Young (Eds.), *Policy-Making in the European Union* (7th edn., pp. 72–114). Oxford: Oxford University Press.

Whitworth, A. (2016). Neoliberal Paternalism and Paradoxical Subjects: Confusion and Contradiction in UK Activation Policy. *Critical Social Policy*, 36(3), 412–431. doi:10.1177/0261018315624442

5

ONTOLOGIES OF POVERTY IN RUSSIA AND DUPLICITIES OF NEOLIBERALISM[1]

Marianna Pavlovskaya

There is no money for your pensions now. But you will somehow hang on. Best wishes for high spirits and health to everyone!
Prime Minister Dmitry Medvedev to retired women of Crimea in May 2016

Thinking about poverty has particular significance for Russia as a post-Soviet society. This is because the majority of the population was born during the Soviet period when poverty did not exist and was not recognized as such in the form that it is today. The notion of poverty was not unfamiliar to Soviet society but it was separated from Soviet time and space: it existed in the past, under the Tsarist regime, or outside of the Soviet Union, in the capitalist West. Relegating the possibility of poverty to the past or to another location provided the Soviet government with a way to deny its existence in any form within the Soviet Union. This denial had both material and ideological foundations. On the one hand, the Soviet state guaranteed minimal levels of social security and consumption. On the other hand, the Soviet ideology of Marxism-Leninism firmly placed poverty within non-socialist societies. Thus, even the theoretical possibility of poverty under socialism was eliminated while it was considered common under capitalism.

Consequently, when post-Soviet Russia radically reset its compass from socialism to capitalism in 1991, poverty was no longer seen as a proximate impossibility. Instead, its presence in Russia became accepted as a natural part of and an unavoidable price to pay for the advantages of a market economy. In contrast to the Soviet past, when differences in material wealth were relatively limited, the post-Soviet transformation produced a society with dramatic inequalities and a large impoverished population. Russia, however, entirely lacking experience with capitalism, was unprepared to address poverty at a societal level. Consequently,

Russian social scientists and the government had to develop from scratch metrics and policies to manage this new population of the poor.

This chapter examines the ways in which Russia has used the new international metrics of poverty designed by the ILO (International Labor Organization) since it first introduced capitalism in 1991. My analysis shows that these metrics measure the poor in a way that normalizes poverty. In particular, I show how the metrics both affirm the presence of poverty and, at the same time, deny its actual scope and extent. That is, they make poverty visible within society but also make it appear limited and manageable despite its pervasiveness. Poverty in Russia does not, however, appear exceptional when compared to the rest of the world; indeed, it is within the "norm" by Western industrial standards. Yet, when compared to the recent Soviet past, the very existence of poverty and its current scale looks like a social catastrophe. The Russian government, however, can avoid comparisons to the Soviet period because the ILO metrics have only been applied since 1991. Measuring and understanding poverty (and non-poverty) in Russia, then, is only possible within and relative to the post-Soviet period.

The Russian government first developed new poverty-related policies during the post-Soviet period which coincided with the global turn toward neoliberalism. Because of this timing, Russia adopted distinctly neoliberal versions of Western social policies which foreground the role of markets and social discipline to alleviate poverty. Had Russia moved towards capitalism in the middle of the twentieth century, for example, it may have adopted more welfare-oriented approaches to address poverty. Given the neoliberal climate of the late twentieth century, Russia, with unprecedented speed, went from full welfare provision under the Soviet system to a state of extreme wealth polarization, pervasive poverty, and authoritarian governance, a state which also increasingly characterizes other Western nations particularly the United States.

The Russian government, however, has a complex relationship with neoliberalism. It clearly adopts neoliberal market-oriented and disciplinary logics yet uses the term rhetorically to negatively characterize Western "liberal" values and policies including those of the Obama administration, to which it counterpoises traditional Russian Orthodox values, a uniquely Russian path to development, and its pride in a strong nationalistic state. Perhaps unsurprisingly, Putin's government was quick to celebrate the new Trump administration, trusting it will lead to a reduction in US opposition to Russian geopolitical ambitions and the removal of international sanctions against Russia. Neoliberal leaders easily find common ground because they share ideologies of markets and strong state control.

The Russian people have, however, responded to economic deprivation, poverty, and disciplinary policies as creatively as they responded to scarcity and authoritarian control during the Soviet period. Under the surface of the formal capitalist economy that generates vast inequalities and poverty, a whole realm of economic practices exists which are driven by ethics of sharing, mutual support, and collective survival, and which work to support livelihoods, people, and places on a daily basis. It is then worth seeing Russia as a realm of multiple economies in transformation that can become, even under the most authoritarian and/or neo-liberal rule, a site of economic possibility and solidarity (Roelvink et al. 2015; Pavlovskaya 2004, 2013, 2015). While discussion of these practices is beyond the scope of this essay, it is important to recognize their role in alleviating the poverty produced by neoliberal capitalism and meager welfare support.

In the rest of the chapter I will first outline the importance of studying Russia as a laboratory for the production of poverty under neoliberal capitalism. I will then discuss the Soviet welfare system and its transformation since the 1990s and the introduction of capitalism. I will then examine the extent of Russian poverty visible in statistics and will show how the new metrics both normalize and hide structural poverty. Underneath these internationally sanctioned metrics, a set of meaninglessly related indicators work to misrepresent the level of deprivation and, therefore, render Russian social policy, informed by these statistics, ineffectual, as the case of unemployment benefits will demonstrate. In the conclusion, I reflect on the implications of the Russian experience with poverty for other societies similarly subjected to neoliberalizing regimes and on the possibility of progressive post-capitalist politics even under such conditions.

Russia as a Laboratory of Poverty for the Neoliberal Age

In his widely discussed book *Capital in the Twenty-First Century*, Thomas Piketty only briefly mentions Russia despite his interest in the trajectory of capitalism and the inequalities it produces. This is perhaps surprising given that Russia, like no other country in the world, implemented, virtually overnight, a radical transfor-mation from state socialism to capitalism, becoming the largest single territory of capital accumulation once its public assets were privatized. Piketty is not alone in paying little attention to this part of the world: liberal and critical researchers alike turn their gaze away from Russia. For them, either Russia is an oligarchic and authoritarian deviation from capitalism and therefore can tell us little about capitalism per se or studying Russia is theoretically and politically uncomfortable given its history of abandoning socialism. Most research on poverty focuses on the, so called, First and Third worlds despite the establishment a quarter of a century ago of an enormous "territory of poverty" (Roy and Crane 2015) in Russia. As a result, the impoverished lives of millions of people do not register within global assessments of poverty; they simply do not exist on the world map.

While some of the harshest outcomes of neoliberal trajectories are made invisible when we ignore the case of Russia, so too is the degree to which such trajectories and outcomes are not "natural" but are of our making. Prior to 1991, Soviet Russia was a society where there was no legal provision for either private property or unemployment for most of the twentieth century. As a result, capitalism needed to be "built" out of whole cloth by state policies that closely followed the prescriptions of the best neoliberal minds that the IMF could find (Offe 1994;

Sachs 1995; Aslund 2001). In this sense, it was "state of the art" neoliberalism, a constructed social reality with nothing natural about it. Therefore, Russian genealogies of capitalism and poverty can be framed in the context of an explicit policy effort which can open new ways of thinking about social change. In particular, development, within Russia and beyond, might best be rethought as not following a predetermined and inevitable path toward "the end of history" (Fukuyama 1989) so that alternative futures may be imagined and politically articulated. Russia, deliberately and decisively, changed its course twice in the twentieth century; despite many undesirable outcomes, the case of Russia pushes us to see social transformations and various economic futures as not only possible but as also always ongoing, incomplete, and the result of a contested political process.

What place could be more intriguing for those who want to understand how contemporary capitalism is constituted and maintained? What lessons could the rest of the world learn from the Russian experience? In Russia the extremes of modern capitalism are allowed to flourish without constraint; indeed, Russia might be the already actualized neoliberal tomorrow of the West. As a real life laboratory of large-scale economic marginalization and poverty, the Russian experience calls for urgent efforts to better understand and resist neoliberalism, and work on alternative futures "here and now" (Gibson-Graham 1996, 2006; Gibson-Graham, Cameron, and Healy 2013; Pavlovskaya 2013, 2015).

Normalization of Poverty through Metrics

In Russia, it is clear that neoliberal reform results in widespread poverty which, twenty-five years on, can no longer be rationalized as the "necessary and short lived pain" of transition. Furthermore, Russia also provides us with a clear case of how measuring and understanding poverty matters, how it allows for some policies and not others, and how it works to reinforce inequalities even as it claims to create knowledge for their alleviation. Like capitalism itself, modes of poverty knowledge in Russia have been adopted/imposed from elsewhere. In particular, Russian policy makers and scholars look to the West, international organizations such as the ILO, and especially the United States, where poverty is understood as a "normal" part of everyday life, for insights into how to know and address the problem of poverty (Collier and Way 2004; Pavlovskaya 2015).

Policy makers and scholars who have accepted neoliberalism also accept, perhaps reluctantly, the inevitability of the existence of poverty in Russia. Making poverty acceptable more broadly, to the society that recently denied its existence, is not, however, a trivial task. It required a complete rejection of Marxist state ideologies, rationalities, and truths that the government and social scientists had produced for decades during the Soviet era. These ideologies had to be replaced with new truths emerging from neoliberal discourses that legitimize individualism, the right to wealth accumulation, inherent inequality, and poverty as an unfortunate but inevitable condition. Social and economic truths are, however, constructed by more than ideological shifts and dispositions; they are established and reinforced through socio-technical practices and methodologies, not the least of which are state sponsored categorizations and collections of data. Indeed, metrics of poverty that conform to international standards (e.g. ILO and others) have played a crucial role in the normalization of poverty because they produce a powerful message that poverty is everywhere in the world and it is acceptable to have it in Russia. These metrics, therefore, do not simply describe poverty, they produce the poor as a new subject and object of policy; they produce a social body that neoliberalism can manage (Hannah 2001; Pavlovskaya and Bier 2012). The relatively new introduction into Russia of not only neoliberal ideologies and policies but also the practices and methodologies of state knowledge production about capitalism (e.g., new categories and techniques for counting and measuring) makes clear how ideology and metrics work together to maintain Russia's neoliberal trajectory.

Welfare and Poverty under State Socialism

In order to appreciate the degree of strain on social reproduction caused by the removal of Soviet era welfare support, it is important to disentangle the advances of state welfare per se from the Soviet authoritarian political system. Neoliberal theorists, however, see welfare as dependency on state authority; they treat them as two sides of the same coin. In their view, state welfare is necessarily joined with political conformism while freedom can only exist under capitalism freed from state intervention (Friedman 1951). Because Russian reformers thought in this way too, they dismantled the Soviet welfare system insofar as it was understood to be integral to the totalitarian state (Pavlovskaya 2015). Yet, totalitarian regimes around the world such as Pinochet's Chile, China, and now Russia have aggressively promoted private markets; it is clear that the connection between capitalism and democracy is contingent rather than necessary. Consequently, neither do the welfare state and authoritarianism need to be theorized as two sides of the same coin; their proximity could be seen as that of two coins put together in a contingent manner. Starting from such an understanding, we can start to (re)imagine post-capitalist (or non-capitalist) democracies with strong welfare support as legitimate, desirable, and possible. In this regard, the experience of the Soviet welfare system is invaluable for appreciating what a society can accomplish by treating basic human needs as entitlements and rights instead of commodities.

Private property in the means of production did not exist under the Soviet system and the state guaranteed jobs to all as a single employer; there was no unemployment (in fact, avoiding work was treated as a problem). Wages and pensions covered basic consumption needs while prices for food items, manufactured goods, cultural services, utilities, and transportation were low and fixed. Such social goods as childcare, healthcare, housing, and education were provided universally, free of charge, and disregarding the ability to pay. The quality and availability of these goods and services obviously varied significantly across Soviet space (they were especially lacking in rural areas, Zaslavsky 1982) but the point is that their provision equalized income differentials and assured social mobility at the large scale. Additionally, the system of the so-called *l'goty* provided benefits (monetized and in kind) to specific population groups such as, for example, labor veterans (those over twenty-five years in the labor force), war veterans, the handicapped, and families with children.[2] Seen as irrational, wasteful, and even "exuberant" from the neoliberal point of view (Collier and Way 2004; Pavlovskaya 2015), the Soviet welfare system worked well for decades by equalizing social differences without explicitly addressing them.

The former Soviet Union denied that poverty could exist within socialism on theoretical grounds. In the 1930s, Stalin declared that the foundations of socialism had been built and the social roots of poverty as well as other "bourgeois" societal ills (such as exploitation, patriarchy, ethnic discrimination, class differences, and so on) had been eliminated. As a result, statistical agencies did not gather statistics on class differences until the 1950s–1960s (Rimashevskaya 2003). Nevertheless, the Soviet government realized the need to address existing differences in material well-being. Statisticians began collecting what was then classified information about income and consumption levels, information that was only made available to economists and sociologists charged with consulting with the government. Because the term "poverty" was reserved for capitalism, Soviet scholars began assessing what they called "low material security" (*maloobespechennost'*) of certain groups from the overall population (e.g., families with several children, the handicapped, or retirees). It was measured against the scientifically determined "minimum subsistence budget" (Rimashevskaya 2003, p. 124). Assessment focused on the availability of food and other everyday expenses but excluded the universally provided free goods such as childcare, housing, healthcare, and education.

Material security was also assessed relative to the wages that the government fixed. Across the entire country, the government set the minimum wage to exceed the minimum subsistence levels by a factor of 1.5 so that a working adult could support a dependent. Low material security meant that income per family member fell below the subsistence minimum. In the late Soviet, it was estimated that 25–30 percent of families had low material security (Rima-shevskaya 2003, p. 122).

While today some scholars argue that low material security under the Soviet system was a form of poverty, it is clear that its nature and scope differed significantly from poverty under capitalism. Importantly, it was not seen as a function of not being able to earn adequate wages but that of having to support non-working dependents (e.g., families with many young children) or not being able to work because of disability or some other condition. Families with low material security still had the same access to childcare, housing, healthcare, and education as everyone else.

From Soviet to Neoliberal Capitalist Welfare

After 1991, private property became legal for the first time in over seventy years which led to the rapid wholesale privatization of national assets and the closure of many long-standing enterprises. Unemployment, now also legal, was rapidly rising, and for those who remained employed, the liberalization of prices diminished wages manifold. Furthermore, any remaining social guarantees, such as free health-care, soon lost their meaning as a wide range of state services quickly disintegrated. Finally, high prices for newly commodified versions of what had been state provided services put them out of reach for the majority of the population.

The devastating effects of these changes on the Russian population quickly became evident in many domains including a demographic crisis unprecedented in peace time (Heleniak 1995; Eberstadt 2010). From the 1990s onward the population of Russia has declined in absolute terms because high mortality rates exceed drastically diminished birth rates while, at the same time, life expectancy fell to its lowest level (for men it dropped in the mid-1990s to 56 years). In other words, "building capitalism" cost Russia millions of premature deaths that critical scholars in other contexts have attributed to the "death-dealing" nature of capitalism that exposes people to economic, social, and physical violence (Gilmore 2007). The violence of poverty inflicted on the Soviet people by "disaster capitalism" (Klein 2008) included job loss, stress, crime and gun violence, deteriorated health, collapse of the public healthcare system and other safety nets, and increased self-destructive behavior and suicide rates.

Many of these problems have been ongoing since the mid-1990s and their persistence over twenty-five years clearly suggests that they are inherent to neoliberal capitalism rather than to social transformation per se.

Ontologies of Capitalist Poverty

The immediate, dramatic, and devastating effects of "shock therapy" and price liberalization on the economic well-being of the Russian population are visible in the new metrics of social differentiation, provided we compare them to the pre-1991 society. In this case, in one year Russian society changed from one of the most equal to one of the most unequal in the world.

Wealth and Income Polarization

Privatization of national assets has led to the exceptional concentration of wealth that considerably exceeds US levels. In the US the infamous 1 percent hold 40 percent of personal assets but in Russia they may hold 71 percent of personal assets and its top 5 percent own 81 percent of all wealth (Zotin and Kvasha 2014). Because most people make a living by earning their income, measures of income inequality are even more important. The popular Gini coefficient, one of the new post-Soviet metrics, shows that income inequality (Figure 5.1) has grown from one

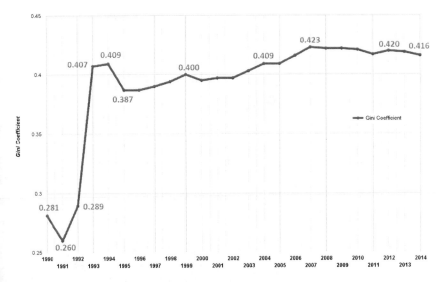

FIGURE 5.1 Income inequality in Russia, 1990–2015
Source: Author based on Rosstat data.

of the world's lowest (0.260 in 1991, comparable to Scandinavian countries) to the world's highest levels (already 0.407 by 1993 and 0.423 in 2007). Income inequality is worse than in the USA (Gini coefficient around 0.411) and remains high whether the economy is doing poorly (such as in the 1990s) or well (such as during high oil prices in the 2000s). In other words, deep inequality has become a permanent feature of Russian society.

Other measures support the story told by the Gini coefficient. For example, the income discrepancy between the top and bottom deciles (10 percent population groups) was only fourfold in the last year of the Soviet period but jumped to fifteen times as early as 1994 and reached seventeen times by 2015. For comparison, decile ratios of ten or more are considered by many experts to be large enough to generate social unrest (Garanenko 2007). Even in the USA, which tolerates high levels of inequality (routine decile rations of ten–twelve), inequality has become a major political concern as manifest in, among other things, the Occupy Wall Street movement. In Russia, despite glaring economic inequality, popular protests target corruption and election fraud rather than inequality.

In short, Russian capitalism led to a rapid, dramatic, and entrenched concentration of wealth and earning power in the hands of a few while the majority of the population has not fared well and many live in poverty.

Rise of Poverty

The Russian liberal reformers of the 1990s, together with their IMF consultants (who included then Harvard economist Jeffry Sachs), convinced politicians and the public that a program of shock therapy would be painful but short lived. Once the wealth-generating capacities of capitalism were activated, all who were willing to work hard would be able to make a living (Sachs 1995). Russian statistics, however, show that the poverty created by capitalism quickly became widespread and, in contrast to what the neoliberal theorists claimed, poverty – like economic inequality – has become a structural condition of Russian society.

According to the Russian Statistics Agency (Rosstat), by 1992 over one-third of the population or almost 50 million people were living in poverty (Figure 5.2). While the poverty rate fluctuated in subsequent years, it never became negligible and today it remains at roughly 15 percent. In other words, a condition of widespread and long-term economic marginalization was established in a country that had no prior experience with structural poverty.

Paradoxically, if we forget about the Soviet period when such poverty was absent, the current poverty rate makes Russia look quite good. For example, the policy makers can claim that poverty declined more than three times from 33.5 percent in 1992 to 11 percent in 2013 (Ovcharova et al. 2014) and, therefore, the new capitalist system, given time, does lift people out of poverty. A similarly rosy picture emerges when comparing Russia to other countries. Because they all have poverty, capitalist Russia does not deviate from the standard social condition. Moreover, Russian scholars cite the World Bank definition of absolute poverty as subsisting on or less than $1.25–$2/day to conclude that the "poverty level in Russia already in the middle of the 2000s was less than 0.0 percent" (Ovcharova et al. 2014, p. 4). The statistics conceal the fact that it is ludicrous for a nation with an advanced space program to compare itself to

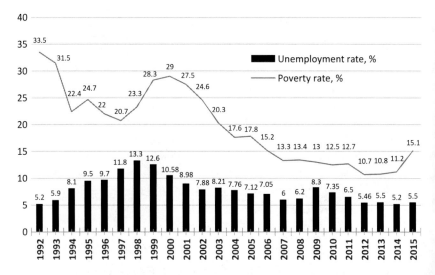

FIGURE 5.2 Poverty rate and unemployment rate in Russia, 1992–2015
Source: Author based on Rosstat data.

the poorest nations of the world. Finally, a poverty level of 15 percent makes Russia, which still considers the USA its primary rival, look good relative to the USA where the rate is similar. In sum, poverty in Russia is no longer seen as an exception, it is commonplace and it is within the statistical norm as demonstrated by comparison with Russia's peers and by a host of international organizations.

Politics of Metrics of Poverty

When Russia began measuring poverty in 1992 using the ILO methodology, researchers reviewed a variety of Western practices and settled on the "absolute" definition of poverty, a measure which roughly paralleled Soviet measures of low material security. In this case, people are poor if they do not earn enough to afford the scientifically determined basic level of consumption: the consumer basket, the monetary cost of which is called the minimum subsistence level (MSL). The rate of poverty is measured as a percentage of the population with a *per capita* income below the MSL. This key metric is used for assessing the state of the economy, socio-economic well-being, and social policy needs.

On the surface, these measures make perfect sense and make Russian data internationally comparable. Yet, national surveys report that two-fifths of the population self-identify as poor – a much larger share than the official poverty rate of 15 percent. While survey measures are subjective, the differences between them and the official statistics suggest that the latter may underestimate the level of on-going economic marginalization. Moreover, the discrepancy is not just a technical error. Because the consistent use of statistical categories actively shapes the social body (Hannah 2001; St. Martin 2009; Pavlovskaya and Bier 2012), Russian metrics of poverty are not innocent. They, in fact, obscure the true scale at which neoliberal capitalism produces and reproduces poverty.

While determining poverty rate appears straightforward, (e.g., percentage of population with income below minimum subsistence level) it actually hinges on three separate metrics which together inform social policy: the minimum subsistence level (MSL), income per capita, and minimum wage. These metrics each have the capacity to shift the poverty line, affect the overall size of the poor population, and determine individual eligibility for social assistance.

To make social policy meaningful, the MSL should properly reflect the cost of basic necessities so that a reasonable poverty line can be set. The minimum wage should exceed the MSL so that working adults can earn enough to provide for basic necessities. Households with per capita income below the subsistence minimum (i.e., poverty line) would then be considered poor. The actual relationship between these indicators, however, tends to obscure more than they clarify relative to the question of poverty.

The Secrets of the Minimum Subsistence Level (MSL)

The consumer basket and the corresponding MSL (Figure 5.3) are defined by the federal government for three population groups (children, adults, and the elderly) every three months. The consumer basket includes both food and non-food items which are revised every five years to better reflect available products and current prices. The consumer basket has regional equivalents because what is essential varies from region to region as do prices.

The state can and often does directly alter the size of the impoverished population by lowering or increasing the MSL threshold. The concern is that these fluctuations affect eligibility for social assistance because they may throw into or lift out of poverty millions of people at once. For example, in 2015 the increase in MSL by 26 percent[3] made the population below the poverty line larger by 3 million while in 2016 the government inexplicably lowered the MSL despite the fact that the cost of living and inflation were going up.

More importantly, however, the MSL has diverged from the cost of basic needs since the very start of the capitalist period. At the end of the Soviet period, it was set at 135 rubles and if the same value had been applied after the shock therapy of 1992, 70–80 percent of population would be in poverty due to plummeting income levels. Because capitalist social welfare policy is only meant to help relatively small groups of people who are in need of temporary assistance, poverty at the scale of the entire society could not be addressed (Rimashevskaya 2003, p.123). Hoping that capitalism would soon start creating well-paying jobs and solve this large scale problem, Yeltsin's government decided to revise the MSL down to 60 rubles (less than half of the previous amount) in order to redefine poverty as the experience of only the very poorest and to bring the national rate down to a more acceptable 33.5 percent (Rimashevskaya 2003, p. 124). This still large but artificially lowered figure is now used as the starting point for analyzing relative change in poverty over time. It obscures the overwhelming scale of economic marginalization in those first years of the transition but it serves very well to demonstrate the subsequent reduction of poverty.

Beyond alterations of the MSL, changes in its composition have also affected the poverty rate.

For example, more than once, the government modified the ratio between the cost of food and other items in the consumer basket (Rimashevskaya 2003, p. 124; Ovcharova et al. 2014, pp. 6–8). The 2000 revision still excluded from consideration costs for healthcare, education, and social services because it was assumed that, as under the Soviet welfare system, these services were available at the minimum level free of charge (Ovcharova et al. 2014, p.8). By that time and further on, however, expenses for healthcare, education, utilities, and transportation had all become a major cost.

Since 2013, only norms for basic food consumption (in kilos) are specified while the cost of other goods and services in the consumer basket is simply set to

50 percent of the cost of food (Federal law 2012) despite rapidly rising prices for non-food items. Because the MSL value sets the poverty line, a proper assessment of the basic subsistence needs provides a foundation for a sound social policy. The way the MSL is currently determined underestimates, by a factor of 2.5 or even 3, the costs of basic necessities, which considerably reduces the size of the population in poverty.

Elusive Per Capita Income

Determining the national or regional poverty rate involves calculating the share of population that earns income below the MSL. The distribution of income throughout the population is done based upon macro-economic tools. The statistical models calculate income per capita for the entire population (including income earners, their dependents, etc.) and determine how many people fall into the group with per capita income below the poverty line. The national per capita income consistently climbs above the MSL which creates a sense of growing affluence (Figure 5.3) and declining poverty (Figure 5.2). If we recall, however,

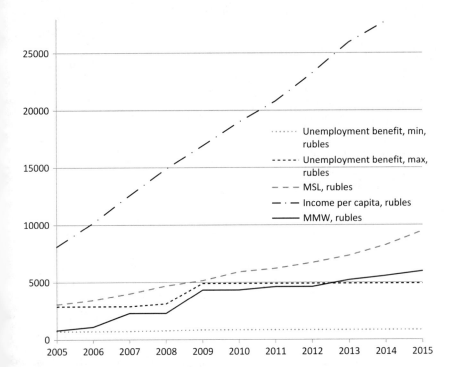

FIGURE 5.3 Income per capita, MSL (minimum subsistence level), MMW (minimum monthly wage), and unemployment benefit limits, 2005–2014
Source: Author based on Rosstat data.

that the MSL should be three times higher, the poverty level and per capita income would be very close to each other, showing a much larger poverty rate.

In addition, per capita income is statistically corrected to adjust for undeclared income which increases the earnings by 20–30 percent. The income per capita is corrected uniformly for all income groups although higher earning groups have larger undeclared income. Per capita income on the bottom, therefore, is over-estimated with the effect of again reducing the population below the poverty threshold (Ovcharova et al. 2014).

Moreover, income per capita is calculated as an average value which obscures the fact that income distribution is skewed with many low income earners at the bottom and a small group of high income earners at the top. Scholars contend that a median income (which is considerably lower than the average) better reflects this distribution and would be more useful for determining the size of population in poverty. In short, the macro-economic procedures that measure per capita income also contribute to considerably underestimating the population in poverty and the demand for social assistance.

The Non-Compliant Minimum Monthly Wage

The last metric vital to the calculation of poverty measures is the minimum monthly wage (MMW). MMW has the status of law and serves to regulate wages and calculate unemployment payments as well as taxes, fines, and other fees. By Russian law, MMW should exceed the minimum subsistence level. During the Soviet period, the minimum wage was indeed set at 1.5 of the MSL to assure that a working adult could support a dependent in addition to herself (Rimashevskaya 2003, p. 122). Soon after 1992, however, MMW lost its ability to keep up with growing living costs and quickly fell below the post-Soviet MSL (which itself was already more than halved by reformers in the attempt to reduce the poverty rate). Initially, the reformers thought that this inversion would be temporary but it kept growing such that by 1999, for example, the minimum monthly wage comprised just 11 percent of the MSL despite the fact that legally it had to exceed it (Rimashevskaya 2003, p. 125).

The current MMW still remains considerably lower than the MSL (Figure 5.3). The government declared that the two indicators should finally converge by the end of 2017 but this remains to be seen because the powerful industrial lobby opposes such attempts.

The point is that the government policy with regard to minimum wage, in violation of the law has kept it below the subsistence minimum for the last twenty-five years. This reversal of these legally set thresholds leads to systemically suppressed wages and is particularly harmful for those with low income. This situation clearly supports neoliberal economic policies that enable high levels of exploitation of the working classes and entrenches them in poverty. At the same time, the Russian government continues to regularly set its minimum monthly wage and publish related statistics as if there is nothing wrong here. This very act ironically signals that the government does not ignore labor regulation and complies with the international expectations and requirements.

To sum up, the key metrics of poverty used in Russia – MSL, per capita income, and MMW – relate to each other in such a way that they obscure the true dimensions of economic marginalization. While their ability to effectively inform social policy is limited at best, their continued use by the government, as if they had meaning, makes the level of poverty in Russia appear both "normal" and manageable.

Working People as the Poor

Finally, that poverty is chronic and structural rather than a temporary outcome of the transition is supported by the prevalence of the working poor in Russia. As others have noted (Hoynes et al. 2005), contrary to widely spread claims, employment in the capitalist labor market does not necessarily provide a way out of poverty. Since the introduction of capitalism in Russia, a large segment of working people have lived in poverty. For example, those Soviet state employees who were not immediately laid off continued to work for many years for drastically devalued wages. This was especially true for many professional workers who were amongst the first of a new class of working poor. Today, employees who work within Putin's government or in certain private companies do earn relatively good wages, but other working people, including professionals, continue to earn meager wages that trap them in poverty. Thus, the working poor, who today are often young and educated, have become a permanent fixture of the Russian neo-liberal economy. Moreover, their share among the poor has been growing and since 2013, for example, they make up an outstanding 63 percent of the poor population (Ovcharova et al. 2014, p. 20).

While some suggest that working people locked in poverty are specific to Russian capitalism (Rimashevskaya 2003; Ovcharova et al. 2014), the growing working poor population is becoming a worldwide trend. It is also present in the USA. As a result of an ongoing shift to neoliberal post-industrial work regimes, people work long hours at several jobs but cannot lift themselves out of poverty because of low wages (Peck 1996; Beck 2000). In Russia, this situation developed in the very first years of capitalism and, as suggested above, might foretell the contours of a neoliberal future in which most jobs have no protections and wages below the subsistence minimum are normalized.

Why Help the Unemployed?

That material comfort in Russia is not well related to jobs is suggested by Figure 5.2, in which poverty and the unemployment rates 1992 through 2015 are counterpoised. If employment provided sufficient wages and job loss caused poverty, then poverty and unemployment rates would vary somewhat together: low unemployment would coincide with low poverty and vice versa. The graph suggests, however, that in Russia poverty and unemployment rates have been generally out of sync and, indeed, have been most of the time opposite each other.

Liberal social assistance, however, presumes that job loss causes poverty and employment lifts people out of it. It also presumes that capitalism generates economic opportunities for the poor in the form of jobs that the poor are expected to pursue. Welfare programs in the USA provide short-term unemployment benefits and job placement services, such programs also require the unemployed to look for jobs and, occasionally, get retrained. Moreover, unemployment benefits must be less attractive than the most marginal employment in order to encourage people to cycle back into the workforce as soon as possible.

To deal with the unemployment that appeared in Russia after 1991, the Russian government adopted rules that are even more neoliberal in spirit than those in the USA. In Russia support is provided for up to 24 months and during the first year unemployment benefits initially constitute 75 percent of the last salary and slide to 45 percent after a few months. These payments cannot, however, go beyond the minimum and maximum limits set by the government. During the second year, the benefit is set to the minimum level only. The set limits on the benefits, however, ensure that they cannot support household needs. For example, in the mid-2000s the maximum limit was still close to the minimum subsistence level but since then the MSL continued to increase while the benefit limits have practically stayed the same (Figure 5.3). Currently, the minimum level is set to only one-tenth of the MSL (about $14 per month at the current exchange rate) while the maximum is about half of the MSL (about $82 per month). If we recall that the MSL underestimates the costs of living by a factor of 3, the monetary value of the unemployment benefits virtually disappears.

It is hard to imagine how one would survive their unemployment without relying on other sources of support from, for example, family, friends, and other networks (Pavlovskaya 2015).

Moral Standing, Self-Discipline, and Desire to Work

In addition to negligible benefits, there are also strict requirements that the registered unemployed must meet. They must show up for events and trainings, re-register every ten days, and accept the second job offered in order to not be bumped out of the system. A job is considered acceptable if the pay on offer is above the subsistence minimum (or its fractions for part-time employment) which, as we have seen, will not lift the unemployed out of poverty. To reduce government payments, legislators aim to shorten the period of coverage, reduce the size of payments, and limit eligibility to particular populations (e.g., exclude those who never worked). Furthermore, legislators attempt to insure that recipients are only those demonstrating a high moral character and will to work by, for example, requiring the registered unemployed to participate in uncompensated public works projects near their place of residence (e.g., cleaning streets, planting trees, etc.) (Mintrud 2016).

It is, perhaps, not surprising that only one-quarter of the estimated 4 million people who are currently unemployed have registered with an employment agency. This is similar to the current situation in the USA where those registered to receive unemployment benefits fluctuate between 25 percent and 40 percent of the unemployed, reaching an all-time low of 23 percent in 2014 (Delaney and Scheller 2015). While the need for support certainly remains high amongst the unemployed, they are deterred from seeking assistance as neoliberal policies increase targeting, means-testing, and other disciplinary measures (Soss et al. 2011; Schram 2015). Instead of providing compassionate government support to the poor and the unemployed, neoliberal social policies in Russia, as in the USA, increasingly marginalize them.

Invisible Economies of Cooperation

Nationalism and geopolitical confrontation are needed to divert attention from low wages and poverty, especially when the government does not have a policy response to the negative consequences of neoliberal capitalism, a system it not only imposed but also continues to support. The government's lack of response was symbolically captured in a recent remark made by the prime minister. Medvedev, during a recent visit to the Crimea, responded to a group of retired women requesting an increase in their meager pensions by saying: "There is no money for your pensions now. But you will somehow hang on. Best wishes for high spirits and health to everyone!" Then he walked away (Gazeta.ru, 2016). What do people do when the government abandons them even during times of extreme hardship, as in the case of elderly women trying to survive in the recently annexed Crimea? Or when, as we have seen, the government not only ignores but also actively obscures, via state metrological practices, the long-term marginalization of what is likely a considerable majority of the Russian population?

Some studies suggest that with no formal jobs paying a living wage and no meaningful social assistance, 14–25 million people have turned to the informal economy, where formal capitalist and state institutions do not have the same control over economic practices and where people can organize social reproduction on their own terms (Pavlovskaya 2015). The diverse economies (Gibson-Graham 2006) they create often work to support livelihoods instead of profits in the direst of the times. While much informal economic activity is undesirable and likely to involve exploitation, also emerging are non-capitalist economic practices that require cooperation, sharing, and mutual support; people build alliances to survive and even manage to provide modest but comfortable consumption levels for their families (Pavlovskaya 2015). This is not to say that the informal economy as a whole should be celebrated, but in the face of persistent large-scale poverty in Russia and lack of a viable social policy, people are finding creative ways to secure social reproduction and live well by participating in distinctly non-capitalist practices.

Conclusions

The post-Soviet transformation produced a dramatically polarized society with a large population of the poor. Since 1992, the poor have constituted between 33 percent and 10 percent of the Russian population, or anywhere between 43 and 15 million (Figure 5.1). Russia, along with capitalism itself, developed from scratch a set of metrics and policies designed to address and manage this new segment of the population. As a result, poverty in Russia is understood to be an unfortunate but "normal" condition as in other developed capitalist countries. Official statistics, academic policy reports and articles, as well as mass media have played an important role in normalizing poverty as well as obscuring its extent and its detrimental effects.

In this chapter, I have focused on those key metrics, suggested by other countries and international organizations, that are used by the government to simultaneously assess and, as I have shown, systematically obscure the depth and persistence of poverty in Russia. A close examination of the most important measures of poverty (e.g. minimum subsistence level or MSL, per capita income, and minimum monthly wage or MMW) reveals their collective role in establishing the foundations for government proclamations concerning the level of poverty and for government intervention in poverty alleviation. In particular, we have seen how the MSL grossly underestimates the cost of subsistence, how per capita income overestimates the wages earned by the lowest income groups, and how the minimum monthly wage has lingered below the subsistence minimum for a quarter of a century. Nevertheless, these metrics are routinely used by policy makers, politicians, and bureaucrats to provide evidence that the poverty rate is decreasing and that its level is within what is considered "normal" in the West. At the same time, and since the advent of capitalism in Russia, the population of the Russian poor has expanded to include not only the unemployed, the retired, those with many dependents, and the handicapped, but also working age, able bodied, and even many employed adults.

The Russian experience deserves more attention than it now receives from critical scholars because it powerfully puts into relief, as in a laboratory setting, the work needed to produce and maintain neoliberal capitalism. The case of Russia disrupts the illusion of capitalism's promise of prosperity for working people and it exposes the everyday violence of neoliberalism produced by low wages, precarious jobs, absent social mobility, and meager social assistance. Most Russians do not dream of capitalist riches, they want secure livelihoods and meaningful lives which they increasingly find only within non-capitalist spaces where diverse economies of cooperation are emerging.

Finally, the Russian experience has profound implications for understanding how neoliberalism works or might work in other national and international contexts. It powerfully demonstrates what happens to a society that implements capitalism via a strong state whose aim is to protect and enhance capital accumulation. Russia has the unique advantage of still remembering the elaborate social welfare of the Soviet period although this memory is being quickly erased. This recent history makes it clear that socialized welfare is practically possible and necessary. People in Russia and elsewhere must continually challenge the neoliberal state to provide the basic standards of well-being that they should see as their right and not a market commodity.

The case of Russian neoliberal capitalism also makes clear that economies are decidedly more contingent and constructed than commonly thought; while this case demonstrates how a particular economic form can be adopted out of whole cloth and imposed from the top down, it also reveals how maintaining any economy requires a host of cooperating metrics and related technologies of assessment. If policy effort can change a society from socialism to capitalism, it can also change its social assistance systems in many other big and small ways, including establishing sound welfare support. Meanwhile, the vast population of the un- and under-employed, those who cannot survive on their state benefits or formal wages, necessarily engage in economic activity that is, like themselves, unacknowledged. In this sense, what the government misses and what we are called to reveal is another economy out of which we might produce new post-capitalist imaginaries that foreground collective ways to care.

Notes

1 Acknowledgements: Support for this work was partially provided by PSC-CUNY grants 65805 and 78704. Funding for the two-year-long faculty seminar on neoliberalism that inspired this book and this chapter was provided by the Dean of Arts and Sciences at Hunter College. I am thankful for the opportunity to get to know and work together with Sandy Schram who was the major energetic force behind the seminar and the book and whose work enriched my thinking about poverty in Russia. I am grateful, as always, to Kevin St. Martin for his continued support and feedback on the draft of the paper.
2 Examples of *l'goty* included, for example, special food items for holidays, extra living space, trips to health resorts, school meals, free public transportation, discounts on utilities and medications, and so on.
3 MSL went up from 7688 rubles in the first quarter of 2014 to 9662 rubles in the first quarter of 2015, or by 26 percent.

Bibliography

Aslund, A. (2001). *Building Capitalism: The Transformation of the Former Soviet Bloc*. Cambridge: Cambridge University Press.
Beck, U. (2000). *The Brave New World of Work*. Cambridge: Polity.
Burawoy, M. (1997). Review Essay: The Soviet Descent into Capitalism. *American Journal of Sociology*, 102(5), 1430.
Collier, S. J. (2011). *Post-Soviet Social: Neoliberalism, Social Modernity, Biopolitics*. Princeton, NJ: Princeton University Press.

Collier, S. J., and Way, L. (2004). Beyond the Deficit Model: Social Welfare in Post-Soviet Georgia. *Post-Soviet Affairs*, 20(3), 258–284.

Delaney, A., and Scheller, A. (2015). A Lot Fewer Americans Get Unemployment Benefits Than You Think. *Huffington Post*, March 13. Retrieved from: www.huffingtonpost. com/2015/03/13/unemployment-benefits-rate_n_6832552.html

Eberstadt, N. (2010). Russia's Peacetime Demographic Crisis: Dimensions, Causes, Implications. Retrieved February 2, 2017, from: www.nbr.org/publications/element.aspx? id=446

Federal law (2012). Federal law, December 3, 2012, N 227-FZ "On national consumer basket for Russian Federation." Approved by State Duma on November 20, 2012. Approved by Federation Council on November 28, 2012. In Russian: Федеральный закён ёт 3 декабря 2012 г. N 227-ФЗ "О пётребительскёй кёрзине в целём пё Рёссийскёй Федерации" Принят Гёсударственнёй Думёй 20 нёября 2012 гёда Одёбрен Сёветём Федерации 28 нёября 2012 гёда

Fukuyama, F. (1989). The End of History? *The National Interest*, Summer, 3–18.

Friedman, M. (1951). Neo-Liberalism and its Prospects. *Farmland*, February 17, 89–93.

Gazeta.ru (2016). Медведев на вёпрёс ё пенсиях в Крыму: денег нет, нё вы держитесь. Retrieved February 3, 2017, from: www.gazeta.ru/business/news/2016/ 05/24/n_8672513.shtml

Gibson-Graham, J. K. (1996). *The End Of Capitalism (As We Knew It): A Feminist Critique of Political Economy*. New York: Guilford Press.

Gibson-Graham, J. K. (2006). *A Postcapitalist Politics*. Minneapolis: University of Minnesota Press.

Gibson-Graham, J. K., Cameron, J., and Healy, S. (2013). *Take Back the Economy: An Ethical Guide for Transforming Our Communities*. Minneapolis: University of Minnesota Press.

Gilmore, R. W. (2007). *Golden Gulag: Prisons, Surplus, Crisis, and Opposition in Globalizing California*. Berkeley: University of California Press.

Garanenko, A. (2007). Terribly Rich. Izvestia, August 9. In Russian: Гараненкё, А. Страшнё бёгатые. Известия, 9 августа. Retrieved April 3, 2017, from: http://izves tia.ru/news/327476

Hannah, M. G. (2001). Sampling and the Politics of Representation in US Census 2000. *Environment and Planning D: Society and Space*, 19(5), 515–534. doi:10.1068/d289

Harvey, D. (2007). *A Brief History of Neoliberalism*. Oxford: Oxford University Press.

Heleniak, T. (1995). Economic Transition and Demographic Change in Russia, 1989–1995. *Post-Soviet Geography*, 36(7), 446–458. doi:10.1080/10605851.1995.10641002

Hoynes, H., Page, M., and Stevens, A. (2005). *Poverty in America: Trends and Explanations* (Working Paper No. 11681). National Bureau of Economic Research. doi:10.3386/ w11681

Klein, N. (2008). *The Shock Doctrine: The Rise of Disaster Capitalism*. New York: Picador.

Mintrud (2016). Минтруд выступил за ётмену пёсёбий для хрёнических безрабётных, May 13. Retrieved January 31, 2017, from: https://informatio.ru/news/society/mintrud_ vystupil_za_otmenu_posobiy_dlya/

Offe, C. (1994). Capitalism by Democratic Design? Democratic Theory Facing the Triple Transition in Central and Eastern Europe. In H.-J. Wagener (Ed.), *The Political Economy of Transformation* (pp. 25–43). Heidelberg: Physica-Verlag HD. doi:10.1007/978-3-642-52404-2_2

Ovcharova, L. N., Biryukova, S. S., Popova, D. O., and Vardanyan, E. G. (2014). *Level and Profile of Poverty in Russia: From the 1990s until Today*. Moscow: VShE. In Russian:

Овчарёва, Л.Н., Бирюкёва, С.С., Пёпёва, Д.О., Варданян, Е.Г. *Урёвень и прёфиль беднёсти в Рёссии: ёт 1990х дё наших дней.* Мёсква: ВШЭ, 2014.

Pavlovskaya, M. (2004). Other Transitions: Multiple Economies of Moscow Households in the 1990s. *Annals of the Association of American Geographers*, 94(2), 329–351.

Pavlovskaya, M. (2013). Between Neoliberalism and Difference: Multiple Practices of Property in Post-Soviet Russia. *Europe-Asia Studies*, 65(7), 1295–1323. doi:10.1080/09668136.2013.822708.

Pavlovskaya, M. (2015). Post-Soviet Welfare and Multiple Economies of Households in Moscow. In Gerda Roelvink, Kevin St Martin, and J. K. Gibson-Graham (Eds.), *Making Other Worlds Possible: Performing Diverse Economies* (pp. 269–295). Minneapolis: University of Minnesota Press.

Pavlovskaya, M., and Bier, J. (2012). Mapping Census Data for Difference: Towards the Heterogeneous Geographies of Arab American Communities of the New York Metropolitan Area. *Geoforum*, 43(3), 483–496. doi:10.1016/j.geoforum.2011.10.007

Peck, J. (1996). *Work-Place: The Social Regulation of Labor Markets.* New York: The Guilford Press.

Piketty, T. (2014). *Capital in the Twenty-First Century*, trans. Arthur Goldhammer. Cambridge, MA: Harvard University Press.

Rimashevskaya, N. (2003). *People and Reforms: The Secrets of Survival.* Moscow: ISEPN RAN (Russian Academy of Sciences). In Russian: Римашевская, Н.М. *Челёвек и рефёрмы: Секреты выживания.* Мёсква: ИСЭПН РАН, 2003.

Roelvink, G., Martin, K. S., and Gibson-Graham, J. K. (Eds.) (2015). *Making Other Worlds Possible: Performing Diverse Economies.* Minneapolis: University of Minnesota Press.

Roy, A., and Crane, E. S. (Eds.) (2015). *Territories of Poverty: Rethinking North and South.* Athens: University of Georgia Press.

Sachs, J. D. (1995). *Rynochnaya ekonomika i Rossia (Market economy and Russia)*, trans. from English. Moscow: Ekonomika.

Schram, S. F. (2015). *The Return of Ordinary Capitalism: Neoliberalism, Precarity, Occupy.* Oxford: Oxford University Press.

Soss, J., Fording, R. C., and Schram, S. F. (2011). *Disciplining the Poor: Neoliberal Paternalism and the Persistent Power of Race.* Chicago: University of Chicago Press.

St. Martin, K. (2009). Toward a Cartography of the Commons: Constituting the Political and Economic Possibilities of Place. *Professional Geographer*, 61(4), 493–507. doi:10.1080/00330120903143482

Zaslavsky, V. (1982). *The Neo-Stalinist State: Class Ethnicity & Consensus in Soviet Society.* Florence: Routledge.

Zotin, A. and Kvasha, M. (2014). All Sides of Inequality. *Kommersant-Den/gi*, 24(15). In Russian: Зётин, А. and Кваша, М. (2014, June 23). Все грани неравенства. *Кёммерсантъ Деньги*, 24(15). Retrieved April 3, 2017, from: www.kommersant.ru/doc/2485570

6

NEOLIBERALISM VIEWED FROM THE BOTTOM UP

A Qualitative Longitudinal Study of Benefit Claimants' Experiences of the Unemployment System

Sophie Danneris

Throughout the western world during the last few decades, substantial transformations have changed the nature of human services in general and of social policy in particular. Neoliberal organizational reforms such as privatization, performance management, and the economic streamlining of services have supported a marketization of social service organizations; as a result, their most important task today is to make dependent clients independent as quickly as possible. In this task, standardization and disciplinary tools such as sanctions, financial penalties, and controlling work processes have been the favorite management tools (Braedley and Luxton 2010; Brown 2003; Schram and Silverman 2012; Schram 2015). Embedded in this neoliberal orientation has been a personalization of the social problems of the clients. This means that matters such as poor health and unemployment, which had once been considered the shared responsibility of the state and the citizen, are now first and foremost treated as personal problems of the individual to be solved through rational individual choices (Schram 2015; Caswell, Eskelinen, and Olesen 2011). Thus, the task of the state is to encourage individuals to see themselves as personally responsible for managing their lives and, using the most efficient tools, to discipline clients by making this a moral responsibility. As Brown puts it, "The state attempts to construct prudent subjects through policies that organize such prudence" (Brown 2003, p. 43). Extending economic rationality to domains formerly dominated by non-economic values enrolls clients in a neoliberal order that normatively constructs them as rational, autonomous, and calculating creatures with the ability to provide for their own needs (Brown 2003). This leaves individuals with full responsibility for their situation, regardless of the circumstances that led to their applying for help – for example a sick child, a severe accident, or unemployment. However, due to their problems, vulnerable welfare claimants are rarely able to live up to this individual responsibility. This means that they fail as economic actors and moral civic beings in the neoliberalized society and that they themselves must seek to change this through individual efforts (Danneris and Nielsen forthcoming; Soss, Fording, and Schram 2011). But how are they supposed to do this?

This chapter attempts to answer this question by gaining insight into how neoliberalism works in local situations and thereby trying to trace the consequences of neoliberalism as we shape policies in our day-to-day practices and lived lives (Braedley and Luxton 2010, p. 20). Based on the understanding that neoliberal policies and practices are not uniform and that their effects depend on the context, the aim is to look at empirical accounts of neoliberalism as a policy regime and explore the nuances in how neoliberalism affects the citizens who are subject to it (Lipsky 2010; Brodkin 2013; Koivisto 2007). This means that the purpose of this chapter is not to trace and discuss the historical and political nature of neoliberal development. On the contrary, this study of unemployed and vulnerable benefit claimants is first and foremost an empirical analysis that examines the neoliberal welfare state from the standpoint of those who are the targets of state intervention (Naples 1998; Patrick 2014). Thus, looking at policy through the eyes of the people that it directly affects, this chapter applies an "everyday world" perspective to the analysis of how neoliberal policies in general and active labor market reforms in particular are implemented. In adopting this perspective, the study reveals a multitude of hidden dimensions of the way in which neoliberalism manifests itself in the daily life of the unemployed (Braedley and Luxton 2010; Danneris 2016).

As has been documented by much research in the field, both theoretical and empirical, the western world's neoliberal misery appears fairly stark and hopeless. However, an examination of how benefit claimants engage with the welfare state in their daily practices reveals nuances, cracks, and non-simultaneities, which challenge a narrow interpretation of the consequences of neoliberalism. These cracks and conflicting real world tendencies indicate opportunities where light shines through and potential pathways become evident.

The Danish Case

In Denmark as in the majority of western countries, neoliberalism has affected the welfare model. The social policy profile of Denmark has undergone a substantial transformation; although it is still defined as a universal welfare state (Larsen 2015), it is now widely recognized that the character of the Danish welfare system is drastically changing. In the domain of employment, which is the subject of this chapter, active labor market policies are developing from a human capital-dominated policy approach towards a work-first policy approach (Goul Andersen 2013; Juul 2010a; Lødemel and Moreira 2014) that seeks the shortest possible route to employment for benefit claimants (Høilund 2006; Juul 2010b; Triantafillou 2012). This development finds expression more or less clearly in several recent labor market reforms and in ways of organizing the work related to moving the unemployed from benefits into a permanent position in the labor market. For example, the formal categories of work capability among unemployed cash benefit claimants have been transformed step by step by political reforms in recent decades. A brief glance at the four most recent reforms of work capability categories will elucidate this.

From 2000 to 2014, there was a drastic change in the categorization of the vulnerable unemployed and, accordingly, in the way this group of clients is portrayed in policies. In 2000, official guidelines from the Danish Directorate General for Employment Placement (Arbejdsmarkedsstyrelsen 2000) clearly explained that front line workers were to place cash benefit claimants in one of five groups, ranging from clients with unemployment as their only problem to clients where unemployment is the least of their problems. In 2004, in the slipstream of a landmark labor market reform ("More people to work"), match-categories were introduced in Danish social policy as a new system of classification. Unlike the former categories, which had focused on the problems of the claimant, match-categories measured the instantaneous distance between the benefit claimant on the one hand and the labor market on the other (Socialministeriet 2001). The basic idea was to view the unemployed with an optimistic neoliberal understanding of the individual's resources, assuming that "everyone is capable" (Bang 2002).

Thus, the point was to look at the resources and possibilities of the benefit claimants rather than their problems and challenges, and to perceive all unemployed individuals as subjects with the ability/capacity to move towards the labor market (Bang 2002), while recognizing their individual pace and the fact that some were closer to the goal than others (Arbejdsmarkedsstyrelsen 2004). With the five match-categories, employment potential was brought to the forefront of job-readiness evaluation, and the claimant was placed in one of five categories ranging from Match 1 (immediate labor market match) to Match 5 (no labor market match).

In 2010, the system of classification was reformed once again, and the number of match categories was reduced from five to three. In this reformed system, the category containing the claimants with the poorest possibilities was renamed so that "no labor market match" became "temporarily passive." Again, the argument for this change was to be found in a fundamentally positive neoliberal view of human beings, stating that no one is without resources and that everyone has labor market potential and the responsibility to exploit this potential (Arbejdsmarkedsstyrelsen 2010a, 2010b).

In 2014, as an important part of the most recent major reform of the Danish cash benefit system, the categories were redefined once more. The concept of match categories was abandoned to pave the way for a new form of classification named "Categories of readiness" (Aftaletekst 2013; Beskæftigelsesministeriet 2013). Since then, all cash benefit claimants have been perceived as *ready*, and categorization has become a process of assessing the sort of activity for which the claimant is ready. Once again, the number of categories was reduced, so only two major groups of cash benefit claimants now exist: "job ready" and "activity ready."

These remarkable changes over the past fifteen years in the categorization of the most vulnerable Danish benefit claimants clearly reflect the neoliberalization of the welfare system; they moved from being initially defined as "suffering from heavy social and/or physical problems" to having "no match with the labor market" to "temporarily passive," and finally to their current definition as "ready for activity," where they are described as those who, "with some help and possibly through a long process/program can be ready for the labor market" (Danneris and Nielsen forthcoming).[1] However, given these substantial and continuous changes, it is remarkable that the group of benefit claimants has not changed correspondingly in numbers or definition. They remain a highly differentiated group of unemployed people with a variety of problems, including poor physical health, mental diseases, social problems, and a lack of the competencies needed for participation in the labor market. If the group of benefit claimants has not changed, we can conclude that the changes in the categorization system reflect a new construction of the "relationship" between the individual and the welfare state. Instead of building a welfare system and implementing policies related to changes in the *group of clients* in need of social services, these changes in the categorization of clients have primarily acted as a political and administrative way of making the citizens *fit into the neoliberal understanding* of benefit claimants and of how they should behave.

Research Approach

In this chapter, I draw on the findings of a qualitative longitudinal study of twenty-five Danish welfare claimants' unemployment trajectories. With the purpose of capturing the complexities and nuances in the encounters between the unemployed and the neoliberal policies to which they are subject, the aim of this methodological approach was to access the claimants' own reality and understandings of the encounters and how their lives progressed through time (Grinyer and Thomas 2012). The qualitative longitudinal research has allowed me to accompany a group of clients as their lives and their relations with the Jobcenter unfolded, and this has provided an exceptional opportunity to explore the processes and dynamics of change as well as the complex interplay of structure and individual agency (Elder 2011; Neale and Flowerdew 2003; Patrick 2014; Verd and López 2011).

Over a two-year period (2013–2015) and in five irregular empirical waves, data was collected intensively from repeated interviews and observations of each claimant's unemployment trajectory (Danneris 2016). The approach to data collection was holistic (Holstein and Gubrium 2003), and contact took various forms, including hour-long biographical and follow-up interviews, observations of meetings with social work professionals, phone interviews, and informal conversations.

Furthermore, the duration, number, and location of meetings varied (for instance, at the Jobcenter, in the claimant's home, or at activation sites). In total, the empirical material consists of eighty-five individual interviews and thirteen observations.[2]

All twenty-five claimants included in the study were formally categorized as "activity ready," which, as described above, indicates that they were assessed as having severe problems besides unemployment. Apart from this commonality, the claimants were highly diverse; they had a multitude of physical and mental health issues, family or social issues such as substance abuse or homelessness, low levels (if any) of education, and minimal or unstable work experience. While a few had only one specific problem (for example a physical problem due to a back injury), most had complex issues pertaining to several problems.[3]

All of the twenty-five claimants were in the range 30–59 years of age, and twelve were men. During the data collection period, they lived in different parts of Denmark, in cities and in small villages. Some lived in their own houses, while others lived in rentals, in caravans, or in the living room of a friend's apartment. Only four of the claimants lived with their spouse, while the rest lived alone or were single parents. Two claimants managed to find jobs during the period and were still employed in the summer of 2015 (Danneris 2016).

In the analysis that follows, the focus will be on the claimants' narratives about their unemployment trajectories. This bottom-up perspective allows attention to the nuances and variations in how individuals meet the state and tackle the meeting in their everyday encounters. In this regard, it is important to note that taking the clients' experiences as the point of departure does not mean that other factors such as the organizational context or the views of street-level professionals are irrelevant to the attempt to understand the relationship between citizens and the state. Neither does it mean that the clients' experiences can be treated as witnesses of the truth about the consequences of neoliberalism. However, it is the underlying assumption of this analysis that benefit claimants have important and unique knowledge through their individual experiences, that this knowledge is relevant, and that it is necessary to gain access to it if we are to obtain a fuller picture of how neoliberalism has affected the welfare system.

Analysis

Through an in-depth analysis of each of the twenty-five claimants' unemployment trajectories, I identified four different coping strategies adopted by the clients in their encounters with the neoliberal welfare system: resignation, action, adjustment, or resistance. The choice of strategies was not related to the individual but changed through time, depending on where the claimant was located in his or her unemployment trajectory. This means that throughout the two years of data collection, the same claimant made use of several or all of the four coping strategies, according to his or her current situation, type of problem, and relation to the employment system and so on. In the analysis below, I will elaborate on each of the four coping strategies by using a main case that exemplifies the strategy in question. In varying forms and at different points in time, the analytical patterns were identified across all twenty-five claimants' trajectories, but for the sake of illustration they will be exemplified through the four stories in the following analysis. Thus, the four cases are neither the "most different" nor representative of a general truth; they are examples from the full sample of unique stories of encounters between benefit claimants and the neoliberal welfare state.

Resignation

The first coping strategy found in the data is resignation, which is characterized by the claimants as a stage during their unemployment trajectory when they have given up their attempts to live up to the current norms proscribing how they should behave. They find themselves in a directionless parallel world and have found that their options for acting on their current situation have been depleted, thus leaving them in a state of resignation. An example of a benefit claimant drawing on this strategy is David. David is in his early thirties and has been unemployed for about four years due to a bipolar disorder and ADHD. He receives stabilizing medication and sedatives, and he spends most of his time alone in his apartment playing games on the computer. David has been provided with several different types of social services. He has a mentor, an at-home supporter who helps him with everyday tasks like cleaning the kitchen and buying groceries, and a social worker at the Jobcenter. In addition, he has an advisor in the criminal system to make sure that he meets the conditions of his parole, a psychologist, and a psychiatrist with whom he meets on a regular basis.

For the last year, David has participated in two different in-job-training programs for a few hours a week. Here, his work readiness (the number of hours he would be able to work, taking his problems into consideration) has been described and assessed by social work professionals, leading to their final decision on his future in the labor market:

> **D**: Now I have been thrown into something that they call a resource program instead of just being on cash benefits, because they can't figure out what to do with me.
> **I**: What does a resource program consist of?
> **D**: Nothing. No, because they can't really find out what … because I am too young to get a disability pension, they say. So the resource program just consists of the same stuff that I have already been doing so far.
> **I**: What do you think of this?
> **D**: I think it is a bit ridiculous, ehm, they can't figure out what to do with me. And then they just put me on a resource program, and then they have an excuse for placing me there for the next 3.5 years.

As David describes in this interview excerpt, the Jobcenter has reached no real decision so far. He does not fit into the available categories because he is too young to be granted a disability pension but at the same time has problems that are too severe for them to find a place for him in the labor market. This short extract from David's narrative exemplifies one out of many situations in the data where the lived life of benefit claimants and the policies targeting them do not match each other. Active labor market policies are based on the understanding that everybody has work potential and that it is the citizen's own responsibility to exploit this potential. In David's case, however, this proves quite difficult. First, as can be assumed from the number of professionals involved in his life, David's disabilities mean that he is not capable of taking on the expected responsibility. He is in need of help every day of the week.

Second, David actually wants to work and contribute to society, but he does not fit into the definition of what characterizes the neoliberal worker; he cannot take any available job, needs substantial support, and will always rely on the government for assistance if he is to participate in the labor market. This means that he does not fit into any of the categories available in the system, which can only define him as either ready for an activity or so disabled that there is no other solution than a disability pension. After several years of trying to change his situation, this has left David in a state of resignation:

> **D**: It is just like they have put me on a shelf and then I can stay there for a while.
> **I**: How long has this been going on?
> **D**: It started two–three months ago and will continue for the next three years. I have threatened them by saying that I will just go out and find a job, but then I will lose all my financial support for medication and stuff. So I feel kind of tied up in a way. ... It is kind of like when you have fought for a long time, it is like they counteract you.
> **I**: So you used to fight more?
> **D**: Yes. But now I have sort of given up.

At this stage in his unemployment trajectory, David is frustrated about the lack of willingness in the system to make a decision about his future, and he now finds himself shelved with no immediate prospect of being removed or any possibility of changing the situation himself. He has no other option than to accept his inability to match the neoliberal understanding of the good citizen and consequently his inability to change the current situation. He has given up.

Action

A different story unfolds in other parts of the data, both at earlier points in David's trajectory and in stages of the other benefit claimants' trajectories. Here the clients make use of an active coping strategy; instead of giving up, they use their available resources to work through their situation and change for the better. An example of this is Harry's story. Harry is in his mid-thirties and is a part-time father with a daughter. As a former drug addict, he has lived a turbulent life, and he has struggled with an ADHD diagnosis and negative experiences from school. However, he managed to complete a formal education as a butcher in his late twenties. Five years ago, Harry applied for sickness benefits after a stressful period at work. After the maximum two years on sickness benefits, Harry applied for social benefits because he still felt unable to work.[4]

Like David, Harry has found himself in stages in his unemployment trajectory where he felt like giving up and just leaving his situation up to whatever social work professional was assigned to his case. However, the last time I met Harry, he had applied a different coping strategy:

> When I got the chance at the butcher's shop where I am now, ... having been there for a month or so, I was just doing the dishes, and I am a skilled butcher. I was looking out the window thinking: "Are you standing here doing the dishes for free, in order to maybe get a job at some point?" and then I started thinking that the tasks I was given were a bit more random. It didn't quite seem they needed me. So at that point I said to my boss: "Listen, this is not working. It looks too much like every other in-job-training program I have attended. I just work for free. It has nothing to do with you, but I just want a real job." And then I quit down there. Ehm, and then I contacted my consultant at the Jobcenter. ... And then I said to him: "Okay, from now on, if you are going to find an in-job-placement for me, it has to be because they are looking to hire someone." Otherwise it doesn't make sense to me. I am 100 percent determined about that.

As this short narrative demonstrates, Harry has expressed his dissatisfaction with the system and refused to submit to it, but instead of applying David's coping strategy, Harry has decided to work through the system. He accepts the fact that he has to participate in another in-job-training program in order for the Jobcenter to assess his work ability and the number of hours a week he will be able to work before he can get out and apply for a permanent position. However, he defines his conditions for the job consultant. He will not accept enrolment in yet another program with no prospect of a real job after finishing the program; instead, he tells his job consultant that if he is to play by the rules of the system, it must be in a way that makes sense to him. Thus, Harry adopts an action strategy by accepting the rationale behind the system but insisting that it must be applied on his terms. Harry's use of this strategy produces the effect he hoped for. The job consultant accepts Harry's terms and soon finds a placement with a boss who has agreed to hire Harry if he shows up and does his job satisfactorily every day for three months. According to Harry, this has made an important difference to him:

I: What difference does it make that there is light at the end of the tunnel now?

H: Well, this is exactly what I have always sought. This, that now I have a way. I have the opportunity to do something actively myself to move forward. And that is finally what I have at hand now, so I'll just catch it with both hands.

I: Yes.

H: Well, this is the first time in many years that I have had the opportunity to move forward.

I: As opposed to earlier when you have felt stuck?

H: But that is how it's been. Well, I haven't been able to do anything active to move forward.

In Harry's case as well as in other trajectories in the data, claimants actually want to participate and become the good citizens that the neoliberal view praises. However, the system has built a wall of processes and procedures that target the unwilling, "bad," or non-responsive neoliberal client, which actually makes it difficult to be the good client demanded by the system. Furthermore, the rigid system processes encourage the job consultant to accommodate demands for registration as proof of development instead of meeting Harry's demands. On several occasions, Harry has tried to take responsibility for his own situation and gone out looking for employment, but he has encountered a system with rules and narrow procedures that the claimant must follow before being able to take a job. As this example illustrates, benefit claimants need substantial resources to be good neoliberal citizens, or, as Harry puts it, "It takes a lot of effort and resources to be sick and dependent on the system."

Adjustment

The third coping strategy identified in the data is adjustment. This strategy corresponds to a stage in the claimants' unemployment trajectory where they feel insecure about what is happening and what is supposed to happen and where they experience their situation as frozen with them unable to see their options to change it. Susan presents an example of a benefit claimant using adjustment as her coping strategy. She is in her mid-forties and lives in a two-bedroom apartment with the younger of her two daughters. She is a trained and qualified home assistant but has a very unstable work history comprising various unskilled jobs, educational failures, and several periods on benefits. Nine years ago, Susan became pregnant with her youngest daughter. At the same time, she started suffering from severe back pain while trying to deal with personal problems (divorce, her mother's cancer, and her eldest daughter's depression), and she has not been employed since then.

At one point in her trajectory, Susan finds herself in a situation where the non-transparency in the system regarding the decisions and actions to be taken in her case leaves her agency dependent on the social work professional in charge of her case. Susan feels as if her life has been put on hold:

> My birthday is coming up soon; it won't be long before I turn fifty and then I just wonder what I will spend the rest of my life doing, you know? As long as you don't have a clear assessment … I just want to figure out where I can work for the rest of my time, right? There are still things in life that I want to do with my daughter. But as long as I don't have any assessment about where I am in my life, I find it very difficult to find some long-term goals. So I'll just wait till tomorrow.

At this stage in her trajectory, Susan has been left so paralyzed that she just waits, adjusts to the condition of not knowing, and lets the institution take over. When Susan has tried to take the initiative to do something, she has found herself being slowed down or completely put on hold due to various circumstances. One of the reasons, Susan explains, is the continuous replacement of the social work professional responsible for her case:

> Since [name of former social worker] quit it has just been a constant stream of different social workers, and then you have to start over every single time — as opposed to having one that you are attached to and can more or less finish it. I know, as many people tell me, that it is impossible because they are moved around. But as for me, I just feel that it is very tiresome. I feel that there will never be an end to this. If I get a new one, she might look at things differently than the others and then I have to start over again and again. They might be close to something, where you think that now something is going to happen, and then I get a new social worker again. This is probably the worst thing about not getting on with it and just being on cash benefits. It is that you don't feel safe and can't tell … and don't even feel that you can trust anyone. Actually I kind of put my life in other people's hands and hope that they can help me. Of course I have to help myself, but in the situation I am in right now, I think that, well, yes, I'll try the best I can to figure it out. Right now I just don't bother anymore. This is where I am now, so they can just do whatever they want with me.

Susan acknowledges that new social workers are inevitable, but when it happens several times it has a great impact on her ability to act and change her situation. Now Susan has moved from progress toward the labor market to a locked situation where each new shift in social worker moves her further away from a job. In the above quote, she refers directly to the neoliberal discourse when she says "of course I have to help myself," but she finds it very hard to do so when the institution appears fragmented and becomes a barrier to her progress. In this stage of her trajectory, Susan wants to give up; even though she tries her best, she encounters institutional factors that significantly constrain her situation. As opposed to earlier stages in her trajectory, she has come to a point where she just adjusts to the institution, takes no action herself, and leaves the future up to whatever social worker is currently responsible for her case.

Resistance

During their unemployment trajectories, several of the claimants represented in the data make use of what I would describe as a resistance strategy in trying to cope with the consequences of being part of a neoliberal welfare system. Resistance as a coping strategy is characterized by narratives about the system acting as an opponent that always challenges and questions the situation and (lack of) resources of the client. André's story is an example. He is in his mid-fifties and lives alone in a small apartment. He is divorced and has three adult children. He has been working since he was 14 years old, first as an unskilled worker and then for many years as a truck driver. Eight years ago, André was involved in two work-related accidents only a few months apart: first, he drove off a cliff in his truck and second, a hoist broke as he was unloading groceries off a truck. In both cases, his back was severely injured and, since then, he has not been able to re-enter the labor market. In the first four years after the accidents, André was eligible for sickness benefits. However, despite no significant changes in his health situation, he received notification from the Jobcenter three years ago that he was categorized as ready for activation and thus no longer eligible except for substantially lower cash benefits. As a consequence of his re-categorization from sick to "activation ready," André had to participate in several in-job training programs to assess his work ability in different fields.

In André's view, he has contributed to society for thirty years, paid his taxes, and been a good citizen, and now, when he is dependent on help from the system, he feels badly treated and neglected while his problems are not recognized or not taken seriously:

> They keep saying all the time that "you have to do this and you have to try this and if you … I think you have so many resources." I am just about to … I lose my temper when they say resources. I am about to throw up over that word. I had a lot of resources once. They are not going to fucking sit there and say that because I have been a blacksmith and because I have been a lifeguard and have worked in my parents' business and have been a truck driver that I have resources. I had some resources once; now I'm broken, now I have no resources left. And in both my mood and my mind, I am completely devoid of resources. Sometimes I don't even have the resources to enter the shower. It is true! It sounds silly. But it is fucking true. I have home assistance every Friday. They keep on talking about resources. I can't sleep.

At this point in his trajectory, André has no resources due to his injuries and feels provoked by the neoliberal resource-orientation shaping the Jobcenter's approach to his situation:

> I can't figure it out, not at all. Back in the old days, well now I say old days – it was about fifteen, ten or fifteen years ago – well then you got a disability pension if you were injured as much as I am. But now you have to work even though you are injured. Who the fuck decided that? If you know what I mean? And even if you don't. And it is not, it is not like the government says. Then they [social workers] say, when you have been at the Jobcenter talking to this young social worker, then she says: "It is the government's fault." But which government? I have been fucking sick during three different government periods, and now the fourth is about to begin.

Like David's extract, André's example demonstrates patterns in the data reflecting a mismatch between reality as perceived by the client and the neoliberal under-standing of the individual citizen which emphasizes how everyone is capable and has resources to be realized in the labor market for the benefit of (not least) the client. In fact, André explicitly states how the resource focus directly leads to systematic neglect of his severe problems. Unlike David, André resists succumbing to neoliberal views. However, the result of his coping strategy is similar to the result of David's. Even though André fights back and refuses to participate in the "neoliberal circus," he is still dependent on it for help and thus must play by the neoliberal rules to receive his benefits.

Concluding Remarks

This chapter has explored findings from a qualitative longitudinal study of the unemployment trajectories of twenty-five vulnerable welfare claimants, focusing on their coping strategies in their day-to-day encounters with the neoliberal welfare state. As the analysis shows, the consequences of being part of the neoliberal welfare system are not uniform but can take several different forms, depending on factors such as the individual client's situation, available resources, and health. David's, Harry's, Susan's, and André's trajectories are unique, but the patterns of difference between neoliberal policy and lived experience found in the twenty-five individual trajectories exhibit similarities through time. From this analysis it can be concluded that the lived experience of some of the most vulnerable unemployed citizens is neither reflected in univocal neoliberal catchphrases stating that "everybody is capable" nor in the political rhetoric that portrays unemployed citizens as resourceful clients able to take responsibility for their own situation. What seems to be needed is a language that, amongst other things, allows recognition of the ambiguities in the trajectories of the long-term unemployed and acknowledgement of the severe problems faced by some claimants. This chapter demonstrates how longitudinal qualitative accounts of the experiences of welfare claimants can be activated in order to critically investigate the relationship between the perceptions embedded in neoliberal policy and the perceptions of those it most directly affects.

Notes

1 Translation of description from a Danish municipality: www.aarhus.dk/sitecore/con tent/Subsites/JobcenterAarhus/Home/Borgere/Uddannelseshjaelp/Aktivitetsparat.aspx? sc_lang=da
2 The national authority of data management has approved collection and management of data – and each client has consented to participation, been given full anonymity as well as the opportunity to withdraw from the study at any time during the data collection period.
3 Several issues, for example the extent of the informants' problems and the longitudinal design, raise central ethical questions besides general ethical guidelines like anonymity and so on. For example the implications of maintaining the researcher–informant relationship throughout two years and how to deal with the special type of knowledge gained by following informants through time. These and other ethical issues have been critically reflected upon elsewhere (Danneris 2016).
4 This reflects Danish legislation on sickness benefits in 2013, which was changed with a new reform in January 2014 that removed the two-year limitation.

Bibliography

Aftaletekst (2013). *Aftale om en reform af kontanthjælpssystemet – flere i uddannelse og job.* Copenhagen: Beskæftigelsesministeriet.
Arbejdsmarkedsstyrelsen (The National Labor Market Authority) (2000). *Vejledning om ændrede rådigheds- og sanktionsregler.* Copenhagen: Arbejdsmarkedsstyrelsen.
Arbejdsmarkedsstyrelsen (2004). *På kanten af arbejdsmarkedet.* Copenhagen: Arbejdsmarkedsstyrelsen.
Arbejdsmarkedsstyrelsen (2010a). *Notat. Ny matchmodel – hvorfor og hvordan.* Copenhagen: Arbejdsmarkedsstyrelsen.
Arbejdsmarkedsstyrelsen (2010b). *Ny matchmodel. Sådan og derfor.* Copenhagen: Arbejdsmarkedsstyrelsen.
Bang, J. (2002). *Arbejdsevnemetode: En teoretisk og praktisk indføring.* Copenhagen: Nyt Juridisk Forlag.
Beskæftigelsesministeriet (Ministry of Employment) (2013). *Alle kan gøre nytte – Udspil til en kontanthjælpsreform.* Copenhagen: Beskæftigelsesministeriet.
Braedley, S. and Luxton, M. (2010). Competing Philosophies: Neoliberalism and Challenges of Everyday Life. In M. Luxton and S. Braedley (Eds.), *Neoliberalism and Everyday Life.* Montreal: McGill Queen University Press.
Brodkin, E. Z. (2013). Street-Level Organizations and the Welfare State. In E. Z. Brodkin and G. Marston (Eds.), *Work and the Welfare State: Street-level Organizations and Workfare Politics.* Washington, DC: Georgetown University Press.
Brown, W. (2003). Neo-Liberalism and the End of Liberal Democracy. *Theory & Event*, 7(1). doi:10.1353/tae.2003.0020
Caswell, D., Eskelinen, L., and Olesen, S. P. (2011). Identity Work and Client Resistance Underneath the Canopy of Active Employment Policy. *Qualitative Social Work*, 12(1), 8–23. doi:1473325011413629

Danneris, S. (2016). Ready to Work (Yet)? Unemployment Trajectories among Vulnerable Welfare Recipients. *Qualitative Social Work*. doi:10.1177/1473325016672916

Danneris, S. and Nielsen, M. H. (forthcoming). Bringing the Client Back in – A Comparison between Government Rhetoric on "Job Readiness" and Experiences of the Unemployed. *Social Policy & Administration*.

Elder, G. H. (2011). Life Course: Sociological Aspects. In N. J. Smelser and B. Baltes (Eds.), *International Encyclopedia of the Social and Behavioural Science*. New York: Oxford University Press.

Goul Andersen, J. (2013). Medborgerskab under pres. In J. Guldager and M. Skytte (Eds.), *Socialt arbejde – Teorier og perspektiver*. Aalborg: Akademisk Forlag.

Grinyer, A. and Thomas, C. (2012). The Value of Interviewing on Multiple Occasions or Longitudinally. In J. F. Gubrium, J. A. Holstein, K. McKinney, and A. Marvasti (Eds.), *The Sage Handbook of Interview Research: The Complexity of the Craft* (2nd edn.). Thousand Oaks, CA: SAGE Publications.

Høgsbro, K. (2012). Social Policy and Self-Help in Denmark: A Foucauldian Perspective. *International Journal of Self Help and Self Care*, 6, 43–64.

Høilund, P. (2006), *Social Retfærdighed: Udkast til en Retslære for Socialt Arbejde*. Copenhagen: Jurist-og Økonomforbundets Forlag.

Holstein, J. A. and Gubrium, J. F. (2003). *Inside Interviewing: New Lenses, New Concerns*. Thousand Oaks, CA: SAGE Publications.

Juul, S. (2010a). *Solidaritet – Anerkendelse, Retfærdighed og god Dømmekraft: En Kritisk analyse af Barrierer for Sammenhængskraft i Velfærdssamfundet*. Copenhagen: Hans Reitzel.

Juul, S. (2010b). Solidarity and Social Cohesion in Late Modernity: A Question of Recognition, Justice and Judgement in Situation. *European Journal of Social Theory*, 13, 253–269.

Koivisto, J. (2007). What Evidence Base? Steps towards the Relational Evaluation of Social Interventions. *Evidence and Policy: A Journal of Research, Debate and Practice*, 3(4), 527–537.

Larsen, C. (2015). Universalisme og befolkningens opfattelse af "de fattige" og "de arbejdsløse" [Universalism and the citizens' view on "the poor" and "the unemployed"]. In C. Larsen and J. Andersen (Eds.) *Den universelle velfærdsstat. Funktionsmåde, folkelig opbakning og forandring* (pp. 119–130). Copenhagen: Saxo.

Lipsky, M. (2010). *Street-level Bureaucracy: Dilemmas of the Individual in Public Services*. New York: Russel Sage Foundation.

Lødemel, I. and Moreira, A. (Eds.). (2014). *Activation or Workfare? Governance and the Neo-liberal Convergence*. Oxford: Oxford University Press.

Naples, Nancy A. (1998). Bringing Everyday Life to Policy Analysis: The Case of White Rural Women Negotiating College and Welfare. *Journal of Poverty: Innovations on Social, Political & Economic Inequalities*, 2, 23–53.

Neale, B. and Flowerdew, J. (2003). Time, Texture and Childhood: The Contours of Longitudinal Qualitative Research. *International Journal of Social Research Methodology*, 6, 189–199.

Patrick, R. (2014), Working on Welfare: Findings from a Qualitative Longitudinal Study into the Lived Experiences of Welfare Reform in the UK. *Journal of Social Policy*, 43, 705–725.

Schram, S. F. (2015). *The Return of Ordinary Capitalism: Neoliberalism, Precarity, Occupy*. New York: Oxford University Press.

Schram, S. F. and Silverman, B. (2012). The End of Social Work: Neoliberalizing Social Policy Implementation. *Critical Policy Studies*, 6, 128–145.

Socialministeriet (2001). *Arbejdsevnemetode. Metode til beskrivelse, udvikling og forbedring af arbejdsevne.* Copenhagen: Socialministeriet.

Soss, J., Fording, R. C., and Schram, S. F. (2011). *Disciplining the Poor. Neoliberal Paternalism and the Persistent Power of Race.* Chicago: University of Chicago Press.

Triantafillou, P. (2012). Decentralization as the Exercise of Power and Autonomy: The Case of Danish Employment Policy. *Journal of Political Power,* 5, 55–71.

Verd, J. M. and López, A. M. (2011). The Rewards of a Qualitative Approach to Life-Course Research. The Example of Effects of Social Protection Policies on Career Paths. *Forum: Qualitative Social Research,* 12(3). Available from: www.qualitative-research.net/index.php/fqs/article/view/1753

7

NEOLIBERAL TALK

The Routinized Structures of Document-Focused Social Worker–Client Discourse

Maureen T. Matarese and Dorte Caswell

Routinization has increasingly become a way for front-line practitioners to make unwieldy caseloads manageable (Lipsky 2010 [1980]). A common tension in modern day social work, the tension between responsiveness and standardization (Hjörne, Juhila, and van Nijnatten 2010), in part surfaces through the use of routines that standardize practice, some argue, at the expense of more personal, individualized service (Abramovitz and Zelnick 2015). While routines are an enduring part of bureaucratic practice in general (Lipsky 2010 [1980]), the advent of neoliberal ideology and its attendant institutional manifestations (New Public Management and New Managerialism) has forced routines to do double duty (White, Hall, and Peckover 2008). Thus, they persist in helping practitioners manage heavy caseloads, while also integrating a business purpose to routine work. Routine documents still record client information but also serve to measure performance and ensure accountability. Book contributor Jamie Peck (2010) has suggested that "the ontology of neoliberalism" involves "an evolving web of relays, routines, and relations" (p. 34).

Soss, Fording, and Schram (2011) have found that the business model is alive and well in the organizational culture of Florida's Welfare Transition program, observed in the "norms and worldviews of street-level workers" (p. 199). While extensive research exists on neoliberalism as it manifests globally, nationally, locally, institutionally, we know very little about how it functions in front-line talk with clients, and yet discourse analytic studies have had dramatic impact on institutional practice (Heritage, Elliott, Beckett, and Wilkes 2007; Waring 2011). This chapter will take a closer look at how neoliberalism and more specifically New Public Management (NPM) works on a micro level in talk between social workers and homeless clients at the front line of policy implementation.

Neoliberalism at the Front Lines

Neoliberalism often institutionally manifests itself through New Public Management (NPM), which organizes and manages non-businesses according to business principles (Diefenbach 2009). Soss et al. (2011) suggest "new public management [has] been deployed as [a] neoliberal response to ... challenges of [organizational] coherence and accountability" (p. 207).

The term "new managerialism" is often used synonymously with NPM, particularly when institutions do not take an expressly NPM approach. According to Abramovitz and Zelnick (2015) new managerialism is the second of three stages of privatization, "import[ing] market philosophy and business principles into non-profit organisations" (Abramovitz and Zelnick 2015, p. 121). These approaches, while promising transparency, efficiency, and equal treatment, are critiqued for routinizing practices at the expense of client voice, a loss of practitioner–client relationships, and practitioner stress and burn out (Abramovitz and Zelnick 2015).

This chapter explores the neoliberal discourses of front-line social workers and their clients in an urban US homeless shelter. Following Lipsky (2010 [1980]) we argue that these front-line practitioners implement policy in their everyday work with some discretion, and like Brodkin (2011) we situate street-level bureaucrats within new managerial institutional space, "highlighting how new forms of process regulation and managerial structures adjust the behaviour of the street-level worker through incentive structures, sanctions, and regulations" (Matarese and Caswell forthcoming, 3). We examine street-level bureaucratic practice as it exists within an NPM institutional space, acknowledging the influence of neoliberal principles that dramatically shape talk between caseworkers and clients.

We focus primarily on routinization specifically through the integration of documentation and forms into social work interactions. Street-level bureaucrats "develop routines to deal with the complexity of work tasks" often "because of the scarcity of resources relative to the demands made upon them" (Lipsky 2010 [1980], p. 83). Routines and particularly documentation within new managerialism not only serve a record-keeping function; they also measure performance by recording accountable actions and completed goals. The tension between being responsive to clients' individual needs and maintaining a common standard of equal treatment is a central dilemma in social work (Hjörne et al. 2010), and making required documentation an interactional routine in practitioner–client meetings serves the interests of time and efficiency.

Discourse analytic approaches to neoliberalism are still scant. Many approaches focus on the analysis of policy (Fairclough 2000), institutional website and publications (Urciuoli 2010), textbooks (Gray 2012), and keywords (Holborow 2012). Several scholars examine neoliberalism as it is socially constructed in moment-to-moment talk. Gray and Block (2012), for example, have begun to examine neoliberal talk in the classroom. In probably the most dramatic example, Matarese (2012) describes how caseworkers' interaction with long-term staying clients compares to talk with short-term staying clients and undocumented clients, revealing that undocumented clients are discursively treated like long-term clients, notwithstanding the length of their shelter stay. Both long-term and undocumented clients endure extensive in situ references to neoliberal ideology, including invocations of increased individual responsibility, accountability, efficiency, and speed to goal completion.

However, seemingly few scholars have examined how the very *structure* of participant turns at talk can reveal an adherence to neoliberal ideology. Matarese and Caswell (2014) show how accountability is socially, interactionally constructed in social work, exposing neoliberal ideologies at work. Matarese (2009) describes how responsibility and accountability are constructed between caseworkers and clients, highlighting that responsibility and accountability are not uni-directionally foisted upon the client but function reciprocally: the responsibility and accountability of the client generating accountability for the social worker, both of whom are held accountable by administration.

NPM-initiated standardized formats are not solely a phenomenon of the United States, but have been analyzed in numerous social work contexts (Høybye-Mortensen 2015). White et al. (2008) have examined an NPM computerized documentation system using discourse analysis. They argue that although the form limits the possible narratives, social workers worked around the form's narrowness. However they find that the dual use of the form for referral as well as for assessment purposes was problematic. In a Danish context NPKM standardized formats have been implemented with unemployed hard-to-place adults, which has been criticized from a practice perspective as well as in research (Caswell, Marston, and Larsen 2010). In a worldwide era of NPM and neoliberalism combined with an increasing reliance on computerized forms of documentation, this study contributes to a growing literature on documentation paying specific attention to micro elements of social work practice.

This chapter examines the use of documentation during caseworker–client talk in an urban American homeless shelter. While we find evidence of managerialism and ergo neoliberal principles, we identify positive and negative consequences of the presence of documentation, routines, and standardization. We argue that form-driven interactions provide limited space for client narrative and extended participation, but they are transparent to the client. While some interactions do have space for extended talk, these are characterized by being less transparent for the client. Our conversation analysis of pauses in particular illustrates the participatory presence of paperwork in practice. To this end, we pose the following broad research question: To what extent is documentation present in these interactions, and to what end? We consider this question in light of how documentation functions in collaboration with other neoliberal, NPM tenets: efficiency and its close cousin, speed.

Research Context

Responding to record numbers of homeless individuals on the streets and in city shelters in 2003, a northeast metropolis in the United States created a plan to drastically reduce those numbers, initiating a plan that included stricter standards for assessment and accountability and increased responsibility for staff and clients (Department of Homeless Services 2002, 2004).

Caseworkers facilitated client movement through the system from entry to departure, coordinating with other city agencies to ensure clients had a stable legal income prior to housing placement. Three meetings, two toward the beginning and one toward the end of shelter stay, relied heavily on documents and forms as a conversational blueprint. Usually the first meeting between a caseworker and client included an intake assessment, which included basic biographical information, including the reasons why the client was homeless, relatives with whom he could live, and so on. Often the second meeting included the psycho-social assessment, which included the psychological history of the client, as well as social issues that may be barriers to housing. The housing application was developed toward the end of a client's shelter stay and, like those previously described, utilized the application's questions as conversational cues.

Check-in meetings did not follow any set series of questions, and while they often concluded with filling out and signing an Independent Living Plan (ILP), they allowed, as we will see, conversational flexibility of a sort. The ILP constituted a contract between the client, the caseworker, and the shelter, providing legal support for the client responsibility policy in cases in which clients were unable to complete the minimal actions necessary to move from shelter.

Methodology

This research is part of an IRB-approved, nine-month institutional interactional ethnography of a city shelter, involving the audio-recording and observation of eighteen caseworker–client dyads (including six caseworkers and eighteen clients), totaling fifty-four audio recorded interactions over nine months. The principal investigator (PI) observed and recorded meetings with clients from shelter entry until housing placement. She took field notes and conducted interviews with all clients at the beginning, middle, and end of their shelter stay and with caseworkers at the beginning, at a mid-point, and at the end of fieldwork. All meetings were transcribed using Jefferson (1984) conventions, which uses font formatting and symbols to represent talk how it sounded. All participants gave informed consent in the language of their choice prior to the first meeting and were able to withdraw from the study at any time for any reason. All names were given pseudonyms and other personal data (names of centers, shelters, social security numbers, etc.) were rendered unrecognizable. The IRB protocol signed by all participants stipulates that research and analyses have no bearing whatsoever on the employment, probation, or promotion of case managers or the placement or sanctioning of clients.

We used discourse analysis (of language in context) and conversation analysis (of participant turns at talk) to examine the transcribed interactions. These qualitative approaches stem from social constructionism and ethnomethodology. The former argues that meaning is socially constructed in situ, and the latter examines the structures and rules of society, which are observable in the satisfaction of them and in the breach of those rules (Garfinkel 1967). Together, these provide a window into the structure of talk, and the circulation of related concepts that collaborate with and enhance that structure. Brodkin and Marston (2013) suggest that:

> a political-*organizational* view puts [Street-Level Organizations] at the center of analysis, offering a different perspective on how welfare states work. It links the micropolitics of SLOs to the macropolitics of the welfare state: it's a ways of seeing big by looking small.
>
> *(p. 18)*

While we do not generalize to anything as broad in scope as "the welfare state" or even "the shelter system," we hope by looking very small indeed that we may provide evidence of the presence of neoliberalism not just in words but in *how those words are organized and presented in talk*. If policy is implemented in the everyday practice of street-level bureaucrats, then the talk of this practice should tell us *how* that policy is being implemented, more specifically; thus showing, as Morpheus so aptly says in *The Matrix*, "how deep the rabbit hole goes."

The excerpts provided in this chapter illustrate discourse practices that cut across the data sample, evolving from iterative analyses of the data rather than *a priori*, hypotheses-driven positions. Routinization of social work interaction through documentation is best revealed through analyses of preference structure, pauses, and word choice. Preference structure explores turns at talk: turn type (questions, answers, promises, requests, etc.), normative turns (Sacks 1992). Turns that violate prior expectation are called "dispreferred" responses; those that satisfy expected turn structure are "preferred." Pauses in talk can signal hesitations, suggesting upcoming conversational trouble. Cohesion and coherence analysis allows us to explore word choice, particularly the clustering, or collocation, of related words and ideas, as well as how they are carried from one meeting to the next (Halliday and Hasan 1976).

While the client is a participant in these interactions, the nature of institutional interaction strengthened by documentation places the role of questioner with the caseworker, putting her in control of question topics and the routine itself; as such we place more focus on the caseworker who implements this documentation in her everyday practice.

We make no generalizations about policy implementation across the country, state, city, or even within the shelter system as a whole. Rather we wish to highlight the utility of discourse and conversation analyses as methodologies for analyzing the production of neoliberal discourses in everyday, seemingly mundane institutional talk.

Document-Focused Routine Talk

The first two excerpts come from talk that uses documents and forms as conversational blue prints. The following is taken from an intake assessment interaction and is representative of most intake assessments the PI observed. The caseworker (CW) meets the client (C) for the first time, explaining the intake assessment and completing it.

Excerpt 1: Intake Assessment

1.	CW:	(laughs) Okay, so today I'm meeting with you- close the door for me?
2.	C:	XXXX
3.		today I'm meeting with you to do your long intake basically **it's a set of questions I'm gonna**
4.		**ask you, about yourself, so I can put it on pa:per,** umm, (.) then, (.) we'll get into your independent
5.		living pla:n **which I've already constructed so we don't- I don't waste too much of your ti:me** I'm
6.		already (.) ahead of the game I'm a little prepared for you today, umm so we'll go over this, (.) I'll
7.		**ask you the questions you answer as honestly as possible I'll write it down, (.) as quick as possible**
8.		and we'll try to get through this as **quick as possible, okay?** (.) you have medicaid?
9.	C:	°yeah°
10.	CW:	are you single, divorced, married,
11.	C:	Single
12.		**(2.4) ((CW writing))**
13.	CW:	thank you ((to another caseworker))
14.		**(.9)**
15.	CW:	umm, you're not a veteran are you? Have you ever been in the army, navy,
16.		(.)
17.	C:	army? no. In my country yes not here.
18.	CW:	do you have your PA- you don't know your PA case number, do you?

Two patterns in the data emerge from this excerpt: documentation-centric talk and the clustering of language around documentation, efficiency, and brevity, illustrating not only routinization but also the business model and its principles at work.

After introducing the procedure for the day, the case worker defines it, making herself the agent who questions and the client the object of the questioning. Practitioner-initiated question–answer sequences are common in institutional interaction. The interactional preferences are clarified in advance here. The questions begin in line 8 and continue to line 18 and beyond.

The caseworker, in saying "so I can put it on paper" (line 4), signals the result of this intake question–answer sequence. She brings the bureaucratic necessity of the paperwork to the foreground, "so" illustrating the result of the talk. Likewise, in line 7 she articulates the process: she questions, he answers, she writes it down, integrating the bureaucratic process into the interaction (as illustrated in lines 10–12 where it follows the aforementioned organization).

New managerialism often emphasizes efficiency and speeding up (Abramovitz and Zelnick 2015), which here are indicated through "not wasting time" (line 5), which she pitches as saving the client's time, and "as quick as possible" (lines 7, 8).

Moreover, the caseworker offers her prior write-up of the client's service plan (ILP) as a signal of preparedness and efficiency. The construction of service plans is meant to be collaborative; however, in the first several meetings some pre-construction makes sense as all clients take the same early steps toward housing at the shelter (getting a tuberculosis test, getting a psychiatric evaluation, acquiring public assistance or other legal means of income). Ritzer (2007) suggests that speed and efficiency are part of "McDonaldization," the treatment of non-businesses (e.g. schools, hospitals) like fast-food businesses. The emphasis on speed and efficiency here are perhaps, like routines, part of the caseworker's need to manage a large caseload. On the other hand, speed and efficiency, like documentation, have a dual function: to assist the caseworker in maintaining a certain level of performance, on which she will be assessed.

Finally, the pause in line 12 should not go unaddressed. When a question is asked, the normative, or preferred, response is to answer, and when a lengthy pause precedes an answer it is usually a signal of upcoming interactional trouble (Pomerantz 1984; Sacks 1992; Schegloff 2007). In line 12, however, the pause precedes the caseworker's next question, indicating instead the participation of the documentation as a silent actant (Latour 1999) that shapes the interaction by being present.

The second excerpt, from a housing application meeting, includes many of the same discourse practices. The excerpt begins after general greetings.

Excerpt 2: Housing Application

1. CW: ((to herself)) no medications. ((to client)) okay, what I'm >filling out here< is your <u>housing</u> application.
2. C: for [°housing alright°]
3. CW: [housing](.) okay? we gonna try to find you somewhere to <u>live</u>. (.) <u>quickly</u>.
4. C: quick (.) <u>rapido</u>
5. CW: <u>rapido</u>.
6. C: hehh
7.   **(.65) ((caseworker types already known information in his housing application))**
8. CW: You don't take no medications <u>right</u>?
9. C: °mm°
10. CW: <u>no</u> medications,
11. C: °yeah°
12.   (.8) ((typing))

13. CW: (sighs)-kay
14.   (.)

15.   CW: Do ya ever use drugs?
16.   C: No
17.   CW: drug?
18.   C: drug? No

As in the prior excerpt, this one begins with an introduction to the application sequence, (lines 1, 3) although it excludes a description of the interactional rules (question–answer sequences). Notwithstanding an introduction to the rules, the caseworker leads the client through a series of questions (lines 7, 10, 15, 17) requiring answers (9, 11, 16, 18). As the client speaks Spanish as his first language, the caseworker restates some questions (lines 10, 17). Moreover, the extended pauses (lines 7, 12) and the micropause (line 14) once again signal the presence of the document as a silent participant, as the caseworker fills out the form. Line 7 is a particularly long silence left open by paperwork. The complete silence here highlights once again the participation of the paperwork.

Routinization, a common coping strategy for street-level bureaucrats, is a double-edged sword, offering benefits and drawbacks. On one hand, both the intake assessment and housing application meetings show talk that is controlled by the caseworker's questions, which almost entirely are derived from required paperwork. The result is limited possibilities for client participation; short answers are preferred. Efficiency and brevity are valued, as the caseworker says "quickly," "rapido." One may once again be reminded both of Lipsky's (2010 [1980]) suggestion of efficiency and routine as a strategy for coping, as well as of the McDonald's drive through. Nevertheless, what participation is required is made transparent from the beginning of the meeting. These routinized meetings are compared with another meeting that uses a form: the ILP meeting.

More Flexible, Routinized Talk

ILP meetings, in contrast, do not begin with an introduction to the paperwork and interactional structure. Rather they function like casual check-up meetings, tailored to the individual concerns of the client and his unique barriers to housing. As a result, the conversation provides extensive space for client talk, shown here in italics. This excerpt is taken from the middle of a typical ILP meeting. These meetings conclude with filling out an ILP form, which will be addressed further in excerpt 4.

Excerpt 3: ILP Interaction

1.   CW: What are you doing to try to get up outta here, Michael?=
2.   C: =*What am I trying to do right now? (.) I've been very, very busy.(.)That's one.(.)Two, the guy*
3.   *that I was working with as a driver, you know the driver that was working with me, (.) he got*
4.   *fired. He got arrested, (.) because he was stealing money. He was doing embezzlement, so*
5.   *I now, 'm doing my truck (.) my route and helping the guy that's driving also do his route. So*

6.   *that's why,=*

7.   CW: =are you <u>driving</u> now?

8.   C: *I <u>wish</u> I was. I don't have my <u>license</u>. **(.6)** But been trying to, you know, trying to find*

9.   *another <u>driver</u>, to do <u>my</u> route, that way, I don't have to be working two, two trucks.* **You**

10.   **know** *that way the guy that's dri- that's doing <u>my</u> route he could concentrate on his <u>own</u> route*

11.   *not do <u>my</u> route and his route. That's the problem there.*

12.   CW: How much money you making? Are you saving [any money?]

13.   C: **[Umm]***I'm not saving nothing what I'm*

14.   *making is sh- <u>shit</u> 'at's why I'm pissed off, because I'm doing double work (.) and they're not*

15.   *<u>paying</u> me.(.) I even took a whole week off, you know, I even told 'em <u>look</u>, you know, that's*

16.   *I how <u>frustrated</u> I was. I was so frustrated that, you know,(.) I'm busting my ass helping them*

17.   *out, and you know, they don't treat me like, you know, like <u>shit</u>? No fuck that. But who*

18.   *come out <u>losing</u>? me.*

19.   CW: °Alright°. (.) What do you want to do to get <u>outta</u> here? Yeah, what are we doing=

20.   C: =What do I want to do to get outta here (.)I'm trying to do <u>anything</u>. (taps bottle on hands)

21.   CW: Anything like <u>what</u> Michael.

22.   C: Whatever' what-

23.   CW: Are you on public assistance?

24.   C: Well, they're only giving me <u>food</u> stamps.

25.   CW: Why?

26.   C: <u>I</u> don't know.

27.   CW: Have you opened a <u>full</u> PA Case?

28.   C: I <u>did</u> I I I I'm still- I <u>passed</u> the 45 days. and then (.) they haven't sent me no <u>letters</u> or

29.   anything.

30.   CW: Okay, I'll check tomorrow and see what's going on with <u>that</u> status, <u>okay</u>? =

31.   C: =Okay.

As mentioned above, this excerpt includes three lengthy narratives (lines 2–6, 8–11, and 13–18), allowing the client to relate his experiences working with a delivery truck. Notably, while client narratives exist, they are initiated by caseworker questions (lines 1, 7, 12). Her question of saving money (line 12), for example, is a commonly asked, required question of all clients, necessary for ascertaining a client's legal income and preparedness for housing. Thus, even the more casual ILP interactions are still guided by caseworker questions, maintaining a level of conversational asymmetry.

These extended narratives, during ILP meetings, end with the filling out and signing of the ILP form. Excerpt 4 is taken from the end of an ILP meeting when the caseworker introduces the paperwork and fills it out with the client.

Excerpt 4: Conclusion of ILP Meeting

1.   CW: I'm gonna do a service plan <u>on</u> you. (.) It's gonna say <u>reactivate</u> public assistance, it's

2.   because you need to get your <u>PA</u> back on. because it's off, (.) follow shelter rules and

3.		regulations, and attend case management meetings with me (.)
4.		and I'm gonna be working a lot closer with you <u>now</u> (.) in order to- so
5.		we can try to move you <u>outta</u> here, <u>okay</u>?
6.	C:	(nods)
7.		**(.34)**
8.	CW:	you need a new <u>psych</u>.
9.	C:	hmm?
10.	CW:	you need a new psych. (.) a new psych.
11.		**(1.70) ((filling out paperwork for psychiatric evaluation))**
12.	CW:	°seven°(mumbles date under breath)
13.		**(1.50) ((typing))**
14.	CW:	So what do you do during the <u>daytime</u>?
15.	C:	Hmm?
16.	CW:	What are you doing in the day now?
17.	C:	In the day?
18.	CW:	Yes
19.	C:	Looking for <u>job</u>. In the <u>city</u>.
20.		**(3.10) ((typing))**
21.	CW:	So this is your new service plan. For this month, alright? **Because you told me** that you
22.		don't have no (.) **public <u>assistance</u> I <u>included</u>** that in this in this month you trying to
23.		activate your public assistance with them because you need to re<u>open</u> it in order for us
24.		to find you any type of <u>housing</u> for us to do any type of assistance right now your
25.		public assistance case is <u>closed</u>.
26.	C:	Right
27.	CW:	you need a new psych- psychiatric evaluation cause you had one- it's been-, you need a
28.		<u>new</u> one. o<u>kay</u>? so I'm going to schedule you for <u>that</u>.
29.	C:	a <u>new</u>, right?
30.	CW:	A <u>new</u> one. I have one but we need <u>another</u> one, cause you've been here three months
31.		it's time.
32.	C:	three <u>month</u>?
33.	CW:	yeah every three months you gotta <u>get</u> one of these. Follow shelter rules and
34.		regulations, attend case management meetings and reactivate your public assistance.
35.	C:	Alright
36.	CW:	Everything that's <u>highlighted</u> in the front we'll discuss here at the <u>back</u>. Client must
37.		Maintain (.) **benefits, entitlements**, this is basically going to <u>XXX</u>, getting your PA
38.		check turned back on I referred you already I already set up the appointment that's how
39.		I did all of that. (.) you'll keep the appointment made for you, You will comply
40.		with all the criteria for public assistance in order to get it <u>on</u>, you'll being all
41.		documentation your <u>referral</u> letter, and so forth and so forth, okay?
42.	C:	Right
43.	CW:	Follow shelter rules and regulations, (.) basically every month we have to do a new
44.		service <u>plan</u> and once we do in between the month just to make sure it's going <u>okay</u>.

45.		You must <u>sign</u> for your bed every night. If you don't sign for your bed every <u>night</u>,
46.		You gonna <u>lose</u> it, you know no fighting [no arguing]
47.	C:	[yeah yeah ye]ah=
48.	CW:	=no none of that. <u>alright</u>? Meet with me twice a week-, twice a <u>month</u> at least.
49.		If I need to see you more I'll send you more <u>appointments</u>. Okay?
50.		this is **the psychiatric evaluation, you need a <u>psych</u>**. I'll refer
51.		you to the psych you keep the appointment with the psych be <u>honest</u> with the psych
52.		and that's basically <u>it</u>. That's everything I've discussed here is highlighted in the <u>front</u>.
53.		If you have any questions you can ask <u>me</u> I need **you to <u>sign</u> it here and date it <u>there</u>**.

This excerpt begins with a phrase used with frequency in this shelter: "I'm gonna do a service plan on you." The use of "on" here underlines the asymmetrical relationship between the agent caseworker and the patient client, putting the client into a position of passive participation in which the preposition "on," is loosely synonymous with "about." This implies that the client is being written *about*, not actively involved in the writing and planning himself.

The prior construction of the service plan, which we also noted in excerpt 1 is alluded to here as well, as the caseworker states "it's gonna say reactivate public assistance." The use of the present participle ("is going") signals that the decision regarding what to include in the ILP has already been decided (line 1–2). Likewise she says "because you told me that you don't have no public assistance I included that in this month" (lines 21–22). The caseworker indicates here that she included acquiring public assistance on the ILP because he informed her during the meeting that he did not yet have public assistance. While the intake and housing meetings had clear introductions, making them transparent, the ILP meetings have no introductory sequence, thus obscuring the ways in which client talk is used in the meeting. Is client talk just to inform the caseworker, or do client admissions during the meeting turn into goals? The pre-construction of the ILP, as in excerpt 1, highlights the tension between efficiency and participation, routinization and individualization. Is the client participating in ILP construction if he is unaware that meeting talk will be translated into goal posts?

This excerpt also invokes policy language, and the caseworker reads requirements to the client verbatim. The client is asked to "follow shelter rules and regulations" (line 33, 43), "attend case management meetings" (line 44), "maintain benefits" (line 37), and "sign for your bed every night" (line 45). This clear use of policy language in the meeting inserts policy directly into the front line. This direct use of policy language brings the voice of the institution to the foreground of the meeting space.

While the intake and housing meetings revealed routines heavily structured by required shelter documentation, ILP meetings included more flexible routines. Without an opening sequence introducing the meeting as one guided by paperwork, the ILP introduced at the end of the meeting sometimes comes as a surprise to the client (from fieldnotes, 2006). Drawing on Brodkin (2011) and Lipsky (2010 [1980]) we suggest that these ILP meetings reveal the ways in which policy tools with particular goals have unintended outcomes. In this case we find a lack of transparency regarding the relationship between what is shared in the meeting and the paperwork introduced at the conclusion of the meeting. While over time a client's exposure to this approach may clarify the routine considerably, long-term clients with experience became frustrated and/or surprised with the relationship between their sharing and the goals set at the terminus of the meeting.

Flexible, Less Routinized Talk

In this final excerpt, we present an example of an interaction that is in no way guided by paperwork. While it includes examples of neoliberal discourses, we focus primarily on the stark shift in the turn type. This meeting begins with the caseworker asking the client to explain himself after a case conference (group session to help a client) turned verbally hostile.

Excerpt 5: Flexible Space for Discussion

```
 1.   C:    All the time I'm going there they say the sa:me thing. blah
 2.         blahblahblahblah. Oh [Mayor], yeah. It ain't
 3.         [Mayor]. (.) Come on. I ain't jum- you- they got
 4.         you jumping through hoops, I ain't jumping through no hoop.
 5.   CW:   Okay, well unfortunately. This is my job, so I have no
 6.         [choice
 7.   C:    [I'm not talking about you.
 8.   CW:   hhhhhhh ((laughs))
 9.   C:    I'm talking about her,=
10.   CW:   =right,
11.   C:    Cause the pressure's on her, right?=
12.   CW:   =right [the pressure's on basically all of us.]
39.   C:    mm-hmm
40.   CW:   So we have to put the pressure on you guys unfortunately
41.         you've been here for nine months, so: now the pressure's on.
42.         it's not like you've been here for si:x,=
```

Notably, there are no question–answer sequences in this excerpt. Rather this excerpt begins with a client-initiated critique of the city's mayor (lines 1–4). He makes a bureaucratic metaphorical reference (line 4), rejecting his engagement in the bureaucracy of the institution. The client suggests that the shelter administration is receiving pressure from the city (line 11), posing the suggestion as a question, and thereby flipping the normative question–answer script for these interactions. The caseworker answers (line 12), suggesting that everyone ("us") is under pressure from the city. The "pressure" here obliquely refers to performance measures required of all caseworkers ("us"), the term "the pressure" obscuring and generalizing the source of the pressure.

This "pressure" links both textually to time-based performance benchmarks (line 41–42) but also intertextually to references regarding speed and efficiency across earlier excerpts, confirming that speed and efficiency, while general coping strategies they may be, are also connected to NPM and neoliberal ways of thinking. The interaction is a collaborative enterprise, as they together create a narrative describing pressured conditions at the shelter. Their narrative is closely linked to time as a measure of performance and thus part of language of new managerialism focusing on efficiency and speeding up (Abramovitz and Zelnick 2015). Van Berkel (2013) has argued that recent policy developments have not only made the clients active, but also the professionals at the front line as well as the organizations implementing the policies. The pressure referred to by the case worker in the excerpt above is a case of triple activation, making the shelter organization, the case worker, and the client active in working towards limiting time spent at the shelter (Van Berkel 2013).

Discussion

Restricted Talk

Documentation created conversational blueprints for verbal interaction between the caseworkers and clients in intake assessments and housing application meetings, as well as psychosocial assessments (not shown). Extended client narratives were rare in the transcripts for these types of meetings, with the one exception "how did you become homeless," which could generate a longer answer. Both participants were constrained by documentation, though the question–answer structure asymmetrically favored the caseworker. Efficiency through routinization and brevity was emphasized. Given the emphasis on client-centeredness in social work (Rogers 1959), conversational asymmetries in these contexts are worth exploring.

There has been some debate about the extent to which social workers can maintain a "relational and narrative approach" (De Witte, Declercq, and Hermans 2015, 1249) when using computerized systems. De Witte et al. suggest it is possible. Our findings do not corroborate De Witte et al., though there are many other meetings and moments that are not focused on documentation over the course of a client's shelter stay. However, meetings focused around intake, psychosocial, and housing largely do not contain spaces for narrative and relational work.

Documentation as Participant

Substantial pauses brought attention to documentation as an interactional participant, albeit an inert one. This finding, in conjunction with question–answer sequences, highlights the ways in which policy and administration constrain casework practice. Drew and Heritage (1992) suggest that institutional interaction is marked by an orientation to "some core goal, task, or identity (or set of them) conventionally associated with the institution" (p. 22). Participants' talk is shaped by the orientation to those institutional norms. The space left in conversation for paperwork reveals both the caseworkers' and clients' orientations to paperwork. The caseworker refers directly to the paperwork, often quoting it directly, while the client's silence while paperwork is filled in is indicative of him waiting for the paperwork to finish and his next turn at talk.

Flexible Talk and Neoliberalism

Routinization was often collocated with efficiency and speed. The caseworker used routines to accelerate individual meetings in order to see as many clients as possible each day. These routinized meetings were transparent, but lacked rich client participation. In contrast, the ILP interactions were less scripted, including space for client narratives, but were less transparent. Both appear to have strength where the other lacks.

Conclusion

Soss et al. (2011) pose the question, "Does the business model function today as a dominant ideology, shaping the norms and worldviews of street-level workers?" (p. 199). Drawing on Goffman (1959), they argue that "if one focuses on the 'front stage' of organizational life, where public interactions and self-presentations play out, the answer would seem to be yes" (p. 199). We, likewise, found that front-line social worker–client interaction appears to include the ideology at the turn and word-level. Neoliberal ideology and NPM operate at a structural level in the meeting talk, by integrating documentation into the structure of interaction amidst a constellation of references to business principles and concepts. Question–answer sequences in bringing documentation to the foreground reveal structural routines in those interactions. Words like "as quickly as possible," "rapido," and "I don't want to waste too much of your time" connect that routine with efficiency and speed, neoliberal, new managerial tenets (Abramovitz and Zelnick 2015). The ILP meetings were likewise constrained by some question–answer sequences, as compared with the final excerpt, which showed more client-directed and perhaps insistent talk (Matarese and van Nijnatten 2015). If policy is indeed put into practice through street-level bureaucrats, then we need more research detailing the ways in which these neoliberal policies manifest themselves in front-line service delivery.

Some scholars argue that front-line practitioners who are working in institutions with few resources and "selective" performance benchmarks on which they are assessed "may go to great lengths to discourage voice, claims making, and the assertion of rights, avoiding – even suppressing – efforts by individuals to discuss their needs and life circumstances" (Brodkin and Marston 2013, 29). Evidence from our study suggests that while we cannot discount the overt and intentional suppression of client voice by workers (an analysis that would require a focus on different discourse features), we have shown that the agent of that vocal suppression is, at least in some degree, the required paperwork that together with performance assessments, benchmarks, and a large caseload makes discursive deviation from documentation challenging. Future research should consider exploring more deeply whether and how voice is suppressed in street-level work, using discourse and conversation analysis as a tool to, for example, look at the *type* of interruptions in these meetings, changes of topic, control of topic, and other language and discourse choices that might convey the suppression of voice.

Appendix: Transcription Conventions (Hutchby and Wooffitt 2008)

(1.8) Pause. The number represents duration of the pause in seconds, to one decimal place. A pause of less than 0.2 seconds is marked by (.)

[] Overlap with a portion of another speaker's utterance.

= Latch: no time lapse between two utterances, used when a second speaker begins their utterance just at the moment when the first speaker finishes.

: Extended sound.

(hm, hh) Onomatopoetic representations of the audible exhalation of air.

.hh Audible inhalation of air. The more h's, the longer the in-breath.

? Rising intonation.

. Falling intonation.

, Continuation of tone.

– Abrupt cut off, speaker stops speaking suddenly.

↑↓ Sharply rising or falling intonation. The arrow is placed just before the syllable in which the change in intonation occurs.

Under Speaker emphasis on the underlined portion of the word.

CAPS Higher volume than the speaker's normal volume.

° Utterance is much softer than the normal speech of the speaker. This symbol will appear at the beginning and at the end of the utterance in question.

> <, < > Noticeably faster (>faster talk<), or slower (<slower talk>) than the surrounding talk.

(would) Transcriber has guessed as to what was said, because it was indecipherable on the tape. If the transcriber was unable to guess what was said, nothing appears within the parentheses.

(XXXX) Indistinguishable speech.

Bibliography

Abramovitz, M., and Zelnick, J. (2015). Privatization in the Human Services: Implications for Direct Practice. *Clinical Social Work Journal*, 43(3), 283–293.

Brodkin, E. Z. (2008). Accountability in Street-level Organizations. *International Journal of Public Administration*, 31(3), 317–336.

Brodkin, E. Z. (2011). Policy Work: Street-level Organizations under New Managerialism. *Journal of Public Administration Research and Theory*, 21(suppl 2), i253–i277.

Brodkin, E., and Marston, G. (Eds.) (2013). *Work and the Welfare State: Street-level Organizations and Workfare Politics*. Washington, DC: Georgetown University Press.

Buttny, R. (1993) *Social Accountability in Communication*. Thousand Oaks, CA: Sage.

Caswell, D., Marston, G., and Larsen, J. E. (2010). Unemployed Citizen or "at Risk" Client? Classification Systems and Employment Services in Denmark and Australia. *Critical Social Policy*, August 30, 384–404.

De Witte, J., Declercq, A., and Hermans, K. (2015). Street-Level Strategies of Child Welfare Social Workers in Flanders: The Use of Electronic Client Records in Practice. *British Journal of Social Work*. First published online: September 8, 2015. doi:10.1093/bjsw/bcv076

Department of Homeless Services (DHS) (2002). *The Second Decade of Reform: A Strategic Plan for New York City's Homeless Services*. New York. Retrieved March 2005 from: www.ci.nyc.ny.us/html/dhs/downloads/pdf/stratplan.pdf

Department of Homeless Services (DHS) (2004). *Uniting for Solutions beyond Shelter: The Action Plan for New York City*. New York: New York City Department of Homeless Services Presses.

Diefenbach, T. (2009). New Public Management in Public Sector Organizations: The Dark Sides of Managerialistic "Enlightenment." *Public Administration*, 87, 892–909.

Drew, P., and Heritage, J. (1992). *Talk at Work: Interaction in Institutional Settings* (Studies in Interactional Sociolinguistics 8). New York: Cambridge University Press.

Evans, T. (2011). Professionals, Managers and Discretion: Critiquing Street-level Bureaucracy. *British Journal of Social Work*, 41(2), 368–386.

Fairclough, N. (2000). Discourse, Social Theory and Social Research: The Discourse of Welfare Reform. *Journal of Sociolinguistics*, 2(4), 163–195.

Garfinkel, H. (1967). *Studies in Ethnomethodology*. Englewood Cliffs, NJ: Prentice-Hall.

Goffman, E. (1959) *The Presentation of Self in Everyday Life*. New York: Anchor Books.

Gray, J. (2012). Neoliberalism, Celebrity and Aspirational Content in English Language Teaching Textbooks for the Global Market. In D. Block, J. Gray, and M. Holborow (Eds.), *Neoliberalism and Applied Linguistics*. New York: Routledge.

Gray, J., and Block, D. (2012). The Marketization of Language Teacher Education and Neoliberalism: Characteristics, Consequences, and Future Prospects. In D. Block, J. Gray, and M. Holborow (Eds.), *Neoliberalism and Applied Linguistics*. New York: Routledge.

Halliday, M. A., and Hasan, R. (1976). *Cohesion in English*. London: Longman.

Harvey, D. (2005). *A Brief History of Neoliberalism*. Oxford: Oxford University Press.

Heritage, J., Elliott, M., Beckett, M., and Wilkes, M. 2007. Reducing Patients' Unmet Concerns: The Difference One Word Can Make. *Journal of General Internal Medicine*, 22, 1429–1433.

Hjörne, E., Juhila, K., and van Nijnatten, C. (2010). Negotiating Dilemmas in the Practices of Street-level Welfare Work. *International Journal of Social Welfare*, 19(3), 303–309.

Høybye-Mortensen, M. (2015). Decision-Making Tools and Their Influence on Caseworkers' Room for Discretion. *British Journal of Social Work*, 45(2), 600–615.

Holborow, M. (2012). Neoliberal Keywords and the Contradictions of an Ideology. In D. Block, J. Gray, and M. Holborow (Eds.). *Neoliberalism and Applied Linguistics*. New York: Routledge.

Hutchby, I., and Wooffitt, R. (2008). *Conversation Analysis*. London: Polity.

Jefferson, G. (1984). Notes on Some Orderlinesses of Overlap Onset. *Discourse Analysis and Natural Rhetoric*, 500, 11–38.

Latour, B. (1999). On Recalling ANT. *The Sociological Review*, 47(S1), 15–25.

Lipsky, M. (2010 [1980]). *Street-Level Bureaucracy, 30th Ann. Ed.: Dilemmas of the Individual in Public Service: Dilemmas of the Individual in Public Service*. New York: Russell Sage Foundation.

Matarese, M. (2009). Help Me Help You: Reciprocal Responsibility in Caseworker–Client Interaction. Paper presented at DANASWAC Conference Gent 20, August 2009.

Matarese, M. (2012). Getting Placed in Time: Responsibility Talk in Caseworker–Client Interaction. *Journal of Applied Linguistics and Professional Practice*, 9(3), 319–340.

Matarese, M., and Caswell, D. (2014). Accountability. In C. Hall, K. Juhila, M. Matarese, and C. van Nijnatten (Eds.), *Analysing Social Work Communication: Discourse in Practice*. New York: Routledge.

Matarese, M., and Caswell, D. (forthcoming). "I'm Gonna Ask You about Yourself, So I Can Put It on Paper": Analysing Street-Level Bureaucracy through Form-Related Talk in Social Work. *British Journal of Social Work* (forthcoming).

Matarese, M., and van Nijnatten, C. (2015). Making a Case for Client Insistence in Social Work Interaction. *Discourse Processes*, 52, 670–688.

Maynard-Moody, S. W., and Musheno, M. C. (2003). *Cops, Teachers, Counsellors: Stories from the Front Lines of Public Service*. Minnesota: University of Michigan Press.

Peck, J. (2010). *Constructions of Neoliberal Reason*. Oxford: Oxford University Press.

Pomerantz, A. (1984). Agreeing and Disagreeing with Assessments: Some Features of Preferred/Dispreferred Turn Shaped. In J. Atkinson and J. Heritage (Eds.), *Structures of Social Action*. Cambridge: Cambridge University Press.

Ritzer, G. (2007). *The McDonaldization of Society*. Thousand Oaks, CA: Sage Publications.

Rogers, C. R. (1959). A Theory of Therapy, Personality and Interpersonal Relationships, as Developed in the Client-Centered Framework. In S. Koch (Ed.), *Psychology: A Study of a Science* (Vol. 3). New York: McGraw-Hill.

Sacks, H. (1992). *Lectures on Conversation*, 2 vols, ed. G. Jefferson. Malden, MA: Blackwell Publishing.

Schegloff, E. A. (1987). Between Micro and Macro: Contexts and Other Connections. In J. Alexander (Ed.), *The Micro-Macro Link*. Berkeley: University of California Press.

Schegloff, E. A. (2007). *Sequence Organization in Interaction: Volume 1: A Primer in Conversation Analysis*. Cambridge: Cambridge University Press.

Scollon, R., and Scollon, S. W. (2004). *Nexus Analysis: Discourse and the Emerging Internet*. New York: Routledge.

Scourfield, P. (2007). Social Care and the Modern Citizen: Client, Consumer, Service User, Manager and Entrepreneur. *British Journal of Social Work*, 37(1), 107–122.

Scourfield, P. (2015). Even Further beyond Street-Level Bureaucracy: The Dispersal of Discretion Exercised in Decisions Made in Older People's Care Home Reviews. *British Journal of Social Work*, 45, 914–931.

Soss, J., Fording, R., and Schram, S. F. (2011). The Organization of Discipline: From Performance Management to Perversity and Punishment . *Journal of Public Administration Research and Theory*, 21(suppl 2), i203–i232.

Urciuoli, B. (2010). Neoliberal Education: Preparing the Student for the New Workplace. In C. J. Greenhouse (Ed.), *Ethnographies of Neoliberalism*. Philadelphia: University of Pennsylvania Press.

Van Berkel, R. (2013). Triple Activation: Introducing Welfare-to-Work into Dutch Social Assistance. In E. Brodkin and G. Marston (Eds.), *Work and the Welfare State. Street-level Organizations and Workfare Politics*. Washington, DC: Georgetown University Press.

Waring, H. Z. (2011). Learner Initiatives and Learning Opportunities. *Classroom Discourse*, 2(2), 201–218.

White, S., Hall, C. and Peckover, S. (2008). The Descriptive Tyranny of the Common Assessment Framework: Technologies of Categorization and Professional Practice in Child Welfare. *British Journal of Social Work*, 39(7), 1197–1217.

PART III

The Neoliberal Disciplinary Regime

Policing Indentured Citizens

8

CRIMINAL JUSTICE PREDATION AND NEOLIBERAL GOVERNANCE

Joshua Page and Joe Soss

In March 2015, the US Department of Justice (DOJ) reported that the city of Ferguson, Missouri had been operating a "predatory system of government." Police were acting as street-level enforcers for a program that used fines and fees to extract resources from poor communities of color and deliver them to municipal coffers. Black residents made up 90 percent of those ticketed for public safety violations and, with the city averaging three warrants per household, fines and fees became almost-universal experiences for poor, black residents.

Under sharp fiscal pressures, city leaders had chosen to offset revenue losses on the backs of poor and working-class black residents. The DOJ Report concludes:

> Ferguson's law enforcement practices are shaped by the City's focus on revenue rather than by public safety needs. ... The City budgets for sizeable increases in municipal fines and fees each year, exhorts police and court staff to deliver those revenue increases, and closely monitors whether those increases are achieved.
>
> *(DOJ 2015, p. 2)*

Payments were pursued so aggressively that they made up one-fifth of the city's entire revenue base in 2013, an 80 percent increase over just two years prior (DOJ 2015).

To generate sustained revenues, Ferguson officials used criminal justice practices to construct and exploit long-term financial debts. Even when subjected to minor fines and fees, Ferguson residents often became ensnared in a perpetual debt trap that led to new entanglements with the courts, additional fines and fees, endless payments on interest and, in some cases, debt-based imprisonment – any or all of which could have ruinous life consequences (DOJ 2015).

"How could this be?" many journalists and public officials asked in shock. The entire story struck many as deeply un-American, and sharply at odds with how governance normally works in the United States. Against this view, we argue that the regime uncovered in Ferguson was no anomaly. Instead, it points us toward practices that are widespread, longstanding, and worthy of far more critical analysis than they have received. In this regard, we advance three main arguments.

First, what the DOJ discovered in Ferguson is not exceptional in relation to the past or present of US governance. Race-, class-, and gender-targeted predation has been a central and enduring theme in American state and nation building, in the structure of our political economy, and in the varied forms of social domination that define American life.

Second, predatory strategies for extracting resources from subjugated communities shift over time, generally reflecting the broader political rationalities of their era. Today, they function as an essential but poorly understood element of *neoliberal* governance.

Third, predation is more than just a repressive taking of freedoms and resources from subordinated groups. It is also a productive force that constructs power relations, subject positions, and terms of civic standing. Among other things, it produces what we call the "indentured citizen."

In what follows, we analyze a complex of criminal justice practices that we conceptualize as predatory, ranging from fine-centered policing to court fees, bail systems, prison charges, civil asset forfeiture, and beyond. These criminal justice practices operate today alongside payday loans, subprime auto financing, toxic credit card deals, for-profit universities, and other efforts to generate revenues by leveraging the vulnerabilities, needs, and aspirations of subjugated communities (e.g., Rivlin 2010; Fergus 2017). Indeed, far from being isolated, they reflect broader shifts in governance that originate and extend beyond the criminal justice arena itself.

Our aim in this chapter is to clarify the origins, operations, and consequences of financial predation in the criminal justice field today. The neoliberal era of governance has been marked by a resurgence and transformation of state predation on poor communities of color. On one side, we argue that scholars and citizens will misunderstand state predation in America today if we fail to theorize its neoliberal character. On the other side, we argue that scholars and citizens will misunderstand neoliberalism in the USA today if we fail to analyze its distinctive predatory forms.

Political Economy, Predation, and Contract

To develop these arguments, we begin from a distinction between contract and predatory conceptions of the state and, more broadly, the political economy. This contrast is often attributed to Douglass North (1981) and invoked to describe Charles Tilly's (1992) "protection racket" model of the resource-extracting state.

More generally, however, the distinction expresses a contrast between broadly liberal views of the state and more critical accounts that begin from the state's role in structures of domination.

Contract conceptions of the state can be traced back to the European social contract theorists of the early modern period. They supply the liberal-democratic image of the state that frames most mainstream studies of US government today. The contract state is grounded in the consent of the governed. Its officials claim to be representative of the public, and they are subject to legitimate criticism for failures in this regard. The contract state fosters economic development in classic liberal fashion – through establishment of property rights, enforcement of contracts, investments in collective infrastructure, and so on. It relates to the people in a manner that is supportive of the *liberal equalities* of democratic citizenship, on one side, and the *liberal inequalities* of market economies, on the other. It funds its own operations through systems of taxation that are accepted as legitimate preconditions for these desired arrangements – "the price of civilization" (Sachs 2012).

In contrast, predatory conceptions of the state begin from a conflict perspective. In this view, resource extraction is a precondition of state making and governance. First, the need for revenues draws the state directly into expropriative projects and creates a structural disposition to serve the interests of capital growth and investment (on which tax revenues depend). Second, although dominant groups may be subject to effective political opposition, they typically shape state action in ways that enrich and protect them at the expense of subordinate groups. Third, in the civic realm, state practices distinguish and empower members of the dominant strata as the "real citizens," who are set apart by the civic exclusion and subordination of other groups.

North's distinction is helpful for summarizing some very broad contrasts in theories of the state. But as a framework for understanding concrete relations and practices, we argue that his account of predation is, in many ways, underdeveloped. Stronger resources for this task can be found in the writings of scholars who have been more marginalized in the academy. Beyond the confines of liberal political economy, particularly helpful historical and theoretical insights can be found in Black Marxist scholarship interrogating what Cedric Robinson calls the history of "racial capitalism"; in feminist scholarship on domestic labor expropriation and social reproduction; and in the burgeoning scholarship on settler colonialism as a racialized project in liberal societies.

Two points of contrast help clarify the significance of this shift. First, for North and many other liberal institutionalists, contract and predatory states are opposites. At a given point in time, a state is, in essence, either one or the other. As a historical matter, North seeks to explain how institutional changes eventually banish predation, produce liberal progress, and establish a contract state (see e.g., North and Weingast 1989). By contrast, scholars such as W. E. B. Du Bois (1935) and Manning Marable (1981) shift our attention from the "essential nature" of the state to a lower level of operations. By focusing on concrete social relations, they provide guidance for empirical analyses of predatory and contractual *governing practices*.

Second, North encourages scholars to ask how contractual institutions work and, separately, how predatory institutions work. By contrast, scholars such as Carole Pateman and Charles Mills (2007) advocate investigating their interplay, asking how the prevailing terms of social contract may presume predation and be organized around the reproduction and advancement of domination.

Indeed, the entwining of predatory and contractual practices is an abiding theme in the history of American political and economic development. In the early Republic, "the growth of a prosperous, liberal democratic society of Anglo-Americans" was made possible by "a predatory state that financed white liberal society through its ruthless exploitation of Indian lands and African American labor" (Young and Meiser 2008, pp. 31–32). Wealth accumulation and national development advanced through practices of dispossession and work enforcement targeting Mexicans in the Southwest (Gonzalez 2013; Rana 2010) and through the extraction of Chinese labor for mining and railroad construction (Takaki 1998; Jacobson 2001). Labor predation operated as well through "bastardy laws," which, for most of US history, transformed the children of unmarried parents (disproportionately poor people of color) into indentured "apprentice laborers" for white land- and business-owners (Gustafson 2016).

The post-Reconstruction era saw the rise of infamous new predatory practices in America, from debt peonage and sharecropping to prison industries and convict leasing. Sharecropping practices extracted labor under exploitative market arrangements secured through inescapable debt. The state held this system in place through laws forbidding wage competition among landowners, the policing of black "idleness" and "vagrancy," brutal violence carried out or permitted by local authorities, and aggressive state enforcement of debtor payments to private creditors (Wright 1997). Likewise, in the wake of the 13th and 14th Amendments, crime and punishment became the basis for a post-slavery system of coercive labor extraction orchestrated by state authority. In the North, "prison industries" turned carceral facilities into factories, and inmates into captive labor pools generating private profits. In the South, chain gangs and convict-leasing contracts were used to reconstruct key elements of the old slavery and plantation arrangements (McLennan 2008; Oshinsky 1997).

Such practices persisted well into the twentieth century. And by mid-century, new and varied practices emerged around the construction of hyper-segregated residential ghettos. Redlining intersected with other state and market practices to exclude black families from conventional home mortgage markets (Massey and Denton 1993). As these practices created long-term inequalities of housing and wealth, they also constructed a powerful opening for predation in the form of contract-to-deed home purchase markets (Satter 2010). "Urban renewal" initiatives – decried as "Negro removal" – advanced a new wave of dispossession targeting black residents of American cities in order to advance state projects and enrich white investors (Pritchett 2003).

The relevant history is too vast to recount here, but this brief discussion suffices to make our point: Liberal development of civil, political, and social citizenship in America has been deeply entwined with shifting practices of predation targeted by race, class, and gender. In many respects, we argue, these practices should be seen as the pre-history of criminal justice predation today. To say this is to suggest that scholars misunderstand criminal justice predation today when we view it – as many do – solely through the narrow lens of crime and punishment. To see the deeper social and political significance of these criminal justice practices, one must locate them in relation to broader developments in the American political economy.

The Neoliberal Character of Criminal Justice Predation Today

The modes of predation carried out through criminal justice practices today share four key features with earlier regimes of predatory governance in the United States: First, they are targeted mechanisms of resource extraction, organized by race, class, and gender, guided by their social and spatial coordinates, and enmeshed in the reproduction of dominant–subordinate relations. Second, they are pursued by a mix of state and market actors under enabling conditions defined by government institutions, laws, and policies. Third, they advance through the construction of *predation opportunity structures* – frameworks that convert the needs, vulnerabilities, and aspirations of subjugated populations into revenue opportunities that can be leveraged for financial extraction. And fourth, they operate – more successfully in some cases than others, to be sure – as mechanisms of state building and maintenance and as bases of accumulation and citizenship for dominant groups.

Now as in the past, however, predation operates as an element of (and thus, adapts to and reflects) the prevailing political rationality of its era. In the United States today, we believe this ordering of the political economy is best thought of as neoliberal in character. Like Wendy Brown (2015) and others, we do not conceptualize neoliberalism as a break with the past. Neoliberalism is not *post-liberalism*. Rather, it is a reweaving of liberalism itself that intensifies some of its elements at the expense of others. Through the concept of neoliberalism, we aim to connect the past and present of liberalism – with an eye toward change and continuity – not to suggest that recent developments are unprecedented.

Broadly speaking, neoliberalism refers to the extension of market rationalities across an expanding range of social, economic, and political relations. Across fields, actors are refigured as *Homo oeconomicus* and positioned in relations of exchange and competition (Dilts 2011). Today, individuals, governments, nonprofits, and a host of other actors are all expected to make prudent choices that enhance their own capacities and lead to a desirable "return on investment" (Schram 2015). Success and failure, deservingness and moral worth, civic standing, and institutional performance are all evaluated in ways that turn market criteria into normative ideals or, conversely, legitimate grounds for condemnation (Brown 2015).

Within the state and across state-led practices, we find that operations in one arena after another have been redesigned to reflect market principles, service corporate interests, enforce market participation, and create new arenas for profitable investment (Soss, Fording, and Schram 2011). Thus, reforms since the 1970s have rolled back the market-constraining effects of state regulations and the welfare state (Harvey 2005; Block and Somers 2014). They have redeployed and expanded state powers for creating markets, absorbing market costs, marketizing public endeavors, and pursuing market-supporting disciplinary projects (Wacquant 2010; Peck and Theodore 2012).

At the most basic level, today's predatory criminal justice practices can be understood as the convergence of two broader trends in the neoliberalization of governance. On one side, they have emerged as part of a broader migration of governmental functions into criminal justice systems. Loïc Wacquant (2010), Bernard Harcourt (2011), Forrest Stuart (2016), and others have stressed how police, courts, and prisons have become repositories for diverse social problems and governmental agendas in recent decades, growing ever more central to governance in a wide variety of domains. With prisons now the largest public mental health facilities (Swanson 2015) and police serving as the frontlines for numerous social interventions (Lyons 2002; Stuart 2016), perhaps the most widely discussed example concerns the traditional functions of the welfare state. In a similar manner, the revenue functions of tax systems are now migrating into policing, judicial, and carceral systems.

On the other side, the turn toward predatory criminal justice practices in local governance can be seen as part of the broader proliferation of what David Harvey (2003, 2005) calls "accumulation by dispossession." Building on traditional Marxian theories of primitive accumulation (Luxemburg 2003 [1913]; Nichols 2015; Ince 2016), Harvey's analysis (2003, 2005) focuses attention on how neoliberalism rhetorically celebrates free-market exchange but advances through the use of state and market powers to forcibly expropriate resources from subordinated groups who are poorly positioned to resist.

At the intersection of these two dynamics, governments and corporations deploy criminal justice practices today as powerful tools of revenue extraction. Consider the fines and fees imposed by police, courts, and prisons, which stand at the center of Alexes Harris's book, *A Pound of Flesh* (2016). About 10 million Americans, disproportionately poor people of color, owe about $50 billion in debt due to criminal justice fines and fees in America today – and make nearly $40 billion in payments on their legal financial obligations each year (Bach 2015; Lind 2015). At the courthouse, officials in many states now charge defendants extra fees to exercise their right to a jury trial, and most states now permit courts to demand fees from defendants who exercise their right to a public defender. For many of these defendants, court involvement also results in substantial additional fees associated with bail. And for those who go to prison, the charges have only just begun. Today, all fifty states defray prison costs by charging prisoners some form of pay-to-stay fees (Brennan Center 2016). Generally these "user" fees focus on room and board, but in some states they extend to medical care and clothing (Shapiro 2016). Beyond the prison walls, probation and parole have also been restructured to generate revenues for state and local governments. In Massachusetts, for example, state collections bring in over $20 million per year from monthly probation fees alone (Massachusetts Trial Court Fines and Fees Working Group 2016).

Nationwide, reports suggest that fines and fees make up as much as 40 percent of annual revenues in some municipalities. Indeed, in the state of Missouri, Ferguson is far from the most dependent municipality: Down the road, Pine Lawn brings in more than 62 percent of its revenue from criminal justice (Better Together 2015). A lawsuit filed in 2016 by the ArchCity Defenders describes the operation in nearby Florrisant (*Plaintiffs v. The City of Florrisant* 2016, pp. 3, 23):

> In 2015, the City collected more than $2,300,000 in court fines and fees and forfeited bond payments, down from [the four preceding years]. The cost to operate the City's Municipal Court, by contrast, was budgeted at roughly $700,000 per year between 2011 and 2015. The City thus netted as much as $2,200,000 in 2011 and still netted $1,600,000 even in its least profitable year. The City's only sources of greater revenue are sales and utility taxes.

Or consider Civil Asset Forfeiture (CAF), a practice that emerged out of the War on Drugs in the 1980s and expanded in the 1990s. CAF allows authorities to seize assets they suspect may be connected to a criminal activity. The burden of proof is then on the owner to show, through a costly court challenge, that the assets have no criminal history. Between 2001 and 2014, an estimated $2.1 billion in assets were seized from Americans *who were not charged with a crime* (Ingraham 2014). In 2013 alone, the police seized assets worth roughly $1.1 billion (Ingraham 2014). An investigative report by *The Chicago Reader* revealed that from 2009 to 2015 the Chicago Police Department brought in nearly $72 million in cash and assets through CAF, retaining about $47 million for itself and sharing the rest of the bounty with the Cook County state's attorney's office and the Illinois State Police. CAF funds were used to finance day-to-day operations and "to secretly purchase controversial surveillance equipment without public scrutiny or City Council oversight" (Handley, Helsby, and Martinez 2016).

Surveying this national landscape, Mary Katzenstein and Maureen Waller (2015, p. 639) conclude that criminal justice institutions today function as a sprawling system for "taxing the poor" through "government seizure." Indeed, Ordower, Sandoval, and Warren (2016, p. 18) argue that in the state of Missouri revenue functions have become so paramount that many criminal justice practices now arguably represent the "exercise of the taxing rather than the policing power of the municipality" and, thus, violate the state's limits on local adjustments of taxes. The authors conclude that criminal justice predation has advanced so far that "the underlying question becomes whether an offender is an offender at all or merely a target wearing a dollar sign" (Ordower, Sandoval, and Warren 2016, p. 24). Rewritten as a neoliberal mode of governance, criminal justice operations today advance "accumulation by dispossession" in a manner that absorbs tax-like revenue functions – and in the process, reconstructs the criminal justice field itself.

The neoliberal turn may be seen equally in a second set of powerful dynamics: the predatory uses of criminal justice to create profitable market opportunities and marketize the state. Policing and punishment have become sites for endless governmental, for-profit, and non-profit efforts to secure moneymaking opportunities. Indeed, resource extraction from legally entangled groups can fairly be described today as a site of dynamic innovation, marked by continual efforts to locate or build new engines of revenue. Through this process, market actors become lodged in core functions of the state; the state becomes reliant on market actors whose cooperation must be induced through profits; and market logics and practices migrate into the everyday operations of public institutions.

Imprisonment in the United States offers a striking example. Today, corporate prison contracts represent a $5 billion industry in the criminal justice field. The leading firm Corrections Corporation of America (CCA, recently rebranded CoreCivic) has been in the prison business since the early 1980s. For three decades, CCA rode the wave of mass incarceration to remarkable levels of growth and profit. As continued carceral growth became less certain in recent years, CCA sought out new opportunities for profit in the area of immigration detention (Wofford 2014). To extend their market reach, CCA officials then worked to convert the detention of women and children seeking asylum into a profitable new market – successfully arguing to the Department of Homeland Security that detention could function as "an aggressive deterrence strategy" to dissuade future asylum seekers (Harlan 2016).

Critics often single out "private prisons" run by companies like CCA, decrying their profit-driven abuses as distinct from practices in "public prisons." Indeed, this was precisely the contrast drawn by Obama administration officials in August 2016, when the US Department of Justice announced that it would begin to "phase out" contracts for the comparatively small number of privately run prisons at the federal level. Framing the decision as a choice between state and market institutions – and citing problems related to poor service provision, administrative costs, and safety and security in the for-profit lock-ups – Deputy Attorney General Sally Yates explained that "these steps would be neither possible nor desirable without the Bureau's superb and consistent work at our own facilities" (Yates 2016).

The announcement was a striking piece of political dramaturgy, performing and shoring up ideological distinctions between state and market. Market profiteering is a social problem, it suggested; government prisons offer an alternative we should embrace as a solution. In reality, however, government prisons today are shot through with arrangements that generate revenues for a blend of public and private institutions. Throughout America's public prisons, for-profit providers prey on captive markets by charging extensive fees to prisoners and their kin for phone calls, video visitation, care packages, prisoner transportation, banking, health care, food, commissary, and education. Public facilities routinely contract out their basic operations in areas such as security, drug treatment, and officer training. Looking deeper still, one finds that many of the nation's "public prisons" are actually designed by private architects, built by private contractors, and financed with bonds underwritten and purchased by the biggest private banks (Sorkin 2013). As Christopher Petrella (2016) rightly explained in the *Boston Review*: "To believe that Yate's directive represents a sea change ... one would have to believe in a deep material distinction between 'public' and 'private' prisons. In reality, this boundary does not exist."

Consider, for example, the arrangements that allow prisoners to sustain connections with their families, friends, and broader communities. In most prisons today, a single telecommunications company is given monopoly control over phone systems, which they leverage to charge exorbitant per-minute rates for phone calls to and from inmates (FCC 2015). The annual value of this industry is estimated at $1.2 billion, generating commissions (or "kickbacks") of more than $460 million for public and private carceral institutions per year (Bunn 2015).

Over the past decade, commercial firms have cultivated markets for prison- and jail-based video interfaces. By arguing that longstanding practices of free, in-person visitation posed security risks, firms channeled social needs for connection into more profitable digital formats. Fee-based video visitation is now replacing free personal visits in many prisons around the country, and JPay Corp has recently extended the model by introducing the "videogram" – a service that allows people on the outside to send thirty-second cell phone videos to prisoners for a fee. JPay maximizes demand for the service by continually sending people reminders of how much it would mean to their loved one inside to receive a personalized video. In this manner, gendered ethics of care are leveraged to produce monetary gains for both JPay *and* state governments, which receive commissions from the company.

Such innovations in the criminal justice field frequently mimic the broader business strategies market firms have developed to pursue what Devin Fergus (2014, 2017) calls "financial fracking" in poor communities. From payday loans to furniture rentals, variable-rate credit cards, and subprime mortgages and auto loans, corporations have devised a remarkable array of predatory techniques that demonstrate how the limited resources in low-income communities can be leveraged in profitable ways. In storefronts throughout America's most disadvantaged communities, one finds "service providers" leveraging social vulnerabilities to move poor people into potentially lucrative contractual arrangements. Here as in the criminal justice field, companies aggressively charge fees not simply to cover operating costs but to generate profit streams. These debt-and-interest schemes are structured so that poor people, without the resources needed to erase the principal, are compelled to make ongoing payments.

In these and other respects, financial predation in the criminal justice arena mirrors predatory market practices more generally. Working creatively within this field, a diverse array of public and private actors work to establish new mechanisms for generating returns on investment. But it is not enough to say that practical operations in the field today follow a neoliberal logic. It is equally important to understand how neoliberal political forces and policy agendas explain, as a historical matter, financialization of the field itself.

A Neoliberal Creation

The financialization of criminal justice practices has grown both wider and deeper over the past twenty-five years, with a burst of onset in the early-to-mid-1990s and a period of rapid expansion during the Great Recession that started in 2007. From 1991 to 2004, prisoners reporting legal financial obligations grew from 25 to 66 percent (CEA 2015). From 1990 to 2014, states charging offenders for probation and parole supervision rose from twenty-six to forty-four (CEA 2015). Over this same period, uses of civil asset forfeiture grew dramatically, as did the rates and levels at which courts imposed monetary bail (CEA 2015).

To explain how these developments emerged, it is helpful to begin with two insights from scholarship on neoliberalism. First, as Jamie Peck (2010) argues, the varied forms of neoliberal governance do not emerge from a single master blueprint but rather through the creative coping strategies of actors on the ground. It is surely true that some neoliberal reforms began as carefully worked out ideological agendas. But, as Peck (2010) points out, we have for some time now lived in a condition of "zombie neoliberalism" in which new developments are driven less by the dreams of a Friedrich Hayek or Milton Friedman than by the ongoing need to cope with the disruptions generated by neoliberal policies themselves.

Marketizing reforms repeatedly generate crises, Peck argues, which then create pressures and opportunities for new rounds of innovation. In this sense, neoliberal governance advances through efforts to manage what Fred Block and Margaret Somers (2014, drawing on Karl Polanyi) describe as the instability and unsustainability of utopian, market-fundamentalist schemes. Such coping tactics reconfigure neoliberal governance, in the criminal justice field as in many others, but generally in ways that lead to new tensions, problems, and modes of resistance.

Second, for explanatory purposes, it is important to accurately define a recent shift in criminal justice predation. As described earlier, it is simply not true that, in the USA, the 1990s marked the onset of predatory practice in the criminal justice field. The historical difference is that – from slave patrols to the convict leasing system and beyond – criminal codes and practices primarily have been used to facilitate *labor* extraction. What is more novel in the contemporary scene, and what must be explained, is the extent to which criminal justice predation has been *financialized*.

Posed in this way, efforts to explain the recent trajectory of the criminal justice field clearly fit into a broader line of analysis in the study of neoliberalism. Since the 1970s, a broad array of policy reforms in the United States have financialized government operations and obligations in piecemeal ways designed to manage structural contradictions and crises. From this perspective, the financialization of criminal justice predation appears far less distinctive. Indeed, it reflects what Greta Krippner (2011) describes as the paradigmatic coping mechanism of neoliberalism: the dissipation of state crisis through the financialization of state functions and practices.

To understand the growth of financial predation in America's criminal justice systems, one must begin – not inside the criminal justice field itself – but with the construction of what a 2012 Pew report called "the local squeeze." In the last decades of the twentieth century, a number of political and policy developments combined to produce immense fiscal pressures on local governments. Since the 1970s, neoliberal reforms have devolved a wide range of functions and responsibilities to lower levels of government (Donahue 1999). At the same time, a number of policy changes combined to deprive local governments of the resources needed to meet these obligations.

Pro-market reforms concentrated wealth and income at the top of the social order and shielded corporations and the affluent from taxation (Hacker and Pierson 2010). After California passed Proposition 13 in 1978, all but four of the fifty American states imposed restrictions on local governments that further limited their ability to raise taxes. Local governments borrowed to meet their rising revenue needs and, through a variety of new bond and credit strategies, took on large interest-bearing debts that eventually proved tremendously costly in their own right. And then, when the Great Recession hit, these chronic shortfalls were transformed into a full-blown fiscal catastrophe. As the housing bubble burst and the economy went into a tailspin, local governments suffered dramatic declines in state aid, property taxes, and sales taxes. By 2009, state aid and property taxes together covered a smaller share of local expenditures than at any time since the Census began tracking these funds in 1972. Then, in fiscal year 2010, local governments lost an additional $25 billion in state aid and property tax revenues.

With powerful forces arrayed against raising taxes or federalizing responsibilities, municipalities found themselves in an unsustainable position they had little ability to change (Ludwig 2015). To understand how they coped, we must turn to a second leg of our explanation: the racialized politics of criminality and the pursuit of social order through expanded practices of policing and incarceration that are signature characteristics of the American neoliberal state (Wacquant 2010). We need not rehearse here the broad bipartisan political story of the carceral turn – from the war on crime, through the war on drugs, to broken windows policing, and the rest. It suffices to note that, by the 1990s, a large and growing system for policing, adjudication, and incarceration was in place. Moreover, the 1990s was a particularly intense decade of moral panic over "underclass pathologies," driven by powerful discourses of social disorder and calls to get tough on crime and other "bad behaviors."

Political pressures to crack down on the "undeserving" combined with limited local control over sentencing, probation, and parole to make it exceedingly difficult for municipal officials to cope with their fiscal crisis by cutting investments in public safety and crime management (an austerity-politics response more common for social services). But the same political pressures that blocked criminal justice cutbacks offered a uniquely hospitable environment for a different response to fiscal pressures: *converting* criminal justice systems into revenue streams. In the name of "law and order," cities and counties created new violations, added on supplemental fines, and raised fine levels. In the name of protecting taxpayers from a further fleecing at the hands of criminals, they piled up fees of all sorts – from pre-trial, through court appearances, and on to probation and parole. And in the name of an aggressive war on drugs, they developed and expanded Civil Asset Forfeiture procedures to seize cash and goods suspected to have illicit origins.

These actions appeared to many as a win-win, a meeting of virtue and necessity. Local officials were getting tougher on criminals, pursuing public safety more vigorously, and meeting the community's significant fiscal needs all in one swoop. And not surprisingly, financialization of the criminal justice field was an exceedingly popular idea among the powerful commercial firms who were flocking to government in the 1990s as new outsourcing initiatives opened up markets for lucrative public-private contracts. Indeed, to explain the financial turn in criminal justice, one must incorporate a third and final element of neoliberal reform: the political campaign to "reinvent government" by privatizing and marketizing policy practice more generally.

Because growing fiscal pressures at the local level and the rise of the carceral state coincided with widespread privatization in American governance, corporations were presented with attractive new opportunities for profitable investment. The entry of these firms into the field should be seen – not as a first-order cause in this context – but as a *byproduct* of changes in criminal justice that accelerated predation and shaped its trajectory.

If only fiscal pressures and "tough on crime" agendas had been at work, we would expect local governments to have pursued only changes that enriched government and advanced social control – and to have jealously guarded revenues against market competitors. That, of course, is not what happened. The broader push to privatize state functions and apply market models to governance directly financialized the criminal justice field in a number of new ways. Here as elsewhere in governance, for-profit actors flooded the field, bringing along the conventional revenue-maximizing focus of market firms and shareholders. Contract-for-payment and pay-for-performance now became organizing principles of administration. This development, in turn, changed the contours and culture of the field, filling criminal justice policy networks with organized actors who pushed payment-centered innovations. And frequently, these innovations were brokered to ensure that governments would receive a set percentage of revenues generated by market firms' new practices – and thus, would support their expansion.

Neoliberal Modes of Legitimation

Critical historical scholarship has interrogated the ongoing challenge, visible from the outset, of how dominant groups could justify predatory takings while maintaining an ideological self-image of the USA as a thoroughly liberal contract state. Solutions came in many forms. White elites deployed the doctrine of *Terra nullius*, for example, to deem Native lands "uninhabited and ungoverned" and, thus, existing in a quasi-state of nature legitimately available for the taking (Pateman 2007; Bruyneel 2007). During and after slavery, constructions of racial and gender difference were fashioned and deployed to justify the violent expropriation of labor and land, and to construct a delimited white-male *herrenvolk democracy* (Du Bois 1935; Wolfe 2001). Public officials used state laws, policies, and delineations of citizenship to underwrite and legitimate predation – in ways that made their violent takings appear (to themselves and other elites) both legal and morally defensible (Rana 2010; Smith 1997).

Now, as in the past, legitimating discourses of predation reflect and reinforce dominant governing rationalities. The strength and scope of market fundamentalism helps us understand why state and market actors operate from a perspective that makes ongoing criminal justice predation appear permissible, reasonable, and right.

In her powerful analysis of neoliberalism as a de-democratizing force, Wendy Brown (2015) highlights how this rationality erodes the public nature of state institutions and any ethos in which public things are seen as held in common and valued for their commonality. Neoliberalism, she argues, substitutes market transactions – purchasing, consuming, exchanging, competing – for shared participation in common institutions and shared valuation of collective public goods. Return on investment becomes a critical benchmark for success in all endeavors. Public institutions strive to cover their own costs in a "self-sufficient" manner and orient themselves toward publics, increasingly, as producers exchanging goods with consumers.

Living under this logic, Americans have learned to expect the "user fee" as a basis for funding public institutions, and to take a skeptical view of arrangements that enlist us all – even non-users – in underwriting shared institutions through taxes. The shift toward this consumer-purchasing logic has transformed our public parks, public health programs, and public universities, reaching deep into the corners of almost all our public institutions.

State predation in the legal arena is often legitimated on precisely these grounds. The targets of predation, in this frame, are just the paying consumers of government services (Eisen 2015). As a legitimating device, the discourse of "user fees" works by assimilating predatory practices into normal state operations and equating predatory targets with the citizen-consumer role normalized under neoliberalism.

By contrast, a second legitimating discourse operates by constructing a symbolic contrast between citizens in full standing and the suitable targets of predation. The real citizens in this rendering are "taxpayers" who lead "self-sufficient" lives – those who have earned and deserve a legitimate place as recipients of the benefits and services associated with the contract state. They are the makers who have been repeatedly victimized by the takers (the street criminals, the welfare queens, the undocumented immigrants, and all the rest).

The people paying fines and fees, in this framing, are the civic failures of neoliberalism who have mismanaged their own lives and refused to take personal responsibility. These are the latest of liberalism's others, the underclass "free-loaders" who disrespect authority and prey on those who "play by the rules." When authorities force them to pay up at the courthouse, such people are only getting what is coming to them. They are paying back the civic debt they owe. They are finally being forced to pitch in their fair share.

But of course, such figures are more than *just* the latest of liberalism's others. Their specific cultural resonance is rooted in old discourses of race and criminality that scholars such as Khalil Gibran Muhammad (2010) remind us have been deeply and distinctively lodged in state institutions and practices throughout American history. Against this backdrop, lower-class black Americans today are, in a sense, always-already positioned as suspect figures – likely criminals, or "takers" in some way, who owe a civic debt that justifies making them pay up.

Indentured Citizenship

As it rewrites the relation of state and market, neoliberalism reconstructs the political citizen as a marketized subject (Brown 2015; Crenson and Ginsberg 2002). Indeed, many critical studies of neoliberalism interrogate shifts in citizenship ideals, emphasizing the rise of the dutiful worker citizen, the consumer citizen, the managed citizen, the custodial citizen, and more (Wolin 2008; Soss, Fording, and Schram 2011; Lerman and Weaver 2014). Alongside these forms, criminal justice predation produces the *indentured citizen* as a key political figure of the neoliberal era. The civic position of the indentured citizen is structured by terms of debt and discourses of indebtedness. Through predation, the indentured citizen is brought into being as a different kind of governable subject; the state–citizen relation is rewritten around a market model of creditor–debtor relations.

Financialized criminal justice practices do not simply take through force or make coercive use of involuntary labor: They generate legal and civic violations that they then leverage to move individuals into positions of financial obligation. Through this process, debt itself becomes the marker of a distinctive civic status rooted in violation of the social contract.

Thus, unlike some earlier targets of state predation, indentured citizens are not privately owned as chattels and may not experience unremunerated labor. They retain a variety of formal legal rights, even when a subset of these rights is stripped away through legal entanglement. The terms of their citizenship are refracted through the lens of debt, rendering their citizenship morally suspect and materially reconstructed.

Through predatory practices, alleged *civic* debts are made politically legible and governable through their conversion into quantified *financial* debts – which then become the basis for attenuating various rights of citizenship and making them conditional on the civic obligation to pay. Once debt is established, new fees and expenses often mount quickly. From this point onward, the foremost civic obligation becomes the act of making reliable payments to public and private creditors. When indentured citizens fail to meet this "civic minimum" (White 2003), they risk incarceration or other state actions that further erode their rights and standing.

Critically, the indentured citizenry in America today is far larger than the incarcerated or even convicted population. First, even among those who are arrested or charged with crimes, many are never convicted of anything. Second, beyond the people who are directly assessed fines, fees, and so on, one must include a far larger group of secondary targets – that is, the people who come to bear the financial burdens of predation and find themselves drawn into relations of ongoing debt and payment.

Here as in the past, gender is critical for understanding the organization of state predation. Women are, of course, direct targets of state predation alongside men. But it is important to recognize both the greater prevalence of men among direct targets of policing and incarceration, and the fact that it is women who shoulder the primary burdens of financial extraction through the criminal justice system.

Roughly one in four women in the USA have a family member in prison – a number that rises to 44 percent among black women – and women make up an estimated 83 percent of family members covering costs for incarcerated populations (Ella Baker Center 2015). It is typically women who co-sign the bail contracts, who cover the fines and fees and prison charges while men are imprisoned, and who take on additional debts when the men return to the community branded an "ex-felon" and find they are unable to secure work (Katzenstein and Waller 2015).

Among families trying to maintain contact with a prison inmate, an estimated one in three goes into debt (Ella Baker Center 2015). And in states such as Florida and Wisconsin, unpaid criminal justice debts transfer to the family estate after an ex-prisoner dies (Lind 2015). Payments on such debts leave many women unable to keep up with living expenses, including food, utilities, and rent. Such dynamics combine with others to push a significant number of women into the kinds of eviction processes analyzed in Matt Desmond's widely discussed book *Evicted* (2016).

Through this process of secondary stigmatization and extraction, women who have not themselves been charged with criminal violations become indentured citizens in their own right. As predatory state practices expand, they reconstruct both sides of the state–citizen relationship. Thus, in the city of Ferguson, the municipal court ceased to "act as a neutral arbiter of the law or a check on unlawful police conduct. [It began to use] its judicial authority as the means to compel the payment of fines and fees that advance the City's financial interests" (DOJ 2015). At the same time, criminal justice predation also transformed Ferguson citizens by further "undermin[ing] community trust," cultivating fear and avoidance of public authorities, and breeding a combustible mix of frustration, anger, and expectations of injustice.

Predation and Resistance

Though it remains legal and widespread, criminal justice predation has become the target of growing political resistance. The contours of critique are, in some cases, politically telling. On the left, progressive liberals such as Senator Bernie Sanders (2015) and scholar James Galbraith (2009) equate predation with profiteering by market firms, faulting government only for failing its obligation to protect the citizenry. On the right, libertarian conservatives such as Rand Paul (2015), George Will (2012), and the Cato Institute (2010) decry predation by state authorities as a classic example of "big government" run amok. Each side applies its own forms of erasure to obscure politically inconvenient storylines and single out its perennial *bête noir*.

Alternative grounds for critique and resistance can be found in scholarly and activist discourses addressing neoliberalism. Here, the tidy opposition of state and market gives way to a critical analysis of how states have been marketized and how markets have become state projects. In America today, criminal justice predation operates through hybrid governing practices. It blurs state–market boundaries as it draw diverse actors together in projects of dispossession targeting marginalized populations.

While political partisans may not highlight these interplays, they are resonant features of life in targeted communities. It is little surprise that insurgent movements like #blacklivesmatter call to end "money bail, mandatory fines, fees, court surcharges and 'defendant funded' court proceedings" and equally insist on stopping "the privatization of prisons, jails, probation, parole, food, phone and all other criminal justice related services" (MBL 2016). Like the recent and widespread protests inside US prisons (Woolf 2016), the movement for black lives is partly a struggle against predation itself – and against the significant role predation plays in making the celebrated "liberal-contractual" relations of more advantaged Americans possible. In this sense, they should be recognized as counter-movements to neoliberalism – the driving force of predation within and beyond the criminal justice field.

Such disruptive resistance should not surprise anyone. As Onur Ulas Ince (2016) rightly stresses, the history of expropriation and dispossession has always *also* been a history of political resistance, from the anti-enclosure riots, Diggers, and Levellers of sixteenth- and seventeenth-century England to slave revolts, mutinies on the sea, and colonial rebellions of various sorts up to the present day. It is through such acts of mass resistance that political communities from time to time are able to undermine prevailing regimes of predation, reorganize the capitalist state, and create, at least for a while, a more just and democratic system of societal institutions.

References

Bach, D. (2015). UW Project Focuses on Fines and Fees that Create "Prisoners of Debt". *UW Today*, December 4. Retrieved from: www.washington.edu/news/2015/12/04/uw-project-focuses-on-fines-and-fees-that-create-prisoners-of-debt/

Better Together (2015). *General Administration Study #2: Municipal Structure, Powers, Funding, and Operations*. Retrieved from: www.bettertogetherstl.com/wp-content/uploads/2015/12/Better-Together-General-Administration-Report-2-FINAL-.pdf

Block, F., and Somers, M. R. (2014). *The Power of Market Fundamentalism: Karl Polanyi's Critique*. Cambridge, MA: Harvard University Press.

Brennan Center for Justice (2016). *Is Charging Inmates to Stay in Prison Smart Policy?* Retrieved from: www.brennancenter.org/states-pay-stay-charges

Brown, W. (2015). *Undoing the Demos: Neoliberalism's Stealth Revolution*. New York: Zone Books/Near Futures.

Bruyneel, K. (2007). *The Third Space of Sovereignty: The Postcolonial Politics of U.S.–Indigenous Relations*. Minneapolis: University of Minnesota Press.

Bunn, C. (2015). Prison Phone Rates Generate Billions for Companies. *The Chicago Defender*, October 21. Retrieved from: http://chicagodefender.com/2015/10/21/prison-phone-rates-generate-billions-for-companies-cause-stress-for-black-families/

Cato Institute (2010). *Policing for Profit: The Abuse of Civil Asset Forfeiture*. Retrieved from: www.cato.org/events/policing-profit-abuse-civil-asset-forfeiture

Council of Economic Advisors (CEA) (2015). *Fines, Fees, and Bail*. Issue Brief, December. Retrieved from: https://obamawhitehouse.archives.gov/sites/default/files/page/files/1215_cea_fine_fee_bail_issue_brief.pdf

Crenson, M. A., and Ginsberg, B. (2002). *Downsizing Democracy: How America Sidelined Its Citizens and Privatized Its Public*. Baltimore, MD: Johns Hopkins University Press.

Desmond, M. (2016). *Evicted: Poverty and Profit in the Modern City*. New York: Penguin Random House.

Dilts, A. (2011). From "Entrepreneur of the Self" to "Care of the Self": Neoliberal Governmentality and Foucault's Ethics. *Foucault Studies*, 12, 130–146.

Donahue, J. (1999). *Hazardous Crosscurrents: Confronting Inequality in an Era of Devolution*. Century Foundation Report.

Du Bois, W. E. B. (1935). *Black Reconstruction in America: An Essay Toward a History of the Part Which Black Folk Played in the Attempt to Reconstruct Democracy in America, 1860–1880*, Vol. 6. Oxford: Oxford University Press.

Eisen, L-B. (2015). *Charging Inmates Perpetuates Mass Incarceration*. Brennan Center for Justice. New York: NYU School of Law. Retrieved from: www.brennancenter.org/sites/default/files/publications/Charging_Inmates_Mass_Incarceration.pdf

Ella Baker Center (2015). *Who Pays? The True Cost of Incarceration on Families*, September. Retrieved from: http://whopaysreport.org/who-pays-full-report/

Federal Communications Commission (FCC) (2015). *FCC Takes Next Big Steps in Reducing Inmate Calling Rates, Also Seeks Comment on Reforms for Video Visitation and Additional Reforms for International Rates and Ancillary Charges*, October 22. Retrieved from: https://apps.fcc. gov/edocs_public/attachmatch/DOC-335984A1.pdf

Fergus, D. (2014). Financial Fracking in the Land of the Fee, 1980–2008. In R. Cramer and T. Shanks (Eds.), *The Assets Perspective* (pp. 67–97). New York: Palgrave MacMillan.

Fergus, D. (2017). *Land of the Fee: Hidden Costs and the Decline of the American Middle Class*. Oxford: Oxford University Press.

Galbraith, J. (2009). *The Predator State: How Conservatives Abandoned the Free Market and Why Liberals Should Too*. New York: Free Press.

Gonzalez, G. (2013). *Guest Workers or Colonized Labor?: Mexican Labor Migration to the United States*. London: Routledge.

Gustafson, K. (2016). *The Legal Manufacture of Hardworking Bastards: Marriage, Bastardy, and Apprenticeship Laws and the Policing of Race and Labor in North Carolina, 1741–1870*. Unpublished Manuscript.

Hacker, J. S., and Pierson, P. (2010). *Winner Take All Politics*. New York: Simon and Schuster.

Handley, J., Helsby, J., and Martinez, F. (2016). Inside the Chicago Police Department's Secret Budget. *The Chicago Reader*, September 29. Retrieved from: www.chicagoreader. com/chicago/police-department-civil-forfeiture-investigation/Content?oid=23728922

Harcourt, B. (2011). *The Illusion of Free Markets*. Cambridge, MA: Harvard University Press.

Harlan, C. (2016). Inside the Administration's $1 billion Deal to Detain Central American Asylum Seekers. *The Washington Post*, August 14. Retrieved from: www.washingtonpost. com/business/economy/inside-the-administrations-1-billion-deal-to-detain-central-american-asylum-seekers/2016/08/14/e47f1960-5819-11e6-9aee-8075993d73a2_story. html?utm_term=.d8c38824c285

Harris, A. (2016). *A Pound of Flesh: Monetary Sanctions as Punishment for the Poor*. New York: Russell Sage Foundation.

Harvey, D. (2003). *The New Imperialism*. New York: Oxford University Press.

Harvey, D. (2005). *A Brief History of Neoliberalism*. New York: Oxford University Press.

Ince, O. U. (2016). Bringing the Economy Back In: Hannah Arendt, Karl Marx, and the Politics of Capitalism. *Journal of Politics*, 78(2), 411–426.

Ingraham, C. (2014). Civil Asset Forfeitures More than Double under Obama. *The Washington Post*, September 8. Retrieved from: www.washingtonpost.com/news/ wonk/wp/2014/09/08/civil-asset-forfeitures-more-than-double-under-obama/

Jacobson, M. F. (2001). *Barbarian Virtues: The United States Encounters Foreign Peoples at Home And Abroad, 1876–1917*. London: Macmillan.

Katzenstein, M. F., and Waller, M. R. (2015). Taxing the Poor: Incarceration, Poverty Governance, and the Seizure of Family Resources. *Perspectives on Politics*, 13(3), 638–656.

Krippner, G. R. (2011). *Capitalizing on Crisis: The Political Origins of the Rise of Finance*. Cambridge, MA: Harvard University Press.

Lerman, A., and Weaver, V. (2014). *Arresting Citizenship: The Democratic Consequences of American Crime Control*. Chicago: University of Chicago Press.

Lind, D. (2015). At Least 2 States Let Prisons Charge the Families of Dead Ex-Prisoners for Their Food and Health Care. *Vox*, October 16. Retrieved from: www.vox.com/2015/ 5/26/8660001/prison-jail-cost

Ludwig, M. (2015). Across the South, Many Jails are Illegal Debtors' Prisons. *Truthout*, September 17. Retrieved from: www.truth-out.org/news/item/32832-many-jails-are-illegal-debtors-prisons

Luxemburg, R. (2003). *The Accumulation of Capital.* New York: Routledge.

Lyons, W. (2002). *The Politics of Community Policing: Rearranging the Power to Punish.* Ann Arbor: University of Michigan Press.

Marable, M. (1981). *Blackwater: Historical Studies in Race.* Dayton, OH: Black Praxis Press.

Massachusetts Trial Court Fines and Fees Working Group (2016). Report to Trial Court Chief Justice Paula M. Carey. November 17. Retrieved from: www.mass.gov/courts/docs/trial-court/report-of-the-fines-and-fees-working-group.pdf

Massey, D. S., and Denton, N. A. (1993). *American Apartheid: Segregation and the Making of the Underclass.* Cambridge, MA: Harvard University Press.

McLennan, R. M. (2008). *The Crisis of Imprisonment: Protest, Politics, and the Making of the American Penal State, 1776–1941.* New York: Cambridge University Press.

Movement for Black Lives (MBL) (2016). *End the War on Black People.* Retrieved from: https://policy.m4bl.org/end-war-on-black-people/

Muhammad, K. G. (2010). *The Condemnation of Blackness: Race, Crime, and the Making of Modern Urban America.* Cambridge, MA: Harvard University Press.

Nichols, R. (2015). Disaggregating Primitive Accumulation. *Radical Philosophy*, 194, 18–28.

North, D. (1981). *Structure and Change in Economic History.* New York: W.W. Norton.

North, D., and Weingast, B. (1989). Constitutions and Commitment: The Evolution of Institutions Governing Public Choice in Seventeenth-Century England. *The Journal of Economic History*, 49, 803–832.

Ordower, H., Sandoval, J. S. O., and Warren, K. (2016). *Out of Ferguson: Misdemeanors, Municipal Courts, Tax Distribution and Constitutional Limitations.* Saint Louis University Legal Studies Research Paper No. 2016–2014.

Oshinsky, D. (1997). *Worse Than Slavery: Parchman Farm and the Ordeal of Jim Crow Justice.* New York: Free Press.

Pateman, C. (2007). The Settler Contract. In C. Pateman and C.W. Mills (Eds.), *Contract and Domination* (pp. 35–78). Malden, MA: Polity.

Pateman, C., and Mills, C.W. (2007). *Contract and Domination.* Malden, MA: Polity.

Paul, R. (2015). Statement posted to Twitter. Retrieved from: https://twitter.com/randpaul/status/631608896826777600

Peck, J. (2010). Zombie Neoliberalism and the Ambidextrous State. *Theoretical Criminology*, 14(1), 104–110.

Peck, J., and Theodore, N. (2012). Reanimating Neoliberalism: Process Geographies of Neoliberalisation. *Social Anthropology*, 20(2), 177–185.

Petrella, C. (2016). No Easy End to Prison Profiteering. *Boston Review*, August 25. Retrieved from: http://bostonreview.net/us/christopher-petrella-doj-private-public-prisons

Pew Charitable Trusts (2012). *The Local Squeeze: Falling Revenues and Growing Demand for Services Challenge Cities, Counties, and School Districts.* Retrieved from: www.pewtrusts.org/en/research-and-analysis/reports/0001/01/01/the-local-squeeze

Plaintiffs v. The City of Florissant (2016). No. 4:16-cv-1693. United States District Court for the Eastern District of Missouri Eastern Division.

Pritchett, W. (2003). The "Public Menace" of Blight: Urban Renewal and the Private Uses of Eminent Domain. *Yale Law and Policy Review*, 21(1), 1–52.

Rana, A. (2010). *The Two Faces of American Freedom.* Cambridge, MA: Harvard University Press.

Rivlin, G. (2010). *Broke, USA: From Pawnshops to Poverty, Inc. – How the Working Poo Became Big Business*. New York: Harper Collins.

Sachs, J. D. (2012). *The Price of Civilization: Reawakening American Virtue and Prosperity* New York: Random House.

Sanders, B. (2015). Sanders, House Leaders Introduce Bill to Ban Private Prisons Retrieved from: www.sanders.senate.gov/newsroom/press-releases/sanders-house-leaders-introduce-bill-to-ban-private-prisons

Satter, B. (2010). *Family Properties: How the Struggle Over Race and Real Estate Transformec Chicago and Urban America*. New York: Metropolitan Books.

Schram, S. F. (2015). *The Return of Ordinary Capitalism: Neoliberalism, Precarity, Occupy* New York: Oxford University Press.

Shapiro, J. (2016). State-By-State Court Fees. National Public Radio, May 19. Retrievec from: www.npr.org/2014/05/19/312455680/state-by-state-court-fees

Smith, R. M. (1997). *Civic Ideals: Conflicting Visions of Citizenship in U.S. History*. New Haven, CT: Yale University Press.

Sorkin, M. (2013). Drawing the Line: Architects and Prisons. *The Nation*, August 27 Retrieved from: www.thenation.com/article/drawing-line-architects-and-prisons/

Soss, J., Fording, R. C., and Schram, S. F. (2011). *Disciplining the Poor: Neoliberal Paternalism and the Persistent Power of Race*. Chicago: University of Chicago Press.

Stuart, F. (2016). *Down, Out, and Under Arrest: Policing and Everyday Life in Skid Row* Chicago: University of Chicago Press.

Swanson, A. (2015). A Shocking Number of Mentally Ill Americans End Up ir Prison Instead of Treatment. *The Washington Post*, April 30. Retrieved from: www washingtonpost.com/news/wonk/wp/2015/04/30/a-shocking-number-of-mentally-ill-americans-end-up-in-prisons-instead-of-psychiatric-hospitals/?utm_term=.5d786e 2a2d44

Takaki, R. (1998). *A Different Mirror for Young People: A History of Multicultural America* New York: Seven Stories Press.

Tilly, C. (1992). *Coercion, Capital and European States, A.D. 990–1992*. New York: Wiley Blackwell.

United States Department of Justice Civil Rights Division (DOJ) (2015). Investigatior of the Ferguson Police Department, March 4. Retrieved from: www.justice.gov/ sites/default/files/opa/press-releases/attachments/2015/03/04/ferguson_police_depa rtment_report.pdf

Wacquant, L. (2010). Crafting the Neoliberal State: Workfare, Prisonfare, and Socia Insecurity. *Sociological Forum*, 25(2), 197–220.

White, S. (2003). *The Civic Minimum*. New York: Oxford University Press.

Will, G. (2012). When Government is the Looter. *The Washington Post*, May 18 Retrieved from: www.washingtonpost.com/opinions/when-government-is-the-looter/ 2012/05/18/gIQAUIKVZU_story.html?utm_term=.39ee5e4589d5

Wofford, T. (2014). The Operators of America's Largest Immigration Detention Center Have a History of Inmate Abuse. *Newsweek*, December 20. Retrieved from: www newsweek.com/operators-americas-largest-immigrant-detention-center-have-history-inmate-293632

Wolfe, P. (2001). Land, Labor, and Difference: Elementary Structures of Race. *The American Historical Review*, 106(3), 866–905.

Wolin, S. (2008). *Democracy, Incorporated: Managed Democracy and the Specter of Invertec Totalitarianism*. Princeton, NJ: Princeton University Press.

Woolf, N. (2016). Inside America's Biggest Prison Strike: "The 13th Amendment Didn't End Slavery". *The Guardian*, October 22. Retrieved from: www.theguardian.com/us-news/2016/oct/22/inside-us-prison-strike-labor-protest

Wright, G. (1997). *Old South, New South: Revolutions in the Southern Economy Since the Civil War*. Baton Rouge: LSU Press.

Yates, S. (2016). "Reducing Over Use of Private Prisons." Memorandum for the Acting Director, Federal Bureau of Prisons (August 18).

Young, R., and Meiser, J. (2008). Race and the Dual State in the Early American Republic. In J. Lowndes, J. Novkov, and D. T. Warren (Eds.), *Race and American Political Development* (pp. 31–58). New York: Routledge.

9

NEOLIBERALISM AND POLICE REFORM

Leonard Feldman

Scholars of police reform, noting some of the difficulties involved in relying on the US courts and constitutional jurisprudence to limit police violence and reform police practices, argue that the more systemic efforts of the Department of Justice (DOJ) in transforming whole departments constitute a more promising avenue of change. Indeed, they argue, the attempt to rein in police violence and halt racially discriminatory police practices may be more fruitfully pursued at the *policy* level, in the shadow of the courts, than directly in the courts themselves. The tendency in the literature is to make a contrast between the more individualized remedies of criminal prosecutions and civil litigation, on the one hand, and the more structural reforms of DOJ interventions. For instance, Chase Madar (2014) writes, "far more useful are the DOJ Civil Rights Division's root-and-branch interventions into violently dysfunctional police forces, triggered by 'patterns and practices' of systematic rights violations rather than any one particular incident." There is a good deal to recommend this position, but two additional points should be made about the DOJ investigations: First is the frequent and central role of political protest in triggering the investigations. Second is the prominent role of neoliberal techniques and approaches within both the investigative reports and the memoranda of understanding or consent decrees that usually result from DOJ investigations. Highlighting them can help make clear what is distinctive in this reform effort, in contrast to the turn to the courts. Ultimately, I suggest that we might characterize these reform efforts as a redeployment of neoliberal techniques for more democratic ends.

In this chapter I examine how governance technologies closely linked to neoliberalism, such as quantitative performance measurement, managerial audits, best practices, and benchmarking, are being redeployed in the service of police reform. I first describe how neoliberalism as a political form involves the development of particular technologies of measurement, observation, and coordination. Then I consider how these play out in the governance of policing, in the implementation of CompStat in the 1990s and in recent efforts by the Obama administration to reform municipal police departments, including the Department of Justice "pattern or practice" investigations into excessive force and systemic racism in local departments. I argue that Department of Justice findings reports combine legal-juridical, muckraking, and managerial frames, and that the implicit alliance between protest movements such as Black Lives Matter and the Civil Rights Division shows the way in which, in very particular contexts, a social logic of surveillance can redirect the neoliberal audit in the direction of democratic oversight.

My argument proceeds in the following steps: First, drawing on the work of Wendy Brown, I examine the role of specific governance techniques such as benchmarking, best practices, and quantitative performance measurement as they are described in the literature on neoliberalism and as implemented, specifically, in the administration of police in (a) the rise of CompStat and (b) the use of "best practices" in the President's Task Force on 21st Century Policing. Then I turn to the specific efforts of the Department of Justice to reform local police departments, briefly looking at how agonistic political action has played a central role in triggering Department of Justice investigations and showing how neoliberal governance techniques and rationalities such as experimentalism, benchmarking, and best practices get incorporated into what are essentially legal reports concerning systemic police law-breaking. In particular I show how the use of quantitative benchmarking for judging incidences of police violence involves the creative redeployment of CompStat techniques from their traditional analysis of criminal violence to the analysis of police violence. In arguing that neoliberal governance rationalities play a role in police reform efforts, I do not mean to deny the well-documented role of neoliberal policies in facilitating or producing the intensified policing of urban space and the refocusing of punitive and carceral mechanisms on subjects who fail to self-regulate according to market norms (Rose 1999; Wacquant 2009; Harcourt 2011; Soss et al. 2011). I rather wish to supplement that picture with an account of how neoliberal governance logics can become attached to different political projects. The Department of Justice reports involve such a redirection, as they bring together features of a traditional legal brief, a journalistic exposé, and a neoliberal audit.

Benchmarking and Quantitative Performance Measurement

Recent work in political theory suggests that the importation of market logics into the state constitutes one of the paradigmatic features of neoliberalism. According to Wendy Brown (2015, p. 34), this "economization of law" includes the application of market rationalities to state institutions: "Centralized authority, law, policing, rules, and quotas are replaced by networked, team-based, practice-oriented techniques emphasizing incentivization, guidelines, and benchmarks." Brown (2015, p. 122), extending Foucault's insights into neoliberalism as a governing rationality, sees contemporary neoliberalism as producing its own distinctive "administrative form" – governance, as opposed to government. Governance, Brown argues (2015, p. 123), "signifies a transformation from governing through hierarchically organized command and control – in corporations, states, and non-profit agencies alike – to governing that is networked, integrated, cooperative, partnered, disseminated, and at least partly self-organized." Brown argues that neoliberal governance is not agent-centered, as compared to older models of authorities and subordinates. Rather, governance is "institutionalized in processes, norms and practices" (Brown 2015, p. 124). This means a transformation from hier-archical commands and straightforwardly punitive techniques to more supposedly collaborative forms whereby workers in an organization are made increasingly responsible, while their entrepreneurial activity is guided by "benchmarks and inspection" (Brown 2015, p. 127). Best practices and benchmarking are promi-nent techniques of contemporary neoliberal governance, whereby organizations emulate their more successful competitors. As Brown writes (2015, p. 136):

> "[B]enchmarking" may sound like a fancy word for goal-setting, but its meaning is rather different. Benchmarking refers to the practice of a firm or agency undertaking internal reforms on the basis of studying and then importing the practices of other, more successful firms or agencies.

"Best practices," according to Brown (2015, p. 135), marketize institutions and domains that were at least partially insulated from economic rationality. Best practices and benchmarking thus position organizations in competition with each other even as they seek to emulate each other through relentless comparison via a standardized metric. Furthermore, the basis of comparison is usually some quantita-tive measurement of performance. As Bruno (2009, p. 278) argues, "benchmarking helps decision-makers to reach consensus by translating political problems of collective action into statistical issues of quantification."

Brown shows how these neoliberal governance rationalities have insinuated themselves into the management of academia. For faculty, the norms of profes-sional success have been transformed, from teaching and research that serves the public good to individualized and entrepreneurial standards achievement, measured through market-friendly indicators such as grant funding and citation counts:

> This professionalization aims at making young scholars not into teachers and thinkers, but into human capitals who learn to attract investors by networking long before they "go on the market," who "workshop" their papers, "shop" their book manuscripts, game their Google Scholar counts and "impact factors," and, above all, follow the money and the rankings.
>
> (Brown 2015, p. 195)

There is, indeed, a broad range of literature that (a) examines the use of quantitative performance measurement in evaluating academic professors and (b) links this trend to the neoliberalization of academia. But Brown may be said to too quickly connect practices of governance and techniques of measurement and ranking as integral and necessary parts of the same political project – neoliberalism. As Feller (2009, p. 328) writes, "The analytical issue that emerges from this discussion is how most properly to couple propositions relating to international trends towards neoliberal modes of governance … with those that describe and account for similar trends towards program management and performance measurement." The use of numbers to assess performance long predates neoliberalism and the new public management. As Le Galès (2016, pp. 15–16) cautions, "a large part of the quantification or the strengthening of the spirit of managerialism does not fall under neoliberal dynamics. The logic of the rationalisation of activities, including through measurement and quantification, has a long history." This does not mean that one should not theorize the way technologies, practices, and concepts connect in ways that render them part of a distinct ideological and political project. But it does mean that one should assume that those connections are *contingent* articulations.

Scholars have tended to be critical of the application of best practices, benchmarking, and quantitative performance measurement metrics to their own practice as academics, as well as to the institutions and practices of the welfare state. I argue that much of this critical literature applies well to data-driven trends in policing as well, such as the CompStat system discussed in the next section. Nevertheless, I also argue that these techniques associated with neoliberalism can be (and have been) redirected, and form a significant element in recent efforts to combat police violence. My point is neither to besmirch critics of the neoliberalization of higher education, nor is it to foster a dismissive attitude towards the efforts of the Department of Justice to achieve structural reforms of American police departments. Rather, my point is that the political effects of the incorporation of governance techniques and rationalities that go by the name of neoliberalism are highly contingent, context dependent, and not always de-democratizing.

Data-Driven Policing and Its Limits

Neoliberal political rationality can be understood as one that subjects state actors, decisions, and processes to norms of market efficiency and quantitative performance measurements. As William Davies (2014, p. 28) puts it, "The neoliberal state is an aggressively utilitarian state, in the sense that it seeks to make all political, legal and public action subject to quantitative empirical evaluation." The paradigmatic case of neoliberal rationality in policing is surely the CompStat system, developed by the NYPD in the 1990s and quickly adopted by other large police departments, which inaugurated an era of quantitative performance measurement. There are at least three respects in which CompStat represents a neoliberal governing rationality: First, it is promoted as the importation of accountability systems from the corporate sector into the administrative state. William Bratton (New York Police Department Commissioner from 1994 to 1996) and his co-author William Andrews are quite explicit about this:

> Like the corporate CEOs of that era, we began with a large, unfocused, inward-looking, bureaucratic organization, poor at internal communication or cooperation and chronically unresponsive to intelligence from the outer world. We reduced layers of management, drove responsibility down to the operating units, improved communication and data processing, tightened accountability, and rewarded results. In short order, we had the NYPD's bureaus and divisions *competing with criminals, not with one another*.
>
> *(Bratton and Andrews 1999)*

The NYPD was to "compet[e] with criminals" largely through better data. But more fundamentally, the turn to CompStat as a management philosophy represents the hallmarks of neoliberal political rationality as Brown (2015, p. 132) identifies them: devolution and responsibilization – pushing decision-making down to lower levels of the organization while "moral[ly] burdening … the entity at the end of the pipeline."

Second, CompStat, while promoted as introducing accountability into policing, actually transforms accountability, as police become less accountable to the communities in which they serve and more accountable to their leaders (Potter 2015), an aspect of what Brown describes as neoliberal de-democratization. Finally, whether understood as leading inexorably to actual quotas for arrests and summonses or, as instituting "performance goals" to "maximize employee performance" (Bronstein 2015, p. 583, citing Operations Order No. 52 from Police Commissioner, NYC Police Department), CompStat ended up generating a fixation on quantitative measures of performance (Potter 2015).

CompStat's purpose was to generate comprehensive statistics on crimes – with data and mapping of crime that would enable police commanders to hold subordinates responsible for crime levels, and develop specific strategies for response (Eterno and Silverman 2010). Two perverse outcomes have been noted in the literature: First, police departments respond to the imperative to improve their numbers (i.e. reduce crime) by reclassifying certain reported events as not-crime, or as misdemeanors as opposed to felonies. Second, the focus on quantitative performance measurement leads to pressure on police officers to meet informal (and officially denied) quotas of arrests and summons. As Bronstein (2015, p. 565) notes, "While CompStat was revolutionary for the NYPD, its unintended consequence appears to be a department-wide fixation on quantifying enforcement activity." There is no necessary link between a focus on quantified measures of criminal activity and quantified measures of enforcement activity. After all, police departments could emphasize a qualitative shift in policing (e.g. from one driven by arrests and summonses for quality of life offenses to one focused on colla-borative problem solving and increased visibility) and then attempt to identify a causal relationship between that shift in policing and a reduction in criminal activity. Instead, it appears that the data-driven quantifying approach simply migrated from the crime side to the enforcement side. This turn to numbers did not require any link between increasing arrests and summonses and decreasing the crime rate. Rather, it appears as though CompStat ushered in a new police rationality (numbers-driven, where "hard" quantitative measures of both crime and police performance are prioritized over qualitative assessments) that made statistical performance measures dominant. The "numbers game" thus designated strategies to lower crime statistics through underreporting and strategies to keep numbers of arrests and summonses high. Bronstein (2015, p. 564) cites an interview with a retired NYPD detective who articulates the shift to a quantitative rationality: "It used to be, 'what's his story?' Now it's, 'what are his numbers?' That's all they care about. CompStat was great, but now they [have] started putting numbers on everything." In combination with broken windows policing, the "results" for low-income communities of color were ever-increasing contacts with police and the criminal justice system more generally, intrusive police surveillance, criminal records for misdemeanor offenses, and the associated social costs of what Lerman and Weaver (2014) call "custodial citizenship."

The quantification of policing has followed a market logic, where the broader social goal (reducing crime) has been transformed into a productivity metric (measuring number of arrests and summonses). Police officers are subjected to a regime of responsibilization, urged to be more entrepreneurial and "proactive" in producing more arrests. However, focus on quantitative performance measurements comes to an abrupt halt when it comes down to documentation of the use of force. Indeed, the sustained public attention to racialized police violence in the aftermath of Ferguson has revealed that a key impediment to police reform is the *absence*, not the presence of practices of governmentality such as the collection of good quantitative data: The US government simply did not track the number of police killings nationally, much less other data concerning the circumstances of the violence such as the racial identity of the victim and perpetrator or whether the victim of the homicide was armed or unarmed (Lowery 2014). It took projects such as *The Guardian*'s "The Counted," again, inspired by popular political protest, to remedy that. James Scott (1998) examines the relationship between the rise of statistics and the expansion of state power. Measuring, quantifying, calculating, render a society legible to the state. By contrast, "an illegible society ... is a hindrance to any effective intervention by the state, whether the purpose of that intervention is plunder or public welfare" (Scott 1998, p.78). While US society has been rendered legible by the precise mapping of crime data, it is local police departments who have, up until very recently, remained illegible to the federal apparatus: The absence of state-collected data on police killings by the United States federal government marks a peculiar lacuna: How is it that the state cannot employ its paradigmatic mode of visioning when it turns its lens away from the population and resources it manages and towards the organization of coercive power that assists in that managing? It was only as a result of the efforts of journalists and activists to create a comprehensive accounting of police killings since 2013 that the DOJ's Bureau of Justice Statistics changed its own practice of data collection – from requests for voluntary reporting by local departments to an approach that searched media and utilized information from medical examiners and coroners to supplement that reporting (Banks et al., 2016; see also Bialik 2016). Not surprisingly, the state's effort to offer an accounting of its own violence lagged behind the efforts of non-state social movement and journalistic actors.

Benchmarking and Best Practices in Police Reform

A task force, established by presidential executive order in 2014, with a staff provided by the Department of Justice's community policing division, published its recommendations after conducting a series of "listening sessions" with police, civilians, academics, and politicians. The final report of the President's Task Force on 21st Century Policing is largely framed by the goals of "building trust" between police and community, and promoting "procedural justice" whereby improved perceptions of the fairness, professionalism, and impartiality of the police lead to increased public compliance.

While those are the goals, the main mechanism for achieving them is the articulation and promotion of best practices, a term which is repeated twenty-eight times in the report. Indeed, the central mission of the Task Force is the formulation of best practices, as articulated in the 2014 Executive Order establishing it, and included in the report's appendix:

> Sec. 3. *Mission.* (a) The Task Force shall, consistent with applicable law, identify best practices and otherwise make recommendations to the President on how policing practices can promote effective crime reduction while building public trust.
>
> *(President's Task Force on 21st Century Policing 2015, p. 79)*

The report situates the Department of Justice as a kind of partner and coordinator in the consensual goal of promoting best practices, not an overseeing political authority with the capacity to compel change. For instance, when discussing the need to develop stronger forms of civilian oversight, the report justifies the necessity of doing so not in order to combat police abuse, but rather "to strengthen trust with the community" (Task Force 2015, p. 26). And the role of the Department of Justice is not to compel such reforms. Rather:

> the U.S. Department of Justice's Office of Community Oriented Policing Services (COPS Office) should provide technical assistance and collect best

practices from existing civilian oversight efforts and be prepared to help cities create this structure, potentially with some matching grants and funding.

(Task Force 2015, p. 26)

While the task force report situates the Department of Justice in a collaborative relationship with local police departments, once the DOJ opens an investigation into a police department for systemic violations, its relationship to the offending department shifts to a mixture of collaboration and coercion. In Cincinnati, Schatmeier (2013) argues that the success of the DOJ monitoring process hinged on its incorporation of "soft law" techniques to supplement and modify the traditional "command and control" approach. Schatmeier (2013, p. 573) describes this as a process in which "the parties set benchmarks and develop plans for achieving them in lieu of the regulator deciding which approach the regulated agency must follow." In a Collaborative Agreement that amended its more traditional Memorandum of Understanding, benchmarks were established, and the traditional court supervision of the agreement between the department of justice and the city's police department was supplemented by Rand Benchmark auditing (Schatmeier 2013, pp. 573, 570). Nevertheless, DOJ pattern or practice investigations often result in a consent decree that is enforced by the courts, or in a settlement agreement operating under the threat of litigation, meaning that soft law and hard law are combined.

But there is another dimension of "soft law" worth noting. More broadly, Department of Justice resources are finite; thus, they select only a small number of police departments where police violence has become already politicized (either by protest movements or by political leaders) for investigation and eventual transformation. One study documented thirty-eight police departments subject to formal investigation by the Justice Department and nineteen of those cases resulting in a Consent Decree between 2000 and 2013 (Rushin 2014). Nevertheless, the goal is to shape police department policies more broadly: In addition to using benchmarking and best practices within their agreements, the DOJ hopes to establish benchmark policies to be emulated by non-investigated departments. Indeed, as Chanin (2011; see also US DOJ 2001) notes, the settlements established with police departments through the "pattern or practice" investigations tend to follow a "best practices" template established by the Department of Justice, with model use of force policies, accountability structures, and data collection procedures. By spreading best practices policy through the threat of investigation and litigation, the DOJ is creating a hybrid of "command and control" and more lateral norm diffusion.

Department of Justice Policy Reform's Roots in Democratic Protest

There appears to be no systematic process governing the Department of Justice's opening of an investigation into a municipality's police department. Rushin

(2014) describes various ways the DOJ identifies targets of investigation: the role of academic studies into particular departments, existing civil litigation against police, department whistle-blowers, and media reports of both systemic police misconduct and particularly shocking individual cases. What needs to be acknowledged is the way the latter – media coverage of cases – is itself frequently triggered by popular political protest against racialized police violence. For instance, in Cincinnati, riots protesting the killing of an unarmed African-American teenager, Timothy Thomas, led the Cincinnati mayor to request DOJ intervention (Schatmeier 2013, p. 557). Similarly, in Baltimore, the mayor requested a full-scale civil rights investigation by the DOJ in the wake of protests over the death of Freddie Gray in police custody (Broadwater 2015). And the DOJ's investigation of the Ferguson, Missouri, police department was initiated in the immediate wake of the Black Lives Matter protests in that city following the killing of Michael Brown by Officer Darren Wilson (Apuzzo and Fernandez 2014). Whether the protests' effects are mediated through the actions of local officials such as mayors, or without such mediation, they are clearly playing a significant role in setting the Department of Justice's agenda in terms of which police departments it chooses to investigate. Any attempt to evaluate the institutional effect of popular protests, such as those of the Black Lives Matter movement, should recognize their role in prompting official action. (At the time of my writing this, the nominee to be the next Attorney General, Jeff Sessions, if confirmed, appears likely to end the investigations entirely, or drastically curtail them, as a result of his view, expressed during his Senate confirmation hearing, that they unfairly stigmatize the police [Fritze 2017].)

Agonistic democratic action is not only an instigator for DOJ intervention: In addition, citizen "sousveillance" (Mann and Ferenbok 2013) of police encounters with civilians gets incorporated into the official findings section of their reports. For instance, the report on the Chicago Police Department frequently cites cell-phone videos of police violence to contradict police officers' accounts. The report notes that the videos' relationship to officer testimony suggested a much deeper and extensive problem of excessive force since "the inaccurate descriptions of events that *were* undercut by video we reviewed bore striking similarities to descriptions provided by officers in numerous cases with no video" (US DOJ 2017, p. 36).

The report stops short of urging more, and more organized, citizen surveillance of police activity, as is promoted by groups such as Copwatch. Indeed, the Chicago report marginalizes the agency of the observer taking the video, describing the video as an object without an author that "surfaced":

> In one incident captured on cell-phone video, an officer breaking up a party approached a man, grabbed him by the shirt, and hit him in the head with a baton. In his reports, the officer, using language very similar to that used in many other reports we reviewed, falsely claimed that the victim had tried to

punch him. Before the video surfaced, the officer's supervisor had approved the use of force and the victim had pled guilty to resisting arrest. The officer has since been relieved of his police powers and is facing criminal charges for his conduct.

(US DOJ 2017, p. 39)

The report does not take this as an opportunity to articulate and defend the principle, currently contested, of a Constitutional right of individuals to film the police. Rather, the report uses this as an opportunity to promote a policy of police body cameras. Thus, as in the case of the democratic protests that sometimes prompt DOJ investigations, the cell-phone video evidence within the report signifies the underacknowledged dependence of the official investigations upon non-institutional, agonistic democratic action.

Policing the Police through Quantitative Performance Measurement

If agonistic democratic action is at the origin of Department of Justice investigations, and if policy reform is the goal via the court-monitored consent decrees that are its conclusion, in between lie various neoliberal practices of governance and measurement. The Department of Justice reports combine multiple frames of analysis. I argue that the reports combine the frames of the journalistic exposé, the legal brief, and the performance audit. The exposé side of the reports is the one that, not surprisingly, receives the most attention from coverage of the reports by journalists themselves. For instance, newspaper articles of the DOJ report on Ferguson emphasized the evidence of systemic corruption (the explicit reliance of the city on police and court-administered fines) and overt racism of city employees. Here the basic idea is the exposure of malfeasance, especially through vivid anecdotal evidence or accounts of systemic practices and policies.

The legal brief side of these reports can be found in the way that the DOJ frames its evidence: It articulates the Constitutional standard for distinguishing excessive from reasonable force, and then asserts that it will demonstrate, with the evidence provided, as it says in its report on the Chicago Police Department, that it has "reasonable cause to believe that the unreasonable force we identified amounts to a pattern or practice of unlawful conduct" (2017, p. 25).

Department of Justice reports combine these two frames when they document shocking evidence of excessive force, link that force to a systemic issue such as a problematic department policy, and compare both the policy and the incident to an established legal standard. For instance, in their report on Chicago, the DOJ finds:

The use of unreasonable force to quickly resolve non-violent encounters is a recurrent issue at CPD. This is at least in part because CPR's policy permits the use of Tasers in situations where it is unreasonable ... Some CPD officers resort to Tasers as a tool of convenience, with insufficient concern or cognizance that it is a weapon with inherent risks that inflicts significant pain. Use of a Taser "is more than a *de minimis* application of force" and is a "very significant intrusion on [a person's] Fourth Amendment interests." *Abbott v. Sangamon County, Ill.*, 705 F.3d 706, 726, 730 (7th Cir. 2013). In an incident we reviewed, a man died after hitting his head when he fell while fleeing because a CPD officer shot him with a Taser. The man had been suspected only of petty theft from a retail store. IPRA deemed this use of a Taser justified.

(2017, p. 33)

The report establishes that such police killings are not shocking aberrations but systemic patterns by bringing forth evidence of many such incidents and by connecting those individual incidents to bad policies.

But it turns out that DOJ investigators also put numbers on everything, including police killings and other use of force incidents. DOJ investigations establish evidence of unconstitutional, illegal, and policy-violating uses of force through a CompStat-like approach to quantitative performance measurement. However, instead of measuring police productivity against a norm or quota, they establish excess violence against quantitative benchmarks of "normal" force rates. For instance, in their investigation of the East Haven Connecticut Police Department for racially profiling Latino drivers for traffic stops, the DOJ uses benchmarking across squads within the department, and benchmarking in comparison of individual officers:

We similarly found some EHPD officers with massive disparities in their stops of Latinos as compared to other officers in EHPD. Indeed, one officer had a stop rate of Latinos of 40.5%, an extraordinary deviation from the baseline of other EHPD officer activity. EHPD accordingly permitted officers with stops rates of Latinos that approached one in two or one in three to operate without oversight or discipline, strong evidence that EHPD at the very least enabled their discriminatory conduct.

(US DOJ 2011b, p. 7)

In their investigation of the New Orleans Police Department, the DOJ establishes a benchmark "use of force" rate per arrest nationally, not to establish the excessive force of the NOPD but to infer that the police department has a culture and practice of *underreporting* use of force:

We reviewed all uses of force reported by NOPD officers for the month of June 2010, 34 reports in all. During this same month, NOPD effectuated 6,787 arrests. Nationwide, estimates of force rates vary, but generally range from approximately 2–5 percent (i.e., for every 100 arrests, officers use reportable force in approximately 2–5 arrests). Thus, in the month of June 2010, if NOPD officers were using force at the national average rate, one would expect to have seen between approximately 135 and 340 uses of force, rather than the 34 NOPD reported.

(US DOJ 2011a, p. 14)

In this way, the report *normalizes* a certain level of police violence – "using force at the average national rate" – in order to diagnose the deeper problems related to excessive force in this case, concerning the systemic lack of accountability and review of all incidents of police use of force.

In addition to establishing numerical benchmarks of "normal" police use of force, a frequent technique employed in DOJ is a random sample audit. For instance, in their review of the Newark Police Department, the DOJ randomly selected 100 use of force incident reports from a nine month period and deter- mined that one-third of them were excessive, based on the testimony of the officer alone (US DOJ 2014). Similarly, in their report on the Baltimore police department (US DOJ 2016), the DOJ investigators used random sampling to audit arrest reports, stop-and-frisk stops of pedestrians, and instances of non- deadly force in order to demonstrate pervasive and consistent racial disparities across the range of coercive police actions.

Finally, in the DOJ investigation of the Washington, DC, police department (Yeomans 2006), the investigation even benchmarked a "normal" rate of *excessive* force. They consulted experts to identify what would constitute a "normal" rate of excessive force in a "well-managed and supervised" department (1–2 percent of all uses of force) and then identified, through random sampling, that in the DC case 15 percent of uses of force were excessive. Similarly, the DOJ even bench- marked the violence of police dogs, establishing that "in tightly run canine pro- grams, bites occur in only about 10 percent of deployments" whereas in the period under review, the Washington canine unit saw "bites nearly 70 percent of the time the canines were deployed" (Yeomans 2006).

In the DOJ investigations, CompStat's quantification of policing is redirected from an emphasis on "performance" measurements along the lines of productivity and efficiency towards an analysis of discriminatory enforcement, underreporting of force, and excess violence. The DOJ investigations and reports, I argue, are a hybrid technology: Institutionally, they are prompted in part by bottom-up agonistic democratic protest, but are conducted as top-down assertions of centralized federal authority. Substantively, they combine the form of the journalistic exposé with the neoliberal audit. I would like to cautiously suggest that the DOJ approach in these cases offers evidence for the political value of what Sanford Schram (2015, p. 174) calls "work[ing] through rather than around neoliberal policies to address the inequities they create" and what James Ferguson (2009, p. 173) describes as "the possibility of a truly progressive politics that would also draw on governmental mechanisms that we have become used to terming 'neoliberal'."

Ferguson's examples of such a possibility are instructive. In discussing cash grants for the poor in lieu of traditional welfare state programs as neoliberal, Ferguson claims (2009, p. 174) that, despite the redistributive ambitions, such proposals also involve "recognizably neoliberal elements, including the valorization of market efficiency, individual choice, and autonomy; themes of entrepreneurship; and skepticism about the state as a service provider." More broadly, Ferguson asks us to think about "techniques" as migratory, but in a different way than Brown's account of the "promiscuity" of neoliberal frames and technologies, in which, for instance, the best practices approach transforms different domains in a way that renders them all fundamentally alike. Ferguson emphasizes the way in which the process of diffusion, migration, and uptake can transform their political effects: "Techniques, that is to say, can 'migrate' across strategic camps, and devices of government that were invented to serve one purpose have often enough ended up, though history's irony, being harnessed to another" (2009, p. 174).

Thinking about the Department of Justice investigations into local police departments as a hybrid technology has broader implications for how we think about the relationship between neoliberal governance methods and democratic practice. While Brown is surely right to emphasize the profoundly depoliticizing and dedemocratizing effects of the proliferation of market logics and market metrics to an ever wider range of institutions and spaces, it is important not to overdetermine the conclusion theoretically in advance of an investigation into the specific ways benchmarks, best practices, and performance metrics are utilized.

Another technology central to policing – surveillance – might serve as a useful case in point. Police surveillance powers are expanding dramatically, through everything from social media and high altitude aerial surveillance to sophisticated data-mining and the Department of Homeland Security "fusion centers." But surveillance technologies in the form of police-worn body cameras are already being promoted as a panacea for police violence, promising to offer hard evidence of excessive force and a deterrent to brutality in the first place. Skeptics rightly worry that such cameras will be one more tool of civilian surveillance by the police, that the audio-visual data's being administered by police departments will lead to its concealment, and that, far from being an objective record of events, the framing effect of the camera will encourage the public's identification with the police. These concerns should not, however, lead to the conclusion that video surveillance is essentially a tool of domination. Public surveillance (or better, sousveillance) of the police, in the form of cell-phone videos, streamed online and eventually taken up by the news media, are an important democratic iteration of the technology (Squillacote and Feldman n.d.).

Indeed, one way of understanding the core meaning of democracy in the context of a complex state apparatus is in terms of social surveillance. For instance, Rosanvallon (2008) sees a compatibility across and between surveillance of parts of the state administrative apparatus by independent commissions, internal organizational audits along the lines of the New Public Management, and the surveillance of social movement organizations, media, and at the broadest level, the internet. ("The internet," he writes, "is … creating an open space for oversight and evaluation. The Internet is not merely an 'instrument': it *is* the surveillance function" [2008, p. 70].) Thought of this way, the linkages I articulate between the Department of Justice investigations, the form of the neoliberal (or New Public Management) audit, and social movement activities of surveillance and denunciation are less surprising than one might suppose given the left critique of neoliberalism. Those linkages might even be said to indicate the health and vitality of institutional and extra-institutional democratic practice.

Bibliography

Apuzzo, M. and Fernandez, M. (2014). Justice Dept. Inquiry to Focus on Practices of Police in Ferguson. *New York Times*. Retrieved from: www.nytimes.com/2014/09/04/us/politics/justice-dept-to-investigate-ferguson-police-practices.html

Banks, D., Ruddle, P., Kennedy, E., and Planty, M. (2016). Arrest-Related Deaths Program Redesign Study, 2015–2016: Preliminary Findings. Bureau of Justice Statistics. Retrieved from: www.bjs.gov/content/pub/pdf/ardprs1516pf.pdf

Bialik, C. (2016). The Government Finally has a Realistic Estimate of Killings by Police. Retrieved from: https://fivethirtyeight.com/features/the-government-finally-has-a-realistic-estimate-of-killings-by-police/

Bratton, W. and Andrews, W. (1999). What We've Learned about Policing. *City Journal*. Retrieved from: www.city-journal.org/html/what-we've-learned-about-policing-11790.html

Broadwater, L. (2015). Baltimore Mayor Seeks Federal Investigation of Police Department. *Baltimore Sun*. Retrieved from: www.baltimoresun.com/news/maryland/politics/bs-md-ci-doj-partnership-20150506-story.html

Bronstein, N. (2015). Police Management and Quotas: Governance in the CompStat Era. *Columbia Journal of Law and Social Problems*, 48(4), 543–581.

Brown, W. (2015). *Undoing the Demos: Neoliberalism's Stealth Revolution*. New York: Zone Books.

Bruno, I. (2009). The "Indefinite Discipline" of Competitiveness Benchmarking as a Neoliberal Technology of Government. *Minerva*, 47(3), 261–280.

Chanin, J. (2011). *Negotiated Justice? The Legal, Administrative, and Policy Implications of "Pattern or Practice" Police Misconduct Reform*. PhD Dissertation, American University School of Public Affairs. Retrieved from: www.ncjrs.gov/pdffiles1/nij/grants/237957.pdf

Davies, W. (2014). *The Limits of Neoliberalism: Authority, Sovereignty, and the Logic of Competition*. London: Sage.

Eterno, J. and Silverman, E. (2010). The NYPD's CompStat: Compare Statistics or Compose Statistics? *International Journal of Police Science and Management*, 12(3), 426–449.

Feller, I. (2009). Performance Measurement and the Governance of American Academic Science. *Minerva*, 47, 323–344.

Ferguson, J. (2009). The Uses of Neoliberalism. *Antipode*, 41(s1), 166–184.

Fritze, J. (2017). Jeff Sessions Voices Concern about Use of Consent Decrees for Police. *Baltimore Sun*. Retrieved from: www.baltimoresun.com/news/maryland/politics/blog/bal-jeff-sessions-voices-concern-about-use-of-consent-decrees-for-police-20170110-story.html

Harcourt, B. (2011). *The Illusion of Free Markets*. Cambridge, MA: Harvard University Press.

Harmon, R. (2012). The Problem of Policing. *Michigan Law Review*, 110, 761–817.

Le Galès, P. (2016). Performance Measurement as a Policy Instrument. *E-Prints – Centre D'Etudes Europeennes*. Retrieved from: www.sciencespo.fr/centre-etudes-europeennes/sites/sciencespo.fr.centre-etudes-europeennes/files/1606%20Le%20Gales%20Performance%20Measurement.pdf

Lerman, A. E. and Weaver, V. M. (2014). *Arresting Citizenship*. Chicago: University of Chicago Press.

Lorenz, C. (2012). If You're So Smart, Why Are You Under Surveillance? Universities, Neoliberalism, and New Public Management. *Critical Inquiry*, 38(3), 599–629.

Lowery, W. (2014). How Many Police Shootings a Year? No One Knows. *Washington Post*, September 8.

Madar, C. (2014). Why It's Impossible to Indict a Cop. *The Nation*. Retrieved from: www.thenation.com/article/why-its-impossible-indict-cop/

Mann, S. and Ferenbok, J. (2013). New Media and the Power Politics of Sousveillance in a Surveillance-Dominated World. *Surveillance & Society*, 11(1/2), 18–34.

Potter, G. (2015). Police Violence, Capital and Neoliberalism. *Imagining Justice*. Retrieved from: http://uprootingcriminology.org/essays/police-violence-capital-neoliberalism/

President's Task Force on 21st Century Policing (2015). *Final Report of the President's Task Force on 21st Century Policing*. Washington, DC: Office of Community Oriented Policing Services.

Rosanvallon, P. (2008). *Counter-Democracy: Politics in an Age of Distrust*. New York: Cambridge University Press.

Rose, N. (1999). *Powers of Freedom: Reframing Political Thought*. Cambridge: Cambridge University Press.

Rushin, S. (2014). Federal Enforcement of Police Reform. *Fordham Law Review*, 82, 3189–3247.

Schatmeier, E. (2013). Reforming Police Use-of-Force Practices: A Case Study of the Cincinnati Police Department. *Columbia Journal of Law and Social Problems*, 46, 539–585.

Schram, S. (2015). *The Return of Ordinary Capitalism: Neoliberalism, Precarity, Occupy*. New York: Oxford University Press.

Scott, J. (1998). *Seeing Like a State*. New Haven, CT: Yale University Press.

Soss, J., Fording, R., and Schram, S. (2011). *Disciplining the Poor: Neoliberal Paternalism and the Persistent Power of Race*. Chicago: University of Chicago Press.

Squillacote, R. and Feldman, L. (n.d.). *Police Abuse and Democratic Accountability: Agonistic Surveillance of the Administrative State*. Manuscript submitted for publication.

United States Department of Justice (US DOJ) (2001). *Principles for Promoting Police Integrity: Examples of Promoting Police Practices and Policies*. Retrieved from: www.ncjrs.gov/pdffiles1/ojp/186189.pdf

United States Department of Justice (US DOJ) (2011a). *Investigation of the New Orleans Police Department*. Retrieved from: www.justice.gov/sites/default/files/crt/legacy/2011/03/17/nopd_report.pdf

United States Department of Justice (US DOJ) (2011b). *Findings Letter RE: Investigation of the East Haven Police Department*. Retrieved from: www.justice.gov/sites/default/files/crt/legacy/2011/12/19/easthaven_findletter_12-19-11.pdf

United States Department of Justice (US DOJ) (2014). *Investigation of the Newark Police Department*. Retrieved from: www.justice.gov/crt/about/spl/documents/newark_findings_7-22-14.pdf

United States Department of Justice (US DOJ) (2016). *Investigation of the Baltimore Police Department*. Retrieved from: www.justice.gov/crt/case-document/baltimore-police-department-findings-report

United States Department of Justice (US DOJ) (2017). *Investigation of the Chicago Police Department*. Retrieved from: www.justice.gov/crt/case-document/file/925771/download

Wacquant, L. (2009). *Punishing the Poor: The Neoliberal Government of Social Insecurity*. Durham, NC: Duke University Press.

Yeomans, W. (2006). *Findings Letter re Use of Force by the Washington Metropolitan Police Department*. Retrieved from: www.clearinghouse.net/chDocs/public/PN-DC-0001-0002.pdf

PART IV

Urban Governance

At Home and Abroad

10

NEOLIBERALIZING DETROIT

Jamie Peck and Heather Whiteside

Introduction: Detroit as Target

"It's there for the taking." That is how Fred Siegel of the Manhattan Institute described Detroit in the summer of 2013, as the city tumbled inexorably towards what would be the largest municipal bankruptcy in US history. It was a flippant remark that spoke volumes about the conservative movement's strategic line on the still-unfolding financial crisis that had been enveloping cities across the country in the years since the Wall Street crash of 2008. And it also represented a blunt summary of the ideologically consistent but in practice continuously evolving position of the Manhattan Institute, a New York-based think tank that since the late 1970s has been at the forefront of the development of a distinctively neo-liberal approach to urban policy, including workfare, zero-tolerance policing, and a pro-corporate development ethos. "The depth of corruption and dysfunction [in Detroit] is so fantastic," Siegel continued, "it's so far that you might describe it as Third World dysfunction. There is no need [for conservatives] to gin it up. It's just right there" (quoted in Gold 2013, p. 2). The financial travails of Detroit would be an opportunity for conservative intellectuals and opinion shapers to rail, once again, against the poisonous legacy of New Deal urbanism, and to repurpose their parables of welfare dependency and governmental failure, this time to frame and facilitate a first-world model for financially mandated structural adjustment at the urban scale. Detroit was going to have to pay the price for what Siegel's Manhattan Institute colleague Steven Malanga (2013a, p. A13) pointedly described on the *Wall Street Journal*'s op-ed page as "tin-cup urbanism."

The political rationalities and policy technologies of neoliberalism are well suited to these moments (and sites) of crisis. In fact, it could be argued that they have been made, and repeatedly remade, for these very circumstances. There is blame shifting happening here, but also quite purposeful forms of social, institutional, and spatial targeting – all sutured to a favored package of policy "solutions." And while there are plenty of repeating refrains and routines, the fact that the terrain and the targets are always moving means that what is better understood as a contradictory process of neoliberal*ization* can in practice only operate as an adaptive mode of governance, a "flexible credo" (see Peck 2010). In the context of the extended fallout of the Wall Street crash of 2008 and the Great Recession, what began as a banking (and financial) crisis was duly rescripted, in a now-familiar fashion, as a crisis of *and for* the social state, not least at the urban scale. This, in turn, has been associated with new rounds of improvised crisis management, creative institutional destruction, and experimental reregulation. Prior to the bankruptcy declaration of 2013, Detroit had already been placed under the control of an emergency manager – corporate restructuring specialist Kevyn Orr – whose appointment over the heads of elected local officials and the mayor was an initiative of Republican Governor Rick Snyder, courtesy of brazenly anti-democratic state law PA 436–2012. Subject to what Orr liked to call "the rule of reason," the city's accelerated restructuring was being guided by the principles of technocratic financial management, in effect a normalized mode of neoliberal governance based on the principles of privatization, outsourcing, governmental purging, and lean administration. Reflecting a political culture in which most forms of public-sector investment and sociospatial redistribution are liable to be reflexively tagged in the pejorative language of "bailouts," local-government profligacy and "deadbeat cities" are frequently indicted:

> [T]he hard truth is that Motown is a victim of its own political vices and a bailout would merely forestall the necessary rehab … Misrule has resulted in the nation's highest violent crime rate, worst schools, blight and corruption … As history shows, sending more cash to Detroit won't fix its breakdown in self-government. Another bailout would merely support its toxic political culture of neglect and corruption.
>
> *(*Wall Street Journal *2013, p. A14)*

The roots of this toxic culture are often laid at the door of "the man who killed Detroit" (Malanga 2013b), Mayor Coleman Young, whose two decades in office (1974–1993) began with the oil crisis and a worldwide recession, spanning the extended restructuring of the auto industry and the progressive detachment of the US federal government from urban financing and urban policy. For conservative critics, his was the unapologetic face of New Deal urbanism, the personification of Big Municipal Government, a tax-and-spend Democrat ruling almost uncontested over a city scarred by too much bureaucracy, too much welfare, too much union power, too much regulation, too much federal largesse, and not nearly enough free-enterprise spirit, individual responsibility, and fiscal control. To a considerable degree, these fed into normalized understandings: "To suburban whites ... the disintegration of cities like Detroit [was] irrefutable evidence that the politics of liberalism, and the programs of the Great Society in particular, had been a terrible social and economic mistake" (Thompson 2001, p. 242).

Rationales of this sort effectively established the pretext for an unprecedented assault on public-sector programs, public-sector employees, public-sector unions, and public-sector pensions, not only in Detroit but in cities across the country (see Tabb 2014; Davidson and Ward 2017). In this context, a neoliberal version of what "history shows" would be pre-emptively stitched together with a new generation of technocratic, autocratic, and postdemocratic interventions, variously justified in terms of an austere policymaking commonsense, the rule of financial reason, and (even) a twenty-first century reboot of "Caesarism" (see Gillette 2014; Eide 2016; cf. Peck 2017).

The critical analysis of neoliberalism, it follows, must involve acts of deconstruction as well as reconstruction. With this as its goal, the chapter develops a reading of neoliberal urbanism through the prism of Detroit, exploring the extended prehistory of the city's bankruptcy filing and fiscally cleansed present. Like the character in Hemingway's *The Sun Also Rises* who, when asked how he ended up bankrupt replied *both ways*, "gradually and then suddenly," financial default was for Detroit above all an historical process more than it could ever be reduced to some legally bracketed event. It was an historical process, furthermore, that brings vividly to light the social, spatial, and scalar dynamics of neoliberalization, across the long arc from defensive entrepreneurialism to disciplinary financialization.

In a somewhat more abstract register, this extended case also speaks to the character of "neoliberal urbanism" as an analytical frame, mid-level concept, and conjunctural formation (see Theodore et al. 2011; Peck et al. 2013; Hackworth 2016; Peck 2017), and as a signifier for a rolling and roiling process of restructuring, enacted in the name of free markets and smaller states, that in its contradictory practice is neither static nor singular. It is never static in the sense that neoliberalization denotes a direction rather than a destination: rather than proceeding in a linear fashion towards some more market/less state equilibrium, neoliberalization follows a zigzagging path of creative destruction grounded in the dialectical interplay of deregulatory rollbacks and the variously crisis-assisted, experimental, and strategic rollout of corporate-centric and market-friendly modes of governance. It is not singular in the dual sense of the absence of a paradigmatic "master transition" or definitive case, coupled with conditions of contradictory coexistence, in which actually existing neoliberalism is unable to stand on its own (or monopolize the social field), but can only be found in context-specific conjunctures, recombinant forms, and volatile hybrids. Together, these conditions of existence mean that neoliberalism is not just contingently but *necessarily* variegated, mutating, unevenly developed, shape-shifting, and site-shifting; that it is marked by family resemblances, recurring tropes, and patterned routines but at the same time exhibits the characteristics of a non-repeating and open-ended historical process;

and that its contradictory historical geographies are therefore always in the making, flanked as they are by ongoing dynamics of contestation, crisis, and consolidation.

Reading the Detroit case in these terms means taking account of what has been an extended and especially checkered history of neoliberal restructuring, refracted through a *constitutive* politics of race, in which the intersecting dynamics of deindustrialization, suburbanization, segregation, and municipal-state incapacitation have combined to produce an overdetermined and by any measure structural crisis, to which an accumulating series of reactions and responses have amounted to radically less than a resolution. When it comes to the question, then, of why it was that Detroit went broke, and why its metastasizing state of bankruptcy far exceeds the legal or technical definitions of the term, there is no shortage of circumstantial causes – or for that matter culprits. Local journalist Nathan Bomey's pithy checklist is arguably as good as any:

> The contraction of the U.S. auto industry. White flight and the exodus of wealth that began in the 1950s. Discriminatory real estate practices. The 1967 riots. Regional political discord. Pervasive government corruption. A lack of corporate social responsibility. The destruction of black neighborhoods to make room for highways.
>
> Former mayor Coleman Young. Former mayor Kwame Kilpatrick. Former president George W. Bush. Wall Street bankers. A dysfunctional mass transportation system. Shattered public schools. The disintegration of the job market.
>
> Predatory lenders. The Great Recession. A collapse in home prices. Greedy unions. Democrats who were in bed with unions. Republicans who tried to kill unions. Republicans who were in bed with big business. Skyrocketing taxes. A failure to collect those taxes. Crime-ridden neighborhoods. Police brutality. Police lethargy. Drugs. Blight.
>
> Neglectful City Council members. Hapless bureaucrats. Generous pensions. Gold-plated health care benefits. Overspending. An explosion of debt. A culture of denial.
>
> *(Bomey 2016, p. 1)*

By way of a prequel of sorts to the recent round of critical analyses that have problematized the neoliberalization of Detroit in the restructuring present (see Akers 2015; Peck 2015; Peck and Whiteside 2016; Hackworth 2016), the chapter returns to the final decades of the twentieth century, in particular to the mayoral administration of Coleman Young (1974–1993), in order to reassess what Hackworth has called conservative "parables" of the Motor City, which have been purposefully mobilized for their negative demonstration effects, ostensibly as proof of the "failures of Black militancy and Keynesianism" (2017, p. 549). Counter to these revisionist conservative histories of Detroit, we will develop the argument that Coleman Young's Detroit was, at the same time, a protean site for the *production* of emergent forms of neoliberal urbanism, just as its constrained circumstances illustrated many of the practical and political *limits* of progressive governance in the context of devolved financial discipline. The chapter's conclusion returns to post-bankruptcy Detroit, where "Made in Detroit" can be read not just as a hipster marketing slogan, more as a question concerning the source, character, impact, and provenance of this stressed and incomplete process of neoliberal transformation, a question of the ongoing *remaking* of Detroit.

Between Entrepreneurialism and Empowerment

No figure looms larger in revisionist conservative historiographies of Detroit than Coleman Young. It was Young, the one-time labor organizer and socialist firebrand who as mayor, in the words of James Q. Wilson (1998, p. 3), had rejected racial integration and balanced economic development "in favor of a flamboyant black-power style that won him loyal followers, but he left the city a fiscal and social wreck." It was Young the "closet Marxist" (Mitsotakis 2013, p. 2) who in the course of "his 20-year reign [had] ignored crime, inflamed racial tensions and built a patronage machine" (*Wall Street Journal* 2013, p. A14). And it was Young who for the right would symbolize for the realm of urban governance a variant of the pathologizing trope of "welfare dependency," with all of the same racial signifiers, a "tin-cup" entitlement culture based on the cultural suppression of entrepreneurialism and self-reliance under which "the increasingly distressed city became a fiscal ward of the state and federal governments" (Malanga 2013a, p. A13).

These arguments have been afforded a degree of academic credibility – and indeed a broad measure of mainstream policymaking acceptance – in the shape of Edward Glaeser's influential version of neoclassical urban economics. The book that secured the Harvard economist's reputation as a globally renowned urban guru, *Triumph of the City*, is a freewheeling celebration of the benefits, not to say glories, of a pre- and post-New Deal amalgam of deregulated urban development, freed from governmental interference and powered by a combination of human capital and competitive spirits. Written, marketed, and promoted with the assistance of the Manhattan Institute (where Glaeser is a long-established senior fellow), *Triumph* borrows liberally from the narrative conceits of Freakonomics-style popular economics and the new genre of feel-good urbanology to construct a bracingly affirmative account of the power and potential of cities, with but one notable exception – Detroit. Motown duly serves as the anti-competitive counterpoint and "the book's prime example of decline" (*Economist* 2011, p. 92), an industrial-era anachronism and a "toxic" expression of municipal welfarism (Glaeser 2011, p. 57). Young is taken to personify what Glaeser calls the "edifice complex," an excessive reliance on grandiose infrastructure projects; he is accused of playing Robin Hood by not only raising the taxes but then by redistributing, therefore practically inviting businesses and the aspirant middle-classes to escape to the suburbs. More perniciously, however, Detroit under Coleman Young is presented as a textbook illustration of the so-called "Curley effect," a model of "racial favoritism" in which local political leaders harvest electoral rewards by catering to the dominant ethnic group in the city, while actively marginalizing others. Despite the fact that the Curley hypothesis was dressed up with algebraic "proofs," and named as if by misdirection after an Irish-American mayor of Boston, it is the failed development strategies, affirmative-action policies, and "righteous anger" of Coleman Young that is afforded critical-case status, since it was in Detroit that the "effect" could be connected to a pattern of predicted outcomes in which not only jobs, white residents, middle-class families, and enterprising individuals but "civilization [itself] had fled the city" (Glaeser 2011, p. 55).

In the wake of Detroit's accelerating financial crisis, post-2008, this (per)version of historical causality has been deployed – to considerable effect, it must be said – to rationalize, to justify, and to legitimate new rounds of social-state purging, privatization, public-service triage, and neoliberal policy experimentation. As Jason Hackworth has argued, conservative parables of governmental profligacy, racialized dependency, cultural dysfunction, unchecked union power, and entrepreneurial deficit have been (re)mobilized in order to paint Detroit as a bastion of municipal socialism and welfare-state bloat, as a Great Society dystopia, when in fact the city has been subject to decades of classically neoliberal restructuring:

> Far from being a profligate quasi-socialistic local state, [Detroit's] governance has been characterised by brutal budget cuts to virtually every one of its departments and intense collaboration with the private sector for 60 years. Though Coleman Young ... is often framed as a misguided socialist by neoliberals ... he is arguably more remembered by Detroiters as being a handmaiden for the automakers ... [In accordance with neoliberal principles, public] spending has been cut, unions decimated, taxes slashed, services streamlined, and yet neither meaningful investment nor social stability has returned. It is difficult to frame Detroit as an over-interventionist collectivist government, if one is interested in historical fact.
>
> *(2016, pp. 543–44)*

Analysts of the actually existing history of the Coleman Young regime disagree about some things, it is true, but there is near consensus around the fact that the mayor, from the outset, was both a fiscal realist and an economic-development pragmatist. His public-service reforms, just as they were motivated by the pressing need to tackle institutionalized racism (especially in the police service) and advancing affirmative action, were also governed by principles of conservative fiscal management. Shrewd observers rated it as a "notable achievement" that the city had remained "intact" after Young's first year in the "God-awful job of

Mayor of Detroit," given the scale of the challenges that had been inherited: "The city payroll was met each week, with the help of a few hundred layoffs. The garbage got picked up. The teachers didn't strike. The police didn't revolt" (Tyson 1975, pp. 237–238). With little or no alternative but to govern as a fiscal conservative, Young proved to be a skillful interlocutor between the city's frag- mented constituencies, fashioning a "financial leadership strategy [and] governing style" around an often volatile mixture of interests that included "interest group politics in the New Deal tradition; a tough bargaining position with the unions; active confrontation with opponents and critics; and maintaining the independence of city management structures, that is, protecting them from what have been called fiscal managers" (Rich 1989, p. 234). Few others could have straddled (indeed for the most part managed) these often-conflicting interests the way that Young did, a man whose own biography expressed "the contradictory relationship between big business, big labor, and the black community" (Hill 1983, p. 106).

The trials and tradeoffs associated with navigating conflicts and contradictions of this magnitude have led some to characterize city management as exhibiting an effectively decades-long "regimeless" mode of governance (Reese and Sands 2013), but in many respects Detroit was one of the pioneers of the pro-corporate, real-estate based model of downtown development (see Orr and Stoker 1994; Eisinger 2003). Young put his political machine, not to say his own energy and charisma, at the service of a business-friendly revitalization effort, cultivating elite partnerships with prominent figures from the business community like Henry Ford II (whom he liked to call Hank the Deuce), General Motors' president Elliot Estes, oil baron and developer Max Fisher, and property magnate and investor Al Taubman. Dedicating both public dollars and political capital to major redevelopment projects may have resembled a classic case of growth-machine politics, at least on the surface, but Detroit was a site for the production of frustrated prototypes, at best. When Young was first elected to office, the city was already on a steep path of economic decline, an existential (pre)condition that in a material sense preempted much of the realistic scope for rational economic planning or strategic prioritization (Hill 1983; Rich 1989; Boyle 2001). With development strategies pursued in the face of persistent negative economic growth, as a creative and proactive player on the metropolitan political scene, the mayor evidently felt that there were few, if any, alternatives to working tirelessly on cementing the alliances with those corporate, financial, and development interests with residual commitments to downtown.

Young's early 1970s election may indeed have been "a black political victory, pure and simple," and his administration would move with urgent purpose to combat "blackjack rule by police," while opening up African-American employment opportunities across the public service, but economic development and job creation were overriding priorities for this self-proclaimed "pragmatic radical" from the beginning too (Darden et al. 1987, p. 216; Hill 1983; Young with Wheeler 1994, p. 212). At first, the model of governance was effectively corporatist, the mayor working with local business and labor leaders to broker major development projects with the assistance of significant federal funding. Having secured more than $2 billion in federal support for his public-private partnership program under the Ford administration, Young would later capitalize upon much closer ties to President Carter, of whom the mayor had been an early supporter. Carter's urban-policy program was all but made in Detroit, with key political operatives relocating to Washington, DC, as federal funds were soon flowing back to the Motor City. What Edward Glaeser would subsequent diagnose as the mayor's "edifice complex" can be seen in less pejorative terms as "a successful partnership [forged] with a select group of private-sector interests to pursue a classic downtown-renewal strategy based on bringing upscale commercial establishments, hotels, apartments, and convention facilities to Detroit to offset the decline in manufacturing industry" (Orr and Stoker 1994, p. 51). The Young administration's strategy was to parlay those powers that remained at the city's disposal into a network of economic-development agencies within which the capacities of the public and private sectors could be combined – organizationally, financially, and through interlocking directorships – in pursuit of what Richard Child Hill called a "corporate center strategy." In its most fulsome expression this envisaged:

> [A] riverfront teeming with the tourist and convention crowds, a strong "first downtown" serving as the financial pillar to the region's economy, a "second downtown" thriving on "culture and silicon," a surrounding expanse of neighborhoods whose population stability and economic well-being [would be] assured by the retention and attraction of modern industries to renovated industrial corridors and port facilities. This is the best of all possible worlds: the full flowering of the Detroit Renaissance.
>
> *(Hill 1983, p. 105)*

In this context, the appeal – both material and symbolic – of large-scale, "visible," and landscape-altering development projects is not difficult to understand (see Thomas 2013). As historian Kevin Boyle (2001, p. 122) assessed the situation, "Young needed help – any help – and it is easy to see how he could have been seduced by the promise of a new factory, sports arena, or high-rise."

That this "conserving strategy" effectively failed, concerned as it was to *restore* Detroit's economic fortunes, says at least as much about the scale of private-sector disinvestment from the city during the 1970s and 1980s, coupled with unprecedented rates of white flight and inner-city deprivation, as it does about some endogenous form of governance failure (see Thompson 2001; Shaw 2009). Specialists in the comparative analysis of urban-political regimes, in fact, score Detroit according to its structural location in the "least advantaged bargaining context" available to Western cities, one of private-sector dependency in which those nominally in charge possess "few choices" since the initiative is with business.

subject to the vagaries of market conditions (Kantor et al. 1997, pp. 352–353). Coleman Young may have enjoyed a substantial level of political autonomy, courtesy of his practically unassailable electoral position, but his policymaking capacity and room for political-economic maneuver were both profoundly constrained, in turn, by the city's fiscally hobbled state and by the centrifugal forces of deindustrialization and suburbanization.

During the time that Detroit enjoyed (preferential) access to federal funds, the preconditions for what has been labeled a "vendor regime" strategy were in place, albeit one in which the mayor's office could be said to have been reduced (though never naively) to "facilitat[ing] business privilege" (Kantor et al. 1997, p. 360). Once Reagan was in the White House, the foundations of Detroit's fragile public-private partnership quickly began to unravel. The president whom Young had famously called "Old Pruneface" abruptly installed an effectively *anti*-urban program, slashing federal transfers to the cities, and to Detroit in particular (see Figure 10.1). Now that what Young liked to refer to as his city's "Jimmy Carter dollars" had stopped flowing, his capacity to deliver public-sector funding for development projects was sharply attenuated. Worse still, federal finances had been used to underwrite general revenue spending for several years, as the tax base continued to shrink (Anton 1983; Young with Wheeler 1994). At the beginning of the Reagan years, Young vividly portrayed the city's vulnerable state this way: "This is not a TV Western and there is no cavalry out there galloping to our rescue. All we can do is circle the wagons – and live or die based on our own strength" (quoted in Fireman 1981b, p. 11A).

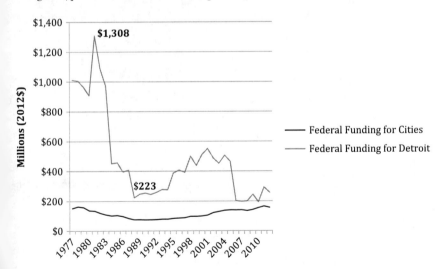

FIGURE 10.1 Federal funding for cities vs. for Detroit
Source: Authors' calculations based on the *Fiscally Standardized Cities* database, Lincoln Institute of Land: http://datatoolkits.lincolninst.edu/subcenters/fiscally-standardized-cities/

In fact, Detroit was already teetering on the brink of bankruptcy. Following a close call with insolvency in the mid-1970s, paralleling the New York City crisis, an initial round of structural changes had been pushed through, but by the end of the decade it was clear that "the glue … was coming apart," and that the city was on a path to become a "fiscal leper," having lost access to the open bond market, in the absence of "fundamental, not makeshift, changes in [its] revenue structure" (Rich 1989, pp. 246, 258, 237). In 1981, Young launched what amounted to a "save-the-city plan," described as an "all-or-nothing strategy" for averting financial default (Fireman 1981c, p. 1A). The city's financial situation was undeniably dire, but there was little or no evidence that this could be accounted for by budgetary profligacy or municipal mismanagement. A blue-chip commission empanelled to investigate the rapidly advancing budget crisis (chaired by a retired senior executive from Ford, Fred Secrest) had concluded that "the city's budget crisis was not attributable to poor fiscal management but to a variety of factors beyond the city's control, including a declining tax base, rising unemployment, shrinking population and rapid inflation" (Fireman 1981a, p. 3A), going as far as to praise the municipality's "excellent financial management" (Secrest Task Force, quoted in *Detroit Free Press* 1981a, p. 8A). Speaking at the Detroit Economic Club, prominent financier Felix Rohatyn, arguably the most important figure in the management of New York City's fiscal crisis, concurred while adding:

> Detroit's problem is *not* a gigantic accumulation of short-term debt as a result of a decade of hidden deficits; it is *not* a result of poor fiscal management, weak mayoral leadership, failure to face problems and lack of co-operation among business, labor and government.
>
> *(quoted in* Detroit Free Press *1981a, p. 8A, emphasis added)*

Rohatyn's credibility had been important to the balancing act that the mayor had to strike ("The iceman cometh. Maybe now the people will believeth," he had told the press), given the need to secure "trust, participation, and sacrifice" across all of the city's constituencies and interested parties (Young with Wheeler 1994, p. 260).

Some of the most difficult negotiations were with the city's unions, where Young (a former union activist himself) engaged in hardball negotiations that he described as "rough [but] the alternatives are much rougher … That's not a threat, it's a fact" (quoted in Fireman 1981a, p. 3A). Confronted with the stark alternatives of "brinksmanship or statesmanship," the unions opted for the latter accepting a package of wage and benefit concessions in exchange for job security (Rich 1989, p. 257). Young's strategy, which he described as a "three-legged stool," the loss of any one of which would leave the city and his administration "on our ass," eventually worked, an experience that had been for the mayor "the ultimate exercise in politics" (Young with Wheeler 1994, p. 261). A municipal default was averted, at the eleventh hour, by the imposition of an austerit budget, a state-approved increase in the income-tax rate for commuters and residents, and an emergency bond issue of $125 million, which was rated as an "extraordinary" accomplishment in the local press (Kushma 1984, p. 10A). Young secured waged concessions from the public-sector unions, including a two-year wage freeze in the early 1980s, and reduced the size of the municipal workforce to levels not seen since the 1930s (Kushma 1984). Six thousand city workers were fired by 1984 and most community recreation facilities (skating rinks, pools) were shuttered, initiatives that the mayor's former press secretary describes as being in an effort to "[keep] a pretty tight rein ... in some very difficult economic times" (quoted in Bomey and Gallagher 2016).

Detroit was actively exploring how it might learn to live in the context of diminished means, to cope with a downsizing economy and a depopulating city, while also authorizing (under profoundly constrained circumstances) strategies of revitalization. Resonances with today's Detroit, in this context, are difficult to miss. It was Coleman Young, for example, who floated the idea – in the context of the financial crisis of the early 1980s – of a "self-service city," in which voluntary contributions and community labor would selectively replace a range of municipal functions, including the adoption of parks and park maintenance, the clearing of vacant lots, the reflation and animation of gift economies, and (even) the recruitment of residents to positions in the police reserves and as fire-department auxiliaries (see Cheyfitz 1980; cf. Boyle 2001; Kinder 2016). While acknowledging the laudability of these and other voluntary efforts, these prototypical experiments in DIY urbanism were criticized at the time for their distributional consequences, since local residents were effectively "compensating for public resources flowing to private corporations" (Hill 1983, p. 112).

Subsequent analyses of the deteriorating fiscal health of US cities would confirm Detroit's uniquely challenging situation: for Coleman Young to restore the levels of public-service provision to something resembling those prevailing when he was about to enter office, in 1972, the revenue-raising *capacity* of the city would have to be boosted by 92 percent by 1982, a deterioration that was attributed to "social and economic trends outside the control of city officials" (Ladd 1994, pp. 241, 255). It is notable, in this context, that Detroit was experiencing an especially aggravated form of fiscal stress, but it was one that was nevertheless *systematically* felt across many of the big-city economies in the United States, where a structural gap had opened up between (constrained) revenue-raising capacities and (often unmet) service needs and budgetary demands. While the fiscal health of the typical big city improved marginally during the 1980s, following the return of geographically uneven economic growth, Detroit was one of a handful of cities in which structural budget problems continued to deepen, presenting an unpalatable choice between severe reductions in public services or large, and potentially damaging, tax increases (Ladd 1994).

In retrospect, the close call with municipal bankruptcy in 1981 bifurcated the Coleman Young years in a more than temporal sense. The vendor regime of the

1970s had been aspirational, purposeful, and in some respects visionary; it had been a time of building, albeit in the face of macroeconomic uncertainty and unrelenting tides of disinvestment, decentralization, and deindustrialization. After the early 1980s, in the final decade of Young's time in office, the vendor regime would visibly fracture as the administration became increasingly embattled, while an inexorably deteriorating set of political and economic fundamentals continued to erode what realistic prospects the city might have had.

At the symbolic heart of Detroit's rebuilding efforts during the 1970s was the aptly named Renaissance Center, the downtown office and hotel complex developed by Henry Ford II, Al Taubman, and financier Max Fisher with a funding package exceeding $500 million, where the City of Detroit's role had been mostly facilitative – land clearance, technical support, and cheerleading. In 1982, Ford pulled his investment out of the loss-making venture that itself was soon in mortgage default. Downtown Detroit has been blighted by an oversupply of office space ever since, every subsequent development project involving public subsidies of some kind to this day (Galster 2012; Reese and Sands 2013). At Young's inauguration in 1974, Ford had spoken expansively of a "new coalition" between business, labor, and government in Detroit (quoted in Darden et al. 1987, p. 216); a decade later it was clear that Detroit needed the auto companies much more than they needed the city, their subsequent involvement in development projects being reduced to matters of "public relations or corporate charity," while the attitude of the remaining business community towards the Young administration veered between appeasement, indifference, and active hostility (Orr and Stoker 1994, p. 58). All along, it had been clear that the political fortunes of the Young administration, and the viability of the city's economic-development strategy, were "inextricably tied to [an] investment agenda set by the corporate business community" (Hill 1983, p. 108).

If Coleman Young had initially ridden into office on a wave of community support, the institutionalization of which squeezed out more autonomous neighborhood organizing initiatives for a while, by the late 1980s his administration was struggling to manage, if not contain, a much more restive array of social movements (see Shaw 2009). For many, the now-notorious case of GM's new plant in Poletown was the tipping point. In 1980, the company had issued a challenge to the City of Detroit to deliver a development site appropriate for the construction of a large-scale plant, larded with all of the usual subsidies. In what immediately became a priority for the administration, an almost 500-acre site was identified in Poletown, the seizure and clearance of which entailed $200 million in direct costs to the City but also the obliteration of a vibrant neighborhood (including two schools, sixteen churches, a hospital, and more than 3,000 residents), overriding what had been a concerted campaign of community opposition (Fasenfest 1986; Darden et al. 1987; Wylie 1989). The company was practically gifted the site, for $8 million, complete with a twelve-year tax abatement, after which it would eventually deliver barely half of the promised 6,000 jobs. The sense of betrayal generated by the Poletown controversy would prove to be a long-lasting one, even if Young claimed (erroneously) that "that one plant makes up for every g–damn thing that went into the suburbs [over] the past 20 years" (quoted in Kushma 1984, p. 10A).

It is no coincidence that Young's successor, Dennis Archer, came to power with the backing of community activists, in addition to pragmatic sections of the business community. Young had notably declined to attend the inauguration of President Bill Clinton, but Archer would be quick to capture what benefits there were from the third-way urban policy that followed. Detroit's (competitively tendered) bid for one of the newly designated Empowerment Zones was considered one of the best prepared, securing the city a $100 million grant and some symbolic visibility, setting the stage for several years of incremental improvements under the new mayor, albeit drawing upon an entirely conventional package of development initiatives, projects, and tropes (Eisinger 2003). Detroit went on to turn every page in the increasingly dog-eared playbook of orthodox economic-development initiatives. There would be new sports stadiums, General Motors would purchase and come to use the Renaissance Center as its world headquarters, legalized casino gambling was introduced (one of Coleman Young's long-frustrated projects), and public-private partnerships like the Riverwalk and Campus Mauritius projects were launched, aimed at downtown restoration and beautification. Ultimately, sustained economic growth would prove elusive and debt-reliant governance would intensify, disciplinary financialization eventually pulling the city's budgetary situation apart by 2013.

Conclusion: Default Explanations

Across the field of critical urban studies, explanatory invocations of "neoliberalism" have acquired something akin to a default position in recent years. Much of this work, understandably, has been concerned with the real-time analysis of the various breaking edges of transformation, often tagged to processual understandings of neoliberalization as an adaptive technology of governance repeatedly reanimated by crisis conditions as well as strategic considerations (see Theodore et al. 2011; Peck et al. 2013). It is not uncommon, however, for work in this vein to rely upon stylized sketches of the past and historically foreshortened forms of analysis, which in some cases may ignore conservative reform narratives in the service of critical genealogies, chronologies, and periodizations (see Jessop 2012). Complementing earlier explorations of the dynamics of municipal bankruptcy and financialized urban governance in the Motor City (see Peck 2015; Peck and Whiteside 2016), the purpose of this chapter has been to revisit and reevaluate the storied time of Coleman Young's Detroit. Young's time in office coincided not only with a dramatic acceleration in the rate of deindustrialization (nationally and locally), remembered by the mayor as "a bleak period of neglect and retrogression [across] the urban scene" (Young with Wheeler 1994, p. 256), but also with the rise of a "new class" of managers and financial technocrats in fiscally distressed cities (Rich 1989, p. 233); all of which would combine in Detroit to manifest as a painful, protracted experience of financialized intermediation, institutionalization, and intensification (Peck and Whiteside 2016).

If bankruptcy is a condition that strikes in two ways, slowly, and then suddenly, Detroit's 2013 default can be seen as a precipitative event many decades in the making. The conservative narrative suggests that by triggering the suburbanization of jobs and middle-class whites, the 1967 riots were Detroit's pivotal moment, even though historical processes of deindustrialization and racial exclusion had been metabolizing for most of the postwar period, the late 1960s rebellion being just one of their overdetermined effects (Sugrue 2005; Fine 2007). Similarly, Detroit's bankruptcy merely punctuated what has been a long-run process of neoliberalization together with all the attendant constraints imposed by trenchant economic stagnation, decades-long credit rating downgrades, and marked revenue loss, leading ultimately to intense debt reliance. Having declared the largest municipal bankruptcy in US history, the city has since been subjected to a politically steered and racially targeted process of financialized restructuring, based on a neoliberal model of technocratic governance, and involving court-administered "adjustment," municipal downsizing, and public asset stripping.

In the world of Realpolitik, Detroit's bankruptcy seems destined to remain an indelible point of reference, moving forward, a moment that will be taken to signify a kind of "reset" in ideological and institutional terms. Detroit is now being repurposed, in leaner form, for new markets and for emergent modalities of market rule. A privatized city has sprouted in the midst of municipal insolvency – Quicken billionaire Dan Gilbert, alone, now owns sixty buildings, or 9 million square feet of downtown real estate (Austen 2014). What was once partnering with (or pandering to) big business under Coleman Young has become outright fire sale under conditions of emergency management. As compensation for their bankruptcy-induced paper losses, bond insurers Syncora and FGIC now own significant portions of city property, including choice parcels of land, buildings, and parking lots. An important pillar of economic revitalization and fiscal recovery now rests with financialized-corporate partnerships of various sorts, from the Red Wings arena (or Little Caesars Arena, renamed in honor of its benefactor Mike Illitch, owner of Little Caesars Pizza, the Detroit Red Wings, along with much Detroit real estate) to soccer stadiums and other investor-led plans for Detroit's urban housing, retail, and entertainment infrastructure. Real estate brokers and P3 investors are having a field day with the redevelopment of bankrupt Detroit, making good on earlier dreams of a fiscally cleansed, investment-opportunity-rich landscape. As the CEO of Detroit's Regional Chamber of Commerce puts it: "The bankruptcy has only made Detroit a more attractive investment ... Bankruptcy isn't a dirty word in business any longer. It often means good investments at a great price" (Sandy Baruah, quoted in Aguilar 2014, p. 1).

Accompanying the new commanding heights (and depths) of urban financial-corporate ownership is the increasingly ubiquitous narrative that Detroit will be saved by the peripatetic class of "creatives," hipster entrepreneurs bringing their ideas, technology, and energy to Detroit, usually from one of the coasts but nearly always from outside. The subjects of this celebrated startup culture, normatively young, degree-bearing, and white as they invariably are, tend to live in entirely different worlds to their (hardly close) working-class, African-American neighbors, the latter being mostly excluded from this development script.

> Nowadays, tales of the city's slow recovery tend to focus on plucky hipsters from Los Angeles or Brooklyn colonizing abandoned spaces, opening pickle companies or tilling little urban agriculture plots. Glossy magazines acclaim Detroit as the next Berlin; never mind that Germany's reunified capital has always floated on a bed of cushy federal subsidies.
>
> (Kimmelman 2017, p. C1)

This can be read as another chapter in Detroit's extended and tortuous history of racialized development, the apparent need to "import" entrepreneurship representing another marker of localized cultural deficits, the pernicious imagery of intrepid pioneers populating the new "frontiers" – for the most part a culturally demarcated archipelago of downtown enclosures – evoking a familiar array of racial, class, and indeed colonial signifiers (see Binelli 2013; Eisinger 2015; Moskowitz 2015; Kinney 2016). As this new population trickles into Detroit, it is worth recalling one of Coleman Young's memorable observations about the city's long-run battle against depopulation: "What's at the root of that loss? Economics and race. Or should I say, race and economics" (quoted in McGraw 2005, p. 28).

Bibliography

Aguilar, L. (2014). Detroit's Challenge: To Spread the Wealth. *Detroit News*, November 17. Retrieved from: www.detroitnews.com/story/business/real-estate/2014/11/17/detroit-bankruptcy-investment/19153475/

Akers, J. (2015). Emerging Market City. *Environment and Planning A*, 47, 1–17.

Anton, T. (1983). *Federal Aid to Detroit*. Washington, DC: Brookings Institution.

Austen, B. (2014). The Post-Post-Apocalyptic Detroit. *New York Times*, July 11. Retrieved from: www.nytimes.com/2014/07/13/magazine/the-post-post-apocalyptic-detroit.html?_r=0

Binelli, M. (2013). *Detroit City is the Place to Be*. New York: Metropolitan Books.

Bomey, N. (2016). *Detroit Resurrected*. New York: W. W. Norton.

Bomey, N. and Gallagher, J. (2016). How Detroit Went Broke: The Answers May Surprise You – and Don't Blame Coleman Young. *Detroit Free Press*, December 19. Retrieved from: www.freep.com/story/news/local/michigan/detroit/2013/09/15/how-detroit-went-broke-the-answers-may-surprise-you-and/77152028/

Boyle, K. (2001). The Ruins of Detroit: Exploring the Urban Crisis in the Motor City. *Michigan Historical Review*, 27(1), 109–127.

Cheyfitz, K. (1980). The Self-Serve City. *Monthly Detroit*, November, 79–82.

Darden, J. T., Hill, R., Thomas, J., and Thomas, R. (1987). *Detroit: Race and Uneven Development*. Philadelphia, PA: Temple University Press.

Davidson, M., and Ward, K. (Eds.) (2017). *Cities under Austerity: Restructuring the U.S. Metropolis*. Albany, NY: SUNY Press.

Detroit Free Press (1981a). The City. *Detroit Free Press*, June 12, 8A.

Detroit Free Press (1981b). Mayor Young. *Detroit Free Press*, September 13, 36A.

Economist (2011, February 12). A Tale of Many Cities. *Economist*, 91–92.

Eide, S. (2016). Caesarism for Cities. *City Journal*, 26(1), 70–75.

Eisinger, P. (2003). Reimagining Detroit. *City and Community*, 2(2), 85–99.

Eisinger, P. (2015). Detroit Futures: Can the City Be Reimagined? *City & Community*, 14, 106–117.

Fasenfest, D. (1986). Community Politics and Urban Redevelopment: Poletown, Detroit and General Motors. *Urban Affairs Quarterly*, 22(1), 101–123.

Fine, S. (2007). *Violence in the Model City*. East Lansing: Michigan State University Press.

Fireman, K. (1981a). Layoffs Loom if Rescue Plan Vetoed. *Detroit Free Press*, April 2, 3A, 13A.

Fireman, K. (1981b). Trials of Coleman Young: Joy – and Fury. *Detroit Free Press*, January 6, 1A, 11A.

Fireman, K. (1981c). Young Goes for Broke with Save-the-City Plan. *Detroit Free Press*, March 23, 31A, 5A.

Galster, G. (2012). *Driving Detroit*. Philadelphia: Pennsylvania University Press.

Gillette, C. P. (2014). Dictatorships for Democracy: Takeovers of Financially Failed Cities. *Columbia Law Review*, 114(6), 1373–1462.

Glaeser, E. (2011). *Triumph of the City*. New York: Penguin.

Gold, H. (2013). Detroit, The Right's Perfect Pinata. *Politico*, August 18. Retrieved from: www.politico.com/story/2013/08/detroit-michigan-conservatives-095630?o=0

Hackworth, J. (2007). *The Neoliberal City: Governance, Ideology, and Development in American Urbanism*. Ithaca, NY: Cornell University Press.

Hackworth, J. (2016). Defiant Neoliberalism and the Danger of Detroit. *Tijdschrift voor Economische en Sociale Geografie*, 107(5), 540–551. doi:10.1111/tesg.12184.

Hill, R. C. (1983). Crisis in the Motor City: The Politics of Economic Development in Detroit. In S. S. Fainstein, N. I. Fainstein, R. C. Hill, D. Judd, and M. P. Smith (Eds.), *Restructuring the City: The Political Economy of Urban Redevelopment* (pp. 80–125). New York: Longman.

Hodge, T. R., Skidmore, M., Sands, G., and McMillen, D. (2015). Tax Base Erosion and Inequity from Michigan's Assessment Growth Limit: The Case of Detroit. *Public Finance Review*, 43(5), 636–660.

Jessop, B. (2012). Left Strategy. *Transform!*, 10, 9–17.

Kantor, P., Savitch, H. V., and Haddock, S. V. (1997). The Political Economy of Urban Regimes: A Comparative Perspective. *Urban Affairs Review*, 32(3), 348–377.

Kimmelman, M. (2017). The Lights Are On in Detroit. *New York Times*, January 11, C1.

Kinder, K. (2016). *DIY Detroit*. Minneapolis: University of Minnesota Press.

Kinney, R. J. (2016). *Beautiful Wasteland*. Minneapolis: University of Minnesota Press.

Kushma, D. (1984, January 1). Detroit Mayor Endures. *Detroit Free Press*, 1A, 10A.

Ladd, H. F. (1994). Big-City Finances. In G. F. Peterson (Ed.), *Big-City Politics, Governance and Fiscal Constraints* (pp. 201–269). Washington, DC: Urban Institute Press.

Malanga, S. (2013a). The Real Reason the Once Great City of Detroit Came to Ruin. *Wall Street Journal*, July 27, A13.

Malanga, S. (2013b). The Man Who Killed Detroit. *Wall Street Journal*, August 2. Retrieved from: www.wsj.com/video/opinion-the-man-who-killed-detroit/86E6D085-86E5-47B2-9DA1-DCD4776674F9.html

Marback, R. (1998). Detroit and the Closed Fist: Toward a Theory of Material Rhetoric. *Rhetoric Review*, 17(1), 74–92.

McGraw, B. (2005). *The Quotations of Mayor Coleman A. Young*. Detroit, MI: Wayne State University Press.

Mitsotakis, S. (2013). Detroit Betrayed: The Radical Wrecking of an Iconic City. *Forbes*, January 13. Retrieved from: www.forbes.com/sites/realspin/2013/01/13/detroit-betra yed-the-radical-wrecking-of-an-iconic-city/#2ac0f8f64476

Moskowitz, P. (2015). The Two Detroits: A City Both Collapsing and Gentrifying at the Same Time. *Guardian*, February 5. Retrieved from: www.theguardian.com/cities/2015/feb/05/detroit-city-collapsing-gentrifying

Orr, M. E., and Stoker, G. (1994). Urban Regimes and Leadership in Detroit. *Urban Affairs Review*, 30(1), 48–73.

Peck, J. (2010). *Constructions of Neoliberal Reason*. Oxford: Oxford University Press.

Peck, J. (2014). Pushing Austerity: State Failure, Municipal Bankruptcy and the Crises of Fiscal Federalism in the USA. *Cambridge Journal of Regions, Economy and Society*, 7(1), 17–44.

Peck, J. (2015). Framing Detroit. In M. P. Smith and L. O. Kirkpatrick (Eds.), *Reinventing Detroit* (pp. 145–166). Piscataway, NJ: Transaction.

Peck, J. (2017). Transatlantic City, Part 1: Conjunctural Urbanism. *Urban Studies*, 54(1), 4–30.

Peck, J., Theodore, N., and Brenner, N. (2013). Neoliberal Urbanism Redux? *International Journal of Urban and Regional Research*, 37(3), 1091–1099.

Peck, J., and Whiteside, H. (2016). Financializing Detroit. *Economic Geography*, 92(3), 235–268.

Ravitch, R. (2014). *So Much to Do*. New York: Public Affairs.

Reese, L. A., and Sands, G. (2013). No Easy Way Out: Detroit's Financial and Governance Crises. Retrieved from: www.dmu.ac.uk/documents/business-and-law-documents/research/lgru/laurareeseandgarysands.pdf

Rich, W. C. (1989). *Coleman Young and Detroit Politics: From Social Activist to Power Broker*. Detroit: Wayne State University Press.

Segal, D. (2013). Motor City Missionary. *New York Times*, April 14, BU1.

Shaw, T. C. (2009). *Now is the Time!* Durham, NC: Duke University Press.

Sugrue, T. J. (2005). *The Origins of the Urban Crisis*. Princeton, NJ: Princeton University Press.

Tabb, W. (2014). The Wider Context of Austerity Urbanism. *City*, 18, 87–100.

Theodore, N., and Peck, J. (2012). Framing Neoliberal Urbanism: Translating "Common Sense" Urban Policy Across the OECD Zone. *European Urban and Regional Studies*, 19(1), 20–41.

Theodore, N., Peck, J., and Brenner, N. (2011). Neoliberal Urbanism: Cities and the Rule of Markets. In G. Bridge and S. Watson (Eds.), *The New Blackwell Companion to the City* (pp. 15–25). Oxford: Wiley-Blackwell.

Thomas, J. M. (2013). *Redevelopment and Race*. Detroit: Wayne State University Press.

Thompson, H. A. (2001). Rethinking the Collapse of Postwar Liberalism: The Rise of Mayor Coleman Young and the Politics of Race in Detroit. In D. R. Colburn and J. S. Adler (Eds.), *African-American Mayors: Race, Politics, and the American City* (pp. 57–79). Urbana: University of Illinois Press.

Tyson, R. (1975). Mayor Young a Year Later. *The Nation*, March 1, 237–240.
Wall Street Journal (2013). Saving Detroit from Itself. July 27, A14.
Wilson, J. Q. (1998). The Closing of the American City. *New Republic*, May 11, 30–38.
Wylie, J. (1989). *Poletown*. Urbana: University of Illinois Press.
Young, C., with Wheeler, L. (1994). *Hard Stuff*. New York: Viking.

11

POLITICAL DISSENT IN AMMAN, JORDAN

Neoliberal Geographies of Protest and Policing

Jillian Schwedler

Jordan is a non-democratic country that has a long but uneven history of vibrant political protest. It is a country of some 7 million people, with a monarchy that hails from the Arabian peninsula and more than half the population as refugees. The capital city of Amman is a sprawling metropolis that just a century ago was a dusty outpost. While the dramatic expansion of the city over the past century created new spaces available for protests – such as locations adjacent to Parliament, the Office of the Prime Ministry, the Professional Associations Complex, and Gamal Abdul Nasser traffic circle (known locally as the Interior Ministry Circle, *Dakhaliya*) – other prominent sites of protest – like the city center – have become significantly less visibile and less disruptive. Some of these changes came by design, as discussed below, but many did not.

Alterations to the city's geography emerged through the creation of entirely new neighborhoods and commercial spaces, and the repurposing of others. The meanings attached to specific places also evolved, resulting as much from the new built environment as from the ways in which people came to use those spaces. Protesters adapted to the changes, adopting new locations and abandoning others.

This chapter explores a geography of dissent in Amman. First, I examine militarization and the increased securitization that emerged first under neoliberalism and now during the crisis temporality of the ISIS threat. Efforts to create or maintain order are not imposed on the spaces of the city, but rather they are directly built into it.

Second, I examine the spatial dynamics of protest and policing, examining how policing practices vary across the city's geography, affected in large part by questions related to class, visibility, and the tribal or ethnic associations of individual neighborhoods. I then examine two protests in particular: the spring 2002 protests against the Israeli invasion of several Palestinian towns, and the March 24 Youth Movement that emerged in 2011.

Third, I examine regime efforts to control spaces of protest in the aftermath of protests, including attempts to strip them of their meaning. I examine erasures, enclosures, and exposures as three techniques for inscribing new meaning on places that came to be associated with political dissent.

State Attempts at Controlling Public Space

As James C. Scott illustrates, all cities are conceived with questions of order and control in mind (1999). The many urban planning documents for Amman imagined new neighborhoods, public spaces, modes of transport, and patterns of leisure activities, all of which required efforts to alter existing spaces or create new ones. The effects of some of those projects, along with the dramatic expansion of the city, had profound impacts on the political work of protests.

It is not that urban planners are directly implicated in the militarization of cities, however. Rather, it is the very act of designing (whether an object, a building, or a city) that resembles the function of the army in the way that both fundamentally anticipate, and encourage specific behaviors. Regardless of intention, the creation of a new city supervised by a limited number of actors, and its control by military elements, insures for designers that their anticipation proves true (Lambert 2015, p. 4).

Thus it is not necessary that urban development projects explicitly embody regime efforts to control or prevent the expression of political dissent, because they already seek to direct and ecourage certain behaviors while discouraging others. They may have aimed to create a sense of national memory, evidenced in the 1955 urban plan and in the King Hussein Gardens project that houses the Royal Automobile Museum. But the greatest constraint on protest and other public expressions of political dissent came through such conventional repressive measures as the imposition of martial law in 1957, the dissolution of parliament and dismissal of the cabinet that year, and the defeat of the Palestinian militias during the Black September civil war of 1970–1971.

Yet some urban development plans – like gated communities, the Abdali project, and high-end commercial districts and tourist resorts – require that explicit techniques of policing and surveillance be built into the plans. Other urban developments and public infrastructure have the capacities for militarized use during periods of crisis times built into them. The first such large-scale urban development project was that of Paris in the late nineteenth century.

Militarization of Public Space

As scholars have long documented, Haussmann's Paris was fashioned in part to adjust the spatiality of the streets to accommodate the needs and hardware o modernizing armies, as well as to inhibit the mobilization and ability of revolutionaries to control certain neighborhoods. Militarizing public space was also a core technique of colonial administration. Lambert notes that, "One of the first decisions of the French colonial administration in Algeria in 1830 consisted in naming the streets of Algiers's Casbah as well as in assigning a number to each home" (2015, p. 5). Surveillance and policing is facilitated through legibility, as discussed in more detail below. The objective of militarization is to create spaces that are controllable through surveillance and policing during periods of normal politics, but immediately accessible to militarized control during periods of crisis.

In Jordan, the militarization of the city is not always visible in the built environment. The city has no central square, and its maze of streets and steep roads are not conducive to the movement of troops or heavy weaponry. But the more recent improvements to the city's infrastructure have militarized capacities. The road past the King Hussein Medical Center was widened and repaved in 2006, almost immediately following the December 2005 hotel bombings. In June 2006, it carried a large contingent of troops and armored vehicles past spectator stands from which King Abdullah and other government officials observed the forces in commemoration of Army Day. The timing of the celebration was saturated with meaning: although Army Day is celebrated annually on June 10, the regime had not mounted large parades for at least a decade (Schwedler 2012). I mentioned to a high-level army officer (not at the event) that I noticed that the medians on the road had been removed so that the troops could march there. He said that the road was also built to be an airstrip if needed.

New overpasses and underpasses are also built to accommodate the weight and width of armored vehicles, as is the Abdoun bridge. The latter extends to a wide road that descends gradually, with branches that curve west toward the airport road and east toward the eastern neighborhoods of Amman. Underneath the Abdoun bridge, a widened road is being constructed to facilitate movement into and out of the city center from the south.

Cities are also militarized in less permanent infrastructure. In normal as well as crisis times, numerous government agencies and security forces engage in the quotidian militarization of public spaces. These include blocked roads, deviated passages, speed bumps, no photography zones, tanks and sandbags, temporary and permanent no parking zones, concrete barriers around buildings, the parking of government vehicles to create blockages or bottlenecks, security points on roads and at hotels, malls, and government buildings. These measures are not merely necessary inconveniences in crisis times of heightened securitization. They are also practices whose irregularity disrupts the routine movement of people as they seek to move within and across the city.

Securitization

Militarization is an aspect of securitization, but the latter extends to an almost permanent and routine surveillance of daily life. Securitization also entails increased mediation by nonhuman actors. Security camera networks and their transactions multiply without human intervention. These also entail a speeding up of transactions. In this way, networks of information – like Internet traffic – is always both human and nonhuman (Grusin 2015, p. xiv). There is an accelerated nonhuman rhythm (phrase borrowed from Grusin 2015, p. xiv).

As is the case with many neoliberal cities, Amman has become increasingly securitized over the past decade. Consumer spaces and financial districts are in need of constant surveillance, to protect foreign investment and agents, whom the government has struggled to attract. The regime has adopted use of cameras and facial recognition software, but not in all parts of the city. Securitization is least visible in west Amman, where it is also most present.

As Fawaz et al. note of Beirut:

> The various security mechanisms of Beirut ultimately consolidate in the formation of an anxious cityscape with varying levels of intensity: "hot" spots – the symbolic centers of political control – where the map reflects an intense concentration of security elements, and "diffuse" areas where the presence of the security apparel becomes comparatively diluted – nonetheless almost always present. Security is furthermore a dynamic and continuously changing concept. It operates within temporal regimes of "crisis time" and "normal time" as well as night/day, weekday/weekend, etc. curing which the cordoned-off areas spill over to their surroundings, including in their bunkers additional streets and blocks, while additional "hot spots" are created and neighborhood-level organization of security patrols and surveillance are deployed.
>
> *(Fawaz et al. 2015, p. 10)*

Attempts to map or identify such blockages will necessarily be valid and accurate for only a moment; the boundaries and intensities of securitization are always in flux. Indeed their unpredictability is a central factor in the functioning of their power. Securitization is therefore not a set of techniques as much as a range of practices that are always changing or potentially in flux. These insights bring the differential geography of securitization into view. They help us to extend our understanding of the control of public space and thus the policing of protest to times and spaces beyond the actual protests themselves.

Crisis Temporalities

Periods of crisis always bring new and deepened practices of securitization and militarization. Following the hotel bombings in December 2005, the city of Amman saw a dramatic increase in concrete roadblocks that prevent vehicles from approaching government buildings and hotels. Security checkpoints upon entering the building became permanent. Shopping malls that already had security at the entrance increased surveillance and also established concrete barriers near major entrances. The crisis temporality of the hotel bombings became semipermanent, a new kind of normal for the capital city.

Curfews are another practice common to crisis temporalities. They illustrate the ways in which controlling bodies by preventing them from exiting their homes or moving in public keeps "unauthorized" bodies both out of our homes and from escaping their own homes (Lambert 2015, p. 5).[1]

With the outbreak of the uprising in 2011 in new crisis temporality emerged in Jordan. Even as the protests died down and the king claimed that politics had returned to a new normal, the outcome was that the escalated securitization never ended. And now with the threat of ISIS and its attempts to launch a major attack inside of the kingdom, the crisis temporality is again the new normal. It authorizes a permanent state of threatened securitization, much like the September 11 attacks in the United States created a permanent state of crisis.

At the same time, the Hashemite regime has aggressively marketed Jordan's "climate of stability" and its status as the moderate and friendly state in the Middle East that the United States and much of the world so desperately wants.

Normal Temporalities

As noted, the militarization and securitization of public space is no less ongoing in normal temporalities than it is at times of crisis. The surveillance and security practices around spaces such as malls and commercial centers, for example, have created an environment in which ostenibly public spaces are really private spaces, unequally accessible and thus subject to all manner of private securitization. The presence and unpredictability as to the location of no parking signs, security cameras, speed bumps, and other blockages of public roads and spaces create obstacles that people need to navigate on a daily basis (Fawaz et al. 2015, p. 9).

During a trip to Amman in 2016, numerous interviewees expressed frustration at the extent to which it has become difficult to park and to navigate traffic in the city. Two people separately told me that they felt that people had become more rude, perhaps frustrated because of the periodic blockage of streets by police vehicles. Drivers are increasingly thoughtless, they told me, stopping their own cars where ever they choose, even in the middle of a traffic circle. While it is unclear if the practice of police blocking road traffic has actually increased, the effect is one of a strong police presence and the randomness of harassment as people try to move about their daily lives.

Securitization has thus become a routine part of life in Amman, its practices reproduced by a range of actors other than the regime.

As Sewell notes:

It is not only states that engage in the policing of spaces – that is, in activities of surveillance and coercion. Both private firms and labor unions police the factory floor, youth gangs cruise their neighborhoods protecting their boundaries against incursions by gang members from other neighborhoods, and eighteenth century neighbors were kept under informal surveillance by gossiping shopkeepers and market women. This private policing ranges from highly formal to extremely informal in both its procedures and its punishments.

(2001, p. 69)

Spatial Dimensions of Protest Policing

Understanding these ongoing and permanent, if changing, forms of securitization facilitates our understanding of how the policing of protest either deviates from or reproduces quotidian forms of policing and surveillance. This section examines some spatial dimensions of protest policing, with particular attention to variations across neighborhoods based on economic status, tribal affiliation, or ethnicity. How do policing practices vary? As one interviewee put it to me, what matters most is not what you say, but who is saying it and where they are saying it.

Neighborhood

In theory, and in police academies, the policing of protest is based primarily on the behavior of the protesters. The police are there to make sure that protesters have the ability to express their freedom of speech but that they do so in a manner that does not neglect the rights and property of others. In practice, the policing of poor neighborhoods and people of color in the United States for example, has always varied dramatically from quotidian policing practices in wealthier neighborhoods. Similarly during protests, patterns of police repression can be contingent on precisely who is doing the protesting, and where. Speaking about the United States, Lambert observes:

> Although the principle of citizenship is based on equality, in reality, we can only observe how, in many of our cities, there are territories of sub-citizenry where the police significantly increases violence, rather than diminishes it.
>
> *(2015, p. 5)*

As we will see below, those policing practices extend well beyond the temporality of the protest event itself.

In Jordan, policing of different neighborhoods varies considerably, in part based on the real and perceived association of certain neighborhoods with different communities of people. Some neighborhoods are associated with certain tribes or other loyalist groups, although those loyalties are often exaggerated. But it is nonetheless true that some communities are more assertive in expressing direct critique of the regime, or even the king, than are other communities. The participation of Palestinians in the protest associated with Jordan's uprising was disproportionately low. As one longtime Jordanian activist told me, "You can yell '*Yoskut Abdullah*' in places like Hay Tufayleh" – a neighborhood in southern Amman that is settled largely by members and relatives from the East Bank town of Tufayleh – "but do it in [Palestinian] Jebal Hussein and you will get tear-gassed." As discussed below, the police may react strongly to a smaller protest but stand by while larger groups say identical things. Most likely, there are strong identity-based reasons why Hay Tufayleh is allowed to say things that the predominately Palestinian area of Jebal Hussein is not.

In many ways, these increased security mechanisms affect a reversal in

> the private/public divide, allowing private control over the use of public spaces. They also establish new social hierarchies defined according to users' competence and the various forms of capital they can activate in this new order. Hence, the implications of security deployment vary considerably across users, depending on one's position in the social, gender, moral, national, and class hierarchies.
>
> *(Fawaz et al. 2015, pp. 10–11)*

Class

Class has always been an important component affecting practices of policing across the geography of a city. Policing is both more present and less visible in many wealthier neighborhoods, where a wide range of surveillance techniques and technologies are built into the architecture of commercial establishments and private residences. Recall that a key dimension of the reconstruction of Paris entailed the movement of working-class people out of affluent areas. Haussmann's reconstruction of Paris explicitly sought to make it harder for insurgents to avoid the artillery and cavalry that could quell their uprising (Jordan 1996, p. 188–192).

As Sewell notes with reference to the insurrections in European capital cities such as Paris, Berlin, Vienna, and Rome:

> Not only did they have densely built poor neighborhoods whose labyrinthine streets were susceptible to barricades, but these working-class quarters were within easy striking distance of the neighborhoods of the rich and of the grand public squares of the ceremonial city.
>
> *(2001, p. 62)*

In Amman, the policing practices between wealthier and poor neighborhoods are significant. In places like the Wahdat refugee camp, the general police routinely patrol the streets, as though they are neighborhood cops. When protests do emerge, security forces make little attempt to stop the protest or clear the streets, monitoring primarily to make sure the crowd does not turn violent. In wealthier neighborhoods, the quotidian policing is less visible, except for traffic officers at intersections and the bored guards who stand in the booths in front of embassies, staring down at their mobile phones and likely texting their friends. But it is also more present, in the surveillance technologies. During protests in wealthier neighborhoods, furthermore, security forces are typically out in force, even if they are not necessarily aggressive in engaging the protesters. But the visibility of the police is exponentially higher, sending a strong signal to protesters. On some occasions, police attempt to prevent protesters from reaching the planned site. This is particularly the case when numbers of people are expected to arrive from other parts of the city or country.

Thus the tactics for policing and repressing protests are in part a function of the space, visibility, and potential for disruption, but they are more significantly a function of class and proximity to high-valued neighborhoods or commercial districts. On campuses and in refugee camps – which are located in all parts of Amman – the typical strategy for policing protests is containment, so that people even just outside the area would probably be unaware of the demonstrations nearby. As a student activist at the University of Jordan told me in 2006, "We can do anything we want, as long as we don't try to leave campus and march [down University Road] toward downtown." In proximity to neoliberal spaces, far less protest activity is tolerated.

Contentious Spaces

Not all spaces are equally contentious. Many sites of protest are chosen for symbolic reasons, such as the Occupy Wall Street movement, or because they are the actual sites of the administrative offices embodying the power against which the protesters aim to make claims. The symbolic meaning(s) of a place also can have profound effects on the impact of a protest, and the political work that it does, as well as the response of the security forces. Protest can entail engaging in an activity that is viewed by some segment of the population or government as unacceptable for that location: sit-ins by blacks in "white only" establishments; "kiss-ins" by queer couples in redneck bars; stamping "keep money out of politics" on US paper currency, and so on.[2] These protests are contentious because they transgress accepted understandings about the appropriate use of that particular place, and by whom.

In the next sections, I explore two sets of protests, bringing to light questions of political geography, visibility, and the meaning of particular public places. The first are the massive protests that took place in Amman (and, indeed, across Jordan) in 2002, in which the regime attempted to use symbolic space to deflate anger expressed by protesters toward Israel and the Jordanian regime (for maintaining the peace treaty), and transform it into support for humanitarian intervention for Palestinians. The second are the March 24 Youth protests that took place as part of Jordan's 2011 uprising, in which a few hundred protesters aimed to set up a permanent "camp" near the Ministry of the Interior until demands for reforms were met.

The Queen's March[3]

In the spring of 2002, Israel invaded several towns under Palestinian control, and Jordanians took to the streets across the country in the tens of thousands, to protest. This included Jordanians in predominately Palestinian areas such as the refugee camps, as well as in the supposedly loyalist and tribal areas. In Amman, the protest continued for seven weeks, with the largest protests spreading over each Friday–Saturday weekend. Some were so large that all of the major intersections of the city came to a standstill. The army came in with tanks to monitor many of the intersections, and to contain the protesters, but it made few efforts to actually end the protest. To do so would have taken extreme repression of the sort the regime has been reluctant to adopt.

A few weeks into the protests, the regime launched a campaign aimed at redirecting the anger of the protest away from demands to abrogate Jordan's peace treaty with Israel, and toward the needs of the Palestinian people as a result of the crisis. That is, it aimed to direct outrage away from critique and instead toward humanitarian assistance. The king announced a fund raising initiative, accompanied by a telethon with many local celebrities and politicians appearing. Jordanians were encouraged to send a text to a specific number from their mobile phones, which would enable them to donate 10 Jordanian dinars, approximately $14, to the humanitarian relief effort.

A second initiative was launched by the Jordan River Foundation, a royally affiliated organization. The event was to be a large march in support of the need for Palestinian humanitarian relief, organized to commence at the Fifth Circle (a traffic circle along Zahran road, leading into downtown Amman). That site held no special or relevant symbolism connected to Palestinians or the particular conflict, and many activists mocked the choice of location, with its five-star hotels including the Ritz Carlton. Queen Rania let the march, accompanied by prominent businessmen, parliamentarians, and other powerful individuals including from many of the prominent tribal families.

While Jordanians were protesting in spaces that signified, either directly or indirectly, the authorities they felt were responsible for enabling Israel's actions, the Queen's March took its assembly of elites and notables just one kilometer away to a UN office of humanitarian affairs. The office was also closed when they arrived.

The importance of the march is that it illustrated the regime's recognition of the national outrage against the United States and Israel, at a time when the regime was deeply committed to maintaining good relations with both states. The alternative march, although it was not joined by average or working-class Jordanians, sought to align the regime with sympathy and caring for the

Palestinians without taking in expressions of outrage at Israel or the United States. The Queen's March conveyed its own meanings, by the symbolism of the destination, but without trying to reinscribe new meaning or its alternative humanitarian message onto the spaces at which tens of thousands of Jordanians were assembling.

March 24 Youth Movement[4]

Jordan's uprising during 2011 received far less attention than did those in Egypt, Syria, Yemen, Libya, and Tunisia, but it was not less significant even if it did not escalate sufficiently to topple the regime. Tens of thousands of Jordanians protested weekly through much of that year, but most of the protests adhered to familiar patterns and took place in the usual symbolic locations. On March 24, 2011, hundreds of Jordanians calling themselves the March 24 Youth began an indefinite sit-in at the Dakhaliya traffic circle, not far from an office of the Ministry of the Interior. As one participant stated prior to the event:

> We are a mixture of free Jordanian young men and women, who are tired of delays and the promise of reform, who see the spread of corruption, the deterioration of the economic situation, the regression of political life, the erasure of freedoms, and the dissolution of the social fabric.
> *(Jadaliyya Reports 2011)*

The riot police showed up in force but with few signs of intervening on the first day. It merely blocked off the traffic circle while some officers spoke to some of the protesters. As had become common at many protests in Jordan, the protesters decided to position themselves as a pro nationalist group. They did not call for the downfall of the regime, and they even brought Jordanian flags and photos of the king to assuage concerns that their protest was going to call for his downfall. A few hours into their protest, a second group that described itself as a Loyalty March, positioned itself facing the March 24 Youth. This group chanted in praise of King Abdullah and launched insults at the March 24 Youth, but the first day of the sit-in was mostly calm, and the evening passed with little incident (Jadaliyya Reports 2011). As one eyewitness described the scene:

> Underneath the bridge was a fairly well-organized group of young 20-something year olds. They had their posters in Arabic and English. They had a truck with a sound system. They had low-level organizers with bullhorns who would walk around making sure their group kept to the sidewalk. They had brooms and garbage bags, and people designated the task of keeping the area clean. They had tents, food, laptops, Internet connections, digital cameras, camcorders, a live feed going, as well as a fire roaring in near-freezing weather. At the tip of the sidewalk, their members were lined up facing the

circle, where across from them was another group, and in between them both were about two dozen policemen.

(Tarawnah 2011)

In the morning, as the Youth began their morning prayers, the Loyalty March began blaring patriotic music over the prayers. One protester told me that the security forces and the loyalists were under the belief, erroneously, that the protesters were made up primarily of Islamists who wanted to call for the downfall of the regime. He said that numerous protesters told them otherwise, but they were convinced that it was an Islamist event.

As the day progressed, busloads of *baltajiya* – pro-regime "thugs" who are not formally employed by the regime but who often arrive to do the dirty work the regime wants done – arrived and took up positions surrounding the peaceful protesters. They began to throw stones and beat on the protesters with their clubs, all the while the Darak forces stood by and did nothing. Many protesters struggled to escape around barricades and over fences that had been rapidly assembled to contain them. In the melee, one Jordanian was killed (Bouziane and Lenner 2011; Tobin 2012). The incident was captured on video and posted to YouTube.

The protest, and its repression, was notable because it took place in the climate of widespread protest across the kingdom. It was also during a period of crisis temporality, with uprisings across the region challenging various regimes. But only this protest was severely repressed in Jordan, although without question the security forces worked hard to contain protest across the country. In that context however, the question arises as to why this severe response to a relatively small protest.

The protest was certainly contentious because it was intended as an indefinite sit-in, much like the one in Cairo's Tahrir Square. From the regime's perspective, preventing the establishment of an ongoing sit-in was probably of the utmost importance. The location of the protest at the Dakhaliya traffic circle was even more contentious. Although the site was not a well-known or possibly ever used site for protest, its location near the Ministry of the Interior suggested that the protesters were attempting to inscribe new meaning on the location. In fact, as we shall see below, they were somewhat successful in that endeavor, even though the protest was crushed on only the second day.

These two examples illustrate the extent to which the meaning and practices of a particular location – that is, its cultural understanding as a place – can produce observable effects in terms of regime response. In the Queen's March, the regime sought to appropriate the pro-Palestinian narrative of the widespread protest, and turn it into a pro-Palestinian humanitarian relief narrative. It did so through the symbolic meaning of the location of the path of the March, ending at a United Nations humanitarian relief agency. In the March 24 Youth protest, by comparison, the choice of a location near the Ministry of the Interior let the regime repress the protesters in a manner they had not done with any of the other protests, the thousands of protests, that had taken place even in the crisis temporality of the Arab uprisings.

After Protests

The policing of protest does not end when protests do. By adopting an analytic framework that examines securitization through the lens of political geography, or place in space, we begin to see broader patterns of control, repression, and the mechanisms that work to silence or obscure a range of practices of political dissent that play out across the spaces of the city.

The March 24 Youth movement attempted to inscribe new meaning onto the Dakhaliya traffic circle, and in many ways it succeeded. The resources of security forces are always significantly greater than those of protesters, which is why the latter need to exploit every sliver of power they can leverage, including the mobilization of meaning. As Sewell puts it:

> Insurgents are normally resource-poor – at least by comparison with the states, established churches, local oligarchies, corporate capitalists, and other entrenched interests against whom they are contending. This limits the forms of spatial agency that are available to them. Whereas business corporations or states can engineer massive changes in the physical environment – by building factories, roads, canals, ports, new urban neighborhoods, and the like – insurgents in contentious politics must generally accept the physical environment as given. Insurgents produce space above all by changing the meanings and strategic uses of their environments.
>
> *(2001, p. 55–56)*

After protests, therefore, regimes engage in practices that work to remove the remnants of any narrative of insurgency and any challenges to their claims to legitimate authority. They do this through a variety of means, some of which are aimed at ostensibly reconstructing areas damaged by the protest, and others of which serve as warnings and reminders to people to consider the consequences before engaging in such protests ever again.

In post-civil war Beirut, the reconstruction of the city functioned not just to repair neighborhoods, but to entirely refashion large districts into elite enclaves. As Mona Fawaz argues, security concerns were primary considerations during reconstruction, manifest explicity in the "privatization of security and its deployment to protect the rich" (Fawaz et al. 2015, p. 9). Post-protest security practices are aimed more at preventing future challenges to elite interests then they are at redressing the grievances, injustices, and inequalities that led people to protest in the first place.

There are three additional techniques that aim to control pubic space connected to protests (and possibilities of expressing political dissent), all of which betray insecurities about losing control of the narratives and symbolism of spaces. Some of these efforts are connected with repurposing spaces, the effects of which are an apparent erasure of revolutionary temporalities, or at least attempts at such erasures.

Exposures

One set of practices or techniques after protests end is to create exposures. Following Michael Brown's death and the large protest in Ferguson, Missouri, the city cut down dozens if not hundreds of hardwood trees that surrounded park where Brown was killed and that stood in front of many private homes and apartment complexes. Such a move is unquestionably an act of violence on a poor community – shade trees and green spaces are often a luxury. In Cairo, numerous trees were also cut down after the uprising, exposing the neighborhood – as it had exposed the neighborhood in Ferguson – to not only a punishment, but also to an increased sense of surveillance and exposure.

As Parker argues, similar techniques have been used in poorer neighborhoods in Amman. He notes that, "wider boulevards were cut through the refugee camps and popular quarters of East Amman, opening them to surveillance and military intervention" (Parker 2009, p. 112).

Erasures

Another set of practices that follow protests entail erasures: efforts to scrub out a particular place, along with the meaning that was inscribed into it as a result of the protest. For example, in Bahrain the regime entirely disassembled the sculpture at the Pearl Roundabout where protesters had assembled in massive numbers. It removed the symbol of the protest in an attempt to erase the temporality that imagined a new future, and to reinscribe the space with the memory of both a failed protest and the regime's willingness to go to great lengths to crush it.

But those efforts have not been successful. Even with the Pearl Roundabout sculpture removed, Bahrainis have continued to stencil images of the sculpture all over Bahrain. The regime whitewashes over the images quite quickly, but those who stencil them take photographs and post them on the Internet, on sites such as www.rebeliouswalls.com. Some have even gotten tattoos of the roundabout sculpture. The regime has tried to erase the symbolic image, even removing from circulation a coin depicting it. Their efforts suggest a desire to eliminate from memory the possibilities that were introduced with the uprising, and the new temporality that came with it.

In Cairo, too, paintings and posters signifying the revolution have since been removed. But people do not stop trying to maintain the revolutionary meaning of the space, even if through small steps such as walking across the square wearing a T-shirt with a provocative, revolutionary message. There, the regime has also tried to introduce new signification in those spaces. For example, in Tahrir, the regime has erected a statue that commemorates and celebrates the contribution of the police to the nation. While in Rabaa, another statue has been erected, this one commemorating the military. These symbols remind Egyptians who came out of the revolution on top.

Both the moves of the activists and protesters, and the efforts of the regime, point to the importance of such public spaces and the meanings attached to them. No one in Egypt mistakes the fact that the current regime means to crush any revolutionary activity. Protest continues, however, although very rarely in Tahrir. It is a mistake to think that the struggle has stopped in such spaces. Using a lens of geography and place, we see that protest extends well beyond conventional spatial and temporal boundaries, to include an ongoing struggle over the use and meaning of public places.

Closures and Enclosures: The Landscapes of Policing

Finally, a third technique has been to try to close public spaces, particularly those that have been used for protest, in order to both reduce accessibility as well as to inscribe new meaning upon them. As with the earlier examples, efforts to change the meaning can, at least for a time, serve to also remind the population of the lengths to which the regime is willing to go in order to limit or silence voices of dissent. In Cairo, the Gamal Abdul Nasser subway station underneath Tahrir has been closed indefinitely, but the symbolism of the square is now so powerful that it is unlikely that what happened there will be forgotten. For the regime, it is at best a bracketing of that new meaning, rather than a full erasure.

A variation on this technique is to reconstruct or repurpose the spaces of protest in ways that aim to create new meanings. In Jordan, one of the most significant developments since 2014 has been the efforts, so far successful, to enclose former sites of protest with fences. This has taken place in at least three locations: at the Fourth Circle, at Dakhaliya circle, and at the field adjacent to the Kaluti mosque.

The Fourth Circle is located at the main office of prime ministry. In the 1990s, it was a common location for protest. At that time, there were no underpasses and overpasses so that protests at this circle could effectively shut down all traffic at the major intersection and create considerable congestion in the city. With the 2000s, however, the high-speed underpasses made it extremely difficult for protesters to stop traffic. Even more, a protest that clustered around the pedestrian area of the square might not even be visible to passersby in cars traversing the underpasses. This is a case of urban development rendering protest less visible, and thus making protesters do lesser or at least different kinds of political work.

With the outbreak of the uprisings in 2011, however, the Circle came into increased use once again. Many different protests were held there, including by the Islamist Salafi protesting to have some of their number released from prison. Tribal groups also protested there to prevent the construction of nuclear energy facilities on their land. Teachers, who had been struggling to develop a union for years, also protested there. And the list goes on. In 2015, however, the traffic circle was fenced off, and the spaces that were previously open to pedestrians were landscaped with trees and flowers.

The pedestrian area around the Dakhaliya traffic circle suffered a similar fate. It, too, has since 2015 being fenced off and landscaped. The large field adjacent to the Kaluti mosque has also been fenced off, although to date it is still a dusty field, perhaps too large for the regime to pay for landscaping. In these and other ways, protest and the policing of protest might better be understood as ongoing processes and practices, not simply undertakings of limited spatial and temporal duration. They entail struggles over space and place, struggles that reveal that the work of protests is not merely about making claims, but also about making meaning in the context of an expanding neoliberal city.

Struggles of Public Spaces

Struggles over public spaces are not limited to interactions between protesters or activists and security forces. They are a routine part of daily life for many who live in Amman, or indeed in any urban or other setting. Regimes draw up plans about how to use and develop public space; people always engage with and traverse spaces in their own ways.

As Parker notes, when the municipal government closed the Abdali transit terminal and moved it farther out of the city, the result was not merely an inconvenienced population. Rather, people created entirely new "informal hubs" for transportation in "defiance of urban planning" (Parker 2009, p. 113). Such efforts and practices are not rare. They are, rather, a routine part of the practices of the population. That is, on a routine basis urban residents in Amman interact with, and resist, the materiality of the built environment. It seems almost sport the extent to which residents rip up and cut out speed bumps intended to slow traffic, removing them in a matter of hours or perhaps days. They also tear down parking signs that are not to their liking and use public spaces in their preferred manner.

It is a losing battle for the regime, in some ways, in that they cannot control all public spaces. Despite the construction of the elaborate and beautiful parks, in the west part of the city, people continue to picnic along the highways, and on public and private land overlooking the Jordan River Valley. They bring chairs, water pipes, barbecue equipment, blankets, and everything to spend the day on the road side.

Protests are not separate from, but rather they are an integral part of, the ways in which people utilize the spaces and places of the city and inscribe them with meanings through their practices. The changing levels of securitization and militarization that characterize the neoliberalization of this and other major urban centers, particularly those that strive to elevate themselves in the global economy and cosmopolitan culture that goes along with it, create new practices as people stubbornly refuse to fall in line.

Notes

1 The violence of the physical structures is made explicit in such moments, but is not absent during "normal" times.
2 Jasper gives numerous examples (1997, p. 6).
3 This section builds on the analysis presented in Schwedler and Fayyaz (2010).
4 This section builds on the analysis presented in Schwedler (2013).

References

Bouziane, M., and Lenner, K. (2011). Protests in Jordan: Rumblings in the Kingdom of Dialogue. In Center for Middle Eastern and North African Politics (Ed.), *Protests, Revolutions, and Transformations: The Arab World in a Period of Upheaval.* Working Paper No. 1, July, 148–165.

Fawaz, M., Harb, M., and Gharbieh, A. (2015). Beirut: Mapping Security. *The Funambulist: Politics of Space and Bodies*, 1(September), 8–13.

Grusin, R. (2015). Introduction. In Richard Gruisin (Ed.), *The Nonhuman Turn* (pp. vii–xxix). Minneapolis: University of Minnesota Press.

Jadaliyya Reports (2011). Jordan's March 24 Youth Sit-in Violently Dispersed. March 26. Retrieved from: www.jadaliyya.com/pages/index/1012/jordans-march-24-youth-sit-in-violently-dispersed-

Jasper, J. M. (1997). *The Art of Moral Protest: Culture, Biography, and Creativity in Social Movements.* Chicago: University of Chicago Press.

Jordan, D. P. (1996). *Transforming Paris: The Life and Labors of Baron Haussmann.* Chicago: University of Chicago Press.

Lambert, L. (2015). Introduction: Militarized Cities, *The Funambulist: Politics of Space and Bodies*, 1(September), 2–7.

Parker, C. (2009). Tunnel-Bypass and Minarets of Capitalism: Amman as Neoliberal Assemblage. *Political Geography*, 28, 110–120.

Schwedler, J. (2012). The Political Geography of Protest in Neoliberal Jordan. *Middle East Critique*, 21(3) (December), 259–270.

Schwedler, J. (2013). Jordan. In Paul Amar and Vijay Prashad (Eds.), *Dispatches from the Arab Spring* (pp. 243–265). Minneapolis: University of Minnesota Press.

Schwedler, J., and Fayyaz, S. (2010). Permitting Protest. In Laleh Khalili and Jillian Schwedler (Eds.), *Policing and Prisons in the Middle East: Ambiguities of Coercion* (pp. 279–294). New York: Columbia University Press and Hurst Publishers.

Scott, J. C. (1999). *Seeing Like a State: How Certain Schemes to Improve the Human Condition Have Failed.* New Haven, CT: Yale University Press.

Sewell, W. H., Jr. (2001). Space in Contentious Politics. In Ronald R. Aminzade et al., (Eds.), *Silence and Voice in the Study of Contentious Politics* (pp. 51–88). New York: Cambridge University Press.

Tarawnah, N. (2011). The Quick Death of Shabab March 24 and What It Means for Jordan. *Black Iris* blog, March 26. Retrieved from: http://black-iris.com/2011/03/26/the-quick-death-of-shabab-march-24-and-what-it-means-for-jordan/ (accessed January 30, 2016).

Tobin, S. A. (2012). Jordan's Arab Spring: The Middle Class and the Anti-Revolution. *Middle East Policy*, 19(1) (Spring), 96–109.

PART V

Forward

Working Through Neoliberalism

12

THE KNIGHT'S MOVE

Social Policy Change in an Age of Consolidated Power

Sanford F. Schram

With the election of Donald J. Trump as president, we confront the possibilities for fundamental transformation of the welfare state along neoliberal lines. While most people may have not voted for neoliberalism, it is distinctly possible that that is what they will get with a Trump administration working in tandem with Republican majorities in the House and Senate. Neoliberalism in fact is today increasingly best characterized as the public philosophy that orients decision-making at the individual and collective level, across all spheres of social life, not just the market but also civil society and the state as well. Across the developed world but elsewhere too, changes in social welfare policies in particular but public policy more generally reflect the growing influence of the market-centered philosophy of neoliberalism (Schram 2015). It has become the default logic for public policymaking today. A long time in coming to ascendancy, neoliberalism arose in response as the welfare state gained traction during and after the Great Depression of the 1930s (Peck 2011). Neoliberalism's basic tenets were promulgated by Ludwig von Mises, Friedrich Hayek, and Gary Becker. It came to be associated with the "Chicago School" of Economics. Especially as articulated by Becker and Chicago School fellow travelers, neoliberalism is centrally about the superiority of economic logic as the basis for all decision-making, public as well as private, collective and individual. A critical feature of neoliberalism is that it blurs the boundary between the market, civil society, and the state. Neoliberalism disseminates economic rationality to be the touchstone not just for the market but for civil society and the state as well. Its emphasis on economic rationality as standing in for what is rational per se promotes marketization of an increasing number of practices throughout society. Most dramatically, it has led to wholesale revision in public policy in a number of domains to be more consistent with market logic in the name of better promoting market-compliant behavior by as much of the citizenry as possible. It places increased emphasis on people practicing personal responsibility by applying economic logic to all forms of decision-making across a variety of spheres of life. People are expected to practice personal responsibility by investing in their own human capital to make themselves less of a burden on society as a whole or face the consequences of a heightened disciplinary regime. It is this last part that is often neglected (Harcourt 2010). Neoliberalism's emphasis on personal responsibility for the choices people make has led to a more get-tough approach to social welfare policy.

The ongoing neoliberalization of social welfare policy itself is now taking place during a time of transformation that is fraught with risks for individuals, families, and societies as a whole, indeed for the global economy overall. The ascendency of neoliberalism as the prevailing rationality of our time is unfolding during what policy analysts call a "critical juncture," where a well-ingrained "path dependency" in social welfare policies has come under increased pressure to change (Pierson 2000). This critical juncture is associated with a cyclical swing back from policy commitments that have dominated the social welfare state in the post-World War II era (Stiglitz 2012). The waning of support for the welfare state is however complicated by changes in the economy in recent years. In today's world, post the Great Recession, when the economy seems to be recovering but in an increasingly unequal way, there is return of what we can call "ordinary capitalism" that has provided a new neoliberal normal of growing inequality and dwindling economic opportunities for people on the bottom of the socio-economic order (Schram 2015, chapter 1). Under neoliberalism's insistence on the pervasive reliance on economic logic as the basis for all decision-making, public as well as private, collective as well as individual, the state buttresses markets rather than counters them and inequality grows virtually unabated, as not a bug but rather as feature of this latest (neoliberal) iteration of the return to ordinary capitalism (Sassen 2006).

In this context, the neoliberalization of social welfare policy indicates a stark shift in orientation. While the state's social welfare policy in capitalist societies has always been attuned to market forces, neoliberal welfare policy represents a significant shift away from a state that sought to buffer the effects of the market for those who were least able to participate in it effectively to now re-purposing the welfare state to be one that explicitly is committed to buttress the market rather than to counteract its most deleterious effects (Schram 2015, chapter 1). Examining changes in major social welfare policy primarily in the USA but also in other countries provides evidence of how the neoliberalization of social welfare policy today includes putting in place a heightened disciplinary regime for managing subordinate populations who are deemed to be deficient in complying with the dictates of an increasingly marketized society where people are expected to leverage their human capital in order to provide for themselves and their families

In what follows, I trace the rise of neoliberalism as the default logic of today' political economy throughout the world. I examine in detail its animating source and its underlying philosophical roots. I review how it has come to be the common sense of capitalist political economies across the globe, and how it operates to structure public policymaking and policy design in those societies. I specify as an example the way neoliberalism has influenced welfare policy implementation in the United States. I conclude with considerations on how to get beyond neoliberalism in social welfare policy via what I call a "radical incrementalism" that makes small changes within the existing social welfare policies that lay the groundwork for more progressive changes down the road. The example provided is the current controversy over repealing Obamacare. If public policymaking were chess, social justice advocates must consider making the "knight's move" to work around the prevailing political limits to progressive change.

The Rise of Neoliberalism: From Explicit Theory to Default Practice

Neoliberalism evolved in the twentieth century from being the preoccupation of economic theorists to becoming the default logic for public policymaking across the globe. At first, it was sustained largely in the writings of Ludwig von Mises and Friedrich Hayek and their followers in the Mt. Pelerin Society (Stedman Jones 2014). It most centrally is reflected in their critiques of the welfare state but especially the thinking of John Maynard Keynes and the idea that the state should be a bulwark to counter the market. For Keynes, only the state was large and powerful enough to counter the excesses that come with swings in the market. The rise of Keynesianism and its emphasis on countercyclical policy provoked a strong reaction from theorists like Hayek in particular.

Hayek believed that the state could not be omniscient and that the decentralized market produced more points of information and was therefore a more intelligent system of decision-making. Hayek's *Road to Serfdom* critiqued the idea of welfare state that would undermine the autonomy of markets. He did concede the need for the state to provide for those who could not participate in the market enough to sustain themselves and their families. Hayek's work went on to prove to be catalytic in rolling back welfare state policies, not just in capitalist societies but eventually also in communist countries after the fall of the Soviet Union.

Hayek, however, was no simple conservative or classic economic liberal who prized individual freedom in some unreflective way. His neoliberalism was well captured when he said:

> We assign responsibility to a man, not in order to say that as he might have acted differently, but in order to make him different. ... It is doubtless because the opportunity to build one's own life also means an unceasing task, a discipline that man must impose upon himself if he is to achieve his aims, that many people are afraid of liberty.

(Hayek 1960, pp. 70–75)

While vigilant in highlighting unwarranted forms of coercion, Hayek was in many ways the father of what would come to be called "responsibilization" and the idea that society needed to be structured to discipline subordinate populations to be economically compliant. Hayek saw neoliberalism in the practices that worked to produce a certain type of citizen/subject who was market savvy and compliant in all their choice making activities.

Milton Friedman was distinctively influential in developing the Chicago School of economic theorizing. His biggest contribution to the rise of neoliberalism was to oppose his ideas of monetarism to that of Keynesianism (Stedman Jones 2014). Rather than an active state counteracting the swings of the market, the state should back away from such fiscal policies that raised or lowered taxes and spending and instead impose a stable monetary system of moderate predictable growth. The goal of the state should not be to aggressively respond to market swings but instead should tamp things down by putting in place a stable flow of money. By the late 1970s, in the USA in particular, the problems of simultaneous high inflation and low economic growth – that is, stagflation – produced growing frustration with Keynesian policies, the election of Ronald Reagan as president, and the institution of Friedman's monetarism as official policy by the US government's Federal Reserve Board, which was charged with primary responsibility for managing the monetary system. Friedman's ideas had gone from the classroom and his textbooks to the halls of government. Now the state's job was not to counter the market but to support it.

The "Reagan Revolution," as it was called, produced reductions in social welfare spending, deregulation of the economy, and tax cuts for the wealthy (Moynihan 1988). It was mirrored in the policies of Margaret Thatcher in her long run as Prime Minister of England (Krieger 1986). It was Thatcher who gave us TINA (there is no alternative) as the most thoughtless version of the need to back away from Keynesianism (Hay and Payne 2015). As this would become a commonplace slogan, the era of big government was over. While poverty rose and inequality accelerated, the momentum had swung away from the Keynesian welfare state toward a neoliberalized political economy where the state facilitated rather than counteracted an economy that had these inequitable outcomes. Growing poverty and inequality were not unintended as much as they were defining features of a system where the state facilitated economic growth that produced winners and losers.

By then neoliberalism was more a "thought collective" than an explicit ideological program (Mirowski 2014). Its tacit nature is represented in how it came to be implicitly associated with what was called the "Washington Consensus" (Williamson 2004). The Washington Consensus involved committing international lending practices to promoting economic liberalization in the debtor countries. Most famously, donors such as the World Bank and the International Monetary Fund came to impose "structural adjustment" policies on the borrowing countries in exchange for the loans received. Latin American, African, and Asian countries in particular commonly found the new terms of loans to involve conditions that led to deregulation of the economy, reductions in taxes, cuts in social welfare spending, and privatization of state operations as well as the imposition of monetarist policies. Problems of growing poverty and accelerating inequality again were immediately noticeable but did not deter the growing insistence for "structural adjustment." The Washington Consensus extended beyond the state to include the non-governmental organizations and others involved in promoting development to economically disadvantaged parts of the world.

Neoliberalism is not anti-liberalism, instead it is a new form of liberalism. It is about both economic and political liberalism (Brown 2015). It is very much an attempt at a return to the classic laissez-faire, free market economic liberalism of Adam Smith. But it is also based in an appreciation that with the New Deal in the USA and social democracies in Europe there was the rise of a welfare state that was justified by a pro-government interventionist form of political liberalism which unavoidably remade the relationship of the state to the market. Neoliberalism might have at its core a wish or desire to roll back the state to return to laissez-faire economic policies and put in place a market fundamentalism. In this sense neoliberalism is a form of conservatism that seeks to undo the welfare state as a counter to the market. Yet, as much as conservatives might have wished that that would happen, they quickly saw that history was not something that could be simply undone.

Instead, neoliberals were with time to appreciate the implications of Karl Marx's understanding of history as an undeniable force in shaping people's ability to act. In 1848, Marx wrote in *The Eighteenth Brumaire Louis Napoleon*:

> Men make their own history, but they do not make it as they please; they do not make it under self-selected circumstances, but under circumstances existing already, given and transmitted from the past. The tradition of all dead generations weighs like a nightmare on the brains of the living. And just as they seem to be occupied with revolutionizing themselves and things, creating something that did not exist before, precisely in such epochs of revolutionary crisis they anxiously conjure up the spirits of the past to their service, borrowing from them names, battle slogans, and costumes in order to present this new scene in world history in time-honored disguise and borrowed language.
>
> *(Marx 1937, p. 5)*

For Marx, people are not completely free to act, individually or collectively, but they are free to act in response to structured conditions in any one place and time. In other words, they have to account for what came before and not simply wish it away. This was very true for neoliberals who wished to roll back the welfare state and enact a return to some type of market fundamentalism.

This points toward what has become a critical feature of neoliberalism, especially in its relationship to the welfare state. While neoliberalism might have wanted to repeal welfare policies, as attempted under Reagan and Thatcher, more often than not, something else happened. Repeal was perhaps Plan A, but given that the welfare state had come to be entrenched, they could not simply undo it. The welfare state had become institutionalized. Its policies had acquired their own path dependency that generated a positive "policy feedback" (as policy analysts call it) (Mettler and Soss 2004). As people came to be accustomed to the benefits they gained from relying on the welfare state, they became more politically supportive of maintaining these policies. So in that sense, there was no real chance of totally going back to a set of policies like those that pre-dated the welfare state. That would be Plan A. And if Plan A was not possible, then a Plan B was needed. If the welfare state could not be repealed so as to reinstate market fundamentalism, then the next best thing would be to marketize the state. Over time, this has come to be a hallmark characteristic of neoliberalism, perhaps more than monetarism, deregulation, and tax cuts. Instead of repealing the welfare state, neoliberalism involves marketizing welfare state operations so they run more like a business in the name of getting everyone involved in them, policymakers, program administrators, and clients, to act in market compliant ways.

In this sense, given the deep path dependencies of the welfare state, neoliberalism is really Plan B for market fundamentalists (Schram 2015, pp. 28–31). It is what they had to do given the historical significance of the welfare state, the path dependency of its policies, the positive policy feedback that they generated and the unavoidable reality that history is a real force that cannot simply be dismissed or wished away. Further, in an age of prolonged partisan polarization and resulting policy gridlock, it is not surprising that the deadlock produces what Jacob Hacker (2004) has called "policy drift," where unchanged public policies drift away from addressing the social and economic challenges people confront in a changing society. Therefore, it is not surprising that neoliberalism is most often confronted with confusion when it is introduced as a topic of analysis. It is less a full-blown ideology than a hybrid practice that has evolved out of historical circumstances. In practice, neoliberalism is not about market fundamentalism as much as it is about marketizing the state. It is less about doing away with the state than getting it to operate in market compliant ways. In fact, it might be best to refer to neoliberalism not as an ideology at all but instead as a more subordinate meaning system, a "practical rationality," that is., the common sense for making public policy today in a post-Keynesian era (March and Olsen 2010).

Jamie Peck (2010) aptly speaks of "zombie neoliberalism," where neoliberal policy changes get enacted simply because they go unchallenged as the default logic for making public policy in the current era. While neoliberalism might have been an explicit theoretical orientation at one point, today it is more an implied understanding of what is to be done. Today, almost no one admits to being neoliberal even if they pursue neoliberal marketizing strategies for changing the relationship of the state to the market. It is generally understood as the common sense of public policymaking in the USA most especially but increasingly elsewhere as well that when the welfare state cannot be rolled back, we search for ways to marketize it so that it becomes less of a counter to the market and something that runs along market lines so as to better promote markets.

Wendy Brown (2015) has insightfully noted that neoliberalism is more about the state than the market. She notes it is most centrally about changing politics so that it too operates in market compliant ways, as in allowing wealth to dominate the electoral process and monied lobbyists to draft the laws that get enacted as well as rewriting public policies to be more supportive of markets and those who dominate them. Neoliberalism's greatest effects are perhaps seen in its being the default logic for the politics of remaking the state, more so than in how it works to reshape markets.

The zombie-like quality of neoliberal thought today is perhaps no accident, as Henry Giroux (2015) notes:

> Neoliberalism is not merely an economic system, but also a cultural apparatus and pedagogy that are instrumental in forming a new mass sensibility, a new condition for the widespread acceptance of the capitalist system, even the general belief in its eternity. Seeking to hide its ideological and constructed nature, neoliberal ideology attempts through its massive cultural apparatuses to produce an unquestioned common sense that hides its basic assumptions so as to prevent them from being questioned.

Therefore, a good case can be made that neoliberalism has gone from being an explicit economic philosophy to an implicit understanding about the politics associated with remaking the state. It is the common sense of the politics of public policymaking. It reflects history as a real force to be contended with. It raises the issue of what Hegel called the "cunning of reason," where actors unknowingly enact what history has led them to do in spite of their own best intentions (Fraser 2009). The thoughtlessness of neoliberalism today may only make it that much harder to counteract. It is something that people do simply because that is the way things get done at this point in time. As a result, neoliberal failures often lead to a doubling-down where they are replaced or modified with other even more intensified forms of neoliberalism. Nowhere is this tragedy more noticeable it seems than when we look at the neoliberal marketization of US welfare policy for the poor.

Marketizing the Welfare State: Neoliberal Social Welfare Policy

Neoliberalism as enacted today is producing nothing less than a regime-wide transformation of the welfare state. We can see this transformation as traversing the continuum of domestic policy across the welfare state. The idea of state policy existing on a continuum is put to good use by Pierre Bourdieu. Bourdieu (1994) has noted that the state is riven with conflict and that it is better to characterize it as a "bureaucratic field." Bourdieu suggests that within this bureaucratic field there is a continuum of domestic policy, with the left hand of the state providing aid and the right hand of the state imposing discipline. Yet for Loïc Wacquant (2009), there has been a joining of the left and right hands of the state in recent years as policies have become more punitive, emphasizing punishing the poor for their failure to conform to social and legal norms, especially regarding work and family. Social welfare and criminal justice policies, for instance, have become more alike, aiding and disciplining the poor simultaneously so that they will be less likely to engage in deviant social practices. Neoliberalism is spreading punishment across domestic policies in the name of disciplining the poor to become personally responsible, market-compliant actors (Soss, Fording, and Schram 2011a).

Yet neoliberalization involves more than punishment in the name of disciplining the poor. The marketization of social welfare policies actually has been the most noteworthy development under neoliberalism. In policy after policy, there has been a dramatic shift to relying on private providers, where clients are turned into consumers who get to make choices, and both are held accountable via performance measurement systems that indicate whether market-based objectives have been met. Examples in the USA include: welfare reform where private providers now dominate in placing clients in jobs, managed-care systems for regulating the private provision of publicly funded health care, Section 8 vouchers for subsidizing low-income families' participation in private housing markets, and education vouchers that subsidize parents' placing their children in private charter schools (where students must score sufficiently high on standardized tests for the schools to continue to participate in the privatized public education system in that locality).

Neoliberalism involves both carrots and sticks; it is about discipline more than just punishment (Soss, Fording, and Schram 2011a, pp. 6–9). Discipline is not just negative in limiting people's behavior; it is also productive in seeking to bring into being a new type of responsibilized citizen/subject who applies economic rationality to all their decision making practices. To help usher in this new citizen/subject, service providers across the social welfare state are also being disciplined in ways that make for profound transformations in the delivery of all kinds of public services. As part of the effort, public policies across the social welfare continuum are themselves undergoing a fundamental transformation as they are being neoliberalized to shift to imposing discipline to achieve market compliance by all actors in the system, service providers as well as clients. From income redistribution programs such as public assistance for the poor to criminal justice policies such as the system of mass incarceration that has arisen in the era of the war on drugs, social welfare policies are becoming more alike as they feature a strong disciplinary approach grounded in marketized operations. Increasingly for-profit providers are required to demonstrate they can meet performance standards. Clients must manage to make do with whatever limited opportunitie the economy provides.

Getting people to be self-reliant in an economy that offers them dwindling opportunities inevitably intensifies the disciplinary core of social welfare's neoliberalization. Today, many people are still struggling with the effects of the Great Recession and the growing inequality and economic hardship it has produced. It has proven to be a pivotal moment not just economically but also politically. Just as the roots of the economic transformation stretch back before the Great Recession, the influence of wealth to forestall state action to address issues of social welfare has been growing for just as long (Bonica et al. 2013). The growing inequality in income and wealth has led to massive expenditures in lobbying by the wealthy to lower taxes, reduce regulation of business, and limit social welfare legislation. As a result, there is now the distinct possibility of the United States moving to a tiered society. At the top, there is a limited stratum of upper-class and upper-middle-class people, ensconced in positions of corporate oversight and needed professional occupations. At the bottom is everyone who is increasingly deemed as not deserving of the state's attention, in part because they failed to position themselves as successful participants for the globalizing economy and are therefore seen as a burden that a globally competitive corporate sector cannot and will not carry. At the extreme, those in poverty are cast aside as disposable populations who are to be monitored, surveilled, disciplined, and punished more than they are to be helped.

The hollowed-out welfare state has less to offer those disadvantaged by economic transformation. Increasingly what it does have to offer is not so much assistance as discipline, discipline focused on getting people to internalize market logic and accept personal responsibility for the need to find whatever means, however limited, to get by in the changing economy (Soss, Fording, and Schram 2011a, chapter 2). This is the core of what is being called neoliberalism, a new liberalism that restructures the state to operate consistently with market logic in order to better promote market-compliant behavior by as many people as possible (Brown 2003, 2006).

Neoliberalizing social welfare programs prioritizes people learning to be economically minded about everything they do so they can more profitably develop their human capital and become less in need of relying on the government for assistance. Everyone must learn to think about all aspects of their lives in terms of return on investment (what is commonly now called ROI) (Heady 2010). Even government programs for the poor come to be centered on inculcating this neoliberal ethos (Schram 2006, chapter 5). The result is that self-governance replaces the government. It is the ultimate form of privatization. Neoliberalism is heavily invested in getting ordinary people to be not just factors in production but sources of capital themselves. Activating those on the bottom of the socioeconomic ladder to participate more extensively in investing in their own futures through acquiring debt, whether for schooling, buying a home, or other purposes, becomes an important source of economic growth in an economy led by the financial industry (Coole 2012).

Yet, for those who fail at becoming, on their own, financially savvy neoliberal citizen-subjects who can develop and leverage their own human capital, the state works to inculcate market-compliant behavior via a panoply of incentives and penalties. And when that does not work, especially as the inequitable economy grows in ways that do not create economic opportunities for them, then coercive controls are imposed. The goal is to control and contain those left behind so as a disposable population they are less of a burden on the rest of society. Social welfare institutions must of necessity be adjusted accordingly. In the transformed context, we see a shift from redistributing resources to the economically disadvantaged to an emphasis on enforcing compliance to behavioral standards so that subordinate populations become less of a burden on society.

Given its disciplinary focus, neoliberal social welfare unavoidably has moralistic and tutorial dimensions, focused on telling the poor how to behave, more so than providing them with needed assistance. The inculcation of personal responsibility becomes central to the welfare state. In this highly neoliberalized paternalistic context, the helping professions that provide the critical social services are inevitably transformed. It is here at this neoliberal terminus that we find a transformed social work, depoliticized and refocused on managing disposable populations. Social work no longer stands outside power but now is more than ever thoroughly assimilated to it. Across a wide variety of populations in need of various forms of assistance and treatment, social work shifts to technologies of the state, forms of governmentality, practices associated with getting served populations to internalize an ethic of self-discipline and personal responsibility. The goal of this responsibilization is for subordinate populations to handle their own problems as best they can on their own, with the aim that they become less of a burden for the constrained state. As a result, they should become more willing to take up whatever limited positions in the globalizing economy that they are afforded.

Social work increasingly comprises forms of psychological services focused on helping realize the disciplinary demands of the neoliberalizing state, which is now ever more dedicated to managing rather than serving disposable populations. When examining changes across a number of different areas of human service provision today, most striking are the parallel shifts in treatment toward a more disciplinary approach to managing service populations (Schram and Silverman 2012). It is the end of social work as we knew it and the ascendancy of a neoliberal regime that disciplines subordinate populations to be market compliant regardless of the consequences.

Neoliberal Governance: Organizational Reforms and New Policy Tools

The marketization of the welfare state involves both neoliberal organization reforms and policy tools to enact its market-centered focus to combating welfare dependency. Neoliberal organizational reforms, such as devolution, privatization and performance management accountability schemes, have been joined with paternalist policy tools, including sanctions – that is, financial penalties – for noncompliant clients, to create a flexible but disciplinary approach to managing the populations being served (Soss, Fording, and Schram 2011b). What we can call "neoliberal paternalism" represents a significant movement to marketize the operations of social service organizations more generally so that they inculcate in clients rationally responsible behavior that leads them to be market compliant, and thus less dependent on the shrinking human services and more willing to accept the positions slotted for them on the bottom of the socioeconomic order (Brown 2006). Organizations are being disciplined so that they can be held accountable for in turn disciplining their clients in this more market-focused environment. Neoliberal paternalism is transforming the human services into a disciplinary regime for managing poverty populations in the face of state austerity and market dysfunction.

This transformed environment involves: (1) deskilling in staffing patterns associated with relying on former clients as caseworkers, (2) marketizing of administrative operations stemming from the reliance on for-profit providers who are held accountable via performance management schemes, and (3) disciplining of clients via paternalist policy tools. These changes in organization and policy were a long time in coming. From the penultimate moment of the welfare rights movement in the early 1970s until the passage of welfare reform legislation in the mid-1990s, the number of welfare recipients stabilized at relatively high levels (even as benefits declined), and recipient families came to have essentially entitlement rights to assistance, albeit modest, and often welfare policies have long been entwined with multiple purposes, among the most important of which have been to return to the roots of social service work and instill or restore morality in the poor so as to assimilate marginal groups into mainstream behaviors and institutions (Katz 1997). Further, as Richard Cloward and Frances Fox Piven (1975) contend, welfare policy has historically served to "regulate the poor," effectively undermining their potential as a political or economic threat. Others have noted that welfare served to regulate gender relations by stigmatizing single mothers receiving aid (Gordon 1994). The stigmatization of welfare recipients as undeserving people who need to be treated suspiciously has not only deterred many welfare recipients from applying for public assistance but also communicated to the "working poor" more generally that they should do whatever they can to avoid falling into the censorious category of the "welfare poor." Welfare reform in the 1990s, however, accentuated the disciplinary dimensions of welfare policy in dramatic ways.

The shift to a more disciplinary approach to managing the welfare poor was facilitated by a concerted campaign by conservative political leaders to replace poverty with welfare dependency as the primary problem to be attacked (Schram and Soss 2001). With this heightened rhetoric about welfare dependency, the importation of behavioral-health models of treatment and associated organizational and staffing patterns came to be seen as not only plausible but desirable. As a result, welfare reform has remade the delivery of welfare-to-work services along lines that parallel addiction recovery programs (see drug treatment example below). Welfare agencies have instituted services that are the social welfare policy equivalent of a twelve-step program: individuals learn in the new "work-first" regime to be "active" participants in the labor force rather than "passive" recipients of welfare (Schram 2006, chapter 7). Such a view of welfare dependency has led to the importation of a "recovery model" into welfare reform, one aspect of which is the staffing of welfare-to-work contract agencies with "recovered" former welfare recipients. While former recipients have been relied on in the past, several studies of welfare reform have in recent years noted that the agencies studied had undergone change such that now about one-third of the case managers are former recipients (Watkins-Hayes 2009; Ridzi 2009). This proportion indicates numbers that go beyond mere tokenism (Turco 2010). One of the virtues of the recovery model is that it is consistent with long-standing calls for a representative bureaucracy (RB) that can practice cultural competence (CC) concerning the unique needs of its clients: a culturally competent bureaucracy is one "having the knowledge, skills, and values to work effectively with diverse populations and to adapt institutional policies and professional practices to meet the unique needs of client populations" (Satterwhite and Teng 2007). A representative bureaucracy that draws from the community it is serving is seen as furthering the ability of an agency to practice cultural competency in ways that are sensitive to community members' distinctive concerns and problems (Carrizales 2010). In other words, RB = CC. The recovery model holds out hope that a more representative bureaucracy will be more sensitive to the ways in which its welfare clients are approaching the unique challenges that have brought them to the agency's doorstep.

Yet there are ironies in this way of moving toward realizing the RB = CC formula. Former recipients, as indigenous workers from the community, under the medicalized version of welfare are seen as former addicts in recovery. If welfare is seen as a dangerously addictive substance, then the implementation of a disciplinary treatment regime is a logical next step. The medicalization of welfare in fact should be seen primarily in metaphorical terms as just described and the main way of providing this medicalized treatment has been to increasingly rely on former clients who have gotten off welfare and can serve as "success story" role models in ways that are consistent with the "recovery model" in addictions treatment (Watkins-Hayes 2009; Ridzi 2009). The decentralized service delivery systems and private providers that so characterize welfare reform are fertile ground for the importation of medical models of dependency treatment. The use of performance management systems is also entirely consistent with the need to track measureable outcomes resulting from the provision of services or the application of treatment to clients.

Under this scheme, case management is a routinized and deskilled position focused largely on monitoring client adherence to program rules and disciplining them when they are out of compliance. There is, in fact, evidence that with the shift to a more decentralized, privatized system of provision, local contract agencies have gone ahead and moved to a more deskilled welfare-to-work case management by replacing civil servants, social workers, and other professionals with former welfare recipients (Watkins-Hayes 2009; Ridzi 2009). In the process, a form of community self-surveillance is put in place that Cathy Cohen calls "advanced marginalization," where some members of a subordinate group get to achieve a modicum of upward social-economic mobility by taking on responsibilities for monitoring and disciplining other members of that subordinate community (Cohen 1999).

While this staffing pattern may at times be relied on for less controversial reasons as a simple cost-saving measure consonant with the business model, it is also entirely consistent with a recovery model philosophy that puts forth former recipients as behavioral role models. These former recipients are frequently referred to in the literature as "success stories" (Schram and Soss 2001). Yet the recovery model suggests they are hired for another reason. The recovery model is grounded in the philosophy that underpins the twelve-step program of Alcoholics Anonymous and its predecessors, which over time has spread to other areas of drug treatment and mental health services, along with the core conviction that clients must be willing to support one another in overcoming their addictions (AA 1953).

Government programs now run more like businesses, and the application of the business model to welfare involves getting case managers and their clients to internalize the business ethic as well. Policy changes emphasize case managers using disciplinary cost-saving techniques to get clients to move from welfare to paid employment as quickly as possible regardless of whether they and their children improve their well-being.

In the new neoliberalized welfare system, local devolution and privatization have been joined by performance management. Performance management accountability schemes measure the performance of private contract agencies to hold them accountable for meeting performance outcome goals. Performance management more than anything else has led many working in the system to suggest that "social work" has been replaced by a much more preferred "business model" (Soss, Fording, and Schram 2011a). Agencies inevitably feel the pressure to outperform the other agencies being evaluated in these performance schemes. Proponents of neoliberal organizational reform predict that local organizations will respond to the competition among provider agencies by innovating in ways that advance statewide goals and improve client services. Devolution will provide the *freedoms* they need to experiment with promising new approaches. Performance feedback will provide the *evidence* they need to learn from their own experiments and the best practices of others. Performance-based competition will create *incentives* for local organizations to make use of this information and adopt program improvements that work.

Studies have suggested several reasons why organizations may deviate from this script in "rationally perverse" ways. Performance indicators provide ambiguous cues that, in practice, get "selected, interpreted, and used by actors in different ways consistent with their institutional interests" (Moynihan 2008). Positive innovations may fail to emerge because managers do not have the authority to make changes, access learning forums, or devise effective strategies for reforming the organizational status quo. Performance "tunnel vision" can divert attention from important-but-unmeasured operations and lead managers to innovate in ways that subvert program goals (Radin 2006). To boost their numbers, providers may engage in "creaming" practices, focusing their services on less-disadvantaged clients who can be moved above performance thresholds with less investment (Bell and Orr 2002).

In this environment, case managers are under constant pressure to get their clients to stay in compliance with welfare-to-work rules and if the clients fail to do so they are penalized with sanctions that reduce their benefits. This preoccupation with monitoring clients for compliance represents a change in the role of the case manager as part of the administrative transformation of welfare policy implementation. The rise of neoliberal paternalism in fact is associated with a shift in the nature of casework, marked by the passage of federal welfare reform in 1996 (Lurie 2006). The prime directives for TANF (Temporary Assistance for Needy Families) case managers today are to convey and enforce work expectations and to advance and enable transitions to employment. Efforts to promote family and child well-being are downplayed in this frame, but they are not entirely abandoned. Under neoliberal paternalism, they are assimilated into efforts to promote work based on the idea that "work first" will put clients on the most reliable path toward achieving a self-sufficient, stable, and healthy family.

Thus, case managers today initiate their relationships with new clients by screening them for work readiness and delivering an "orientation" to describe work expectations and penalties for noncompliance. In parallel with individualized drug treatment plans, welfare-to-work case managers then develop "individual responsibility plans" – or "contracts of mutual responsibility" – to specify the steps that each client will take in order to move from welfare to work. These rites of passage establish a relationship in which the case manager's primary tasks are to facilitate, monitor, and enforce the completion of required work activities. In celebratory portrayals of the new system, case managers are described as being deeply involved in their clients' development, as "authority figures as well as helpmates" (Mead 2004).

In some states, this ethos is expressed by the neoliberal relabeling of caseworkers as "career counselors." The label evokes images of a well-trained professional who draws on diverse resources to advise and assist entrepreneurial job seekers. In practice, however, few aspects of welfare case management today fit this template. It is rare today that welfare-to-work caseworkers have a social work degree of any kind. Many, however, have management degrees from Strayer, DeVry, Capella, or other vocationally oriented schools that line the strip malls across the country. It is common in many states that a sizeable number of case managers are former recipients who qualified for their jobs by virtue of their experience with the system. Under the business model of service provision, the relationship between client and case manager is rooted in an employment metaphor: the client has signed a "contract" to do a job and should approach the program as if it were a job.

The case manager's job is now to enforce that contract, often using the threat of sanctions to gain compliance. As one major study reported, case managers spend most of their time enforcing compliance to individual responsibility plans and very little time counseling clients (Soss, Fording, and Schram 2011a, pp. 223–226). The change is palpable. One former recipient case manager as reported in this study stressed in a most poignantly metaphorical way that welfare is no longer a social service. She suggested it was now herding cattle instead of tending sheep; while a shepherd takes care of the sheep, a cattle herder just runs the herd through a pen in an insensitive fashion.

The shift from tending sheep to herding cattle at one level is not necessarily that significant since both can be interpreted as dehumanizing. Yet the desensitization implied by this way of characterizing the shift is noteworthy in itself. It also points to another problem with performance measurement. The preoccupation with numbers emphasizes meeting benchmarks as the primary goal irrespective of whether the client is actually helped. In the public management literature, this is the problem of suboptimization. Simon Guilfoyle (2012) refers to suboptimization as analogous to synecdoche, in which a part stands in for the whole. Suboptimization occurs when a measure of one particular outcome of service provision implies that other dimensions, usually less measureable, if no less important, have also been met. Suboptimization is rife in human services where the intended outcomes almost always include difficult-to-measure subjective states of being, including improvements in overall well-being. Suboptimization results when outcome goals are achieved in name only and the full spirit of the goal is lost or forgotten in the process. Meeting performance benchmark targets can misleadingly imply that the overall goal has been met when in fact only an indirect indicator implies that is the case. Welfare-to-work targets might be met but all that has really happened is that we have moved clients from the "welfare poor" to the "working poor" with no real improvements in their overall well-being.

Yet suboptimization's deleterious effects go further. They can produce an instrumentalization, a veritable means–ends inversion, where the performance measurement benchmark or target becomes the end in itself. Under these conditions, human service professionals are encouraged to forget about the overall goals of their program and focus exclusively on meeting the designated benchmarks. Once this happens, it is likely that all work with clients is converted into activities associated with meeting the target irrespective of whether the broader goal is achieved. Once an agency puts in place a performance measurement system it risks creating an instrumentalization that changes the very work that human service workers do. With all the debate about "high-stakes testing" under neoliberal education reform, the threat of performance measurement to change how work is done is most popularly discussed in the mainstream media as the "teach to the test" effect, where school teachers teach students only what they need to know to improve their test scores even if this means their overall learning is not really enhanced (because critical thinking skills and other important forms of learning are neglected).

The "business model" may be replacing "social work" as the way to deliver neoliberal, marketized welfare-to-work programming but the results are proving to be devastating for the poor who are increasingly blamed for their welfare dependency as a treatable condition. The result is that more of the "welfare poor" are being made into the "working poor," while their poverty persists but employers increasingly profit (Edin and Shaefer 2016, pp. 157–158).

Getting Beyond Neoliberal Welfare Policy: The Road to Radical Incrementalism

The disciplinary approach to the poor is spreading beyond welfare to other policies and from the USA to other countries (Brodkin and Marston 2013). The results elsewhere are proving no better than in the USA. As more and more evidence mounts about the horrors of neoliberal welfare policies, interest grows in moving beyond neoliberal insistence that the welfare state buttresses markets rather than counters them. Yet, just as neoliberals could not simply wish away the welfare state the same is true for the opponents of neoliberalism. The road beyond neoliberalism is most likely one that goes through, not around it. That means engaging it, not ignoring it, and in the process trying to bend it to better purposes and more humane ends. I call this sort of realistic approach "radical incrementalism," where small incremental steps within the existing regime are strategically taken to lay down a path for eventually getting beyond it (Schram 2015).

The key to practicing radical incrementalism successfully is to avoid replicating the limitations of status quo-reinforcing incrementalism that does little more than put a band aid on a bullet wound to cover over the problems the existing political economy perpetuates, especially for those on the bottom of the socio-economic order. One critical way to do this is to push for small, feasible changes that are directed at revising the embedded power relations that limit addressing a socio-economic problem. For instance, even though they are less redistributive than proponents of a social wage or advocates of social democracy may wish, revised welfare policies that enhance people's ability to participate in markets effectively so as to live decently still today need to be supported, even as we insist that existing social protections be maintained and even improved so that no one has to endure poverty whether they are participating in labor markets or not. Like the paradox of radical incrementalism itself, we need to consider the value in working through neoliberalism in order to get beyond this. Historically, some of the most important political insights come from considering the analytical power o paradox, whether it is Rousseau's musing about forcing people to be free or other paradoxes. In fact, in recent years, there has been a revival of interest in considering paradoxes when examining the strategies of a "new realism" for promoting social change (Coles 2016; Phulwani 2016). The same is true for social policy change today under neoliberalism, with its increasing economic inequality, concentration of political power, and policy gridlock born of partisan polarization. Yet, we can do this; we can do two things at once. We can walk and chew gum at the same time. We can work both sides of the street. We can work through neoliberalism so as to get past it. Rather than bemoaning its hegemonic status, we should begin the process of working through it in radically incremental ways. Right now before neoliberalism imposes any more hardship than it already has done.

In other words, in today's policy climate, we may need to accept that progressive policy change is not a linear matter of building on what came before to make the next steps to better realizing an inclusive social democracy for US citizens. We might need to consider taking to heart literary theorist and father of formalism Viktor Shklovsky's (2005) recommendation that we make the "knight's move." In 1923, Shklovsky was writing as someone concerned about the future of artistic freedom under Soviet communism. He suggested that the knight was a chess metaphor that allowed us to think about how to move forward but under constrained circumstances. The knight could move sideways, jumping over other pieces on the board, it could work around obstacles to get to where it needed to go. Yet, Shklovsky also appreciated that the knight's options for movement were prescribed, its freedom to act differently was constrained by the rules of the game and the terrain of the board at any one point in time. Power, as Michel Foucault recognized, creates its own resistance, both by inciting opposition to its constraints but also then pre-scripting the types of responses that are feasible given that structure of power. Foucault came to be accused of being a neoliberal for suggesting how working through it rather than ignoring it might be the imperative for getting change. Foucault appreciated such an "inside-out" strategy might reduce power's oppressiveness even if only incrementally but significantly, especially for those who suffered most from neoliberalism's disciplinary insistences (Golder 2015). In order to counter the inequities of the market today, we may need to consider how to work through neoliberalism in order to get beyond it.

A controversial example is Obamacare (the Patient Protection and Affordable Care Act of 2010). Obamacare radically revises the health care system in the USA to extend access to care, control pricing, and improve quality by not doing away with the existing mixed system of public and private insurance, but rather by building on that deeply path-dependent system. It holds out the potential to revise the power relationships between the state, insurance markets, and providers. It relies on market exchanges to extend private insurance to the uninsured (publicly subsidized for low-income participants). While polling indicates it is not overwhelmingly popular, costs for co-pays and premiums can be high for the non-poor, and Republicans have moved now to repeal it, it already seems to have come to be embedded in the welfare state, proving difficult to eliminate, thanks in no small part to the benefits it affords people, especially those with pre-existing conditions, families with uncovered young adult children, and women in need of access to preventive services such as birth control. It may have already become path dependent without overwhelming positive policy feedback (Schram 2015).

Obamacare is deeply entwined in the existing public and private system of delivering health care, relying on Medicare, Medicaid, employer-provided insurance, and market exchanges for personal insurance. As a result, Obamacare remains opaque for much of the public and makes it part of what Suzanne Mettler (2011) calls the "submerged state." This situation has perhaps limited its popularity and led to people voting for candidates like Trump without knowing that they would be authorizing repeal of the health insurance they seek to keep (Krugman 2017). It also possibly deceives its opponents that they could repeal it without facing public backlash. It might lead policymakers to be forced to contrive votes for repeal by denying possibilities for incremental reform, hoping that "repeal and replace" will not turn out to be "repeal and repent" (Farrell 2017). With 20 million newly insured at risk of being without the ability to access affordable insurance (with or without subsidies from Obamacare), the political backlash against those who vote for repeal could be significant. But most importantly, the embeddedness of Obamacare makes it difficult to dislodge irrespective of whether it has produced positive policy feedback in the form of increased public commitment to the policy itself. It may have made itself irreplaceable without public support.

Universal coverage, improved cost controls, and a more equitable health policy might be better realized through more dramatic reform such as the institution of a single-payer system. Yet, the politics of today under neoliberalism simply do not allow that. In the meantime, while we are waiting for a more progressive political climate to possibly never come, we might be better spending our time trying to figure out how to work through neoliberalism in spite of constraining insistence on the hegemony of market logic. The case of Obamacare highlights how working through neoliberalism may be the radically incremental thing we need to be doing in order to improve health care for millions of Americans. It may even lay the basis for eventually getting beyond the limitations of neoliberal health policy. Such is how the knight's move may prove effective in an age of neoliberalism. Working through market hegemony may be the best option today and it may lead to a more inclusive social democracy down the road. The paradoxes of politics in an age of neoliberalism need to be given consideration.

Acknowledgements

Thanks are extended to Adam Dahl, Rom Coles, Mitchell Dean, Tom Grimwood, Patricia Jefferson, John Maher, Melania Papa-Mabe, Marianna Pavlovskaya, Matt Sparke, Amanda Tillotson, and Vanessa Wells for helpful comments on an earlier draft.

References

Alcoholics Anonymous (AA) (1953). *Twelve Steps and Twelve Traditions.* New York: Alcoholics Anonymous.

Bell, S. and Orr, L. (2002). Screening (and Creaming?) Applicants to Job Training Programs: The AFDC Homemaker–Home Health Aide Demonstrations. *Labour Economics*, 9(2), 279–301.

Bonica, A., McCarty, N., Poole, K. T., and Rosenthal, Howard (2013). Why Hasn't Democracy Slowed Rising Inequality? *Journal of Economic Perspectives*, 27(3), 103–124.

Bourdieu, P. (1994). Rethinking the State: On the Genesis and Structure of the Bureaucratic Field. *Sociological Theory*, 12(1), 1–19.

Brodkin, E. Z. and Marston, G. (Eds.) (2013). *Work and the Welfare State: Street-Level Organization and Workfare Politics.* Washington, DC: Georgetown University Press.

Brown, W. (2003). Neo-Liberalism and the End of Liberal Democracy. *Theory & Event*, 7. Retrieved from: http://muse.jhu.edu/journals/theory_and_event/

Brown, W. (2006). American Nightmare: Neoliberalism, Neoconservatism, and De-Democratization. *Political Theory*, 34(6), 690–714.

Brown, W. (2015). *Undoing the Demos: Neoliberalism's Stealth Revolution.* Cambridge: Zone Books.

Carrizales, T. (2010). Exploring Cultural Competency within the Public Affairs Curriculum. *Journal of Public Affairs Education*, 16(4), 593–606.

Cloward, R. A. and Piven, F. F. (1975). Notes toward a Radical Social Work. In Roy Bailey and Mike Brake (Eds), *Radical Social Work.* New York: Pantheon.

Cohen, C. (1999). *The Boundaries of Blackness: AIDS and the Breakdown of Black Politics.* Chicago: University of Chicago Press.

Coles, R. (2016). *Visionary Pragmatism: Radical and Ecological Democracy in Neoliberal Times.* Durham, NC: Duke University Press.

Coole, D. (2012). Reconstructing the Elderly: A Critical Analysis of Pensions and Population Policies in an Era of Demographic Aging. *Contemporary Political Theory*, 11, 41–67.

Edin, K. and Shaefer, H. L. (2016). *$2.00 a Day: Living on Almost Nothing in America.* New York: Mariner Books.

Farrell, H. (2017). Republicans Midnight Vote Was about Bridge Building: Actually It Was Bridge Burning. *The Washington Post*, January 12.

Fraser, N. (2009). Feminism, Capitalism and the Cunning of History. *New Left Review*, 56 (March–April), 97–117.

Giroux, H. A. (2015). Neoliberalism, Violence and Resistance: A Discussion on Forthright Radio. *Truthout*, August 24. Retrieved from: www.truth-out.org/opinion/item/ 32464-neoliberalism-violence-and-resistance-a-discussion-on-forthright-radio

Golder, B. (2015). *Foucault and the Politics of Rights.* Palo Alto, CA: Stanford University Press.

Gordon, L. (1994). *Pitied but Not Entitled: Single Mothers and the History of Welfare, 1890–1935.* New York: Free Press.

Guilfoyle, S. (2012). On Target? Public Sector Performance Management: Recurrent Themes, Consequences and Questions. *Policing*, 6(3), 250–260.

Hacker, J. (2004). Privatizing Risk without Privatizing the Welfare State: The Hidden Politics of Social Policy Retrenchment in the United States. *American Political Science Review*, 98(2), 243–260.

Harcourt, B. (2010). *Illusions of Free Markets: Punishment and the Myth of Natural Order.* Cambridge, MA: Harvard University Press.

Hay, C. and Payne, A. (2015). *Civic Capitalism.* Cambridge: Polity Press.

Hayek, F. A. (1960). *The Constitution of Liberty.* Chicago: University of Chicago Press.

Heady, L. (2010). Social Return on Investment Position Paper. *New Philanthropy Capital,* April. Retrieved from: www.thinknpc.org/publications/social-return-on-investment-position-paper/

Katz, M. (1997). *Improving Poor People: The Welfare State, the "Underclass," and Urban Schools as History.* Princeton, NJ: Princeton University Press.

Krieger, J. (1986). *Reagan, Thatcher and the Politics of Decline.* New York: Oxford University Press.

Krugman, P. (2017). Donald Trump's Medical Delusions. *New York Times,* January 13.

Lurie, I. (2006). *At the Frontlines of the Welfare System: A Perspective on the Decline in Welfare Caseloads.* Albany: State University of New York Press.

March, J. G. and Olsen, J. P. (2010). *Rediscovering Institutions: The Organizational Basis of Politics.* New York: Simon and Shuster.

Marx, K. (1937). *The Eighteenth Brumaire of Louis Napoleon,* trans. Saul K. Padover. Moscow: Progress.

Mead, L. (2004). *Government Matters: Welfare Reform in Wisconsin.* Princeton, NJ: Princeton University Press.

Mettler, S. (2011). *The Submerged State: How Invisible Government Policies Undermine American Democracy.* Chicago: University of Chicago Press.

Mettler, S. and Soss, J. (2004). The Consequences of Public Policy for Democratic Citizenship: Bridging Policy Studies and Mass Politics. *Perspectives on Politics,* 2(1), 55–73.

Mirowski, P. (2014). *Never Let a Serious Crisis Go to Waste: How Neoliberalism Survived the Financial Meltdown.* London: Verso.

Moynihan, D. P. (1988). *Came the Revolution: Argument in the Reagan Era.* New York: Harcourt.

Moynihan, D. P. (2008). *The Dynamics of Performance Management: Constructing Information and Reform.* Washington, DC: Georgetown University Press.

Peck, J. (2010). Zombie Neoliberalism and the Ambidexterous State. *Theoretical Criminology,* 14(1), 104–110.

Peck, J. (2011). *Constructions of Neoliberal Reason.* London: Oxford University Press.

Phulwani, V. (2016). The Poor Man's Machiavelli: Saul Alinsky and the Morality of Power. *American Political Science Review,* 110(4), 863–875.

Pierson, P. (2000). Increasing Returns, Path Dependence and the Study of Politics. *American Political Science Review,* 94(2), 251–267.

Radin, B. (2006). *Challenging the Performance Movement: Accountability, Complexity, and Democratic Values.* Washington, DC: Georgetown University Press.

Ridzi, F. (2009). *Selling Welfare Reform: Work-first and the New Common Sense of Employment.* New York: New York University Press.

Sassen, S. (2006). *Territory, Authority, Rights: From Medieval to Global Assemblages.* Princeton NJ: Princeton University Press.

Satterwhite, F. J. O. and Teng, S. (2007). *Culturally Based Capacity Building: An Approach to Working in Communities of Color for Social Change.* Los Angeles: California Endowment and Compass Point Nonprofit Services.

Schram, S. F. (2006). *Welfare Discipline: Discourse, Governance and Globalization.* Philadelphia, PA: Temple University Press.

Schram, S. F. (2015). *The Return of Ordinary Capitalism: Neoliberalism, Precarity, Occupy*. New York: Oxford University Press.

Schram, S. F. and Soss, J. (2001). Success Stories: Welfare Reform, Policy Discourse, and the Politics of Research. *The Annals of the American Academy of Political and Social Science*, 577, 49–65.

Schram, S. F. and Silverman, B. (2012). The End of Social Work: Neoliberalizing Social Policy Implementation. *Critical Policy Studies*, 6(2), 128–145.

Shklovsky, V. (2005). *The Knight's Move*, trans. Richard Sheldon. Champaign, IL: Dalkey Archive Press.

Soss, J., Fording, R. C., and Schram, S. F. (2011a). *Disciplining the Poor: Neoliberal Paternalism and the Persistent Power of Race*. Chicago: University of Chicago Press.

Soss, J., Fording, R. C., and Schram, S. F. (2011b). The Organization of Discipline: From Performance Management to Perversity and Punishment. *Journal of Public Administration Research*, 21, i202–i232.

Stedman Jones, D. (2014). *Masters of the Universe: Hayek, Friedman, and the Birth of Neoliberal Politics*. Princeton, NJ: Princeton University Press.

Stiglitz, J. (2012). *The Price of Inequality: How Today's Divided Society Endangers Our Future*. New York: W. W. Norton.

Turco, C. J. (2010). Cultural Foundations of Tokenism: Evidence from the Leveraged Buyout Industry. *American Sociological Review*, 75(6), 894–913.

Wacquant, L. (2009). *Punishing the Poor: The Neoliberal Government of Social Insecurity*. Durham, NC: Duke University Press.

Watkins-Hayes, C. (2009). *The New Welfare Bureaucrats: Entanglements of Race, Class, and Policy Reform*. Chicago: University of Chicago Press.

Williamson, J. (2004). The Washington Consensus as Policy Prescription for Development, A Lecture in the Series "Practitioners of Development" Delivered at the World Bank on January 13. Retrieved from: www.iie.com/publications/papers/williamson0204.pdf

13

NEOLIBERALISM

Towards A Critical Counter-Conduct[1]

Barbara Cruikshank

In the style of Michel Foucault (2008, pp. 8–9), this chapter asks, Why do so many write "with so much passion and so much resentment against our most recent past, against our present, and against ourselves," that politics, democracy, freedom, and equality are threatened, destroyed, or negated by neoliberalism; that the exercise of power is "depoliticized" by neoliberalism to displace or suppress politics; that individual liberty is no more than an instrument of neoliberal subjection; that our present is dominated by neoliberalism; that we are not free? Why seek the pathway to freedom in critical analysis that exposes and defines neoliberalism or sets political resistance against neoliberalism? I argue that critical conducts – activist and academic alike – too often remain under the spell of the repressive hypothesis and its presumption that freedom and knowledge are external to and under the thumb of power, in this case, neoliberalism. It is as if to resist, we must dare to speak the dirty and frightful word, "neoliberalism," as if to knowingly defy the silence imposed upon the truth by power is to call out the name of that truth.

If neoliberal hegemony determines the reality of the present, however, then from what vantage point is anyone capable of seeing clearly through the fog that engulfs the present? There is widespread disagreement about what neoliberalism is, as we shall see, in part because there is disagreement over which vantage point it is necessary to take: a vision of the past that is lost, of the future to come, or the possession of a critical perspective on the present. Nevertheless, there is broad agreement among its critics on what the proper perspective must achieve; it is necessary to turn neoliberalism into a target of resistance, that is, to essentialize neoliberalism as self-evidently real, if hidden, stable, the name of a grave and unified threat. There is also widespread agreement among neoliberalism's critics that change is necessary to overcome the hegemony of neoliberalism, which defines, determines, and stabilizes the present. Change, then, is understood as the temporal limit of the present. The agent of change, however, does not live in the present, and must be fashioned and brought into being as a collective, a movement, or a revolutionary army by critical conduct, that is, by critical thought, political organizing on the left, solidarity, and unified resistance to neoliberalism.

I am adapting the concepts of conduct and counter-conduct for my own purpose that were introduced by Michel Foucault in lectures given in 1977–78 and now published in translation (Foucault 2008). Those concepts and Foucault's manner of critique are given clarity and breadth by Davidson (2011) and Butler (2004). As Foucault expressed them, between the two, conduct and counter-conduct, there is "an immediate and founding correlation" (p. 196). They are alike in that their coherence comes from practicing certain rules, norms, and strategies for conducting oneself and for conducting others, for exercising power and freedom. The difference between them is that counter-conducts are:

> movements whose objective is a different form of conduct, that is to say: wanting to be conducted differently, by other leaders (*conducteurs*) and other shepherds, towards other objectives and forms of salvation, and through other procedures and methods. They are movements that also seek, possibly at any rate, to escape direction by others and to define the way for each to conduct himself.
>
> *(pp. 194–195)*

I am adapting and extending these concepts to practices of conducting and counter-conducting critical analyses and writing critical theories, to conducting and counter-conducting readers persuaded by critical theory, and to conducts and counter-conducts of exercising power and freedom in resistance.

There is certainly sense in pursuing the "immediate and founding correlation" between neoliberalism as a conduct and critics of neoliberalism as a counter-conduct. It is by giving the status of conduct to the critics, however, that I am able to fashion a critical counter-conduct. And it is for that purpose that I am also adopting Foucault's widely known critical attitude toward the repressive hypothesis, which, in a nutshell, is the seemingly incorrigible presumption that power represses freedom, action, truth, and speech in a zero sum balance. Readers are likely to be familiar with Foucault's critical attitude towards the repressive hypothesis: power does not only repress, but also produces freedom, action, truth, and speech. His reconceptualization of power undercuts claims that revealing the truth hidden behind the mask of power is a pathway to liberation. To name and unmask neoliberalism, then, is not going to overcome the power of neoliberalism, nor will it set repressed resistance free from under the heel of neoliberal hegemony. Neoliberalism, like power, is not a singular or unified agency of repression; it does not have a face. I adopt his critical attitude towards the repressive hypothesis found discernable here in the strategies, norms, and expectations that govern and which set the limits of critical conduct. Those limits, I argue, not only mislead resistance against neoliberalism; those limits have become obstacles to critical thought and action in the present. This is why, as will be explained throughout this chapter, it is necessary to fashion a different form of critical conduct, a critical counter-conduct.

Adamantly, by "critical conduct" I do not mean to evoke what is called "critical theory" in academic circles. Critical theory may be implicated here by the use of that phrase by some practitioners cited here as examples of what I call critical conduct, to be sure. But in no way is this chapter a blanket statement that *all* or even *most* critical conduct succumbs to the repressive hypothesis, only critical conduct that proceeds to name, define, critically analyze, and target neoliberalism as the proper target of political resistance. Wherever the phrase "critical conduct" appears in this chapter, it is an abbreviation of "the critical conduct of those who write and speak with passion, resentment, and conviction, to expose the truth of neoliberalism and do so in resistance to a reality determined by neoliberalism."

What I am calling critical conduct repeatedly insists that neoliberalism is the defining reality of the present and the obstacle to true freedom, democracy, and all hope for a better day. As a consequence, critical conduct closes the door to contingent forces of change in the present and rudely slams it in the face of those who are presently engaged in resistance that is not conducted according to the limits set by critical conduct. Two additional consequences follow from critical conduct setting change at the limit of the present. That temporal limit aligns easily with the repressive hypothesis, which in this instance situates change at the threshold between neoliberal hegemony (repression) in the present and the moment of overcoming the present (liberation). Both the necessary critical vantage point to see neoliberalism for what it is and the very possibility for freedom to act upon that vision are only to be found on the outside or on the other side of the present. Setting change at the temporal limit of the present pitches us into the lurch on the promise of pulling us out. The limits of critical conduct have consequences that impose obstacles to critical thought and action.

The most troubling consequence is the disparagement, devaluation, and displacement of struggles underway in the present that are deemed to be insufficiently unified against neoliberalism, insufficiently radical in their revolt or in their analysis of the present, or so hoodwinked by neoliberalism that they are unable to see what should or must be done. Often enough, however, this chapter suggests a different vantage point to see that struggles underway in the present are organized and conducted explicitly *against* the repressive hypothesis, against the idea that power is unified and singularly repressive. Those in struggle may *refuse*, rather than merely fail, to fashion themselves into the collective agent of change that critical conducts aim to bring into being. Instead, they organize and resist power that is understood to be polymorphous, unevenly and unstably distributed in all kinds of relations, places, among human and non-human forces.

Understanding power as uneven and unstable, rather than repressive, opens the door to contingency. There is no assurance that power can be overcome once and for all, but there is assurance that no singular power, with the possible exception of forcible violence, can remain unified and stable. The same understanding, I will argue later on, should be applied to resistance and to the left. Many in struggles underway refuse to conduct themselves in unified resistance against neoliberalism not only because they do not agree that power is singular and repressive, but more precisely because the uneven, unstable, and contingent distribution of power is painfully evident in the history of struggle. Moreover, in the contingency of struggle undertaken amidst uneven and unstable powers, one should expect surprises; new and unforeseen powers may emerge, there will be unintended consequences of struggle that may redistribute power or give new scope to power for better, for worse, or a mixture of both. Even though resistance may be repressed or met with violence, there is no certainty of the result. It may serve the intention to bring resistance to an end, or unintentionally enliven resistance, draw in new recruits and pull the uncommitted to the side of resistance. So the organization and expression of resistance in ways that defy the repressive hypothesis are made in order to grapple within the uneven, unstable, and contingent distribution of power, rather than to overcome the singular power of repression once and for all. That objective sets a new limit for a critical counter-conduct.

Resistance conducted in ways that run counter to the repressive hypothesis will disappoint the expectations set by critical conduct. Moreover, as is explained below, the expectation of finding and sharing a critical vantage point *on* the present is another limit of critical conduct that is countered by the expectation of finding a critical vantage point only *within* the present. These new limits placed upon critical counter-conducts are evident in new vocabularies, new forms of association, new modes of organizing, in the temporality and scales of struggle underway. For example, affinity, coalition, and intersectionality run counter to solidarity and unity; pre-figurative, alternative, and direct-action *in* the present counter visions for *overcoming* the present; horizontal rather than from above or below; leaderless rather than grassroots; post-politics rather than consensus politics. And running counter to setting the scale of struggle on the state, nation, institutions, law, or ideology, recent struggles set the scale of their conduct at the level of micro-power: community, the street, local, associations of many kinds, the personal, identity, lifestyle, and practice.

I suggest these movements as the proper object of critical diagnosis and as models for critical counter-conduct, one that analyses practices of freedom and resistance already underway as "the diagnostic of power," a phrase and direction for critical counter-conduct signaled by Lila Abu-Lughod (1990). Critical counter-conduct takes the vantage point of what is said and done in the present and expects that change is continuous, contingent, erupting in places and from forces that are unexpected.

Although I originally embarked on this chapter in the winter of 2016, already in this winter of 2017, I feel somewhat vindicated in the argument made then to expect surprises. Over the last few months, the most potent and unexpected resistance to neoliberalism erupted in the electoral arena rather than in the numerous trenches set up and massive protests by the left around the world since the global financial crisis in 2008. Amidst that crisis, hand-wringing on the part of neoliberal capitalism, discussed briefly below, especially finance capital, was matched momentarily by jubilant declarations from the left that the Washington Consensus – neoliberalism – was finally dead. Jubilance was squashed, in part, by bailouts of big banks and industries, refusal by the European Union to bail out member countries, policing and violent repression of protest. And it was squashed also in part by the critical conduct of Naomi Klein, who published an international best-seller, *The Shock Doctrine: The Rise of Disaster Capitalism*, in the summer of 2008, at the height of the crisis. Klein pointed to the history of natural disasters and crises to argue that rather than roiling or ending neoliberal capitalism, they actually smoothed the way for the ascent of neoliberal hegemony. The 2008 financial crisis would be no exception, a conclusion confirmed by Mirowski (2013). Indeed, despite the astonishing number, size, and scale of sustained resistance from the left sparked by the crisis – starting with Iceland's Pots and Pans Movement, M-15 in Spain, Occupy Wall Street, Hong Kong, Greece, those lumped together as the Arab Spring, extending to the Gezi Park protests in Turkey in 2013 – the diagnoses of neoliberalism as hegemonic under examination in this chapter went largely unchanged. Of course, there are important exceptions to what I am calling critical conduct to be found in Amar (2013) and in Soss, Fording, and Schram (2011).

The big surprise finally came in the latter part of 2016 and has culminated, so far, in the election of Donald Trump to the presidency of the United States on a platform of white nationalism, anti-establishment, pro-jobs, anti-global trade, and free spending; the relative success of the Bernie Sanders' campaign for president in the name of political revolution and socialism; the Brexit vote in the United Kingdom; the escalating support for nationalist parties of the far right in Europe. All of which, in the words of Nancy Fraser (2017), "signal a collapse of neoliberal hegemony." Time will tell, of course. These ascendant forces may face the same fate as Syriza in Greece, for example. But to my knowledge, nobody saw any of this coming before the summer of 2016 and few, including the winners, could credibly claim no surprise in the fall of 2016. While it is now shockingly evident that the most potent resistance to neoliberalism is, to date, electoral and largely from right-wing forces, the left-wing models of resistance I use here to model a critical counter-conduct are, I hope, still persuasive. The newly ascendant right-wing forces are no more or less unified, coherent, or expected than the left-wing forces that surged in the recent past. It is troubling that the certainty in which critical conduct held neoliberal hegemony was not shaken despite all the evidence of vitality and open resistance by the left over many years. Just a moment later signs of vitality on the right appear to have shaken the certainty of neoliberalism to the point of breaking. Still, as I see it, the lesson to expect surprises is vindicated.

In what follows, this chapter asks, What is neoliberalism? After a quick survey of the answers given to that question by practitioners of critical conduct and the usage of the concept in political life, the chapter proceeds to point out the agreements and disagreements over neoliberalism to articulate the limits set upon critical conduct. The chapter next proceeds toward and finally arrives upon a critical counter-conduct.

What Is Neoliberalism?

Is neoliberalism an ideology? An economic or political doctrine, or a theory of political economy (Harvey 2005)? A counter-revolution against Keynesianism or a rebellion against the state (Duménil and Lévy 2004)? A state formation, a state of exception, or a global assemblage (Wacquant 2009; Ong 2006, 2007)? An imperial order (Petras 2011)? A revolution in the rationality or purpose of government or of liberalism (Brown 2015; Feher 2009)? A market rationality applied to everything and everywhere or applied in enclaves, certain spheres, regions, or sectors (Ferguson 2006)? A practice of privatization, deregulation, or devolution? A political culture or a cultural politics (Duggan 2003)? The only alternative, either because the left lacks an alternative vision, ideology, or the "decline of socialism" (Brown 2003; Fukuyama 2012)? The only alternative because the left was caught in the grip of neoliberalism, side-tracked by anti-racist and identity politics from advancing a unifying vision of equality and solidarity to overcome neoliberal capitalism (Brown 2003; Dean 2009; Duggan 2003)? The only alternative because the left, caught in the grip of resistance to capitalism, failed to invent its own art of government (Foucault 2008, pp. 93–94)? Or is it the only alternative even in the face of its own failure because neoliberalism's success is due to its ability to pass for "common sense" despite all evidence to the contrary (Mirowski 2013)? Is it hegemonic, under strain, or already surpassed by a new era dubbed "post-neoliberal" inaugurated by the pink tide in Latin America (Brenner, Peck, and Theodore 2010; Petras and Veltmeyer 2014)?

Recently published left-leaning studies define and dispute neoliberalism in all these terms. Without any intended glibness, one could say that neoliberalism is a conceptual contest or conceptual dispute on the left. As is often noted, and in the words of Wendy Larner (2006, pp. 449–451), "the concept of neoliberalism is overwhelmingly mobilized and deployed by left-wing academics and political activists." Others have taken notice of the remarkable profusion of studies taking neoliberalism as the proper object of analysis and resistance, and the no less remarkable repetition that neoliberalism is hegemonic in our time. Some have ably defended doing so (Mirowski 2014). Neoliberalism, despite voluble disagreement over what it is and how to define it, is a term of negative judgment that is difficult to find in use by anyone other than its critics.

To my knowledge, no one advocated for or in the name of "neoliberalism" per se, with the possible exception of the highly secretive Mont Pélerin Society which originated in 1947, whose members founded and headed institutions to spread neoliberalism – unnamed as such and under the cover of calling for market freedom and limited state power – such as the Federalist Society, the American Heritage Foundation, and the Institute for Economic Affairs, among hundreds of others spread around the world. That history is documented by Philip Mirowski (2014). Mirowski suggests that evidence of a neoliberal political movement existed in Latin America and Francophone countries in the 1980s, so that neoliberalism emerged as a critical category earlier there than in the United States, for example, but he does not suggest that movement was conducted openly under the banner of neoliberalism. (p. 18). Nevertheless, since June of 2016, in the moment Brexit shocked the world by voting to leave the European Union, itself an institution for protecting finance capital from democracy, there is more evidence of neoliberalism as the name used by its practitioners for scrutiny under pressure of what was previously called "market competition," "capital account liberalization," "free trade," "globalization," "privatization," "foreign direct investment," and so on (Ostry, Loungani, and Furceri 2016).

What I am calling "critical conduct" is the conduct of scholars and activists who take neoliberalism to be a proper object of critical analysis and resistance. (Emphatically, again, I do *not* mean to implicate critical theory writ large or the Frankfurt School in particular in the category of critical conduct.) Despite widespread disagreement over what it is said to name, amidst a profusion of critical studies, theories, analyses, and protests over nearly two decades, "neoliberalism" is uttered in critical conduct as the defining word of our times. It has taken on a multifaceted character that is singularly and self-evidently bad and only gets worse. "Neoliberalism" names a unity, often with force and agency of its own, that wages successful assaults upon equality, democracy, liberal democracy, democratic citizenship, the environment, the poor, the middle-class, public things, and public life. Neoliberalism is presented as wily and capable of undercutting all efforts to resist its hold on individuals, common sense, government, institutions, and political culture. What hope these studies supply for emancipation or escape from neoliberalism is dependent on the whole-scale rejection of the present. The means and purpose of overcoming the present are also disputed. They range from calls to envision the coming revolution to reviving Enlightenment principles, to take a blind leap of faith that another world is possible or to establish forms of government, old and new, from liberal democracy, radical democracy, communism, and republicanism, to anarchy.

So there is disagreement about what neoliberalism is and how to overcome it yet agreement that it encompasses and defines the present. A norm of critical conduct is discernable: to diagnose the present. There is disagreement also about how to overcome the present, but no disagreement that it is the purpose of critical conduct to get us there. Another discernible norm, then, is for critical conduct to overcome the present. Implicitly there is agreement that critical conduct must define, expose, and target power or, in a word, to essentialize, neoliberalism as the real, determining condition of the present. There is certainly also explicit agreement that the neoliberal condition of the present will be overcome only by resistance. While it is often only implicit that the strategy of critical conduct is to conduct that resistance by dint of its diagnosis, we turn now to one of the more explicit expressions of that strategy.

Bernard Harcourt asserts that for the task of resistance, "properly defining neoliberalism becomes of vital importance" (2010, p. 23). Calling neoliberalism out into the open, naming and defining it, is an urgent matter of critique. The "central task of critique is to lift the veil from the purported orderliness or market efficiency; to unmask the ostensible neutrality of the economic analysis; to expose the distributions that are at the heart of all political interventions" (p. 27). Critical conduct guided by the norms of conceptual definition, exposure, and resistance to power, however, will inevitably generate a tautology: power is hidden because power can mask itself. The singular face of neoliberalism is masked by its own indefinite presence, hidden in the barely perceptible and gentle force of a nudge to do or to choose this over that, narrowing down democratic freedom to consumer choice, reducing citizens to human capital, driving the rampant privatization of public goods and services, and pulling the strings of protest against "too much government." It is the face of a singular power and the essential reality of the present.

While aiming to expose power as the target of resistance, the tautology of power draws instead to conclusions that defeat resistance. For example, Sandy Schram (2015, p. 192) asserts that:

> neoliberalism is the pervasive reality of the state today. It is the common sense of how to get things done. Whenever it fails for whatever reason, it is a good bet that the chosen responses will be to double down on neoliberalism and take it to another level.

Neoliberal hegemony makes itself inevitable by making anything else unthinkable. "The polity/citizenry cannot imagine capitalism's demise because neoliberal forms of discourse have rendered unthinkable more socially just alternatives ... To use a common philosophical term, neoliberalism is hegemonic" (Bialostok, Whitman, and Bradley 2012, p. 79). Neoliberal ideology functions in such a way that it distracts resistance away from itself and away from critical conduct, simultaneously, according to Jodi Dean (2009) and Lisa Duggan (2003). The strategy of critical conduct is to unify resistance into a force that is powerful enough to topple the unity of power. Any resistance that is not conducted by the norms and strategies of critical conduct, then, only serves to secure the veil covering the face of power. The strings pulling unwitting and distracted resistance to the wrong targets (e.g., racism, sexism, environmental degradation, neo-colonialism), into disunity and disconcerted resistance, are held by the invisible hand of power. In short, critical conduct renders resistance underway into an obstacle and into further evidence that power is hidden. The strategy of critical conduct results, then, in taking up a quarrel on the side of the true left against the false left, which dismisses, displaces, and denigrates any resistance underway in the present reality as defined by critical conduct.

Even when the veil of power is lifted, however, the face of neoliberalism remains in dispute, as noted above in the disparate answers given to the question, What is neoliberalism? First, disagreement over the definition of neoliberalism indicates that "lifting the veil" does not expose the real truth to one and all or unify the target of resistance even amongst the practitioners of critical conduct. Rather, it plants the stakes of truth and reality in a conceptual dispute. The many different faces exposed and the proliferation of definitions leaves critical conduct in confrontation with a many-headed beast. Which head must be cut off to bring the beast down? The project of defining and exposing the real truth does not compel any agreement on the definition of neoliberalism, but it does compel critical conduct to repeat the repressive hypothesis as a necessary condition of any definition. Second, added upon conceptual dispute are the difficulties of exposing (epistemology), disagreement over the definition or the face of neoliberalism (power), critical conduct is also engaged in fierce disagreement over the nature of the veil that masks neoliberalism (method), over the proper weapon to slay the beast (mode of resistance), and who is poised to wield that weapon (political subject). These disagreements increase the stakes of critical conduct, planting them deeper into political dispute.

Harcourt also warns that "useful categories – categories that serve to reveal illusions and targets of resistance at one point in time – get in the way of addressing new problems that emerge in later times" (p. 28). That time has come not only with the category of neoliberalism, and not because times change and new problems arise, which of course they do. Rather, the time has come because critical conduct, exposing the truth hidden by power, revealing the true and proper target of resistance, is a conceptual contest that turns its own categories into self-evident realities. To be rendered into "useful categories," not only neoliberalism, but also "resistance," must be accepted as stable, fixed, and self-evident, the site of a singular truth and reality. Any resistance that does not measure up to that category is not real or true resistance. It is the first rule of critical conduct that the self-evidence of categories be accepted as the essential sites of critical thought and action where reality, truth, and power are at stake. Acceptance of that self-evidence is the first rule of critical conduct. It is critical conduct itself that renders neoliberalism an arresting site of contest. I am *not* saying that conceptual dispute stops critical thought and action or turns it into idle speculation. Rather, I am saying that the norms, practices, and strategies of critical conduct are obstacles to critical thought and action.

Towards a Critical Counter-Conduct

Even when neoliberalism is treated as paradoxical it retains the qualities of singularity, "ubiquitous and omnipresent, yet disunified and nonidentical with itself," as Wendy Brown describes it, it is also "the face of an order replete with contradiction and disavowal" (2015, pp. 48–49). Nevertheless, Brown warns against and provides the perspective for avoiding one of the obstacles to critical thought and action produced by critical conduct, essentialism and the self-evidence of neoliberalism as an all-encompassing reality. "Alertness to neoliberalism's inconstancy and plasticity cautions against identifying its current iteration as its essential and global truth and against making the story I am telling a teleological one, a steady march toward end times" (p. 21). That is made possible by taking her perspective from the vantage point of what is said and done in the articulation and utilization of neoliberal rationality. This perspective affords tremendous insight into neoliberalism while avoiding essentialism.

Yet the paradox at the core of her book is not perceived from the vantage point of what is said and done. It appears, instead, at the intersection of two vantage points. The second vantage point is taken from the position of what it is that neoliberalism "undoes"; *homo politicus* is undone by *homo economicus*: "the vanquishing of *homo politicus* by contemporary neoliberal rationality, the insistence that there are only rational market actors in every sphere of human existence, is novel, indeed revolutionary, in the history of the West" (p. 99). Brown does not take the vantage point of what is said and done when she addresses what is undone, but the vantage point of "the West," the conceit of which is a "public life," at its best educated and democratic, represented by "informed political passion, respectful deliberation, aspirational sovereignty, sharp containment of powers that would overrule or undermine it" (p. 39). *Homo politicus* lived in the West, in a sovereign public sphere peopled by sovereign citizens. "In the beginning, there was *homo politicus* …" (p. 87). So begins Brown's compact origin myth of *homo politicus*, whose story begins with Aristotle and who "remains alive and important" through to modernity (p. 98). The implementation of neoliberal rationality through the privatization and marketization of everything, including the public sphere, staged a revolution that stripped sovereignty from *homo politicus*, reducing him to *homo economicus*. *Homo economicus* may be free, but not sovereign. Therein lies the paradox: "the neoliberal revolution takes place in the name of freedom – free markets, free countries, free men – but tears up freedom's grounding in sovereignty for states and subjects alike" (p. 108). By "undoing the *demos*," neoliberal rationality destroyed the only political subject capable of staging a counter-revolution to restore the West.

The vantage point provided by the mythical existence of *homo politicus*, then, provides the wedge for critical conduct in Brown's argument. This raises the obstacle to critical thought and action, whereas the other vantage point, of what is said and done vis-à-vis neoliberal rationality, offers no strategy, subject, or target of resistance. With *homo politicus* vanquished, who is left living in the present capable or willing to wage a counter-revolution against neoliberalism? Assuming we believe in him and desire to resurrect him to re-take his place in the history of the West, how might that be accomplished? Absent *homo politicus*, there appear to be no other resources in Brown's critique of neoliberalism. Perhaps there are such resources, but they are buried deep under *homo politicus*. With no other recourse, neoliberal rationality bears down upon Brown's book and the very possibility of critical conduct.

> Neoliberalism is the rationality through which capitalism finally swallows humanity – not only with its machinery of compulsory commodification and profit-driven expansion, but by its form of valuation. As the spread of this form evacuates the content from liberal democracy and transforms the meaning of democracy *tout court*, it subdues democratic desires and imperils democratic dreams.
>
> *(p. 44)*

Like the other diagnostics of the present noted above, Brown's too draws the conclusion that neoliberalism is totalizing and hegemonic. Neoliberalism has, effectively, thoroughly, and completely overtaken the state, common sense, extinguished democratic freedom, the sovereignty of citizens, and successfully thwarted anti-capitalist and democratic forces and smothered aspirations that run counter to neoliberalism. Neoliberalism is presented as pervasive and spread so deep that there is, in reality, no alternative. Put another way, accepting the self-evidence of neoliberalism as your starting point, and taking the rejection of neo-liberalism as your end point, are the limits set for critical conduct. Brown over-comes the first limit, but not the second.

If you do not accept the limits for critical conduct, you are a neoliberal apologist, at worst, or at best insufficiently critical in your analysis or revolu-tionary in your aspirations. Within these limits, neoliberalism is the only possible target of resistance and "neoliberalism" is the only weapon to slay it in the arsenal of critical conduct. With no toehold for unified resistance "in reality," and with faint hope for mounting such resistance in the present, critical conduct is reduced to Manicheanism: neoliberalism is an unmitigated evil, a target of rejection and refusal, rather than of resistance. Rejecting neoliberalism is good, and to fail to do so is evidence of blindness, acquiescence, cowardice, or the awesome power and total success of neoliberalism. Since there are no cracks in neoliberalism's grip upon the present to exploit from the perspective of critical conduct, and apparently no one but the practicioners of critical conduct have the vantage necessary to diagnose the present for what it is, the question of resistance against neoliberalism is to slay the many-headed monster on the pretense of defining it.

I certainly hear an echo of the repressive hypothesis at work in the oppositional logic – repressed or emancipated – of critical diagnostics. Somehow, it is neoliberalism that stands between us and true freedom. Why is neoliberalism so pervasive and powerful, an insurmountable barrier to freedom? Some critics reply, with the classic tautology upholding the repressive theory of power: resistance to neoliberalism is repressed by neoliberalism (in this usage neoliberalism is clearly both a weapon and the target for neoliberals, as well as for emancipatory projects). Brown succeeds in avoiding that tautology by illuminating the positive power of neoliberal rationality to shape the present. Nevertheless, she is drawn to the conclusion that the neoliberal revolution cannot be turned back. Either way, then, as a repressive force or as a productive force, the power of neoliberalism is tautological and total. As such, resistance must come from somewhere outside neoliberalism.

Others have noted limitations imposed upon critical thought and action by taking up the position of anti-neoliberalism. This is where critical conduct comes in from nowhere to provide the vantage point of normative theory as a toehold for resistance. For example, Clive Barnett (2010, p. 26) writes:

> Neoliberalism as an object of analysis is certainly a critics' term. The explicit formulation of neoliberalism into an object of theoretical analysis ... [indicates] the turning-in of intellectual curiosity around a very narrow space ... As long as this remains the horizon of normative reflection, critical human geographers will continue to always know in advance what they are expected to be *critical of* but will remain unable to articulate convincingly what they are being *critical for*.

Anti-neoliberalism, in other words, is a position that limits critical thought to resistance against neoliberalism at the expense of envisioning a normative alternative to neoliberalism. After introducing another important resource for a critical counter-conduct in additon to Brown, I return to Barnett's call for normative commitment.

James Ferguson (2009) wrote an inspired response to the reduction of critical conduct to a great refusal and narrowing the scope of resistance to anti-neoliberalism. Ferguson's patience is tested by groups he calls "the antis." "Anti-globalization, anti-neoliberalism, anti-privatization, anti-imperialism, anti-Bush, perhaps even anti-capitalism – but always 'anti', not 'pro'" (p. 166). He is also impatient with critical conduct that merely casts judgment and he heeds the call made upon the left to invent or to re-invent the arts of government by Michel Foucault. To do so, Ferguson suggests, progressives and leftists need to think in terms of appropriating neoliberal policies and programs. The cases in point are redistribution schemes and governing techniques of direct cash transfer policies and programs implemented in Brazil, Venezuela, Bangladesh, and Mexico. His focus is concentrated on the ANC's proposal for South Africa's basic income grant (BIG). Conditional (e.g., on kids attending school to qualify for Bolsa Família in Brazil) or unconditional, direct payments provide income without stipulating how income is spent. (Notably, experiments with basic income are currently underway or planned today for locales in several countries, including Canada, Finland, India, Kenya, and the United States.) In South Africa, Ferguson saw basic income as a recognizably neoliberal policy of redistribution: reliance on or bolstering markets; individual entrepreneurship and autonomy; cutting the state out as a service provider; and privatizing social provisions. Advocates for BIG appropriate both "pro-poor" arguments from the left and "anti-poor" arguments from the right: for example, the charge that the nanny state is racist, moralizes over the "deserving" and the "underserving" poor, buys off the legitimate dissent of the poor, and will replace social welfare techniques like the means-test with a universal cash payment. Advocates also swing accusations against big government, corruption, and the dependency produced by the over-weaning nanny state which coddles the poor and their bad behavior, so BIG replaces welfare with individual responsibility, "investing in human capital," and entrepreneurship. There is not one governing rationality, but many, appropriated and re-appropriated by the advocates of BIG, willy-nilly. In Ferguson's view, such policies are never simply either neoliberal or resistant to neoliberalism, a perspective that undermines the antis' critical position from somewhere outside neoliberalism and their stance of resistance to neoliberalism.

If, as "antis," critics of neoliberalism treat programs like BIG as an unmitigated evil to be completely rejected and shunned, the left will never take advantage of the opportunity there is to re-appropriate neoliberalism's policies and programs to fight poverty. His essay comes with warnings neither to embrace nor reject neoliberal policies and techniques, but to ask, are they appropriable? Ferguson gives several other historical examples to show that antis need to reconsider the historical record of how unpredictable policies and programs are, in fact. Once enacted even the purely progressive or conservative policy may be appropriated by the other side.

Ferguson's examples of appropriation are readily generalizable, I believe, even to antis. For example, neoliberal policies and techniques are undergoing appropriation by those struggling against police violence and student debt in the USA. A signature technique of neoliberal policing, CompStat, originally designed to hold police responsible, became a big data technique for tracking and mapping crime. These data techniques are currently being appropriated by those combatting police violence and racial profiling to expose and resist the fully neoliberalized, professionalized, racialized and militarized policing we have come to know under the mantra of "broken windows."[2] Another example is Strike Debt, a campaign to oppose the predatory debt practices of finance capitalism and the neoliberal logic for policies to "liberalize" or "privatize" higher education. It is a coherent neoliberal argument to say that a degree paid for with publicly funded students loans to a for-profit institution is fraud because graduates cannot realize their "human capital" with a "bad" degree. Nevertheless, that argument is being appropriated as an argument that for-profit institutions cannot be "incentivized" to be capable and trustworthy educators because their motive is profit rather than education. That is a neoliberal argument turned against the privatization of education. W do not have to resuscitate *homo politicus* or aristocratic visions of liberal arts education and Enlightenment principles, nor to embrace communitarian visions of liberal arts education to make "good citizens," to defend public provision for higher education. It may even be possible to further appropriate neoliberal techniques and policies ascendant in public schools, public universities, and adapt them for transportation, police and prisons, health care, finance, among other sectors under pressures of withdrawing state funding and encroaching state regulation, marketization, and privatization. Appropriation may fail or succeed (or both) to secure the future of education, and the question now is if appropriation and re-apporopriation will proceed apace. The strategy of appropriation will be sorely tested if it is true that the recent ascendance of nationalism spells the end of neoliberal hegemony.

Ferguson's suggestion that it is possible to resist neoliberalism by appropriating it for the left provides inspiration for critical counter-conduct. I agree with him that by treating neoliberalism as a great and unified evil to draw a line in the sand, critics are telling their audiences that there is no adequate resistance underway. I also agree with the implication of his argument, that any resistance taking the form of rejection, anti-neoliberalism, will find no traction for resistance in the present. However, Ferguson also suggests that the left is exhausted:

> neither the governmental mechanisms, nor the strategies of mobilization, that the left came to rely on in the twentieth century (and which characterized, in different ways, both socialist and social democratic or "welfare state" regimes) are capable of getting the sort of traction they once did.
>
> *(p. 167)*

He cites two reasons why "progressive thought and politics" (p. 168) are incapable of mounting an adequate response to neoliberalism. First, transnational forms of government, finance, philanthropy, and second, the dramatically shrinking formal wage labor sector have rendered leftist strategies and their dreams of social democratic government anachronistic. Yet in his impatience with the "antis," their judgment that neoliberalism is a bad thing and an appropriate target of refusal, Ferguson neglects to see that the antis are not only anti-neoliberal, and left strategy is not limited to "anti" neoliberalism.

Many on the left are actively fashioning strategic and governmental counter-conducts within a present they may even believe is irredeemably neoliberal. They can be found doing so both guided by and standing aside from repressive hypotheses. While Ferguson's patience is tested by the antis' overly quick and facile rejection of neoliberalism, mine is tested by the ways that critical conduct, and in this way like Ferguson, discount, disparage, and disavow the variety and scale of resistance on the left. The antis, so to speak, are in fact contributing to the reinvention of neoli- beralism by resisting, forcing neoliberalism to respond, and maybe also appropriating the neoliberal arts of government in practicing critical counter-conducts, but not in ways that are recognizable, apparently, to Ferguson. And the antis certainly do not satisfy Barnett's call for normative theory to set out a normative vision of what we are *for*, anarchism and participatory democracy notwithstanding.

Like both Barnett and Ferguson, I suspect that little good can come from endlessly repeating that neoliberalism is bad. However, I do not have faith in Barnett's vantage point that abandons critical conduct and the present to assert normative commitments and build a movement on visions of what "we" are *for*. To make good on the promise of normative visions and commitments entails either consensus or coercion to unify others to resist in the name of, and then to live according to, shared and settled commitments. That is no better and no more achievable than the unity called forth by critics in the name of resistance to neoliberalism. What I am aiming at here is the reinvention of critical conduct to avoid its bad consequences, not to abandon the present or the search for critical vantage (be it political, theoretical, or conceptual perspective) on neoliberalism.

Ferguson offers the vantage point *of* the present to locate resources and strategies for resistance to neoliberalism. Whether neoliberalism is conceived as a repressive form of government, an ideology, or as rationality of power that is capable of producing reality and shaping subjectivity, there is a strong tendency in critical conduct to essentialize neoliberalism as hegemonic and insurmountable, barring the possibility that any critical vantage point is possible within the present. And the call to normative commitment takes its critical vantage from outside the present. Ferguson demonstrates that the present does afford a vantage point that offers a non-essentialist perspective on neoliberalism. This overcomes the temporal limit imposed on change by the repressive hypothesis that is set between repression/present and liberation/future. However, why is there not enough vantage from the present for him to see the innumerable signs of vitality on the left in the present?

Despite his valuable contribution, in addition to Brown's, toward de-essentializing neoliberalism, Ferguson essentializes the left as a unified body of shared aspiration that is no longer stabilized and supported by its necessary conditions. In effect, he displaces the left from the present. He can see that power is unevenly and unstably distributed so that neoliberalism is in a continuous state of transformation amidst the appropriation and re-appropriation of techniques and policies of government. However, he does not see resistance and the left in similar terms, as in a continuous state of change and contestation. This is why it is not enough for a critical counter-conduct to avoid the essentialism of the repressive hypothesis and adopt the vantage point of the present. It is also necessary to treat resistance as a diagnostic of power, even if it does not meet your expectations or satisfy your understanding of the proper role, conduct, and purpose of the left.

Critical Counter-Conduct

Rather than banish the concept of neoliberalism from critical conduct and get back to the purportedly real world of politics, my aim so far has been t investigate and counter what is done with the word, how it is used to fight conceptual and political battles, how it came to be an arresting site not of definition, but of conceptual contest, and to treat its usage in critical conduct more as a speech act with real consequences and not as barking in the wind. This is to practice what I now propose as the rules, norms, and strategies for a critical counter-conduct and its "immediate and founding correlation" with critical conduct will be obvious. First, to breach the self-evidence of neoliberalism in the world and in critical conduct, do not argue over what neoliberalism (or power) is, in reality, or call out its name as an act of resistance. Rather, analyze what is said and done in the world and *within* critical conduct; analyze the effects of putting neoliberalism into conceptual and political dispute. That rule guided my analysis of critical conduct and helped to explain how critical conduct poses obstacles to thought and action that is critically necessary to resist neoliberalism.

The effects of critical conduct do *not* repress a more true or politically useful critique. Rather, they displace and disparage resistance underway in the present, including resistance to neoliberalism. The second rule is: do not attempt to expose what (e.g., power) is hidden. Look instead at what is said and done to see how power works (rule #1), and above all, look to resistance underway and practices of freedom as the diagnostics of power in the present. "Protests against neoliberalism" is a misnomer to frame protest from the left if we listen to what is actually said in protests, although neoliberalism is certainly a focal point of resistance in many cases as well, particularly in Latin America and ever more so in the European Union. (It is possible to interpret protest from the right as anti-neoliberal, such as the Tea Party's protest against corporate bailouts and the rising tide of nationalism in the European Union and elsewhere.) For example, anti-austerity was the focal point of Spanish *Indignados* and Greece; anti-redevelopment and anti-gentrification of Gezi Park Protests; global inequality of Occupy Wall Street; prison abolition in the USA, extractivism in Latin America, and there are far too many more focal points of recent and ongoing protest to list, including corruption, environmental degradation, state and police violence, government secrecy and cyber-security, prison abolition, and electoral reform.

Recent protests have been transformative. Strike Debt, as already mentioned, and anti-austerity in Greece transform national and personal debt from something that by right must be paid, into a target of resistance. Critical counter-conducts may resist neoliberalism, not in name, but in its immediate encounter. For example, protests in Ferguson, Missouri targeted the tyrannical system of fines and court fees that locked people into the judicial system and subjected them to police violence and entrenched injustice. That system was built upon rollbacks of public financing for public goods including public safety and justice. Resonating across the country, many new organizations and movements appeared which ran counter to the conduct of the civil rights movement. As a result, rather than appearing as good governance, the withdrawal of public financing came to appear as fostering tyranny and pushed police into acting in patterns deemed by the Department of Justice to be unconstitutional.

Resistances from publicizing state secrets to protest against racial profiling have made security and police over into the forces of imperial and racial tyranny. These and other transformations (distinct from but in kind with what Ferguson terms "re-appropriation") are the effects of resistance underway. It is true that many of these protests are committed to aspirational norms, but more importantly, they are conducted by those norms, such as direct action, horizontalism, non-violence, transparency, real or direct democracy. By refusing to take the form of a party, vanguard, or a revolutionary army, or in some cases refusing to adopt a reformist platform and make demands of any kind, they are conducted and even self-proclaimed as "anti-politics," a refusal to act politically *that* way. They are political counter-conducts.

Political and critical counter-conducts will never match expectations set by the oppositional and Manichean logic of repression–liberation. Critics from the left are quick to point out that recent protest movements failed to become fully revolutionary, failed to slay the many-headed beast or chop off even one of its heads. Protests, it is said, were insufficiently unified, organized, militant, led, too local, and focused on the wrong target. Alain Badiou (2010, p. 5) writes that recent uprisings and protests are "[a]s yet blind, naïve, scattered, and lacking a powerful concept or durable organization." As Badiou casts them, the liberating force of uprisings remains in its infancy, the infancy of the coming revolution. To become mature and capable of liberation, riots and uprisings must harness themselves to the discipline of a "powerful concept or durable organization." Yet, from my perspective, political counter-conducts generate intense instability in all forms of organized and disciplined politics, from the state to social movements. That instability resonates beyond the event of protest, riot, or occupation. I am attempting here to extend that resonance to critical conduct. The strategy I propose for critical counter-conduct is to expect surprises.

There is a purpose as well as strategy in refusing to conduct political action in the terms of organized, disciplined, and unified politics. Rather than pursuing liberation out from under repressive power, and rather than foregrounding the coming revolution, recent protests and uprisings implicitly, and at times explicitly reject the repressive hypothesis. They do not aim to overtake the powers of the neoliberal state and overthrow the system of global capitalism by waging revolution be it violent or non-violent, and instead they practice counter-conducts horizontalism, and direct action, and aim to transform political action in resistance to the limits of action imposed upon politics itself. They reject political vanguard and opt for leaderless movements. They reject preceding resistance on a settled focus of resistance such as neoliberalism or a normative vision and opt for building egalitarian consensus from the ground up amongst anyone who shows up. The profusion of critical counter-conducts, activist practices, "alternative" lifestyle economies, and so forth, evince the vitality of resistance under neoliberalism. A practices of freedom, counter-conducts run directly counter to the idea that neoliberalism has completely overtaken the freedoms of citizens or destroyed the public sphere.

Democratic counter-conducts ("This is what democracy looks like!") do not proclaim the sovereignty of the people or attempt to take over the state; they do not see democracy as a kind of government or a way of establishing relations of ruling others or being ruled by others; they practice democracy as a counter-conduct to organized democratic politics. Among other things, antis debate the Western and imperial bias of "democracy"; whether democracy is, can, or should ever be the form of the state; the forms, inclusiveness, and effectiveness of democratic practices within movements; and what it means to practice democracy in the conditions of the present.

Yet Wendy Brown suggests in the strongest possible terms that neoliberalism effectively banishes *homo politicus* from the stage of history and "undoes" the *demos*. Neoliberal "reorientations also entail an existential disappearance of freedom from the world, precisely the kind of individual and collaborative freedom associated with *homo politicus* for self-rule and rule with others" (p. 110). But what are these new counter-conducts of protest and resistance if not powerful evidence that in the present and under neoliberalism the freedom of self-rule and rule with others are alive and well? Brown mentions recent protests and movements in positive terms, but she disavows the evidence I see by taking her vantage point from the past, from what is lost to the present. By following a third rule of critical counter-conduct, it is possible to see what is new and different without melancholy: take one's vantage point in and from the present. *Homo politicus* may well be dead, and quite sincerely, I hope that is true. I prefer to join in with those making a concerted effort to reinvent politics in and on their own terms. Rather than seeking to revive *homo politicus*, we are trying transform "the West," an ideal built upon slave labor, imperialism, and settler colonialism, to be and to conduct ourselves politically in a different way or by coming to politics just as we are. We even sometimes acknowledge the part of and welcome non-human actors in political life.

Counter-conducts can only appear in critical conduct as more evidence of neoliberalism's hegemony. By countering the idea that the truth will set us free from power, the fundamental pillar of the repressive hypothesis, critical counter-conduct establishes a norm for counter-conduct: Do not wage resistance by speaking the truth to power and do not resist in the hope of freedom to come. Practice freedom and exercise power, not in the name of truth, principles, or aspirations, but as much as possible in full awareness that the conduct you are undertaking is both in your hands and undertaken amidst an uneven and unstable distribution of freedom and power, making it fraught with risks and dangers. Be alert and vigilant at all times and never trust that principles, knowledge, or power will place or keep your political conduct on the right path. I am proposing critical counter-conduct not to more fully realize freedom in the future, but to realize here and now that we are freer than we feel.

Notes

1 It is a pleasure to acknowledge those who read or commented on earlier drafts and presentations of this chapter. Despite their criticism, insight, and aid, all the faults of the essay remain mine to bear. Many thanks to Ivan Ascher, Leonard Feldman, Farah Godrej, Fred Schaffer, Sandy Schram, Jillian Schwedler, and John Seery. I am grateful to acknowledge the inspiration I took while writing this chapter from the members of a graduate seminar, particularly from Siddhant Issar and Candice Travis.
2 See, for example, *Mapping Police Violence* at mappingpoliceviolence.org; *Fatal Encounters* at fatalencounters.org; *Killed by Police* at killedbypolice.net; *The Guardian* project, "The Counted: People Killed by Police in the U.S.," at theguardian.com.

References

Abu-Lughod, L. (1990). The Romance of Resistance: Tracing Transformations through Bedouin Women. *American Ethnologist*, 17, 41–55.

Amar, P. (2013). *The Security Archipelago: Human Security States, Sexuality Politics, and the End of Neoliberalism*. Durham, NC: Duke University Press.

Badiou, A. (2010). *The Rebirth of History: Times of Riots and Uprisings*. London: Verso.

Barnett, C. (2010). *Publics and Markets: What Is Wrong with Neoliberalism?* In Susan Smith, R. Pain, Sallie A. Marston, and J. P. Jones (Eds.), *The Handbook of Social Geographies*. Thousand Oaks, CA: Sage Publications.

Bialostok, S., Whitman, R. L., Bradley, W. S. (Eds.) (2012). *Education and the Risk Society: Theories, Discourse and Risk Identities in Educational Contexts*. Rotterdam: Sense Publishers.

Brenner, N., Peck, J., and Theodore, N. (2010). After Neoliberalism? *Globalizations*, 7, 327–345.

Brown, W. (2003). Neoliberalism and the End of Liberal Democracy. *Theory & Event*, 7, 1. Retrieved from: https://muse.jhu.edu/ (accessed November 10, 2003).

Brown, W. (2015). *Undoing the Demos: Neoliberalism's Stealth Revolution*. New York: Zone Books.

Butler, J. (2004). What Is Critique? An Essay on Foucault's Virtue. In Sara Salih (Ed.), *The Judith Butler Reader*. Malden, MA: Blackwell Publishing.

Davidson, A. (2011). In Praise of Counter-Conduct. *History of the Human Sciences*, 24, 25–41.

Dean, J. (2009). *Democracy and Other Neoliberal Fantasies: Communicative Capitalism and Left Politics*. Durham, NC: Duke University Press.

Duggan, L. (2003). *The Twilight of Equality: Neoliberalism, Cultural Politics, and the Attack on Democracy*. Boston, MA: Beacon Press.

Duménil, G. and Lévy, D. (2004). *Capital Resurgent: Roots of the Neoliberal Revolution*. Cambridge, MA: Harvard University Press.

Feher, M. (2009). Self-Appreciation: or, the Aspirations of Human Capital. *Public Culture*, 21, 21–41.

Ferguson, J. (2006). *Global Shadows: Africa in the Neoliberal World Order*. Durham, NC: Duke University Press.

Ferguson, J. (2009). The Uses of Neoliberalism. *Antipode*, 41(S1), 166–184.

Foucault, M. (2008). *The Birth of Biopolitics: Lectures at the College de France, 1978–79*. Basingstoke, UK: Palgrave MacMillan.

Fraser, N. (2017). The End of Progressive Neoliberalism. *Dissent*. Retrieved January 12, 2017 from: www.dissentmagazine.org/online_articles/progressive-neoliberalism-reactionary-populism-nancy-fraser

Fukuyama, F. (2012). The Future of History: Can Liberal Democracy Survive the Decline of the Middle Class? *Foreign Affairs*, January/February. Retrieved March 29, 2017 from: www.foreignaffairs.com/articles/2012-01-01/future-history

Harcourt, B. (2010). Dismantling/Neoliberalism. *Carceral Notebooks*, 6, 21–32.

Harvey, D. (2005). *A Brief History of Neoliberalism*. Oxford: Oxford University Press.

Klein, N. (2008). *The Shock Doctrine: The Rise of Disaster Capitalism*. New York: Metropolitan Books.

Larner, W. (2006). Review of A Brief History of Neoliberalism. *Economic Geography*, 82, 49–51.

Mirowski, P. (2013). *Never Let a Serious Crisis Go to Waste: How Neoliberalism Survived the Financial Meltdown*. London: Verso.

Mirowski, P. (2014). The Political Movement That Dared Not Speak Its Own Name: The Neoliberal Thought Collective Under Erasure. Institute for New Economic Thinking, Working paper No. 23. Retrieved November 15, 2016 from: www.thing.net/~rdom/ucsd/Borders/The_Political_Movement_that_Dared_not_Speak_its_own_Name.pdf

Ong, A. (2006). *Neoliberalism As Exception: Mutations in Citizenship and Sovereignty*. Durham, NC: Duke University Press.

Ong, A. (2007). Neoliberalism as a Mobile Technology. *Transactions of the Institute of British Geographers*, 32, 3–8.

Ostry, J., Loungani, P., and Furceri, D. (2016). Neoliberalism Oversold? *Finance and Development*, 53, 38–41.

Petras, J. (2011). *Social Movements in Latin America: Neoliberalism and Popular Resistance*. London: Palgrave.

Petras, J. and Veltmeyer, H. (Eds.) (2014). *The New Extractivism: A Post-Neoliberal Development Model or Imperialism of the Twenty-first Century?* Chicago: University of Chicago Press.

Schram, S. (2015). *The Return of Ordinary Capitalism: Neoliberalism, Precarity, Occupy*. New York: Oxford University Press.

Soss, J., Fording, R. C., Schram, S. F. (2011). *Disciplining the Poor: Neoliberal Paternalism and the Persistent Power of Race*. Chicago: Chicago University Press.

Wacquant, L. (2009). *Punishing the Poor: The Neoliberal Government of Social Insecurity*. Durham, NC: Duke University Press.

INDEX

Note: **bold** page numbers indicate figures and tables.